unbound

Also by Annie Zaidi

Gulab (2014)
Love Story #1 to 14 (2012)
The Good Indian Girl (2011)
Known Turf: Bantering with Bandits and Other True Tales (2010)
Crush (2007)

un *bound*

2,000 YEARS
OF INDIAN
WOMEN'S
WRITING

EDITED BY
Annie Zaidi

ALEPH

ALEPH

ALEPH BOOK COMPANY
An independent publishing firm
promoted by *Rupa Publications India*

Aleph Book Company
7/16 Ansari Road, Daryaganj
New Delhi 110 002

First published in India by
Aleph Book Company in 2015

Published in paperback in 2016

ISBN: 978-93-83064-16-8

1 3 5 7 9 10 8 6 4 2

For Ali Jawad Zaidi,
who was the sort of grandpa that every girl needs.

CONTENTS

INTRODUCTION

Annie Zaidi

An odd thing happened soon after I took on the daunting task of editing this anthology. I found myself inscribing my own name on the first pages of the books I had bought. As a student, I was in the habit of writing my name in books I owned but over the years, the more I bought, the less ownership mattered. But now, again, I found myself wanting to stamp certain books as 'mine'—ones by Krishna Sobti, Mahasweta Devi, Sivakami, Salma, Meera, Geetanjali Shree. As soon as I began to feel a kinship with the work, I'd write my name on the first page. I even wanted to make notes in the margins and underline passages with ink.

In this way, I discovered that I belong to the books as much as they belong to me. It was the same impulse that led to me scratch my name on rocks when I climbed the hills near my childhood home. It's a way of saying: I was here. And on several pages written by the women represented in this book, I have found my own self.

When I began work on this project, I struggled with several questions. The biggest one: several women writers are celebrated not just as 'women writers' but as writers, period. Some have won the nation's highest literary honours. Must we continue to put 'women writers' in a box of their own?

Part of the answer came as I read more and more Indian women. Women bring to their writing the truth of their bodies, and an enquiry into the different ways in which gender inequity shapes human experience (and destroys lives). Many women writers also place women protagonists at the centre of their work and many stories set within the household have the power to illuminate the ways in which women's lives are shaped and controlled.

It is worth noting here that there has been a sort of dismissal of 'domestic' fiction in the recent past. Editors and writers, male *and* female, have equated domestic themes with dullness, or the lack of imaginative daring. In fact, there was a time when I (and I'm squirming as I write this) used to say that I didn't care much for 'kitchenized' fiction. It took me over a year of exclusively reading women writers to realize how deep and strong the roots of my own bias were and how foolish our undermining of 'domestic' fiction.

Of course it's domestic! Patriarchy is nothing if not domestic. Besides, there is more sex, violence, politics and overall drama in the average household than, say, the average office. Why are we surprised if domestic settings are chosen for fiction? From such settings emerge stories of great rebellion—and poetry that directly challenges the myths fed to us over thousands of years.

Hindi writer Krishna Sobti had once said in an interview that she wants to have fun, to live and not just write. She also said that families and marriages were anti-art, anti-writing. Yet, it is marriage and family that form the basis of her own writing. Her delicately crafted, aurally delicious novel *Dil-o-Danish* (translated as 'The Heart has its Reasons') is firmly domestic. It tells of endless manoeuvring by women as they struggle for economic security and personal dignity. And while the bold reclamation of a woman's sexuality was one aspect of her novel *Mitro Marjani* (To Hell With You, Mitro), it was also the story of a joint family.

There have been periods in our literary history when it seemed women cared less about craft or form; all they wanted was to be heard. The argument against patriarchy could turn into a howl of rage, as in P. Sivakami's tightly spun novels, or it could be a lucid, almost detached account of Indian women's lives as seen in Mahadevi Varma's essays. Kumudini was wittily subversive as was K. Saraswathi Amma; Rokeya Sakhawat Hossain's anger was brushed with sardonic humour. Rassundari Devi's account was quite simply that—an account of her life, where she expresses more gratitude than rage, while Baby Kamble, Bama, Joya Mitra and Devaki Nilayamgode wrote memoirs that reflect their consciousness as activists.

At various points in our history, the very act of reading and writing was a protest. Most Indians were illiterate but women's literacy was actively discouraged, even prohibited. Only a few managed to document their lives. It is against this backdrop that the introduction to Ramabai Sarasvati's *The High Caste Hindu Woman* says: 'The silence of a thousand years has been broken...' This is not entirely accurate, of course, for women in the thousand years preceding 1887 did write. But in 1887, it was rare for a high caste Hindu woman to express herself in the public domain. To write fluently in English, to travel abroad and to be published in America was very, very rare.

The High Caste Hindu Woman remains relevant even today, speaking as it does about infanticide, establishing clear links between marriage, dowry, caste, religious scripture and the violence done to little girls. A hundred and fifty years later, the sex ratio is still alarmingly low in several parts of the country and the government is still trying to stop female foeticide through law enforcement. Pundita Ramabai's descriptions of the woes of upper caste women ought to be read alongside Baby Kamble's account of the lives of Dalit women, and Bama's autobiography, *Karukku*. All of them speak of a cycle of oppression and the need for literacy and financial independence in order to break this vicious cycle.

India has come far since Independence but violence against women continues to be so common that only the most gruesome acts shake the average citizen out of his/her complacency. Many activists now openly say that the 'freedom' we won in 1947 was a political transfer of power, and that women must struggle for their freedom again. There is a lot of hostility directed at those who are part of this struggle and the abuse directed at women writers is also a reflection of this hostility.

Contemporary writers have faced abuse and threats after having written about bodies, sex, and religious institutions. Tamil poets like Salma and Kutti Revathi were accused of 'obscenity' and threatened with violence. Criticism is often accompanied by sexual abuse and this was painfully evident while I was looking for essays by historian Romila Thapar. I came upon a website discussing her work and one comment described her thus: 'That BIYATCH Romila thapar is nothing but a whore of the commies'. It was both amusing and sad to realize that more money, better education and exposure (mainly to American culture, judging from the language used) has not rid our civilization of men who, unable to disprove a woman's scholarship, start to abuse her sexuality.

In recent years, we also had a senior academic declare in an interview that women writers (with reference to contemporary Hindi literature) are competing with each other to establish who is the greatest whore among them. This is not a far cry from the way male social reformers had, in the early twentieth century, called for a ban on the work of Muddupalani, calling it the work of a prostitute; Nagarathnamma, the woman artiste who salvaged the Telugu classic and republished it, was also dismissed as a prostitute.

Even today women are judged by a different set of social and moral standards than men. It is in this context that an Indian woman must be read, alongside the generations that came before her. We cannot know what to do next unless we know what we have already done, or what was done to us. Ignorance of the past leads to contortions in our understanding of our present selves. For instance, I had grown up believing that there was something remarkably bold and progressive about the Indian political leadership of the pre-independence era. I was proud of the fact that women were given equal voting rights in a sovereign India, which makes us better than the UK or the USA where women had to fight for it. What I did not know is that, initially, the plan was to offer only limited suffrage to Indian women. Reading Sarojini Naidu's impassioned plea to an overwhelmingly male leadership was a real eye-opener. She appealed to their generosity, their sense of justice, even to their dedication to our traditional values. But what if there were no Sarojini Naidu? Would we be marching down the streets even today, chaining ourselves to the gates of Rashtrapati Bhavan, screaming for women's right to vote?

Reading towards this anthology has been a way of looking at the distance Indian women have travelled. Interestingly, the writers themselves seemed to be constantly looking over their shoulders, grappling with a shared history. Myths are referenced, goddesses invoked, legends summoned forth for a conversation. Draupadi and Sita, Amrapali and Akka Mahadevi are addressed with familiarity, as if they were grandmothers lying down in an adjacent bedroom. Rukmini Bhaya Nair writes of Kali's loneliness. Vaidehi writes in Parvati's voice. Pratibha Ray's *Yajnaseni* retells the Mahabharata in Draupadi's voice. Amrita Pritam calls on Waris Shah. Many emerging writers, whose work is not represented here, mainly due to a severe space constraint, continue to build conversations with the past. Anamika, a contemporary Hindi poet, has written poems addressing Tulsi, Amrapali and Jesus Christ. Amruta Patil, an emerging graphic novelist, has written *Adi Parva* with Ganga as the narrator. The urge to re-re-tell the stories that defined our cultural roots is still strong.

Editing this anthology has also been a personal journey. Some books felt like a personal tryst with truth, philosophy and cultural identity. Some were bottled-up forebodings, full of cruel prescience. Others infected me with a grey groping in the midst of bewildering change. Often, I would tweet a few lines as soon as I had read them. I couldn't wait to share with the world a tiny fraction of what I had *right now*!

I am hoping to convey to you, dear reader, a portion of the joy, the rage, the comfort, the kinship that I have found. It was only after reading all these women writers that I was convinced of the need for this anthology, even though other anthologies already existed. The most significant one is an extensive two-volume set edited by Susie Tharu and K. Lalita and I owe them a huge debt of gratitude. They documented all women writers whose authorship of a particular text could be established. Other anthologies have appeared with an emphasis on language, genre, 'new' voices; voices from the eighteenth or nineteenth centuries, saint-poets, and so on.

This anthology does not seek to document *all* literary contributions by *all* Indian women. There are thousands of women writers and it is beyond the scope of a single volume to include them all. I expected to be able to include between eighty and ninety writers. I have done my best to represent each era and region but have limited myself to existing translations or those that are forthcoming shortly.

Apart from the problem of not being able to include all writers, in some cases, it was all but impossible to firmly establish authorship. The Rig Veda refers to female 'rishis' like Ghosa, Lopamudra, and Apala, but scholars do not seem to agree that they authored hymns or verses. I have heard of women like Bavri Saheb, Sheikh Rangrejin and Taj who are believed to have written in the sixteenth and seventeenth centuries but could not find books featuring their original work. It would take several lifetimes to rescue all the texts that have disappeared from print or have never been translated.

We do have access to verses in Prakrit, translated beautifully by Arvind Krishna Mehrotra in *The Absent Traveller*, which resonate powerfully thousands of years later. But while they are written in a feminine voice, and may have been written by women, there is no way to establish individual authorship and therefore I have not included them here. Matters are further complicated by the fact there is a definite tradition of men writing in the first person, from a female perspective. For the same reason, I chose not to include folk literature where it is not clear who the author is.

In trying to decide what to include, I also examined the question of 'Indianness'. Historically, India (Hindustan or Bharat) was an entity that shifted as kingdoms were won or lost, but it was contained mainly within the subcontinent. So, of course I have considered all writers who belong to the current map of India. Partition in 1947 complicates matters but I settled the issue by including writers who were writing extensively and getting published before Partition, like Rokeya Sakhawat Hossain. If they were born before 1947 but most of their writing was published in independent Pakistan or Bangladesh, I have left them out.

Many 'Indian' writers not only live abroad but were born, bred and educated in other nations. I cannot settle prickly questions about cultural versus national identity but I decided to go with some basic rules: I would not privilege Indian writing in English over other languages, especially where good translations are available; I would look for our spiritual, cultural, mythological and political history; I would pick narratives set within India as far as possible. I have avoided diaspora writing, particularly if it is set in other nations.

Genres represented include poetry, drama, novels, short fiction and non-fiction. I tried to focus on writers whose body of work was not restricted to speeches, letters or newspaper columns. I also avoided diary extracts. I very reluctantly excluded the memoirs of Binodini Dasi, Hamsa Wadkar, Protima Bedi—I would urge readers to read those remarkable works. I grappled with the notion of 'writer' for a long while and eventually decided that, at least for the twentieth century, I ought to focus on writers who created a body of work and not just one book. The exceptions are texts that capture a slice of women's history at times when reading and writing was strongly discouraged, if not forbidden, like Rassundari Devi's and Ramabai Ranade's memoirs.

I read and considered the work of women playwrights where it was available in English translation but did not include screenplays and narratives about the making of films. I do believe that film scripts may well be a literary genre of the future. But I also think that we must learn to read screenplays without reference to, without access to, the audio-visual productions they lead to. We should be able to judge them on purely literary grounds, and that time has not yet come. We can, and do, read scripts written for the stage, regardless of the productions they resulted in.

Wherever decisions were difficult, I have weighed in on the side of literary craft and genre-bending abilities. Another deciding factor was the possession of a distinctive voice, a definite way of observing the world and remarking upon it. This is what unites writers as disparate as Qurratulain Hyder, Ismat Chughtai, Irawati Karve, Nayantara Sahgal, Volga and Suniti Namjoshi. They have all pushed the boundaries of content and form while offering a fresh feminist perspective.

I must add that the selection of extracts reflects my own tastes. Apart from craft, I looked for novelty, empathy, a fresh perspective, great historical significance, insights into gender and literary longevity. This is one reason I did not include newspaper or magazine articles (they often require readers to be familiar with the immediate news context) even though the writing of some young women journalists is brilliant and I'm looking forward to the books they will write.

Some omissions still make me anxious. There are writers I definitely wanted to include—Ambai, Gogu Shyamala, Saniya, Mala Sen, Anita Desai, Githa Hariharan to name just a few—but could not get permission to use extracts from their work either due to length or budget constraints. The works of Utsa Patnaik, Vrinda Nabar, Ritu Menon, Kamla Bhasin, Leila Seth on labour, caste, law and gender are also essential reading and I was tempted to include them. But if I went down that road, I would have had to do a volume devoted entirely to non-fiction writing by Indian women.

This anthology comprises a mix of all genres and forms, arranged thematically. I worked under the assumption that most writing falls into broad themes, like love, sex, religion, death, parenting, politics, food, travel. Thus the book would touch upon all things that matter to humanity while reflecting the diversity and great range of women's literature. However, deciding where a particular piece of writing belongs has also been a bewildering exercise. Take, for instance, the poems of Karaikkal Ammaiyar.

They are dedicated to the lord, so I initially placed them in the section on spiritual love. But on a second and third reading, it was clear that the work was firmly rooted in the body, the awareness of impending death and the terror of destruction accompanied by a clear-eyed love for the Lord of Destruction. Similarly, many of Lal Ded's vakhs (verses; literally the word suggests an 'utterance') are about death or the body, the meaninglessness of shame, the quest for Shankara, and the need for escape. It would be easier, perhaps, to say what they're *not* about rather than slot them into any single category.

The novels were equally slippery. I would sometimes place extracts from the same book, even the same chapter, under three different themes. Take Indira Goswami's *The Blue-necked God* where she says what needed saying about widows—starvation, predators, the foolishness of thwarting desire. It is an indictment of organized religion that values ritual over humanity. It is about poverty and pain but it is also full of passages that capture the peace and elevation women hope to find in Vrindavan. Kamala Markandaya's *Nectar in a Sieve* is another complex story—a love story, a parenting story, a story of tentative industrialization and rural famine. In *The Anger of Aubergines* Bulbul Sharma explores women's relationship to food, but, as a natural extension, many of those food stories are about bodies, desire, ageing.

I have also tried to pick extracts that converse with each other, dancing from one 'ras' to another, one shade of human experience to the next: from spiritual longing and religion to secular love and lust, marriage to motherhood, class and caste to politics and administration.

Finally, let me turn to a quote attributed to Hindi-Urdu writer Premchand. He said that a writer's task is not to entertain, or even to hold up a mirror to society; a writer bears a torch that lights our way ahead. I had wondered if this philosophy would hold up over time. If we read a book a hundred, a thousand years after it was written, can it still light our way?

Having read the women who wrote in centuries past, I now believe the answer is: yes! Yes, they continue to light our way ahead.

Spiritual
Love

This section is dedicated to writings that are rooted in spiritual longing and devotion. In other words, a woman's yearning for acceptance and the quest for meaning that reaches beyond the tangible, material realm.

Some of the earliest texts for which women's authorship is acknowledged are by women who gave up their households, converted to Buddhism and left a record of their lives and their motivations in the *Therigatha*. Theris were nuns admitted into the order, albeit reluctantly (according to scholars, women were only let in on the condition that the senior-most nun would remain subservient to a monk), but at least they had the freedom to wander and they were glad to be free of domestic burdens. Other early texts include Andaal's *Nacciyar Tirumoli*, and verses by saint-poets like Akka Mahadevi, and Lal Ded.

It's very likely women wrote of matters other than god, but it was mainly devotional texts that were preserved. Writing skills were rare, after all, and most work survived through an oral tradition. Besides, manuscript making and copying of books was an expensive, labour-intensive business, limited by patronage from royalty or the religious order of the day.

But what is interesting about spiritual writing by women is that it is heavily laced with domestic, secular and sensual imagery. Cooking, cleaning, children waiting to be fed, pots of water, veils, suspicious husbands, lusting strangers, breasts, vaginas—all these aspects of a woman's experience can be found in 'sacred' verses.

Flagrant secularization, romanticization and politicization of the divine was also common amongst Bhakti and Sufi writers. Like Kabir, Bhakti poetesses like Jenabai and Soyrabai sing not only of spiritual hunger, but also of their world, its inconsistencies and divisions. In a casteist world, even the name of god had to be wrested from those who sought to monopolize it. Naturally, women sought social and religious reform too, along with personal freedom. Even the Persian verses written by Mughal Princess Zeb-un-nisa show her yearning, and the weariness of living in a restrictive, judgemental world. God alone seems to offer understanding.

Another interesting aspect of the work of women writers is that many of them wrote verses addressed to masculine gods. They speak of surrender, wanting to let go of fear and ego, but they also make petulant demands, like lovers. They threaten, cajole, sulk, complain of maltreatment or abandonment. They rebuke god for neglect, express exasperation at being made to wait. They even invite punishment.

In this section, I have tried to pick verses that seemed to be especially poised at the intersection between the spiritual, the temporal and the feminine self. There are few contemporary writers here, barring an extract from Urmila Pawar's story, 'Mukti', which is structured as a debate between a Buddhist monk and a Jain nun and it is an interesting retelling of a legendary debate on questions of dhamma and renunciation, self-mortification and ego. However, this is not to say that contemporary writers do not engage with the spiritual realm. Literacy and publishing has changed writing to the extent that brevity, rhythm and orality—integral to the work of poets in the past—are no longer key drivers of popularity. Novelists express the same bewilderment, longing and despair that prompted a lot of the early spiritual writing. But they do so through complex storylines. Modern poets still engage in a direct conversation with the divine, posing new challenges to myth and tradition, and, in doing this, their spirit is not so far from that of the saint-poets.

SANGHA

Therigatha

Translated from the Pali by Caroline Augusta Foley Rhys Davids

Home have I left, for I have left my world!
Child have I left, and all my cherish'd herds!
Lust have I left, and Ill-will, too, is gone,
And Ignorance have I put far from me;
Craving and root of Craving overpowered,
Cool am I now, knowing Nibbana's peace.

MUTTA

Therigatha

Translated from the Pali by Caroline Augusta Foley Rhys Davids

O free, indeed! O gloriously free
Am I in freedom from three crooked things:–
From quern, from mortar, from my crookback'd lord!
Ay, but I'm free from rebirth and from death,
And all that dragged me back is hurled away.

CITTA

Therigatha

Translated from the Pali by Caroline Augusta Foley Rhys Davids

Though I be suffering and weak, and all
My youthful spring be gone, yet have I climbed,
Leaning upon my staff, the mountain crest.
Thrown from my shoulder hangs my cloak, o'erturned
My little bowl. So 'gainst the rock I lean
And prop this self of me, and break away
The wildering gloom that long had closed me in.

URMILA PAWAR

Mukti

Translated from the Marathi by Veena Deo

As the sun moved westward the governor started the proceedings with a brief preface and invited Sariputra to ask his first question. Kundalkesha spoke up in a clear voice, 'Forgive me, governor, but since I have issued the challenge, I should have the right to ask the first question.'

Sariputra responded politely, 'Sister Kundalkesha's proposal is fair. Sister, I will try to answer your question to the best of my ability.'

Kundalkesha sat up and bowed to the governor, Sariputra, and the audience and asked, 'What is happiness? How does one obtain it?'

'Happiness is nirvana and that can be gained by cultivating deep feelings of friendship, compassion, and renunciation.'

'Renunciation?'

'Yes, renunciation. Having seen life fully, a person's ability to look at pain and pleasure with detachment is renunciation.'

'What is good character?'

'Good character suggests following a straight path without violence, thievery, immoral behaviour, falsehood, alcohol, or harm to anyone's body, mind or soul and so on.'

'I understand, Arya. Who should be considered a pure Brahmin?'

'One who has given up bad actions and impure thoughts can be called a Brahmin. I am not saying the Brahmin who is born in the caste, but a Brahmin who has chosen to become pure, still, happy, selfless, and a scholar. Only such a person is truly an Arya, or pure or a Brahmin.'

'What are the eight characteristics of the ocean-like Dhamma?'

'The ocean is deep, and all around us. Similarly Dhamma is deep, constant, and all-encompassing. Like the ocean, the teachings of the Dhamma are consistent and stable. Dead bodies do not last in the ocean. Similarly, evil men cannot stay in the Dhamma.

'All rivers find their way to the ocean and become the ocean. Similarly, all kinds of people can be part of the Sangh and will be known only as Bhikkhugana.

'The ocean accepts rainwater and rivers without losing itself. Similarly when Bhikkhu accept nirvana, nirvana doesn't lose itself.

'The ocean has one taste, saltiness. The Dhamma also has one taste, detachment.

'The ocean has many jewels. Similarly, Dhamma has many precepts:

the four noble truths; the middle path that avoids self-indulgence as well as self-mortification; five hindrances to enlightenment; five controlling factors; seven precepts of enlightenment; and the eight-fold path to nirvana.

'The ocean houses many kinds of large fish and creatures. Similarly, the Dhamma houses many different followers of Dhamma.'

Kundalkesha asked questions and Sariputra answered them as expansively as he could. All listeners learned from his answers.

Finally, she asked, 'Bhantey, one who gives up worldly pleasures and accepts suffering and has conquered pain, is such a person not great?'

'Sister, such a person is not great. Such a person makes his suffering itself part of his character and wallows in it drawing attention to himself or herself. That makes such a person arrogant. And it is stigma on his or her asceticism.'

As soon as she heard the word 'stigma', Kundalkesha's forehead was creased with displeasure. Her eyes narrowed, but she collected herself quickly and said, 'Bhantey, I have finished asking my questions. You must ask your questions of me now. Perhaps you will find answers in your own questions.'

Sariputra smiled kindly and said, 'Sister, if I have failed to answer your questions satisfactorily, I am ready to accept my defeat in accordance with your rules. For me, winning and losing have the same meaning.'

'Bhantey, that is not what I meant,' she said quickly, 'please ask me whatever you wish.'

'Sister, I have your answers for my questions without asking them. Therefore—'

The governor broke in, 'Bhantey, forgive me, but the people here have heard so much of Kundalkesha's brilliance and knowledge. They are curious to hear from her. So please ask her your questions.'

Sariputra looked at the audience and they all nodded in agreement. He looked at Kundalkesha and her eyes seemed to be smiling at him.

'All right then. Sister, I will ask you one question. You have conquered pain. At the root of this pain there is something unsettled, diseased, an ugly desire which has sway over you. What is that one thing?'

'Impossible. Kundalkesha, controlled by something else? This is impossible,' she shot back quickly. 'Bhantey, to use words like diseased and swayed by desire in Kundalkesha's presence is disrespectful.' Her voice rose as she spoke the words. It was clear her tiny body was shaking with passion and her eyes were getting wider and redder.

'Sister. Calm down. I have not used any words that would disrespect you. I have merely asked a question. I am sorry that my words have hurt you.'

The governor stood up to arbitrate and said, 'Bhantey, this is a debate. It is an exchange of ideas. There is no need here to talk about disrespect or apologies. Each person must answer the questions posed as thoroughly as he or she can so the listeners can be satisfied. Sister, please direct your attention inwards and answer the question: what is that one thing that has sway over you?'

Kundalkesha collected herself and turned inwards: My behaviour is as pure as the gold that has come out of the fire. My body, mind, and soul are pure. My intelligence is sharp as a sword and my memory as piercing as the tip of an arrow. Yet what is the one thing that is unsettling, diseased, and attached to desire that has sway over me? What is it?

For several minutes there was silence everywhere. All eyes were watching Kundalkesha. Her face was blanched with doubts and her eyes were unsettled. Suddenly, the audience spoke as if in one voice, 'Victory to Bhantey Sariputra.'

Sariputra got up quickly and raised his arms to quiet the audience. In a calm voice he said, 'Brothers and sisters, those who express joy at someone's pain do not follow Dhamma well. Remember, we are all part of the Dhamma here. Follow its edicts well.'

VIMALA

Therigatha

Translated from the Pali by Caroline Augusta Foley Rhys Davids

How was I once puff'd up, incens'd with the bloom of my beauty,
Vain of my perfect form, my fame and success 'midst the people,
Fill'd with the pride of my youth, unknowing the Truth and unheeding!
Lo! I made my body, bravely arrayed, deftly painted,
Speak for me to the lads, whilst I at the door of the harlot
Stood, like a crafty hunter, weaving his snares, ever watchful.
Yea, I bared without shame my body and wealth of adorning;
Manifold wiles I wrought, devouring the virtue of many.

Today with shaven head, wrapt in my robe,
I go forth on my daily round for food;
And 'neath the spreading boughs of forest tree
I sit, and Second-Jhana's rapture win,
Where reas'nings cease, and joy and ease remain.
Now all the evil bonds that fetter gods
And men are wholly rent and cut away.
Purg'd are the Āsavas that drugg'd my heart,
Calm and content I know Nibbana's Peace.

ZEB-UN-NISA

The Diwan of Zeb-un-nisa

Translated from the Persian by Magan Lal and Jessie Duncan Westbrook

3
O Prophet, o'er the world
Thy soul-compelling banner is unfurled:
    See how thy faith hath spread
Till Iran and Arabia are led.
    Thy lips unclose
Like petals of a newly-budded rose,
    And from them flow
Thy words of wisdom, till not only know
    The sons of men,

But birds within the garden sing again
 Thy words of gold.
O thou whose beauty I with joy behold,
 Nature in truth
Made never loveliness like to thy youth.
 Snared me it hath
Till fain would I renunciation's path
 With patience tread,
And follow where thy holy feet have led.
 But how can I
My cherished joys to my poor heart deny,
 Or, even more,
My cherished sorrows can I yield, for sore
 My heart doth bleed
Where cruel love hath wounded it indeed.
 Look thou and see
Where from my wounds there drops continually
 A crimson flood;
But fragrant flowers are springing from my blood,
 And every thorn
Wherewith my weary wandering feet are torn
 Turns to a rose.
O Makhfi, if the Kaaba keeper close
 To thee his door,
Complain not: thou possessest even more
 A holy place;
For look into the Well-Beloved Face,
 Over His Eyes
Arches more fair than Kaaba gates arise;
 Thy heart shall bend,
Itself an archway welcoming the Friend.

34

Why should we but in the assembly pray
 Only when friends are gathered call for wine?
Lo, I have done with this hypocrisy,
 And ever pray and drink the cup divine.

The fountain of my spirit has run dry,
 So that in tears no more my sorrow flows,
Mute is the heart that wailed continually,

Silent the bulbul in the garden-close.

Here, as we tread the pilgrim's way, we find
   The torch of inspiration like a fire,
Men see it not, so dull they are and blind,
   They yearn not for the garments of desire.

To each was given on the Creation-day
   His fitting portion, his appointed share,
Why should'st thou then demand from destiny
   More joy than others have, less pain to bear?

O Makhfi, for thy counsel all have come,
   Their secrets thou hast kept concealed, apart,
But why should'st thou, who for their sakes art dumb,
   Tell shamelessly the secrets of thy heart?

LAL DED

Lalla Vakyani

Translated from the Kashmiri by George Grierson

8
Let Him bear the name of Śiva, or of Keśava, or of the Jina, or of
the Lotus-born Lord,—whatever name he bear,—
   May he take from me, sick woman that I am, the disease of the world,
   Whether He be he, or he, or he, or he.

93
The soul is ever new and new; the moon is ever new and new.
So saw I the waste of waters ever new and new.
But since I, Lalla, scoured my body and my mind,
I, Lalla, am ever new and new.

98
By a way I came, but I went not by the way.
   While I was yet on the midst of the embankment with its crazy
bridges, the day failed for me.
   I looked within my poke, and not a cowry came to hand (or, *atē*,
was there)
   What shall I give for the ferry-fee?

Translated from the Marathi by Jerry Pinto and Neela Bhagwat

BAHINABAI

Te Sukh Sangta Vaache Pade Maun

Translated from the Marathi by Jerry Pinto and Neela Bhagwat

Such happiness strikes me dumb.
How do I speak of these passionate pilgrims?

Bliss knocks urgently at the doors of my senses.
As if I were sitting by the pulsing life force.

Were I a pot, I'd be submerged
Under water and yet unbroken.

Bahini says: Tukaram saw the signs.
He knew what was going on, in my mind.

RAJAI

Don Prahar Raatr Paahoni Ekaant

Translated from the Marathi by Jerry Pinto and Neela Bhagwat

In the second watch of the night,
Rajai is alone and so is Rukhmai.

'Bai, look at the state of my house,
And then intercede with your spouse.

'Why would he drive a devotee mad?
Fourteen mouths and no grain to be had.

'Were I to get food, begging from door to door,
In what would I serve it? My kitchen's no more.'

Call Rajai a harridan, call her a bore,
I don't care. Just talk to Namdeo.

Ghardhanyaani Kela Guru

Translated from the Marathi by Jerry Pinto and Neela Bhagwat

The man of the house says he's found a guru.
Mother Mesai, now what do I do?

I have a family, hungry mouths to feed.
Namdev, my Lord, pays no heed.

Mesai, I'm asking you for aid.
I can't see anyone else who will help.

My husband has Vitthala on his mind.
And fills the house with others of his kind.

They dance, they sing, they touch each other's feet
They chant Vitthala's name and joy breaks free.

Poor Gonai, you birthed a white stone
Even that Vitthala claimed for His own.

Mesai, how would a woman not be vexed?
Mother, you tell me, what comes next?

JENABAI

Doicha Padar Aalaa Khaandyaavari

Translated from the Marathi by Jerry Pinto and Neela Bhagwat

I have let my veil drop to my shoulders.
Bare-headed, I shall walk through the market.
In my hands the cymbals, on my shoulder the veena
Let who will try and stop me now.
Come wish me well, anoint my wrists with oil.
Jani says: I have become your whore, Keshava.
I come now to wreck your home.

Viveksaagar! Sakhaa Maajha Dnyaneshwar

Translated from the Marathi by Jerry Pinto and Neela Bhagwat

Dnyaneshwar, friend, ocean of wisdom,
I'd take the pangs of being born again
But only if you'd sprout in my belly.
My brother, would you do that for me?

Dnyanadeva, father, I'd surrender to you
Life after life, swears Jani.

MUKTABAI

Sukhaache Shevti, Dukh Aale Bheti

Translated from the Marathi by Jerry Pinto and Neela Bhagwat

First came joy and on the morrow
Hard on her heels, a visit from sorrow.
Just as we settled down to grieving,
She announced that she was leaving.
Joy and sorrow, what's the difference?
Both are sisters, born of ignorance.

Muktai tells Changya: self-born, the soul,
Standing like a banyan, aloof and whole.

Mungi Udaali Aakaashi

Translated from the Marathi by Jerry Pinto and Neela Bhagwat

An ant flew into the sky,
She swallowed the sun.
That wasn't the only wonder:
The barren gave birth to a son.

The scorpion burrows into the underworld
And Shesha touches his feet.
Unto a fly, a hawk is born.

Muktabai watches, laughs.

AKKA MAHADEVI

Songs for Shiva

Translated from the Kannada by Vinaya Chaitanya

63
I am united with the beautiful one who has
No death, no fault, no form.
O mother, I am united with the
Handsome one who has
No end, no break, no compare, no distinguishing mark,

No birth, no fear.
Brave is he, the beautiful one I am joined to;
I am united with the boundlessly expansive
Channamallikarjuna, jasmine-tender.
All these husbands who die and decay—
Throw them in the fire, mother.

64

I touch the feet of Kama once,
Then again, beseech the moon with folded palms:
This separation be damned.
Why must I be perturbed?
Because of Channamallikarjuna, jasmine-tender,
I am obliged to everyone.

113

Like the monkey at the tip of a pole,
Like the puppet at the end of a string,
I played as you made me play,
I spoke as you made me speak,
I stayed as you made me stay:
Till Channamallikarjuna, jasmine-tender,
The machinist of the world,
Said 'Enough'.

135

Desiring, imagining, I sat, O mother, being scorched;
Deluded kissing, I went mad, O mother;
Ever, never giving up, I believed him with joy.
If my god, Channamallikarjuna, jasmine-tender,
Does not like me
What shall I do, O mother?

142

Listen, O sister, I had a dream:
I saw rice, betel nut, coconut
And palm leaf festoons;
I saw the mendicant with small matted locks
And shining pearly teeth,
Come begging, O sister.
I ran after him and caught him by the hand

While he was running away;
Seeing Channamallikarjuna, jasmine-tender,
I opened my eyes.

151
Make me go from house to house
Begging with outstretched palms, O Lord!
Even if I beg, O lord,
See that they don't give.
If they give, O lord,
Make it fall to the ground.
When it falls to the ground, O lord,
See that the dog gets it before I pick it up,
Channamallikarjuna, jasmine-tender.

SOYRABAI

Translated from the Marathi by Jerry Pinto and Neela Bhagwat

Kaa Baa Udaas Maj Kele

Why do you thwart me thus?
Would you call your behaviour just?

We will sit here at your door.
Until we get what we ask for.

With all the others, you're sitting tight.
Soyra says: Vittho, this is just not right.

Kiti Kiti Boloo Deva

How much more must I plead, Lord?
How much more jealousy must I bear?
The love of others touches you.
Why do you refuse mine?

I feel no fear of you now.
Not of you, nor of any other.
How much more must I say, Lord?

I don't care if you bear a grudge.
Soyra says: I'm here. I won't budge.

Sukh Anumatra Nahi Sansaari

Translated from the Marathi by Jerry Pinto and Neela Bhagwat

Not one atom of happiness,
And this is a life sentence.

I can't, I can't focus on that holy name.
I can't conjure up the saints.
My mind won't stop, won't settle.
All day, all day, just tumult.

Nirmala says: Chokha, how do you do it?
How do you hold on to him?

MIRABAI

Eating God

Translated from the Rajasthani by Rahul Soni

33
Rana
this shame is
so sweet

condemn or
commend me
I'll carry on

there's no
turning back
on this
one-way street

hermits
speak wisely
sinners
vilify

but Girdhar's
my master
the sinners
can go die.

83
fever-bird
stop crying
piya-piya

or
I'll tear off
your wings
cut off
your beak
rub salt
in your wounds

I'm aching
for my piya, my lover
I'm his
and he's mine
why should you
call to him

but
if your call
brings him to me
I'll gild
your beak
I'll crown you
king

crow
go tell my lover
his woman
can't eat
without him
she keeps
crying
piya-piya

come back soon
my master

you know all
don't you know
I can't live
without you.

ANDAAL

Nacciyar Tirumoli

Translated from the Tamil by Priya Sarukkai Chabria

Song 8: Dark Rain Clouds Be My Messengers

5
Monsoon clouds you spread and spread
    To hood earth, your torrent slashes
The sky, you shake the honey-heavy blossoms
    Of Vengadam and strew scented petals.
Go tell the dark lord who killed the demon Hiranya
    Ripping him with paws of fury
That he has robbed me of my bangles.
    He must return them to me now.

Whirling clouds you enlarge in anger
and growl across the sky rending it open

with lightning. Spilling honey you tear
flowers, petals spatter like blood on earth.

Go to the fierce lord who roars and mauls
tossing his mane as his paws rip insides out.

Tell him I'm bloodied. He must heal
with long caresses, still me in his thrall.

engorged with anger
nails extending he kills
plunging wrists in blood

from these very hands I seek
fondling
gather in my swollen ripeness

as spilling nectar
my body's bloodflower
bursts

7
The Great Churning bubbled gems and moonmilk
    Conches from the ocean. He sustained this
Upheaval. Descend Clouds below crashing waves, down
    To the glowing feet of Vengadam's lord whose
Long eyes redden in ardor. Rest there my request:
    I beg his great chest is smeared and smeared
By the saffron paste that swathes my breasts.
    He must enter me if only for a day, else I waste away.

Before Time began The Churning
spun constellations from the cosmic

ocean's depths. Lotus-eyed Narayana
dived as Kurma, submerged tortoise.

Submerge clouds, lay me at his feet
and tell him of my eternal surrender-

to satisfy my body's velvet longing
by permeating me over and over.

churn
churn
Time's great ocean, each second, each eternity

                    churn my body's milk
                        adored one
                    churn red my ocean

                    churn out my true self
                    let me rise to cover you
                        or let me die

9

Great thunderheads rearing like maddened
        War elephants over Vengadam's forested emerald
Summit ask him who makes his bed on the colossal
        Coils of the sacred serpent what words he said to me.
He, Protector of the Universe, sole refuge to all is false
        With me, a maiden slender and trusting.
In what light will the world judge him if he betrays
        Me, slays me instead? Shouldn't he protect his name?

Clouds clashing like rutting elephants trumpeting
with trunks entwined over Vengadam's peak

ask him who sleeps on the snake's stupendous
loops to awaken to my distress, to be not twisted

in his words. He, Supreme Guardian of All ignores
me as he slumbers, head secure beneath its hood.

I'm a vine yearning to wrap around him. How
will universes assess him if he lets me wither?

                    coiled twisted thunderheads
                    coiled twisted words of succor
                            ask me

                        tender coiling vine
                        what words of love
                            should be

save yourself resplendence
by loving me
my love expanding over universes expanding

Secular
Love

Love, sex, relationships have been the cornerstones of women's (and men's) writing, starting as far back as the ancient Tamil Sangam era (third century BCE to fourth century CE). Avvaiyar I (the one from the Sangam era), according to legend, was a court poet, and many of her verses are dedicated to a local ruler called Vallai Athiyamaan who also sent her as an ambassador to a neighbouring kingdom. She wrote of love as well as statecraft.

What is interesting to me are the ways in which writing about secular love overlaps with spiritual longing, marriage and children. Molla, one of the earliest known Telugu writers, is credited with a Telugu retelling of the Ramayana. Her verse 'The Sun Moved in the Sky' is a luxuriant passage that describes Sita and Ram meeting, and though the Ramayana may be seen as a devotional text, this particular extract is pure shringar ras (one of the nine rasas, associated with romantic love and beauty).

Alka Saraogi manages to weave together half a dozen themes into her story 'The Death of a Tree'—it is as much about environmental consciousness as urban landscapes, philosophy, love, and the multiple roles played by storytelling in the lives of beleaguered people. This particular extract rests on restlessness in the work place, and loneliness, and of course, the trickiness of love. In the words of the protagonist, Jagannath babu, the biggest drawback of being in love is that 'a person is no longer his own master. Stripped of his ambitions, his beliefs, commitments and even his habits, he becomes a nincompoop. But,' Jagannath babu added (...) 'the fact is that the loss is really a gain.' The story is rich in sensual descriptions of love and tangible loss, though the beloved is neither human nor god.

Kutti Revathi's poem 'Breasts', which created a storm of protest when it was first written, is a poem about emotions rather than bodies. Yashodhara Mishra's short story, on the other hand, is a wonderful inquisition into our need for human touch, a need which drives a woman towards a man regardless of love or the expectation of permanence. The extract from Vibhavari Shirurkar's *Kharemaster* describes a man's first steps towards intimacy with his teenaged wife at a time when girls of nine were considered too old for marriage.

Krishna Sobti's *Sunflowers of the Dark* describes child abuse, deceit, frigidity and the delicacy of sexual moods. It speaks without shame and with a great deal of tenderness about sexual fulfilment. The work of Muddupalani takes us to an India that was joyfully erotic. Some of her verses might make modern readers blush but her celebratory approach to sex is unrivalled.

One of my favourite pieces on love is a poem by the Malayalam writer Rosemary: 'What I Have to Tell You'. She outlines the confidence and trust that define love so simply that it is both startling and heartbreaking.

ROSEMARY

What I Have to Tell You

Translated from the Malayalam by J. Devika

You
must not fear my love.
It expects nothing from you.

You
should not mistrust my friendship.
It does not wish to own you.

Once upon a time,
on a dark, dark night,
the spirits came
and stowed away in my heart
a hoard of love.
That gift was given
while I was asleep.
When I awoke,
love surged over the
banks of my heart.
The sad, the lonely,
came to snatch it away.
Love brimmed full, though.
I poured it into goblets.
I wandered
beneath the boundless sky,
across vast open spaces,
along deserted paths.
I held in my hands
the overflowing goblet.

You
should feel not guilty
about my love;
I do not hold out to you
what I took back from another;
have I not told you

of the love that withers unfelt,
of the goblet that brims over?
I want to make some things clear.
If you come to me someday
do not assume the gestures
of the king
who goes to meet his slave.
I do not need rent-free land,
or provinces to rule.
Do not wear the mien
of a god
before his devotee.
I have no boons
to ask of you.
My soul is not arid
that it should be filled
with your radiance.
Like one emperor to another,
like one friend to another,
come to me
as an equal.
Like a flute
pursuing the tune,
like the question
seeking its answer,
may your steps be
as light
and as carefree...

VELLI VITIYAR

Translated from the Tamil by George L. Hart III

Kuruntokai 58

YOU TELL ME I AM WRONG, MY FRIEND

You tell me I am wrong, my friend,
that I should stop seeing her.
Yes, I know it would be good

if I could do what you say,
but my pain
is like butter melting
on a ledge scorched in the sun
while a man who has no hands or tongue
tries to save it.
It spreads through me
no matter what I do.

Kuruntokai 130

HE WILL NOT DIG UP THE EARTH AND ENTER IT

He will not dig up the earth and enter it,
he will not climb into the sky,
he will not walk across the dark sea.
If we search every country,
every city,
every village,
can your lover escape us?

(The friend speaks to the heroine about her lover, who has left on a journey and not returned.)

AVVAIYAR

Translated from the Tamil by George L. Hart III

Kuruntokai 28

WHAT SHE SAID

Shall I attack these people, shall I strike them?
I do not know.
Or shall I find some reason and cry out
to his city that sleeps
not knowing my suffering
while the moving wind swirls
and pulls me to and fro.

YOU CANNOT COMPARE THEM WITH A LUTE

You cannot compare them with a lute.
The tenses are wrong, the meanings unclear,
and yet the words of a little son
fill a father with love.
The words of my mouth are like that also,
O Netuman Anci
who have taken many enemy forts with guarded walls,
for they make you show your love.

MOLLA

Ramayanam

Translated from the Telugu by B. V. L. Narayanarow

ARE THEY LOTUSES?

Are they lotuses
or the arrows of Cupid?
    Difficult to say
    of her eyes.

Are they sweet chirpings of birds
or of celestial women?
    Difficult to say
    of her words.

Is it the moon
or the looking glass?
    Difficult to say
    of her face.

Are they golden pots
or a pair of *chakravaka* birds?
    Difficult to say
    of her breasts.

Is it a flow of sapphires

or a flock of bees?
  Difficult to say
  of her hair.

Is it a sand dune
or a dais for Love God's wedding?
  Difficult to say
  of her thighs.

People got confused
as they watched
elegant her.

MUDDUPALANI

The Appeasement of Radhika

Translated from the Telugu by Sandhya Mulchandani

107
'Her crestfallen face,
Quivering lips and trembling body,
Shining eyes tearful,
Even Manmatha would pity her,
As she stands at the gate,
Stunned,
Awaiting my return...
How did I remain so unmoved?
So unthinking?

108
'She dislikes sleeping on the bed
Preferring my chest
She dislikes sitting on a chair
Preferring my lap
She dislikes eating sweets
Preferring my lips
She dislikes listening to the rudra veena
Preferring my voice
She cares not to call her maids

Prefers to call only me with love
Such an embodiment of goodness,
Have I forsaken.
Can this be anything but a curse from the Almighty?

109
'Seeing her get dressed heightens my love
Even reapplying her bindi, she pleasures me
Refreshing her make-up, she excites
Moving her thighs, she allures
Embracing me tightly, she attracts
Changing postures, she whets my lust
Rearranging the flowers on the bed, she seduces
Artfully, she alternates
Fuming and forgiving
Pleading and cajoling
Respecting and teasing
Adept at making love
She rules over me
I cannot bear being separated from her any longer!

110
'Her breasts heave
Hair spills over
Her bindi smudges
Eyelashes flicker
Sighs turn to groans
Sweat runs down her cheeks
I remember
Our satiating intercourse
In the very depths of my mind.

111
'Trembling thighs, loosened sari and marked lips,
Sweating face, dishevelled hair and bindi smudged,
Smeared sandalwood, heightened sighs and quivering breasts,
Swaying gait, love uncontrolled and exhaustion
After making love, as semen pours,
I imagine my love standing beside me.

112
'Bashful she still beckons,
Fearless and standing tall
Touching me, squeezing me against her breasts,
She revels in delighting me
Teasingly, loosening her clothes
Pressing her thigh to mine
Slapping me gently on my cheek
She fills me up with desire.

113
'Stylish and artful, she kisses me lovingly
Appreciated and adored for her beauty
Lauded and praised for her experience
Lively and spirited is she
Who else would have such vitality?
Who else, except her?

114
'Many have I seen
Many have I talked to
Many have I made love to
But she
Her style, her beauty, her talent
Are exceptional.
The ecstasy of our union
I've felt with no other,
She, the only deserving one.

115
'As I enter her, she opens her eyes wide,
Eyebrows rise,
Feigned anger colours her face,
"O! you pitiless man,
Surely a god without sympathy threw me at you!"
She says, coquettishly closing her eyes,
Content.

116
'As I make love over and again
With force and passion,

She half opens her lotus eyes,
Smiling sweetly, she encourages,
"Wonderful…That's the way…
This is good…Excellent…Don't stop!" she says,
Seductive.
With such words, she allures,
Can I ever forget her sweet voice?

117
'Pressed against me,
Her breasts touching my back,
Lower back pushed against my thighs,
Radiant thighs spread wide,
Fingers running through my hair,
She pleases me so…
How can I stand being separated from such a one?

118
'With great passion, she embraces
Slipping her hand into my dhoti
Raising her thighs as I press mine,
She responds with pleasure.
Pressing again, with mounting desire
Getting on top of me, with desire swelling,
Satisfying my manliness…
She holds our bodies together,
Like a creeper does a tree…
She does a "snake crawl" over me with passion,
Can anyone else do this?
None except her!

Sunflowers of the Dark

Translated from the Hindi by Pamela Manasi

A lone cottage amidst the wilderness of Corbett Park. Diwakar and Ratti sat facing the fireplace, held in the grip of stolen time. Ratti carefully swept all the niches and corners of her mind, dusted the picture frames and turned dates on the calendar. She traced the movement of Diwakar's arm as he added another log to the grate. Sparks flew from embers and were lost in golden fire. He looked into her eyes, searching for the whirlpools rising within him.

The glass was still in Ratti's hand, her gaze resting on its surface. Smiling, she said, 'How long do you take to finish a large?'

Diwakar chuckled. 'Why? Want to compete with me?'

'No. Today, I want each sip to be long. Long and endless. Let it be dawn by the time I finish.'

The smile playing on Diwakar's lips stilled. He pulled her close, looked into her eyes and whispered, 'Understood.' Ratti did not stir. The trials of an unlived childhood, the freedoms and constraints, the borders of her solitary life clouded her eyes. When she clung to Diwakar, there was a tremor in her arms, a painful throbbing in her breast. Nestling her in his arms, he led her to the bed and laid her down gently.

'Do you like it here, Ratika?'

'I feel wonderful, Diwakar. Like I've never felt before.'

Fondling her lap, he said, 'There's a bigger sanctuary here, Ratika— more peaceful than any other—here within you.'

Ratti basked in the warmth of his gaze. Then gazing at the dim-lit room, she said, 'The footsteps I hear outside my solitary cottage are yours. But at this moment, it seems I am you, and you are me.'

Diwakar smiled. 'So my wise Ratti has a third eye.'

'Yes. Those who have nothing else have it. They endure, and they wait.'

Diwakar bent down over Ratti as if to gather all of her into himself. She caressed his nape, smooth as silk. For an endless moment, Diwakar hung from a fine string, lighter than a breath, connecting him to her. Floating. He closed his eyes and let his fingers stray, undoing the buttons at her throat, mapping her feverish body with his hands.

Here. Right here. Yes. Ratti's hands stilled Diwakar and pulled him out of that wave. She kissed him, woman anew, a whole woman. Caressed the rough velvet of his chest with her fingers, her lips.

Steeped in the glow of the fading fire, the room seemed ethereal. And the two of them, two deities on an altar. Questing the potion of life from wellsprings hidden deep.

'Ei, what are you thinking?'

Ratti smiled. 'I am not thinking anything. I am waiting for you, watching the road. When will you reach here?'

'You simple little girl!' Touched, Diwakar's laugh filled the room. He cupped her face and kissed her, long and slow. He breathed her in, caressed her, and then unfurled her. Ratti tightened her arms around him, wanting to contain a waterfall, poised on the brink. Diwakar gently kissed her forehead, her hair. 'Ratti, let go. Let me love you. Because we want to...just for each other. Let go, Ratti...'

She kissed him back greedily, possessively. Her fingers slipped between his thighs. They moved slowly, on a swing of desire. Until Diwakar began to tremble. He softly mouthed her nipples, now rigid, her belly. Then moving further down, below her navel, he kissed her there, tracing patterns with his tongue, his fingers. And Ratti's gentle hold on Diwakar's back became an iron grip.

'Come...come...come...'

Moving astride, Diwakar cradled Ratti's head with a hand, and she tore off the cover, pulling him down into her depths. As her body danced to his rhythm, a spiralling pleasure, sharp and new, coursed through her. And Ratti seemed to laugh from behind the veil of her mind and body. Diwakar paused for a second to look into her eyes, and then he lost himself. He didn't hear her moan.

A fish writhing on the shore was swept in by a whirlpool, and hearing Ratti's silent scream, Diwakar too found his release. When he parted, pearls cascaded down her legs, lighting up Ratti's decades-old darkness.

Diwakar enfolded Ratti and stroking her hair, asked, 'I want to know, Ratika...'

She touched his lips. 'Never before. You have washed away my curse, Diwakar.' Then holding his palms over her eyes, she asked, 'Was I too something?'

He sprinkled tiny kisses all over her, then nuzzling her lap, murmured, 'There is a forest of sapphire in here...tall evergreen trees...a fire rages at the mouth of this cave. An erotic fragrance drenches the mind and body. Blooms of paradise filter through the tranquil shade of those trees and snowcapped peaks...'

Ratti laughed and pinched his nose. 'I'll hit you now! Am I a woman or a map?'

'Really?' Laughing, Diwakar held Ratti's glowing face in the hollow of his palms. Then just as she was slipping away, he pressed her down and kissed the inside of her thighs, softly, urgently, filling her with warmth. And parting them, he entered her, his tongue deep inside her mouth, as if in search of something.

◆

Ratti opened her eyes to find Diwakar fast asleep. She quietly left the bed. Gazing at Diwakar, she felt the silence of an aeon empty itself from her womb and cling to his sleeping form, vanish under his eyelids. The tranquil rise and fall of his breaths, blue music of the deepening night, made her taut with desire and she yearned to be under his skin again. Lying before the fading warmth of the glowing logs, a languorous exhaustion filled her limbs. Pleasure. Bliss. Sap dripping on green boughs. The touch of fingertips on her skin. O fire, this infinite, indefinite joy of your warmth, like the union of lovers. You have ignited a blaze in Ratti's desert solitude. Grant me just one more moment, so I can awaken the divine in me, just one more time.

She felt herself all over, reverently. Everything is just as it was...and yet it isn't. Amazed that Diwakar had truly fathomed her depths, Ratti softly brought his name to her lips, as if to herself, for the first time.

A Matter of Choice

As she rose to higher ranks in her profession, she began to acquire from the market all that seemed valuable in the eyes of her friends and colleagues. But living in that house which had started looking more like an ad in a magazine, Manisha increasingly felt that she had innumerable days of loneliness to count there. And amidst all that if ever a male friend or associate offered a compliment or a meaningful gaze, she cast it out of her mind and body as a proposition fraught with hassles and trouble.

Then followed this meeting with DK. What was it that Manisha got from him that evening? What promise did she see in him, during that meeting or later at home when she could not put thoughts of him out of her mind? Whatever was he able to give Manisha? Who did not know about DK's wife and children, his worldly success and prosperity, and his flamboyant life? Where was a niche there for Manisha that he could hope to fit into? In fact, even the attractive female stenographer at the office flaunted her close association with DK like a devotee sporting the flowers left over from the deity's adornment. And yet, one wonders, how much does DK let the others participate in his life? He does not even let them use his full name; he has given them just the abbreviated initials to address him by or even to profess their intimacy with him.

For Manisha, where DK was concerned, it was simply a matter of experience—an experience that was nothing new. In fact, she was familiar with it. Yet, it was like a whiff of cool air on a muggy afternoon. DK had managed to convey this feeling during their very first meeting at the party. She felt as if her body that had over time deadened into steel was slowly regaining its magnetic power.

Probably for the first time in ages, Manisha did not bother about the man who sought her company. She did not gauge his eligibility. Nor did she bother to consider what quality in herself attracted him towards her. She heard the door-shackle clank; and that was all. She opened the door and said:

'Come. Come inside.'

After exchanging pleasantries and meaningful glances in the midst of friends for several days, one day DK proposed that they go over to a certain place together after office hours. She readily agreed. When they were alone, she did not resist his extended hand.

On returning home, she tried to slowly untangle the yarn of her experience step by step, replaying every single moment of that evening.

What did she feel when DK touched her with his hands and his lips? Was she thrilled? Or was she passionate about it? Or was it simply an overwhelming experience of fear and confusion? It was none of these things. There wasn't either happiness or gloom in there. The experience was like that of the crumbling of a wall that had stood needlessly as an obstacle all the while, and the incredible journey over the mound of rubble one step after another to cross over to the other side. She was neither astonished nor disappointed at what she saw on the other side. She had physically arrived at the forbidden destination. That was all.

Till the time she entered her house, she was afraid of herself. Manisha was apprehensive that the moment she saw her face in the mirror, she might turn away in shame. She thought she would be reproachful of herself. Surprisingly, that did not happen.

It then occurred to her that she did not remember when last she had felt the touch of human hands on her body. Was it when she had fever that showed no sign of remission for a week, and the doctor Ms Sen had examined her pulse and checked her blood pressure? And also examined her chest and stomach with a stethoscope, and pressing the sides of her stomach asked her if she felt any pain? She could not think of any other human touch that she had experienced in days before or after that occasion. Once in a while, Ma, when she was alive, would massage her hair. She would carefully separate the strands, and keep rubbing oil through the roots and massaging for a long time. 'You can wash it away in the morning. Oily hair is such a thing of shame for you girls these days.' Six years had passed since Ma died. She could hardly remember oiling her own hair, ever since. Could she recall the feel of Ramesh's touch? Yes, but she had succeeded in pushing it away to the backyard of her memory. Even those rare moments, stolen from public gaze at some quiet corner of a restaurant or in a park, had been fraught with so much caution, fear and care for self-respect. Also, at that tender age one's future looked so bright and full of promise that the smallest scratch seemed risky enough to mar it.

Such thoughts were occurring to Manisha for the first time in her life. And she found it strange that although her hands touched things like tables and chairs, files and papers all the time, she hardly ever got to touch another human being even casually. Living in the midst of people and spending much of her time in a crowded human melee didn't change this fact. In her childhood she used to pick up their neighbour's baby in her lap and hug her and tickle her. As a grown-up girl, she played bohu-chori and kabaddi with other girls, putting their arms around each other's waists, pulling each other's braids and giggling away. She also remembered how, as a child, she would sometimes pick up a stray puppy from the roadside, chase little dragonflies and feel with her palm the throbbing abdomen of tiny frogs. Was it a natural urge to move towards another living body just to feel the existence of life akin to one's own?

'Truly, Mani,' Rita Apa would often ask, 'what do you gain in deliberately getting friendly with someone who would simply rob you of your reputation, let alone shouldering your responsibility?'

'Even a tree wilts away and hardens into wood if it receives no water or air,' she wanted to tell Rita. 'When you try driving a nail into it, no sap oozes from it. I too was becoming lifeless, like the tough bark of a tree that was soft once. That was when another human being's hand caressed mine. The only solace was that it was a human touch—enough that it was no demon or ghost or beast. Do you believe me? Just to be able to touch another human being like yourself! It is a human touch in the first place; that it belonged to a man came next. It didn't matter if the man wasn't a god or a fictive hero drawn from the imaginary world of some novel or film.'

And then it began. She gradually started discovering touch, layer by layer, and taking it in step after step. A few drops of moisture were enough to revive a dying bud lying in a neglected corner of a garden. Soon, it would spread its petals in full bloom. Just because she could not grow along with the other flowers in the richly manured flowerbed or enjoy the streaming water flowing on to its bed everyday, must she wither and fall dead? Should she let herself die?

Breasts

Translated from the Tamil by N. Kalyan Raman

Breasts are bubbles, rising
In wet marshlands

I watched in awe—and guarded—
Their gradual swell and blooming
At the edges of my youth's season

Saying nothing to anyone else,
They sing along
With me alone, always:
Of Love,
Rapture,
Heartbreak

To the nurseries of my turning seasons,
They never once forgot or failed
To bring arousal

During penance, they swell, as if straining
To break free; and in the fierce tug of lust,
They soar, recalling the ecstasy of music

From the crush of embrace, they distill
The essence of love; and in the shock
Of childbirth, milk from coursing blood

Like two teardrops from an unfulfilled love
That cannot ever be wiped away,
They well up, as if in grief, and spill over.

Kharemaster

Translated from the Marathi by Yashodhara Maitra

Indu tai had, so far, never answered back. He looked at her present stance and replied, 'All right, you do whatever suits you.' He remembered that when Indu had refused to learn the alphabet, he had threatened to send her back to her parents. She had been completely taken aback and had agreed to learn. Till today his word had been law. He had thought of himself as the master of all he surveyed. But that was clearly not so any longer.

He realized that he had taken Indu for granted. He had not noticed that she worked very hard all day long. She took very good care of him, and remembered all the little things that pleased him. Now, hereafter, he decided, he must also be sensitive to her. Indu tai had brought all the family idols to Ghodnadi with her. She performed the puja ritual faithfully. Although Kharemaster did not believe in worshipping idols, he did not express his disapproval.

He consciously changed his attitude and behaviour towards Indu tai. He was then about twenty-six and had graduated fully into manhood. The nine-year-old girl who had entered his life was now about sixteen and had blossomed into womanhood. Desire for her stirred in him, but a strange reluctance held him back. He remembered what had happened to Thaki in Bombay. Thaki was Indu tai's age and was completely innocent in matters of sex. On the night of her garbhadhan—the consummation ceremony—she fainted with fright and was bedridden for several days. Indu tai had already reached puberty while they were in Bombay. So his mother had arranged for the consummation ceremony according to custom.

In those days, in Maharashtra, a great debate raged over the Age of Consent Bill. A bill was being considered to provide that if the woman was younger than twelve, the husband should not have sexual relations with her. If he did so he could be convicted and sentenced for life. Raosaheb Rege and his friends were fighting for the passage of this bill. In Madhavbag in Bombay, thousands attended meetings, protesting this law. In Pune, Agarkar and his group were agitating that the law be enacted. Kharemaster pushed aside his mother's plans and flatly refused the performance of this rite.

At Ghodnadi, however, they were just the two of them. Kharemaster's passions were aroused whenever he looked at Indu. But she had such an innocent look about her that he would be reminded of the Thaki episode.

He was worried that if he were overeager, Indu would be frightened and lost to him forever. How could this girl be so unaware of the relationship between a husband and a wife? Was it possible that women did not have any instinct for sex?

Although she was innocent in such matters, he realized that in running the household, Indu was by far his better half. It was Indu tai who had made this house into a home. For the first few days, he paid close attention to all the domestic details, but soon felt that he was ignorant about many things. He didn't know what the vegetables were called, whether they were fresh or not, what quantity should be bought—he had to bow to Indu tai's judgement in many such matters. This had a beneficial impact. Indu lost her diffidence and gained confidence. Kharemaster began slipping off his pedestal.

A natural occurrence that helped to remove the barrier between them was Indu tai's menstrual period. In those days, during her menstrual cycle, a woman actually had to sit outside the house, like an outcaste. For those three days of impurity, she was forbidden to do any of the household chores. Naturally, the man of the house had to shoulder these responsibilities. Who else would bring drinking water, cook the meals and perform the household chores? Kharemaster hadn't faced this problem in Bombay, since Aai had been there to manage the house. But the first time that Indu tai had her period at Ghodnadi, Kharemaster was in deep trouble. He had to sweep, cook, and wash the clothes and dishes, before he left for school at eight! He rebelled! And took recourse to questioning this practice of periodic abstinence from work. 'Forget this taboo and carry on as usual,' he told Indu tai. But she opposed the idea. 'In the Brahmin circles we will become outcastes. Shall I ask Gopika bai to make a simple meal of bhaji and bhakri for us?' But as there were frequent differences of opinion with the priest's family, Kharemaster didn't like taking his help in such times of trouble. So he braced himself and tried to do all the chores. After he had swept up the house, he went to fill water at the communal tap. Seeing that a man had come, the women at the tap stood aside. But when Kharemaster began filling his ghagar without the required 'purification', the women began whispering amongst themselves. Kharemaster was taken aback. For the first time he learnt how difficult it was to practise what one preached.

Although he had been accustomed to doing housework under Phatak mami's guidance, he had never cooked a meal before. Now that he was cooking under Indu tai's tutelage, his male ego was further threatened. Each time he had to ask her advice. 'How much salt should I add? Is this much chilli powder right? How do I give the phodni?' And, as Indu tai could not enter the kitchen during those days, each time he had to ask her a question he had to go to her, where she stood, outside the door. She would answer him, cover her mouth with her sari padar and giggle. And after all this, when the cooking was done, he had to serve her the meal outside, and serve himself in the kitchen.

With the first mouthful, both would realize that either there was too much salt or too little, the spices were all wrong and both would break out into laughter. All this served to bring them closer together, make them more each other's equals. Slowly, Kharemaster began cooking without direction. On the fourth day, he had to purify Indu tai by pouring a bucket of water on her. The sight of her body, through her wet clothes was, he felt, his reward for three days of hard work.

ALKA SARAOGI

The Death of a Tree

Translated from the Hindi by Vandana R. Singh

Like so many other human traits it's possible that the desire to narrate stories is also genetic—at least that appears to be the case with Jagannath babu. We know this because every now and then, the story of Jagannath babu's own life creeps into his narratives. This has happened so often that over the years, people listening to his stories have an improvised feature film about Jagannath babu's family running in their heads. As soon as Jagannath babu begins a story, all of them tune in to the films. Everyone has given faces to the now familiar characters and imagined them in specific settings. No one will ever know how different each one's film is from the other's imagined reality, even though they are all based on the same story.

In everybody's film, Jagannath babu's father lives in the last house in a blind alley of north Calcutta's Shyam Bazaar. He sits in a wheelchair, weaving one story after another and is happiest when people visit him. Jagannath babu's mother does her household chores mechanically. Not a hint of a smile ever touches her face. She is a manly woman with a hard face and a person of rare grit and determination. Her resolve to fight the poverty, disease and disability that have burrowed into her life is so strong that she refuses to sit idle even for a minute. For her, taking care of her disabled husband is a duty that god himself has entrusted her with. While discharging this duty she is never indolent or tired and doesn't procrastinate even for a moment. As Jagannath babu had once said, those who have to cope with the disability of someone close to them find strength by seeing their lives as a duty to be performed.

Jagannath babu's two elder sisters are always busy too, either giving dance and music lessons, or stitching and embroidering. Whenever they find time from these activities, they convert a wooden stool into a planchette by writing the Hindi alphabet on it with a piece of chalk. They then place a small bowl upside down on the stool and with their fingers on the bowl, start inviting all kinds of spirits to move it across the letters. They are especially keen on inviting Gandhi's spirit, though they can't quite understand why he mostly sits quietly inside the bowl, making it motionless. But Gandhi's muteness never frightens the two girls because they know that his is a great soul. They know that he will never harm them. One day the elder sister had seen an article in the newspaper,

'Gandhiji's soul depressed in today's India'. It then became clear to her why his spirit almost never communicated anything. Sitting in his wheelchair, Jagannath babu's father had also thought of a story with the same title.

Sometimes spirits are violent and can cause physical discomfort to the person who calls them: a feeling of suffocation, echoing sounds in the ears and so on. On such occasions, one has to beg forgiveness with folded hands, plead and implore them to go back to where they came from. At times, spirits, especially those of near and dear ones, do not want to go back. When this happens, Jagannath babu's older sister first cries her heart out. She then puts the fear of her mother into the spirit and begs it to go away.

In our films there are several other captivating details and anecdotes that are related to Jagannath babu's family but we cannot narrate them here. The predetermined title of the story reminds us that this is not its central theme. Well, such reminders were never necessary for Jagannath babu or his wheelchair-bound father as they composed and narrated one story after another. It never happened that they started telling one story and drifted into another. They've always been perfect storytellers and knew exactly how much to say, how to say it and, most important of all, what to say and what not to say.

As it happened, Jagannath babu stayed on in this particular job for six years. This unusual behaviour on Jagannath babu's part was enough to make his acquaintances wonder if all was well with him. In any case, they were convinced that his staying on for six years in the same job could only be on account of some extraordinary reason. The first thought that crossed everyone's mind was that Jagannath babu had fallen in love. After all, women in workplaces are like flowers in full bloom and, like bees, men seem to naturally hover around them. Recently, a bank from America set up a branch in Calcutta. One look at the trendy hairstyles and smart outfits of the girls who worked there was enough to foretell that everyone in town was going to open an account with the bank. Sure enough, newspapers soon carried articles announcing the closure of two of Calcutta's oldest foreign banks. A hospital specializing in heart bypass surgery in Calcutta with female staff raising heavily made-up eyes from their computers to admit patients is believed to have a waiting list running into several months.

There were reasons behind the assumption that a woman was behind Jagannath babu's lingering on in this particular office. It was located in a posh area on the ninth floor of a multi-storeyed building where the chance of meeting an attractive female co-worker was much brighter than elsewhere. After all it is money that is a magnet for beauty. That Jagannath babu was under a spell was further confirmed when he suddenly started chatting about 'birds'. Whatever Jagannath babu said now was received with knowing smiles. When Jagannath babu plunged into a lengthy description of a yellow-and-black bird with a red beak and an enchanting call, people found it impossible to suppress their mirth.

There was something in Jagannath babu's personality which naturally attracted people towards him. It was perhaps an inner happiness which can only come from seeing life as a story and nothing more. No one had ever seen Jagannath babu downcast or miserable. Even when he talked of his disabled father, his mother who made pickles day and night to run the household or an elder sister who died mysteriously on stage during a snake dance from a rib-punctured lung, he conveyed a sense of satisfaction at being able to gauge the mystery of existence. However, he never said what had happened to his younger sister in any of his stories.

We knew that his mother, after being widowed, had taken up some kind of penance and had given up eating cereals, salt and sugar and always walked barefoot for the rest of her life. The devotion with which she had taken care of her husband paled into insignificance when compared to the zeal with which she took to enlightening the world about Jamuli Sati, a matriarch in their lineage who had willingly gone up in flames on her husband's pyre a few hundred years ago. Jagannath babu's mother walked long distances in processions to propagate the spiritual powers of Jamuli Sati and so impressive was her evangelical crusade that photographs of Jamuli Sati soon adorned many walls and a temple built in her honour became progressively grander. Jagannath babu himself once said that it was on Jamuli Sati's orders that his mother had cheerfully accepted the decision of her only son to remain a bachelor.

Nobody who knew of the magnetic pull of Jagannath babu's personality was really surprised at the possibility that a girl with an enchanting voice, draped in a yellow-and-black sari, had fallen head over heels in love with the charmer. In their heart of hearts they were all very happy for him. There must be some sadness, some loneliness lurking inside his man—how was it possible that a man who lacked these emotions could ever exist on earth? So what if all this was happening rather late in his life; at least now Jagannath babu had found love, the most passionate emotion known to man. Perhaps it was in quest of this experience that he had been wandering from office to office. Was it not Jagannath babu himself who, in narrating one of his stories, once said that love is the only experience when man is completely purged of all egoism; when the self doesn't matter at all?

Talking of his mother's obsession with Jamuli Sati after his father's death, Jagannath babu said that any kind of religious fervour happens usually because of the absence of love. Man's desire to make someone the object of his love never dies and the imagination seeks a substitute in faith or religion to make one rise above the petty self.

Marriage

This section is given over to marriage, its joys and comforts as well as the difficulties it poses, not only in terms of sustaining a long-term relationship but also the fear of being left on the outside, or, once in, being kicked out of the institution. Where it is not enforced or mandated, marriage is still so much the norm—and for women, held up as a one-time investment in future security—that living outside the institution leaves them extremely vulnerable.

In this anthology, I treat marriage as a distinct section, separate from love, although the two are deeply enmeshed. Marriage will always encompass love, sex and children, but it is primarily an institution governed by law, with deep economic, legal and social implications for the human beings involved. Traditional marriage laws pushed several women to the margins of society: widows; unmarried women; women in extra-marital relationships with married men; wives who have been abandoned.

Readers will note that I have included extracts about education in this section. I have done so because it appears the primary obstacle to education—or other forms of empowerment—is marriage, or the fear that it will interfere with a woman's role as a wife and with the inequality built into such a relationship. Withholding education was not so much an attempt to discriminate against little girls as it was an attempt to take away agency from adult women.

Women who know the world, who can negotiate the world without men, pose challenges to patriarchal constructs. Learning brings confidence. It gives to women the necessary intellectual tools with which to argue against unjust systems. Pundita Ramabai was able to argue fiercely against the Manusmriti only because she could actually read all the ancient scriptures. But almost as soon as women began to learn how to read, they also wanted to write. Rassundari Devi's autobiography tells us not only of her great struggle to read and write, but also how much work 'housewives' actually do.

Women writers have looked beyond the happily ever afters. Mamta Kalia's 'After Eight Years of Marriage' is a straight look at how the average woman experiences the average marriage. Her poem 'Brat' addresses the control of a mother's womb, and it makes a wonderful accompaniment to the passage extracted from Volga's story 'The Experiment'. The story examines a man's fear of confident, independent women who don't believe in marriage. Attia Hosain's *Sunlight on a Broken Column* is about feudalism and class, which are the principal forces guiding arranged marriages, and the extract chosen for this section touches upon it lightly through the banter of a younger, more rebellious generation.

Kamala Das's autobiography is a telling account of how women, even educated and relatively privileged women, have very little actual control over their destinies, and how depression and loneliness weighed down her marriage. Indira Goswami's *The Blue-necked God* describes the horrific condition of widows living in Braj.

Geetanjali Shree's *Mai* is about patriarchy, bullying, the subsumption of a woman's identity, and the chain-links of oppression: father-in-law to mother-in-law to daughter-in-law to grandchildren. It also touches upon a woman's burden of trying to set her children free while living in an oppressive atmosphere.

ATTIA HOSAIN

Sunlight on a Broken Column

Aunt Saira, frowning with concentration, pulling names out of her memory said anxiously, 'What does one do about Bhimnagar? Now that he has married some half-caste from Calcutta and insists on taking out both wives together, what does one do? One cannot condone such behaviour.'

'Have you written Sheikh Waliuddin's name yet? If not, do so,' said Uncle Hamid.

Waliuddin was a lawyer who found politics more rewarding than his practice. His political beliefs veered in any direction that promised power. He was as friendly with Congress leaders as Muslim League ones. He won followers by making use of men with influence whom he won over with service and flattery.

'That man,' exclaimed Aunt Saira, 'that man who instigated Shia-Sunni riots for the sake of becoming a leader? Everyone knows he secretly encouraged the rioting, and then came out as the hero who stopped it.'

'I am not concerned with his methods. All I am concerned with are the results. Which reminds me, don't forget Agarwal,' interrupted Uncle Hamid dryly.

'Agarwal?' Saleem repeated the name as if searching for something.

'His daughter used to be at school with me. Sita Agarwal,' I said.

'Sita?' Kemal said sharply.

'Do you know her?'

'Slightly. Met her in London.'

'You have never mentioned her.'

'There was no occasion to,' Kemal said curtly.

'The world is a small place, they say,' Saleem smiled. 'Even London is microscopic when one Indian wishes to avoid another.'

'I must go to Amirpur's for bridge,' Uncle Hamid said.

'That reminds me,' Aunt Saira said. 'What about Dr and Mrs Lal? The way Amirpur dances around that woman is shocking.'

'Nonsense! Scandalous nonsense!' said Uncle Hamid as he was leaving the room. 'Mrs Lal is a charming woman.'

'I can't understand what you men see in her. Bold and pushing,' Aunt Saira called after him. 'The spectacle men make of themselves! All the ministers spinning round her....'

'Clever woman to achieve what seems to be the general purpose,' said Kemal.

'Such dreadful people one has to meet!' she sighed. 'Things have

52   *Unbound*

changed so much. But you must learn what your position in life is, and where you belong.'

'We were left in no doubt about that on quite a few occasions in England—we coloured people,' Kemal smiled.

'I like my position in life,' laughed Saleem. 'It is very comfortable. When I was young I thought otherwise, but that was adolescent masochism which I mistook for Marxism. Mind you, I still appreciate its principles, but I am no Lenin and can establish no Soviets...'

'Linen serviettes?' Aunt Saira frowned. 'I do not know what you are talking about.'

'How fortunate you are, Mother. Oh, brave old world!' Saleem laughed and kissed his mother.

She smiled happily and kissed both her sons. 'I am going to rest now. Will you children get the invitations ready? The cards and envelopes are in your father's office downstairs.'

'I'll get them,' said Saleem and went down the stairs with his mother.

Kemal sat staring out of the window. He never argued with his mother when she talked to him about understanding his heritage and culture; but I knew, because he confided in me, that his readjustment was not as easy as Saleem's.

He said very quietly, as if talking to himself, 'When I was a boy I used to sit at this window and look at the hills and the lake. Nothing has changed. I can still see a man's profile in the shape of that peak over there; the same noises come up from the bazaar below; the same human ants move about. The toy yachts becalmed on the lake have not finished the race which started when I was a boy. The house has not changed, the garden hasn't changed, the gardener hasn't changed. These hill people grow no older. They treat me like a little boy. The coolies are the same, in the same rags, with the same smiles and smells. I feel I have never been away. Then I talk to Father and Mother and their friends and I know I have been away for more than ten years. We talk without knowing what has happened to each other in the course of these years, not even external things. How much greater is the ignorance of the changes within that cannot be described but only felt! At least, when people are near each other they have some slight indication... Yet I am expected to think and behave as if I had never been away, as if the patterns of my thoughts should be familiar to those who have stayed behind. Do you understand me?'

'I do understand. Do you know why? Because without having gone away physically as you did I have never lived completely with the others.'

'I recognized that about you quite quickly. That is why I could talk to you and no one else. And now,' he smiled, 'I can tell you something which proves my point about my mother, about our not understanding each other. I had been back scarcely a week when she asked me whether I would consider marrying you.'

'She asked *you* to marry *me*?'

'She said, "Now that Laila is nineteen it is time to think of her marriage. What could be better than to keep the family undivided?..."'

'And the house, and the property,' I added.

'You are being unkind, Laila. I think she genuinely meant it...not from a material, but a human point of view.

'It is lucky when they coincide. But what did you say?'

'I said, "Damn it all, Mother, I'm not going to commit incest." Because that is how I thought of you from the first—as a sister. Not that she understood.'

Saleem stamped up the stairs into the room, 'What is the matter? Why do you both look so solemn?' he asked.

I smiled. 'I have the right to be. Kemal has refused to marry me.'

'Kemal has refused to marry you? Add me to the list. I've done the same.'

'You have?' Kemal and I said together.

'Well, Mother put the proposition to me...'

'To you too? She seems to be very impatient. I had better find someone for myself before she gets quite desperate. And what did you say?'

'I said, "Mother, I don't love the girl".'

'Thank you for being honest,' I laughed.

'I mean not that way,' Saleem said quickly. 'And she said, "Love?" in a very superior, shocked manner, eyebrows lifted, nostrils quivering, "Love? No one in decent families talks of love".'

We burst out laughing together, and I said, 'I've been told I'm not loved; I've been rejected twice; and I couldn't be happier. Thank you both with all my heart. I may have hated you as husbands, but I love you as friends.'

'A more lasting relationship, I assure you,' said Kemal.

'In sickness and in health until death do us part,' laughed Saleem. 'And now to our task! Let us slay the social dragons.'

RASSUNDARI DEVI

Words to Win

Translated from the Bengali by Tanika Sarkar

I was immersed in a life of labour, I hardly knew how time went by. Little by little, a desire took shape in my mind and I came to be possessed by a single wish: I will learn to read, and I will read a sacred text. I began to resent my own thoughts. What is wrong with me? Women do not read, how will I do it, and why does this bother me so! I didn't know what to do. It isn't as if all our ways were evil those days, but this certainly was. Everyone got together to deprive women of education. It must be said that women of those times were most unfortunate, they were hardly any better than beasts of burden. However, it is useless to reproach others about this, that was what fate had decreed for me. Really, how cross those old housewives would be if they saw a woman with as much as a piece of paper in her hands. So, how was I to learn anything? But my heart would not accept this, it was forever yearning. I began to ponder: as a child I had learnt something at that school at home from the other students who used to recite the letters loudly. Would I remember any of that? Slowly, with great effort, I managed to recall the thirty-four letters, the vowels and the spellings. That, again, was something that I could recite but not write. What was I to do? Truly, if no one teaches you, you can't learn a thing. Moreover, I was a woman, and a married one at that. I'd die if someone was to rebuke me. Nor was I supposed to talk to others, so my fears kept me nearly mute. I prayed all the time: Lord of this world! If you teach me yourself, I shall certainly learn. Who else will teach me if you don't? These thoughts were always with me. Many days passed thus.

Then I had a dream: I was reading the manuscript of *Chaitanya Bhagabat*. When I woke up, an unearthly joy possessed my body and heart. I kept closing my eyes even when I was fully awake, I kept going back to the memory of the dream. It was as if I had been given a priceless jewel. As my body and mind filled with delight, I began to wonder: 'Isn't it strange? I have never seen this book before, I wouldn't even recognize it. Yet I was reading it in my dreams. I can read nothing at all, let alone something like this, it is impossible. Even then, I am blessed that I was at least able to read it in my dream. Since I am always praying to god to teach me to read, he has allowed me to do so in my dream, for he never actually did teach me. This is, indeed, a great blessing, thank the lord for blessing my birth, for fulfilling my deepest desire.' I was so happy.

I began to think, 'This house has many books, maybe *Chaitanya Bhagabat* is also there.' But what difference could that make to me? I didn't know how to read, I couldn't even identify the book. So I resumed my prayers: 'Lord of the poor! Lead me to the book that I saw in my dream. You have to do this, who else can bring *Chaitanya Bhagabat* to me?' Thus I spoke to the Great Lord.

What miraculous proof I had of the wonderful mercy of the Compassionate One! As I was brooding, he heard my wish and he set about granting it immediately. My eldest son was eight years old at the time. As I sat cooking in the kitchen, I heard karta say to him: 'Bepin, I have left my *CB* here. When I ask for it, bring it in.' He left the book there and went away.

I heard all this from the kitchen with great delight. I rushed over to look at the book. Thanking the lord for listening to my prayer, I opened it and felt it all over. Manuscripts were very different from the printed books of these days. They used to be pressed between wooden slats which were colourfully illuminated. Since I didn't read at all, I memorized the illumination in order to identify the book.

When the book had been taken inside, I secretly took out a page and hid it carefully. It was a job hiding it, for nobody must find it in my hands. That would lead to severe rebukes and I would never be able to put up with that. It was not at all easy to do something that is forbidden and then to face the consequences. Times were very different then, and I was an exceptionally nervous person. Such days! One was entirely in bondage and my fears were great. That page was a headache. Where could I hide it that nobody would come across it? Eventually, I decided that it must be a place where I would always be present but which nobody else visited much. What else could it be but the kitchen? I hid it under the hearth. But there was never any time to look at it. I finished cooking very late in the night. After that was over, the children started waking up, one after the other. And then it was pandemonium! One says, Ma, I need to pee, another says, Ma, I am hungry, and yet another says, Ma, take me on your lap, while someone else wakes up and starts bawling. I had to look after them all. After that it got even later, I couldn't fight off sleep any more, there was no time to study the page. I could see no way out of it. How can one learn without a teacher? I could silently say a few letters to myself, but I could not write them. It is impossible to master the word without knowing how to write. I saw no way of reading that page, however hard I thought about it. Moreover, the fear of exposure was always there.

Helplessly, I prayed to the lord: 'Great Lord, do help me to read this, who else is there to teach me?' Thus I prayed all the time but I would also despair at times. Even if someone did teach me the letters, where was the time to pursue that? Why cherish an impossible dream? At other times, I would hope again. Since the Great Lord himself has planted this hope in me, he will not thwart it. So I held on to the page. Even though I hardly had the time to glance at it, I would occasionally keep it in my left hand while I was cooking, and sometimes I would steal a look at it from under the veil. The letters, however, remained inscrutable.

My eldest son was practising his letters on palm leaves at that time. I hid one of them as well. At times, I went over that, trying to match letters from that page with the letters that I remembered. I also tried to match the words with those that I would hear in the course of my days. But after a quick look at them, I would hide them under the hearth once more. I spent quite a bit of time in this fashion.

Ah, what a sad thing it was! Such misery, only because one was a woman! We were in any case imprisoned like thieves, and on top of that, reading was yet another crime. It is good to see women having an easier time of it now. Even if someone has a daughter these days, he educates her carefully. We suffered so much just to learn to read. Whatever little I learnt was entirely because god was kind to me.

The man who was my master was a good person. But it is most difficult to abandon the custom of the land. That is why I suffered so. However, why dwell on past misfortunes! Those days, people were convinced that it is sinful to educate women. Why blame them alone, even now there are those who go up in smoke at the thought. It is useless to blame them either. Time is a priceless treasure. Those times and these are so different, if we compare them, we won't be able to count the changes that have happened. If people from those times were to see the ways of today, they would die of grief and horror. Actually, we happily accept whatever the Great Lord decrees at a particular time. Women would then wear coarse clothes, heavy ornaments, an armful of conch shell bangles, their foreheads would be smeared with vermilion paste. It didn't seem so bad then. We ourselves didn't dress quite like that, but even so, I shudder to think of what we had to wear then.

Anyway, the Great Lord had taken care of me all that while, I was happy and contented. I can only say that whatever he does is providential. As a child, I had been made to sit in that schoolroom, and now that helped me a lot. I could match the letters I remembered with those on the palm leaf and on the page. I read to myself, in silence. All day, I would try to go through this in my mind. With tremendous care and effort and over a long stretch of time, I learnt somehow to limp and stammer across *CB*. Those days, we did not see printed letters, the handwritten letters on the manuscripts were immensely difficult to read. My reading was so painfully acquired! Even after such effort, I didn't know how to write. It takes a lot to be able to write—paper, pen, ink, inkpot. I would need to spread them all around me and then sit down to write. I was a woman, and on top of that, a married one. They are not meant to read and write. The authorities have decreed that this is a cardinal sin for women. How could I have tried to write in that situation? I was so scared of rebukes. So I killed my desire for writing and I would only read, and that, too, in secret. Even that had so far been beyond my wildest dreams. It is almost an impossible achievement, it was possible in my case only because the Great Lord himself guided me with his own hands. The fact that I could read at last was enough for me, I didn't think of writing.

PUNDITA RAMABAI SARASVATI

The High Caste Hindu Woman

Translated from the Marathi

MARRIED LIFE

Although the ancient law-givers thought it desirable to marry girls when quite young, and consequently ignored their right to choose their own husbands, yet they were not altogether void of humane feelings. They have positively forbidden parents and guardians to give away girls in marriage unless good suitors were offered them.

> To a distinguished, handsome suitor of equal caste should a father give his daughter in accordance with the prescribed rule, though she have not attained the proper age. *Manu* ix., 88.

> But the maiden though marriageable, should rather stop in the father's house until death, than that he should ever give her to man destitute of good qualities. *Manu*, ix. 89.

But, alas, here too the law is defied by cruel custom. It allows some men to remain unmarried, but woe to the maiden and to her family if she is so unfortunate as to remain single after the marriageable age. Although no law has ever said so, the popular belief is that a woman can have no salvation unless she be formally married. It is not, then, a matter of wonder that parents become extremely anxious when their daughters are over eight or nine and unsought in marriage. Very few suitors offer to marry the daughters of poor parents, though they may be of high caste families. Wealth has its own pride and merit in India, as everywhere else in the world, but even this powerful wealth is as nothing before caste rule. A high caste man will never condescend to marry his daughter to a low caste man though he be a millionaire.

But wealth in one's own caste surpasses the merits of learning, beauty and honour; parents generally seek boys of well-to-do families for their sons-in-law. As the boys are too young to pass as possessing 'good qualities', i.e., learning, common sense, ability to support and take care of a family, and respectable character, the parents wish to see their daughters safe in a family where she will, at least have plenty to eat and to wear; they, of course, wish her to be happy with her husband, but in their judgement that is not the one thing needful. So long as *they* have fulfilled the custom, and thereby secured a good name in this world and heavenly reward in the next, their minds are not much troubled concerning the girl's fate.

If the boy be of rich or middle class people, a handsome sum of money must be given to him and his family in order to secure the marriage; besides this, the girl's family must walk very humbly with this little god, for he is believed to be indwelt by the god Vishnu. Poor parents cannot have the advantage of marrying their daughters to boys of prosperous families, and as they *must* marry them to some one, it very frequently happens that girls of eight or nine are given to men of sixty or seventy, or to men utterly unworthy of the young maidens.

Parents who have the means to secure good-looking, prosperous men for their sons-in-law, take care to consult the horoscopes of both parties in order to know the future of their daughters; in such cases, they are anxious to ascertain, over and above all things, that the girl shall not become a widow. If the daughter's horoscope reveals that her future husband is to survive her, the match is considered very satisfactory; but if it reveals the reverse, then a boy having a horoscope equally bad is sought for, because it is sincerely believed that in that case the guardian planets will wrestle with each other, and, as almost always happens, that the stronger, i.e., the husband's planet will be victorious, or else both parties will fall in the conflict, and the husband and wife will both die together. A friend of mine informed me that three hundred horoscopes were rejected before one was found which agreed satisfactorily with her sister's guardian planet. Undoubtedly many suitors, who might make good husbands for these little girls, are for this reason rejected, and unworthy men fall to their lot; thus, the horoscope becomes a source of misery instead of blessing.

It not infrequently happens that fathers give away their daughters in marriage to strangers without exercising care in making inquiry concerning the suitor's character and social position. It is enough to learn from the man's own statement, his caste and clan, and the locality of his home. I know of a most extraordinary marriage that took place in the following manner: the father was on a religious pilgrimage with his family, which consisted of his wife and two daughters, one nine and the other seven years of age, and they had stopped in a town to take rest for a day or two. One morning the father was bathing in the sacred river Godavari, near the town, when he saw a fine-looking man coming to bathe there also. After the ablution and the morning prayers were over, the father inquired of the stranger who he was and whence he came; on learning his caste, and clan, and dwelling-place, also that he was a widower, the father offered him his little daughter of nine, in marriage. All things were settled in an hour or so; next day the marriage was concluded, and the little girl placed in the possession of the stranger, who took her nearly nine hundred miles away from her home. The father left the place the day after the marriage without the daughter, and pursued his pilgrimage with a light heart; fortunately the little girl had fallen in good hands, and was well and tenderly cared for beyond all expectation, but the conduct of her father, who cared so little to ascertain his daughter's fate, is none the less censurable.

When the time to conclude the marriage ceremony draws near, the Hindu mother's affection for the girl frequently knows no bounds; she indulges her in endless ways, knowing that in a few days her darling will be torn away from her loving embrace. When she goes to pay the customary visit to her child's future mother-in-law many are the tearful entreaties and soul stirring solicitations that she will be as kind and forbearing toward the little stranger as though she were her own daughter. The boy's mother is moved at this time, for she has a woman's heart, and she promises to be a mother to the little bride. On the day fixed for the marriage, parents formally give their daughter away to the boy; afterwards the young people are united by priests who utter the sacred texts and pronounce them man and wife in the presence of the sacred fire and of relatives and friends. The marriage being thus concluded, it is henceforth indissoluble.

> Neither by sale nor by repudiation is a wife released from her husband; such we know the law to be which the Lord of creatures made of old. *Manu* ix., 46.

Marriage is the only 'Sacrament' administered to a high caste woman, accompanied with the utterance of Vedic texts. It is to be presumed that the texts are introduced in honour of the man whom she marries, for no sacrament must be administered to him without the sacred formulae. Henceforth the girl is his, not only his property, but also that of his nearest relatives.

> For they (the ancient sages) declare that a bride is given to the family of her husband, and not to the husband alone. *Apastamba II., 10, 27, 3.*

The girl now belongs to the husband's clan; she is known by his family name, and in some parts of India the husband's relatives will not allow her to be called by the first name that was given her by her parents; henceforth she is a kind of impersonal being. She can have no merit or quality of her own.

> Whatever be the qualities of the man with whom a woman is united in lawful marriage, such qualities even she assumes, like a river united with the ocean. *Manu* ix., 22.

Memories of Our Life Together

Translated from the Marathi by Maya Pandit

ANASUYABAINCHE PURANA (ANASUYABAI'S PURANA)

Around this time, a woman called Anasuyabai came to Pune. She was well versed in Sanskrit and was accompanied by her husband and old father. She used to read the Holy Bhagawata like Pundita Ramabai. She would set the verses to a tune and chant the text like a puranika (preacher) while she explained their meaning. She made a presentation once at our house, and later at several other houses too. One day a reading was arranged in the Vishnu temple, which was also known as Joshi's temple. It was usually women who went to this temple. Once the program was arranged, the women who were there decided on a plan of action. 'We won't leave any place for the wives of the reformists to sit. We'll leave the assembly hall of the temple empty for them, but we'll occupy all the places in front of the sanctum. Then they will have to go and sit with the men in the assembly hall. And anyway, don't they sit together with the men when they attend those meetings? On chairs, too. As if they were their equals! Why would they need a separate place here?'

I learned of this plan from a couple of my friends. I normally used to mix both with the orthodox women and with the reformists. Naturally, I had friends in both camps, and did not like this plan to segregate us. I felt aggrieved and insulted. I would have easily upset their plan had I come to know of it a couple of hours earlier. But I had no such time. As it was, I got to the temple a little late. It was only then that I came to know of their plan. But by that time it was too late. The temple was already packed with people. I had no choice but to go and sit where Pundita Ramabai and the other reformist women were sitting. But I was unhappy. I kept thinking of going home. A place was made for Anasuyabai between the reformists and their wives.

Around twenty minutes after the reading began, I whispered in Pundita Ramabai's ear, 'I am not well today. I feel rather giddy. I think I'll go home.' Saying so, I left.

On my way home, I kept on feeling that I had acted very wisely, that I had done a very brave deed. And in that jubilant mood, I narrated the whole incident to Taisasubai, who was sitting outside on the verandah. I told her everything. I told her how the women in the temple were in league against us, how they had made us sit with the men and occupied all the places in the sanctum, how all this had angered me, and finally, how I had decided not to sit with the men and marched home.

I was speaking with great confidence and pride, as if what I had done was very commendable and would meet with everybody's approval. And Taisasubai was, indeed, pleased with me. She said in a very encouraging tone, 'Well done! You should always use your reason like this. That is the proper way to behave in public life. Then people will not speak ill of you. These newly educated young men—what do they know of the ways of the world? They will ask you to do anything. But you should know better than that. You don't have to do everything that they ask you to. And don't worry if they get angry about it. Let them. Don't you fuss over them at such times because it is in their nature to get angry like that. Whatever the reason, they will always take it out on their women. Why, they seem to consider that heroic! God alone knows what makes them think that. It's beyond me!'

She spoke at length, encouraging me to 'behave with reason' for the sake of people. Her affectionate words and concern for me made me feel gloriously happy.

But this glorious happiness of mine did not last even for two hours. And that wasn't all. I was to learn a major lesson of my life. And never did I dare make such a mistake again.

When in the evening he returned home, I went to him as usual, to help him undress. As soon as he saw me, he asked me, 'What's wrong with you today?'

'Nothing whatever,' I replied innocently.

And no sooner did I give this reply than I remembered that I had left the temple on the pretext of being unwell. I was terribly confused. What would I say if he demanded an explanation? Fortunately, he didn't ask me anything; but then he did not say even a word to me. I was waiting there to collect the clothes he had taken off. But instead of giving them to me, he hung them on the peg by himself. I stooped down to remove his shoes, but he quietly pushed my hands away and removed them himself. I stood there, rooted to the spot for some more time, but no conversation of any kind ensued. My heart beat faster with a strange sense of foreboding. All my pride just vanished into thin air and I grew extremely apprehensive. It was his custom to chat with me at least for some ten minutes after he came home. This routine would be interrupted only when he was accompanied by his friends or was busy with some urgent work. But today there was no such reason as far as I could see. 'Then why does he behave like this?' I wondered. His behaviour did not change during the meal either. Usually he told me whether he had liked or wanted a particular dish. But today, everything was indicated with gestures. Nobody seemed to notice this, but I certainly did! Immediately! And became even more worried. 'If he doesn't like what I have done, why doesn't he scold me?' I thought. I would have preferred it had he scolded me, even if it was in front of the others. But his reticence was causing me so much suffering and I had to endure it mutely.

As usual, I went upstairs and began to read the book from the place I had left off last night. We used to receive these books from the Dakshina Prize Committee. Usually, I would be told to mark that particular word or sentence which I had read erroneously; but that night, the few mistakes that I deliberately made went without any comment. When he pulled the covers over himself, and turned his face to the other side, I knew that this was a signal to me to stop my reading. I put the lamp away and set the book down. The servant came with ghee as usual to massage his feet. I said, 'Today you are not required to do it. Go away.' I started rubbing his feet with the ghee myself. I wanted him at least to say, 'Now that's enough!' But no, he went off to sleep as soon as I started rubbing his feet. Usually, after an hour's massage, he would extend his other foot and ask us to start working on that. But today, I don't know how, he did not forget his resolve of silence even in his sleep. He didn't speak a single word. And turning on the other side, he pretended to be fast asleep.

Up to this time, I was really dozing even while rubbing his feet. But when I saw him feigning sleep, I realized that the opportunity to speak was completely lost. I couldn't sleep now and felt absolutely miserable. I even cried for a long time. I was dying to say to him, 'What's the reason for this silence? You've never treated me like this before.' I wanted to beg him to forgive me, but the words just refused to come out. It is very difficult for the proud nature of youth to speak even though the mind has become meek enough to do so. I couldn't bring myself to utter a single syllable even though I resolved a thousand times to speak. Whenever I tried to speak, I realized that he, too, was awake, and then all my resolve would just melt away. The whole night passed like this. Both of us hadn't been able to sleep a wink. At the break of dawn, he got up and left the room. I was extremely disappointed and cried a lot at this unbearable punishment. Then I washed my face clean with cold water and went downstairs, but I was feeling absolutely wretched.

GEETANJALI SHREE

Mai

Translated from the Hindi by Nita Kumar

We were always picking on those purple, sometimes raw green, seeds. There would be the sound of the gate opening. Without bothering to check who had come, Dada would say, 'Go inside, Sunaina, ask them to send some refreshments.' At that moment I could see the woman in myself.

Dadi, Mai, Hardeyi, no woman went out in front of him. We could only wonder, has Dada ever seen a woman or not?

But that headmistress arrived and someone chased me inside. Dadi was resting, Mai was massaging her and Dadi kept muttering about the falsity and lowness of womankind. Then she began to abuse Mai.

'Gave me a bad coin, that's what they did. My poor son...'

Mai did not say a word, just went away, and returned in a while with a bottle of oil and began to oil Dadi's hair.

They had jointly made up some excuse so that we could not leave the courtyard. But even without knowing much, the little we understood made us find a chance to reach the roof. From up there we had seen the oily, shiny, buffalo-like woman, a beaded purse swinging in her hand, the obscene flesh on her chest shaking. She walked ahead and behind her was a young man, perhaps her son.

We did not understand anything and then came the age when we understood even what did not exist. And after that came the age when it seemed sheer melodrama to 'understand' everything. All these phases of understanding got so entangled that now it is impossible to find one balanced viewpoint to fix on. Is it not melodramatic to 'understand'? Is it real to not understand? This is so difficult. Only now and then, just like that, the vision of that boy with his face down, walking behind that woman, flashes by. Was there a shade of some familiar face on his face? Some floating shadow from our home that had fallen on his? Part of a nose, or lip, or something else, from one of us?

Can it ever happen like that? Can someone perish after having been nameless, unknown, and no one aware that a written word existed and is now totally erased? If you bury a tale forever, will it not trip up someone sometime and make itself heard? If someone starts digging there by chance, will it not blurt out its story?

This is so frightening. To put someone beyond death, and make him nameless, invisible. To empty someone into non-existence.

When does one ever put up a curtain in an empty room? On our part we did something too to contribute to so many stories remaining untold, being buried unceremoniously. As if they had never existed.

We had scolded Mai that she let Dadi say all that she did. Mai told me that Dadi's bald spot was not from old age. Dadi used to hide in the storeroom when Dada was drunk and he would pull her out by the hair. Mai said that Dadi's and her jati was the same and she could not turn away from her own kind. And I experience a strange weakness in finding the reflection of both these women in myself. I cannot blame them whose face and body can clearly be glimpsed in my own.

The headmistress had met Dada in his sitting room. There was a time when she would come. There was a time when she never came again.

The life of the house continued according to its rules. Dada, his eyes closed, waving his hands with pleasure, kept enjoying his music. But none of the rest of us was free to sing or to dance. He was in his bath one day and Mai passed by humming something. He immediately came out and opened the door from his sitting room to the courtyard. Mai quickly covered her head and stood to one side—

'Who was singing? Was someone singing?'

That was all and he disappeared without waiting for an answer. I can swear that Mai never ever hummed again.

The dilemma was that we were both ready to learn music and dance. Subodh began to go to guitar classes in his school. There was nothing like that in my school. Apart from regular classes there was one subject, Home Science—cooking, sewing, knitting—in which I was not interested. I got after Mai and she spoke to Nagji Appa's sister in the club and arranged for her daughter's teacher, Ustad Nanhe Khan, to come to our house to teach me dance. He would have to climb over the barbed wire at the back and come in through the courtyard. After everything had been arranged, Nanhe Khan messed it all up. He did not understand the subtlety of the arrangements. After leaving the courtyard he decided that it would be easier to exit by the front gate and take a rickshaw in the bazaar. Dada caught him, gave him a talking-to, discharged him...

Mai's finalized, arranged plans were left unexecuted. Dada's one bark sent the artiste far from our house forever.

Then Dada had the barbed wires at the back tightened up. He recited something to me in Sanskrit, the meaning of which was that women who sang or wore bells on their feet were bad women, and one whose teeth were a little protruding was a wise woman.

But Dada was in favour of my learning English. It was Dada who sent Subodh to a boarding school with some actual English teachers to turn him into an 'English' officer. The first time Subodh came home he had forgotten Hindi somewhat. When we were served okra at lunch, he could not remember that it was called bhindi. 'Give me that...that...that...' he pointed, dumb. Mai laughed.

Dada sent me too to the mission school in town which, in our nice, hot country, was misnamed 'Sunny Side Convent'. Dada wanted me to learn English.

But not speak it. Or Hindi either. That is, not speak at all.

Even when Dadi broke her leg, Dada did not come to see her. He would call us to get the news and ask Babu about everything. We were the ones who told him that Dadi was all right after her operation, had been unconscious but was now awake. Now and then Dada's lip could be seen trembling behind his moustache.

INDIRA GOSWAMI

The Blue-necked God

Translated from the Assamese by Gayatri Bhattacharya

One day, she crossed the roof of this temple, intending to go to this mysterious place. But as she was about to go down the steps, the sadhus who stayed in the temple said to her, 'Since you are new here, it will be better if you do not go there.' These words from the sadhus who slept on string cots on the roof and who passed their spare time playing the pakhwaj, only increased Saudamini's curiosity. Bowing respectfully in front of the priests, she replied, 'Every inch of Brajdham's land is of interest to me.'

She climbed down the broken and faded old steps. She saw an old unused well, the top of which was covered with a few moss covered wooden planks. Nearby were some small and dark dilapidated rooms that looked more like pigeon holes than human habitations. A large group of widowed radheshyamis dwelt here. They were grossly undernourished, and wore dirty and faded old dhotis. But their foreheads shone with bibhuti (sacred ash) and lines drawn with holy sandalwood. Seeing Saudamini, the old women came out of their pigeon holes and surrounded her inquisitively.

'Ladies, how do you make your living here?' Saudamini asked.

The 'ladies' looked at each other. Then one of them, sunken eyes shining with the brightness of the sun, replied, 'When necessary, we sit at the gates of the Tortoise Temple, and at Rangaji and beg. When there is no other way, we spend the whole night in front of the temple, waiting and hoping for the malcha offerings.

'But if you had become radheshyamis singing bhajans in the temple, you would have been assured of at least two square meals a day,' said Saudamini.

All the women cackled with laughter on hearing this, and one of them started singing mockingly, *'Sethbari's bhajan ashram, Gopinath's bhajan ashram, Borbag's bhajan ashram, the stable's bhajan ashram!'*

'Listen,' she said, 'The accountant got so fat on the radheshyami's money that he cannot get up now. You must be new here, not to know this. This fat man sat and watched all the radheshyamis, their thin hands and feet, and starving bodies. He came to know which of them would kick the bucket, and when! He also came to know which dying radheshyami had how much money, and where. He found out everything. Everything!'

Again the old women cackled with laughter.

'One day, this wicked man was observing our legs. As soon as we knew this, we fled and saved ourselves. Otherwise he would have kicked us out. See, look at our legs.' And they pulled their tattered clothes up to their knees and exposed their legs.

Saudamini hurriedly stepped back a few steps in fright and shock. All these women were sick! They had leprosy.

'My dear girl, we like begging at the Banke-Behari lane, at the doorway of Shahji Temple, on the steps of Daman Mohan... People like you go there.' And saying this, one of the women started stroking Saudamini's hand with her own hands. Saudamini went stiff with fright! But the ghostly woman seemed to get a peculiar satisfaction. Encouraged by the act of the first woman, another started touching the gold bangles on Saudamini's wrist, while yet another said, 'Give us some donation to keep us alive. You people live to eat, but we need to eat something in order to live. Give us something to keep us alive.'

In the meantime, another group of old women came out of the small rooms and surrounded Saudamini. They started feeling and touching her soft young body, and then started scratching her all over in a strange and feverish excitement. Saudamini's hair came loose and cascaded down her back, her blouse was almost ripped off and, if some sadhus had not arrived at that moment, the women would have probably taken on the nature of wild wolves.

One of the sadhus shouted at the women, 'Get out! Get out, you demons! Do you think there is no one to help her?'

Immediately all the old hags disappeared inside the pigeon holes.

The sadhu rebuked Saudamini, 'Did I not tell you that you should not venture alone to these places? These old women can devour people. Come, I will see you on your way. And let me tell you another thing. These women are very unfortunate. I am told that you have come with the intention of making Braj your permanent home. Give some thought to the welfare of these women whenever you have the opportunity.'

Saudamini wiped the perspiration off her neck and face as soon as she stepped on to the main road of Gopinath Bazaar. The bhajan ashram here had not yet closed its doors and an old widow was standing in the middle of a group singing bhajans to the accompaniment of small cymbals. A sentry sitting at the doorway, whose function it was to keep the accounts, was silently chanting the Lord's name with prayer beads. Every so often he would open his eyes and observe the radheshyamis, to see whether they were all really singing. These women were compelled to sing even if they were starving. They had to sing the Lord's praises as loud as they could even if they were on the verge of choking. Saudamini noticed that, although they sang without stopping, very often their eyes would turn to the line of vegetable vendors. She noticed that the only buyers of the rotting, dried up vegetables that were heaped on one side were the poor radheshyamis.

Saudamini returned home, and entered her dark room again. She was trying her best to forget her loneliness, but it was not easy. Sometimes she would scrutinize her own body. She had a lovely, soft young body. Even the mental imbalance and torture of the past seven years had not been able to leave any permanent mark on this lovely body. Try as she might, she could not come to terms with the condition of her life or her situation. Was there anyone else, she wondered, who had suffered as she had, who had been compelled to face a situation like hers?

VOLGA

The Experiment

Translated from the Telugu by Alladi Uma and M. Sridhar

In the meanwhile a good flat comes up for sale. Even after taking loans, she is short by a lakh and a half.

'Ask your father and get it,' says Sandhya in her usual manner.

'Go ask your father and get it,' says Narendra.

'My father has given whatever he has to. It's your father who has to give.'

'My father need not give anything at all. Why are you talking as if my father has to give you a dowry?'

'He needn't give me anything. Don't you have a right to property?'

'What if I have? It will come at its time. I don't give them a paisa from my earning. Why should I ask them? Moreover, there are two sisters to be married.'

'That's what I'm worried about also. If he gives everything to your sisters and there's nothing left? As it is, your people can't stand me,' Sandhya says vengefully.

'You only want money, don't you?—I'll get a loan on my LIC Policy. Will get PF Loan. I'll take a loan. I'll bring it somehow, okay? But I won't ask my father.'

'Take loans, go on paying interest and ruin the home. You can't touch the LIC and the PF. If you have an accident in the future, what will happen to me?'

Narendra is totally distraught. Sorrow engulfs him. Sandhya has an eye even on the money that she'll get when he dies.

Why such hell for him? What sins has he committed? All men torture women, it seems. Even when he's good, why is he being tortured? Does marriage mean one torturing the other? His goodness is being taken for good-for-nothingness. Should he live for the wife who is looking forward to the money she'll get after his death? Is there any meaning to this existence?

Tears are streaming down Narendra's eyes.

'You may not be man enough to get money. But why do you cry like a woman? It's I who should cry about your uselessness.' Unable to control himself, he hits her.

Sandhya is enraged even more.

Narendra hits her again. He hits her again and again and stops when his hands hurt.

Dispossessed of his anger, looking at himself, he weeps. He has hit his wife. He has hit a woman. Why has he become like this? Who between them is the devil now?

When he tries to speak to Sandhya, she gets wild and hurls abuse at him.

The very next morning she goes to her parents' house. Narendra reaches his father's house. A week, ten days pass by.

Then for a compromise, mediators enter the field. People from each side present their arguments. The mediators convince them that they have to put up with it no matter who is at fault.

They chide them saying, isn't it natural for a husband and wife to quarrel or to hit each other sometime? They begin to make plans for their being together.

Narendra's people lay down the condition that Sandhya can come back if she is willing to live with his people and not separately.

Sandhya's people demand that since not just living separately but being with Narendra is itself not safe for her, he should come to their house.

For the health of Sandhya, now in her fourth month of pregnancy, it's best to be in her parents' place. Using this, they strengthen their claim that Narendra should go to her place. Narendra doesn't give in.

'I am vacating the house, take your things away,' says he.

Both take away their own things.

Narendra feels he has got back to his old life.

He is looking after his sisters' education. He is making them read good books.

To learn to play the violin, he goes to a music teacher. Now and then Shantamma thinks of the happiness her son has lost and sheds tears.

'Ma, I am now quite happy. Don't make a fuss.' Saying this, he brushes the topic aside.

Five months pass.

He gets a call at his office one day.

'Sandhya has delivered. A baby boy.'

Doesn't say which hospital. Doesn't invite him either.

Sorrow gushes out from within him. He has a son. He has become a father. He is unhappy. How will they bring up the son? Is it possible for him and Sandhya to bring him up? What will happen to him because of their quarrels? He goes into the bathroom, cries as much as he can, washes his face and comes out.

By the time he comes back to his seat, he finds Sunanda there. Narendra's face glows with happiness. A new enthusiasm fills his body. In the recent past, Narendra has never felt such a feeling in body and mind.

Sunanda wants to come back to Hyderabad. She wants to hand in her transfer application and has come to give the responsibility to Narendra to follow it up.

Narendra asks her to come home, but she says she has checked into a hotel. Narendra goes with Sunanda to the Secretariat and does all the work enthusiastically.

By the evening both reach Sunanda's hotel. After washing her face, she orders coffee and asks: 'Now, tell me. How's your married life?'

'Married life? Where's it? I have come out of it six months ago.'

Sunanda is stunned. Narendra relates everything.

'I have a son now. I don't know what to do. I am not happy. Now they will try to win me over through the little one. I have no desire to see her face.'

Sorrow overwhelms him again. This time Sunanda feels sorry for him. He himself is responsible for ruining his life, she thinks.

She holds Narendra's hands in her own and says:

'Don't worry. Try to set things right. What's the point in feeling bad?'

Sunanda's touch gives him a lot of relief. He feels he has gained a lot of courage.

'Sunanda—if you come here, maybe my loneliness will go,' he says eagerly.

Sunanda smiles, withdrawing her hand.

My Story

MENTAL DEPRESSION

My mother-in-law grew visibly upset whenever anyone looked in through our windows. She grumbled about the inconveniences of our flat, which included the elderly maidservant who had turned disobedient, the cook who cheated at accounts and the proximity of girls who lured me out of my home to play a version of hopscotch with them on the terrace.

Our next-door neighbours were the Marathes whose second daughter at that time was a popular film actress with a busy schedule. Her name was Usha Kiran. Her two younger sisters became my dear friends, and during the four weeks preceding the Ganesh festival, we rehearsed on the terrace for hours every evening, the many items of entertainment such as the Gujarati garba, the Punjabi bhangra and the Hindi play.

The youngest girl, Pushpa, was gifted with a rich, vibrant voice. She taught me the Marathi filmsong, '*Nachatho Varuni Anand... Vachavi Pava Govind...*' In their company I forgot the bitterness of life and became for a few short hours the carefree person that I was before I came to Bombay.

My mother-in-law sulked, for she felt that I was spending too much time away from my child and my domestic responsibilities. Whenever she said disgruntled things, my husband grew angry, and his anger was directed against me and the baby. The servants could not get on with my mother-in-law. We are going back to Malabar, they said everyday, we cannot bear such nagging. My husband was also missing his evenings with the young man at the YMCA, and with me he was terse and impatient.

One day, being able to bear it no longer, I sent the cook to a chemist's shop for a dozen tablets of barbiturates. No chemist would give them without a doctor's prescription. The cook, on his return, empty-handed, told me with tears in his eyes that he too would take some tablets if I decided to kill myself. Then the maidservant came up to me and said that she was planning to get run over by a bus. I cannot live on like this, she said. All three of us were miserable. My husband stopped me from going up to the terrace for the rehearsals in the evening. You must remember you are a wife and mother, he said. My friends passing our window glanced at me with pity in their eyes.

Then I settled down to housekeeping and sewed the buttons on and darned our old garments all through the hot afternoons. In the evening I brought for my husband his tea and a plate of snacks. I kept myself busy with dreary housework while my spirit protested and cried, get out of this trap, escape... In the mornings, when my husband left for work, I ran behind him and stood near the corner of the road where the cows were loitering and the crows pulled out fishbones from the open garbage boxes. Then I watched him walk away with his briefcase towards the railway station to catch the first train to Churchgate. It was only after my return that I bathed or changed my dress.

Often, from behind the house and from the dirty seashore, the smell of rotting fish would enter our back verandah, from which I watched a municipal school's children parade in the morning singing a patriotic song and the huts of the bootleggers who buried their wares in tins at night and slept on charpoys in the day, while the sun climbing over them, burnt their skin black. The bootleggers were full of distrust for strangers and once or twice when I went strolling past their colony, they turned their hostile eyes towards me.

Of the many huts, one was bigger and its occupants were better dressed. The man was short and handsome with yellow skin. His dress was a white singlet and a pair of khaki shorts but they were washed every day by his wife who seemed to love working for him. She used to bring for him glasses of milk while he lay on a charpoy under a tree, dozing. She fed him well and although from my height I could not hear what she was telling him, by the look on her face, I could make out that they were lovewords. He was silent and sullen as all men are when they are being loved too deeply by a woman. He used to gaze at her indifferently while she turned her back on him and walked back to their hut.

Everybody in that colony showed him respect, even the police constables who used to come in trucks off and on to poke the ground with long iron rods to see if anything had been buried there. He would laugh aloud, seeing them at it. On some days when he was not very sleepy, he would play with his little sons throwing them in the air and catching them while they chortled with joy. He liked to watch his wife washing their rounded bodies near the hydrant soaping them and rubbing hard until they turned a burnished copper. He was obviously proud of his progeny.

One day while I stood leaning over the railings of my verandah watching him sleep, he opened his eyes all of a sudden and looked at me. They were eyes reddened with sleep and desire. I felt uneasy while they grazed my limbs and withdrew to my room in a hurry. One morning we woke up hearing a commotion in the backyard and saw the police take him away in their truck. They had at last found the liquor which he had made at night in his hut and stored in two wooden barrels. His wife ran behind the truck with the end of her pink sari flying for a few yards, but he did not once look at her. He sat on one of the barrels looking like a king, his handsome face impassive and cold.

When my mother-in-law's dissatisfaction increased and the servants became constant grumblers, my husband decided to send us all back to Malabar. The decision was welcomed by all. One of his uncles came to Bombay to take us home. He was to stay for three days only but, being a dandy, had got made two suits of sharkskin for the Bombay trip. He was a great one for girls, a man with a reputation and so the first thing he wanted to know from me was the address of a nurse named Meenakshi who had come to Bombay from our village to take up a job in one of the city hospitals.

I did not know such a person. He was very disappointed, but with determination went out each morning to enquire at every hospital for Meenakshi, for whom he had made such delicious plans and also the pink sharkskin suits.

When we left by train at last, we found as the occupant of one berth a well-known Congresswoman who was delighted to meet our uncle and together they enjoyed a lengthy conversation that lasted until three in the morning. My mother-in-law was tired and slept soundly on the train. I lay near the baby listening to the talk which sounded hypocritical and comic. I have always been cherishing certain high principles, said the lady and my uncle said, of course, of course, what else should a lady cherish...

After Eight Years of Marriage

After eight years of marriage
The first time I visited my parents,
They asked, 'Are you happy, tell us.'
It was an absurd question
And I should have laughed at it
Instead, I cried,
And in between sobs, nodded yes.
I wanted to tell them
That I was happy on Tuesday
I was unhappy on Wednesday.
I was happy one day at 8 o'clock
I was most unhappy by 8.15.
I wanted to tell them how one day
We all ate a watermelon and laughed.
I wanted to tell them how I wept in bed all night once
And struggled hard from hurting myself.
That it wasn't easy to be happy in a family of twelve.
But they were looking at my two sons,
Hopping around like young goats.
Their wrinkled hands, beaten faces and grey eyelashes
Were all too much too real.
So I swallowed everything,
And smiled a smile of great content.

Brat

Looking at my navel
I'm reminded of you, Mamma.
How I lay suspended
By that cordial cord inside you.
I must have been a rattish thing,
A wriggly roll of shallow breath.
You, perhaps, were hardly proud
Of your creativity—
Except for the comfort
That I looked like Papa
And not like the neighbour
Who shared our bathroom.

Children

At first I wanted to call this section 'motherhood' but there is more to bringing up children than that word suggests; even 'parenting' feels inadequate. Child-rearing is a mixed bag of work and emotion but children continue to have a great hold over women's lives even after they have grown up. The works included in this section capture the risks, the hardship, the love and loss that parenting entails.

Manju Kapur's essay ('Name: Amba Dalmia') about losing a daughter on the cusp of adulthood and trying to come to terms with the loss is a heart-rending read. It sits well beside Ajeet Cour's powerful memoir wherein the author describes the anguish of watching her young daughter die in a hospital in a foreign country.

Baby Kamble's memoir, *The Prisons We Broke*, describes the Mahar community's great poverty, ignorance, and the lack of hygiene or healthcare support that kills many women in childbirth. Cornelia Sorabji's essay describing a royal adoption reflects the need to have a child, if only in name and title, without much concern for the child's feelings.

Mannu Bhandari's *Bunty* looks at a child whose mother tries to find love after a divorce. The extract I've picked describes the young boy's first exposure to sex, and how distressing it is for him since he has already learnt to think of nudity in terms of shame and sin.

Nabaneeta Dev Sen's poems reflect the different ways in which a mother responds to children. They capture the joy of watching one's own baby turn into a chatterbox, the sense of identification with the earth itself, but they also see each child as a lone tree on a desert island, and as an abandoned creature screaming for love. Gagan Gill's poem, on the other hand, is a potent mix of ideas about home, a place where a child is welcome. A woman's body, after all, is a child's first home.

Lila Majumdar was one of the few writers in the twentieth century who wrote stories mainly for children. An extract from one of her stories included here taps into children's appetite for stories, and it signals how they are moulded and, in a sense, mothered by the person who tells them stories.

MANNU BHANDARI

Bunty

Translated from the Hindi by Jai Ratan

Even a long night's sleep could not dispel the image of Mummy's and Doctor sahib's nakedness from Bunty's mind. When he woke up, he found that Mummy and Doctor sahib were gone, leaving their naked bodies behind, wrapped in semi-darkness.

Was what he had seen at night a reality? Could such a thing really happen? His gaze travelled to the dressing table. Could it be the effect of that magic phial? He vividly remembered that last night that phial was not there. Then from where had the bottle appeared now?

'...Bunty bhaiyya, when she made the Rajkumar sniff the bottle it completely befuddled his mind. He couldn't recognize his father. Nor his mother. He even forgot who he was...'

Bunty tumbled out of bed and ran out.

He was running across the verandah when he heard Mummy's voice from the dining room. 'So you're up, Bunty? Hurry up, son. Or you'll be late for school.'

He thought of going to Mummy and having a word with her. But no. Would his Mummy recognize him? And what if she slapped him? Last night too Mummy had forgotten who she was.

Ami and Joat were getting ready for school. He was pleased to see them. He caught Joat's hand. He wanted to reassure himself by hearing his own voice. It would exorcise the fear from his mind. Sometimes one's own voice can be so comforting.

'You seem to be a late-riser, Bunty. Don't you get late for school? There's hot water for you in the bathroom. Wash yourself and get ready.'

Joat's face, her voice, her words, put him at ease. He felt at peace with himself. Whenever he saw Joat, he felt drawn towards her; it was good to just look at her.

He quickly entered the bathroom. But as he closed the door, fear gripped him. He urinated and came out without waiting for the morning motion. He wanted to remain in touch with the living world. Even faces can be reassuring.

They sat down to breakfast. Mummy was putting butter on bread and passing it on to Doctor sahib. In his milk-white clothes he looked fresh and prim as if he had walked out directly from a laundry. He dabbed his lips with the napkin as he nibbled at the toast. Bunty's mind was not there, nor was he taking any particular notice of Ami and Joat. All the time, the Doctor was at the periphery of his mind. One moment he saw him properly clad and the next, utterly naked.

While making toast or sipping tea, Mummy's body also became naked. He felt he had chanced upon a great secret. First fright, then revulsion and now fear and revulsion, both, led to a desire to witness that scene again.

As he went in to bathe and took off his clothes, he felt a sudden thrill. He mentally compared his body to the Doctor's. When he grew up, would his body be like his? As he handled himself, a strange tremor ran through his body. For the first time, he became conscious of the fact that he was also a somebody, that he had also a secret possession.

Listening to the teacher in the class, Bunty saw even the teacher without his clothes. Then he saw Joat standing before him, sometimes in her own form and sometimes in Mummy's. He tried to peer through her dress. He found no resemblance to Mummy. Maybe she would become like her when she grew up.

To his dismay, this scene kept repeating itself wherever he went.

As the evening approached, all his feelings vanished except a sense of guilt. He felt he had been doing something dirty. Why did Mummy come here? Why did she bring him along with her? In school, he could not concentrate on his studies even for a minute. What would happen to his studies? He crossed his fingers. No, no, he would not think of those things again. He had loaded himself with sin. But what was the way out? He felt he was wallowing in helplessness. And as the night advanced, this sense of guilt changed into fear. But what kind of fear and whose fear? He just did not know. Yet, there was something which invisibly held him in its clutches...

'Bunty, have some palav. Don't you like salad? It's good to eat salad. Ami, what will you have? Bansilal, get me some potato curry.' The clutter of dishes, the tinkle of cutlery. The people sitting round the table blurred into confusion and then submerged into darkness. The darkness grew more intense.

Sitting by his side, Mummy patted Bunty's head. 'Go to sleep, son. I'm with you. I've told Bansilal. He will sleep in the verandah near your door. I'll keep the verandah light on. And then there are Joat and Ami. Go to sleep. Be a good boy.'

As Mummy got up and turned off the light, all the darkness of the room found its way into Bunty's heart and got solidified there. Did they know how agonizing congealed darkness could be?

Then he heard Mummy's room closing and the blue light spread before Bunty's eyes. And then the same cavalcade... Bunty firmly crossed his fingers.

The whole night Bunty kept wandering among strange people, unknown faces and in unfamiliar places. What brought him to such uncongenial spots among a swarm of naked people—all of them stark naked. They came and they went. They stood there and pissed shamelessly. He was also moving about naked among them. When he felt the urge to piss, he planted himself in their midst and urinated with brazen abandon. He went urinating on and on. He wondered how his body could hold so much urine.

To his horror, he realized that he had wet his bed. And when he realized what he had done, another kind of fear gripped him. Not so much fear as embarrassment akin to his being caught naked in the midst of people.

Translated from the Bengali by the poet

Antara—1

Antara rising from primordial water
Like the first sun, forever new, forever old
You made me a universe
History and pre-history filed through me hand in hand
In gradual evolution.

Antara, because of you
I've earned the right to
Enter the tenfold halls of my foremothers

Clutching your baby hands in my fist
I hold the future in my debt forever
Antara, in an instant you have filled all time
By your grace I am coeval with the earth today.

The Twittering Machine

I have a picture postcard
Stuck on my kitchen wall

Spreading out slender wire branches
Across a bright blue sky
And setting four tiny wire birds upon them
Mr Paul Klee has created a funny little machine
With a great big lever attached to it
As if
The moment you turn it on
The tiny wire birds will start twittering
Wielding their thin wire tongues

He has called it
The Twittering Machine.

Whenever I see the picture I think of you
Four little wire birds
Are hidden within your tiny body
And the lever is held in your small fist
Before you could start talking
You have become a chatterbox
Our very own little Twittering Machine
The one we have made
Filling the bright blue sky

Children

Children
Whirling like tops inside my brain
Leaping clapping shrieking creaking
Upon the rusty springs of my nerve-ends

Children
Each a solitary palm tree
In a desert island

Sucking up subterranean waters
To bear branches of bitter bronze fruits

Childspeak

Whenever I see you
That exiled, homeless, street-child within me
Starved for days
Makes a great clamour
Millions of lice under her matted hair
Blood oozing from her chapped skin
Her cries scare the neighbourhood crows away

Every time she sees you
Every time she sees you

That naked street-child starving within me
Abandons her games in the dust

And stretching out her arms against the wind
Wails in hunger:
'Give me love!'

At this, her playmates,
The crows and the street-dogs
Stop their games of snatch and tag
And stand still for two minutes
Upon the garbage heap

GAGAN GILL

Child, Go Home

Translated from the Hindi by Lucy Rosenstein and Jane Duran

Child, go home.
Your home is nowhere?
Then go back to the womb.
No mother's womb?
Go to father's semen.
Your father is nowhere?
Go to mum's tubes.
Is the egg there barren?
Then, little one, flow away
in her menstrual blood
just as her longing
goes down the drain—
go that way too.
Let the girl be.
Child, go home.

BABY KAMBLE

The Prisons We Broke

Translated from the Marathi by Maya Pandit

There is a saying that a black cow can survive even on thorns. Our women were like that proverbial black cow. Even on occasions when they had a right to be indulged a bit, they had to fill their stomachs with thorns to stay alive.

Daughters usually went to their mothers' house for their first delivery. Not that there was a great deal of difference between the house of their parents and that of their in-laws! Poverty and adversities were the same for Mahars everywhere. The one thing that was found in abundance was firewood. And so the girl, after her delivery, was given plenty of hot baths. And that used to be so painful! Actually, the ordeal would begin from the time the labour pains set in. In the first place, the girl generally would be very young as all girls were married off at a very tender age. Obviously, they were physically quite underdeveloped at the time of their first pregnancy. The labour pains would continue for quite a long time, sometimes for even three or four days. The whole of the maharwada, in fact, would gather around the house. Women, in any case, did not have much work to do at home so they would simply flock to the house where a delivery was taking place. The ignorant midwives would keep thrusting their hands into the poor girl's vagina to see how far the baby had progressed. Invariably, the vagina would get swollen, obstructing the baby's path. The girl could overcome all obstacles and have a safe delivery only if her luck held strong! It was a battle with death. Her parents would be in a petrified state till she delivered the baby. They did whatever they could for her safety; that is, whatever did not cost any money. The poor girl would keep screaming aloud in pain and their hearts would be rent apart. The girl's mother especially would be in a state of utter shock and bewilderment. People would suggest a hundred different things to her. The elderly women would come up with their own advice, 'You should go to the stream and take a bath. Keep the wet sari on. Then go and pay a visit to our goddess Lakamai and pour water over her stone. Pray to her for an easy delivery. Don't forget to ask her to allow your daughter to return to her husband's place safe and sound along with the baby!'

Then the poor mother would hurry to the stream to bathe and then pour water over all the saffron-coated stones of goddess Lakamai, worship them with haldi and kumkum and pray for her daughter's safe delivery.

Her teeth would chatter with cold and fear. When finally her daughter gave birth to the baby, the relief that she felt would be so intense that she would nearly faint. But the ordeal would not yet be over for the poor girl. Helpless, she would lie completely at the mercy of the women surrounding her. Her vagina would be swollen stiff as the surrounding women kept thrusting their hands inside. There would be several wounds and cuts inside, which throbbed with unbearable pain. For want of cotton or cloth pads, blood continued to flow. Why, the girl would be fortunate if her family could find even some dirty rags for her. This was the extent of their poverty!

Then the girl's mother would heat some water. In the meanwhile, her father would dig a pit in one corner of the hut for her bath. The soil dug out from the pit would be spread all over the hut. Once the pit was ready, they would spread sticks on top of the pit, put the spade and other tools used for digging inside the pit, and make the new mother sit upon the sticks. Then they would give her a bath with scalding hot water. They would massage her as well, but of course, without any oil. This went on till she started sweating profusely. Then they would spread dry paddy upon the floor. That would be her bed for the next twelve days. She was made to lie naked upon it, her sari spread over her as cover. After the hot water bath, she was given the hot coal treatment, that is, pieces of burning coal were kept around her to keep her warm. This made the poor girl sweat even more, as if she was having another hot bath. Only after all this torture was over, was she was allowed to sleep. Then the newborn baby would be given a bath with hot water. People lived in filth, yet no one told them about the use of soap. Women would spit on their palms and clean the baby's face with the saliva. Then they bathed the baby till it became completely exhausted. Both water and fuel were free of charge, anyway! So there might even be two baths a day.

The crushed jowar would be cooked till it was soft; some jaggery and a little oil would be added to it before it's given to the mother. It was believed that the baby would not suffer from stomach aches if the mother was fed such soft gruel. The hungry mother would quickly pour it down her throat and, feeling utterly exhausted, throw herself down on her straw mattress and close her eyes. Sleep would be instant and peaceful as her stomach was full. A neem twig would be hung at the doorstep as a sign that the house had a new baby. A visitor had to stop at the entrance for five minutes and spit three times before being allowed to enter. This was supposed to ward off any evil spirit that might have accompanied the visitor.

Of course, it was only the more fortunate who could enjoy the luxury of eating cooked jowar, though this was the cheapest grain available. Many new mothers had to go hungry. They would lie down, pining for a few morsels while hunger gnawed their insides. Most women suffered this fate. Labour pains, mishandling by the midwife, wounds inflicted by onlookers' nails, ever-gnawing hunger, infected wounds with pus oozing out, hot water baths, hot coals, profuse sweating—everything caused the new mother's condition to worsen and she would end up getting a burning fever. On most occasions, it was tetanus. The family would have to look after the infant on the one hand and the suffering mother on the other! There would be neither food nor money! Only unlimited grief and suffering! The fever was often called madanvayu. Heated discussions would follow. Many remedies, which did not cost any money, would be freely prescribed and followed.

Some women would become possessed and the spirit of some goddess would speak out, 'This girl is possessed by an evil spirit. The hadal from that place, Shertati, possesses her. She has come into the house lodged in the feet of a neighbour. The girl met the spirit's eye exactly at twelve o'clock. Now I'll tell you what the remedy is. Take some oil, jowar, beaten jowar, kajal, kumkum in a bowl, move the bowl over the girl's body and then put it under the banyan tree at midnight. That evil bitch ties a swing to the banyan tree and sits swinging there to her heart's content. She is evil, I tell you, evil! She'll simply take away the body she possesses.'

The suffering of the woman would be beyond endurance. Even the onlookers found it difficult to watch her plight. Her family would smear her forehead with ash from the chulha. Two or three days would pass like this. People around her would try to soothe her with kind words. Life in that poor mother would gradually diminish and she would finally sink. Many young girls on the threshold of life succumbed to death. One in every ten lost their lives during childbirth. Infants died as well. The fear of death drove people to the Goddess Satwai and they would perform all the customary rituals.

On the fifth day, a ritual called the Pachvi would be performed. On this day, there would be a lot of work in the house. If no dead animal could be found in the village, an animal would be killed as a sacrificial offering to the goddess. The new mother, it was believed, needed to eat five particular organs of an animal on this day. The elderly women in the house would wake up early and polish the floor and the chulha with cow dung. The new mother would be given a hot water bath. Four dry jowar sticks would be placed in the four corners of the house. The women in the family went and stood in front of the queue if a dead animal was being skinned, and staked their claim on the five organs required as offerings to the Goddess Satwai. The butchers would nod with understanding and give the women the required organs—the kidney, the stomach, the liver and an organ with several veins that looked like a slipper and the large intestine full of fat.

The women collected these in a big earthen pot and immediately carried the pot home to cook the organs to a soft pulp. At sunset, the women would get busy. First, they would take seven small stones, wash and arrange them on the bath pit in a line and smear them with haldi and kumkum. A big earthen pot would be kept on the bath pit and a lamp of kneaded flour lighted inside. Then the black soot from the flame would be gathered and applied on the stones. The cooked limbs would be offered as the sacrifice. Then the mother would be covered with a blanket and the baby put at the feet of the goddess, that is, in front of the seven stones. After this, the mother would be given a large plate full of the cooked organs. After the meal she would be made to wipe her tongue with a tattered piece of jute cloth. It was believed that by doing so she would prevent the baby from getting stomach aches. Then the new mother and her mother had to keep vigil the whole night without even a wink of sleep. No rat was to be allowed inside. It was believed that the Goddess Satwai and the God Barama visited the house at midnight to write the baby's future on its forehead.

The Adoption

This was rather an interesting zenana. I remember so well my first visit. I was led through the outer courtyards of the usual rajbari, past the two painted lion-dragons, which helped the armed watchmen to keep guard, through narrow passages and a rather attractive rose garden to the women's staircase. And here my guide left me and fled incontinent, for, as I soon found, the zenana was guarded by peacocks, warranted to peck the eyes out of any male creature whomsoever.

They were terrible protectors, pouncing silently, despite a be-ringed right ankle; and all my security of womanhood and draperies did not prevent a chill clutch at my heart as they came to reconnoitre. I think they must have been clever as well as terrible, for it takes a little observation to separate men and women from each other in a Bengal cold-weather season, when men also wrap themselves in Kashmiri draperies.

But the peacocks never, I am told, made a mistake. 'Yet father, brother, sons-in-law, the zenana amlas (officers)? How about these, Rani sahiba?' I asked.

'Oh,' she told me, 'the birds are chained up till they learn the faces of the privileged ones.'

And it was then, I suppose, 'upon the head' of the privileged ones to see that their class was not enlarged.

In the course of time my rani had her suggestions ready. Choice of a son for the dead raja was difficult; for many things had to be avoided. He might not be an only son, and the fiction of sonship must be observed. No one could be adopted whose mother the late 'father' could not have married. This excluded her first choice, the son of her husband's sister.

Again, the boy must not yet have been admitted into the spiritual sonship of his own family. This barred among others a charming boy whom I myself saw invested with the sacred thread. 'But you can't have him, Rani sahiba; all his spiritual value is already pledged to the uses of his natural father. His prayers cannot help Raja sahib.' And she understood this far better than the mundane obstacles, which I had to allege later against other selections.

Finally, however, a boy was found of the right class, and caste, and possibility of real sonship; and I was as excited as the zenana over the great ceremony which would presently go forward.

And now the day itself was here, and I was set down at three o'clock of a morning at the foot of the hills in what looked like remarkably pretty country.

'If Miss sahib cares to wait till the dawn hour or for a night of the moon, she will see the wild peacocks come out of the jungle and dance.'

I did so want to ask if the peacock sentries were allowed to go to the wild peacocks' ball just once in a way and if sentry peacocks retired from service were to be professional chaperones at dances; but such frivolity would not have been understood, so I exercised a wise restraint.

'And, if the Miss sahib will come in the days of cold and stay in the little bungalow beyond the canal, she can join in the big shikar. Oh, a very big shikar is necessary every year to kill the things that are not peacock-people in that same jungle which climbs to the hill tops.'

We drove in an ancient phaeton for a few miles, and I was getting restive at the incongruity of an English phaeton for this hour and this countryside and this occasion, when my guide spoke once more: 'At the fourth mile the carriage road stops; the Miss sahib will forgive that there will then be conveyances of the country.' The Miss sahib rejoiced.

The country was indeed lovely. To my right gleamed the sluggish canal, slimy and shiny as a snake, drowsing between mud banks. This is the chief waterway for country boats laden with hay, or for the 'green' boat, the local houseboat, perilous as to kitchen and stuffy as to cabin, but most picturesque to the eye of the onlooker. Now we had come upon a boat at anchor, and a very populous green boat taking an entire colony to another part of the country. The mother was cooking the evening meal safely on shore, and a small 'goose boy', aged four and dressed in an amulet, was trying with a long thin wisp of cane to gather his chickens back to the boat. Beyond the canal the horizon had been pushed away and away, and it was some time before I realized that the gigantic 'love-in-a-mist' plant-like trees were dying bamboos. They gave a weird cobwebby effect to a landscape in which indeed nothing at that moment seemed real.

To my left the low shrub was full of things to see: birds and lizards, jackals and khargosh, a million butterflies—while here, close by the road, was a sacred tree shadowing an army of mud horses.

The god at the foot of the tree was fond of riding, so pilgrims brought him little mud-horses for keepsakes. To the rani the same pilgrims brought a cow apiece. In a minute we had come upon their grazing-ground—the loveliest sight, for the dainty little creatures had to be milk-white, and were stalled in the temple fields—a pleasing harmony in white and green.

Straight from the grazing-ground began the ascent of the hills to the great temple itself. When I came to travel this bit, I had already long since changed to my 'conveyance of the country'. It was a red-enamelled carrying-chair, most comfortable, but oh, so noisy! for my lusty Ooriya carriers shouted at the top of their voices 'hum-hum, hum-hum, hum-hum', between middle C and its octave, till they got tired, when they would begin on the higher note and end on the lower.

'What does it *mean*?' I begged, thinking a meaning would help me to bear it better.

'Oh just mad talk,' they said grinning, and went at it again.

The wood was thickening, planted with white-barked trees slim and tall, and dressed in spring clothes of the colour of the olive groves at Bordighera.

Before I had done loving the trees we had arrived at the temple, and the bearers set me down in a lane of flag-staffs, their light-hearted welcome all aflutter—red and blue, pilgrim-colour, sun-yellow and deep amber, earth-brown, and wheat-colour... It is impossible to describe the effect.

Between the flags I walked to an enclosure made of plaited twigs. It shut in a great pond fed by a sacred spring. The rani bathed in this pond, and then walked past more little flag decorations to her special temple house. Here she sat watching the preliminary ceremony in the old old temple, grey stone against forest green. Nothing there was, to outward seeing, which kept it from being the temple of all the world. Shiva and his bull, and other gods and godlings, lived within doors. The ceremony was performed in the verandah, facing god's out-of-doors, and all the beauty of that temple not built with hands.

The actual adoption was very simple indeed. The boy's father and mother stood on one side of him and the rani on the other.

'Will you give?' 'Will you take?' were asked and answered; and there was my rani with a boy of her very own, who should save the soul of the dead raja, and fill up all that was wanting in her sonless hearth.

As for the boy himself—he was wide-mouthed, wistful, with the listening look of the deaf-mute. But he was neither deaf nor mute; his expression was but the result of an intense desire to please. He had seen his very own mother give him away, not sadly but with much self-gratulation. 'The family would all now belong to raj-people.'

He had heard his merits and demerits discussed by a hundred folk, and he was nine years old, old enough to understand. His temperament was such that the greatness and importance thrust upon him were lost in the hurt of losing his own people, and in the desire to please these other great ones.

'Well,' I said, as he sat wearied out with the day, a pathetic wee figure, 'tell me all about it.'

'I was bathed and had new clothes and my head was shaved. So I am a "son given", and my mother cannot love me. It is sin.'

Name: Amba Dalmia

Name: Amba Dalmia
Dates: 19 May 1980–19 November 2001

I was fifty-three when my daughter died.

Even now I do not think I can describe the endless night of 18 November, the visit to the hospital, the return home, the hours that passed, the collective silence of relatives as they gathered in our drawing room.

I remember a frantic burning itch unfurling beneath my skin. For weeks no salve, no ointment, no ice, no heat made any difference.

My reproductive system shut down, this time for good. A hazy disbelief shrouded everything; my mind was doing its best to bar the outside world entry.

The years ahead lay heavy on my heart. I saw myself being pushed down the desolate trajectory of my life—without joy, without hope, each day as bleak as the one before.

So far as I was concerned all the children of the world should die, die at the height of their youth and beauty, die with their lives ahead of them, die and leave their parents grieving, even as I was grieving.

Every morning I opened the newspaper to the obituary page, to examine the only item that interested me, the death of the young. Ghoulishly, I devoured confirmation that I was not alone.

Although this did nothing to ease my sorrow, I persisted in searching for dead children. Suffering had made me a monster.

Through the day the only pleasure I could anticipate were the sleeping pills at night. My continuing existence tore at me. I, the old parent, inhabiting the minutes, the hours that rightfully belonged to the next generation.

I had failed in my most basic duty: I had not been able to protect my daughter.

You don't let your child go out in unsafe situations. And on that particular night of 18 November 2001 she was unsafe enough to die.

◆

When I returned to work after two months (I taught in a college), it was with the slow painful walk of a cripple. My words came with difficulty, each lecture presented hurdles I stumbled over.

She had been the same age as these milling students, students walking, eating, studying, secure that to live was their birthright.

What did they know about birthrights? They who looked at me with large tender eyes, they whose gaze I avoided while walking stiff-faced down corridors.

In the staff room, I spent my time staring dully out of the window, my back resolute against sympathy aimed in my direction.

Stay away from me.

I resent your kindness, your determined advance upon my space, anything you say that expresses solidarity, the slightest reference to what happened.

I wished to have nothing to do with the social face of grief.

From time to time I recall with shame the condolence visits I had once paid. How useless I was on those occasions; I with the fixed smile, the trite sympathy, the fearful, there-but-for-the-grace-of-god-go-I feeling in my heart. I had gone in the service of you-are-not-alone but now I understood how much bereavement isolates, and how little difference any interaction makes.

The companionship I sought was of fellow sufferers. You, I will listen to. I respect you, your pain, your endurance, your survival.

One mother: The day you come home from the funeral, the first time you put food into your mouth, that is the moment you have decided to live.

I stare at the black-and-white portrait of her daughter. The face in three-quarter profile, the wide open, smile. I used to call her teeth piano keys, she said.

Piano keys. Nice image. We smile painfully.

It has been two years since her daughter died. She was thirty-three. (Twelve years older than our daughter. Twelve more years of life.)

In some ways the second year is harder, she continued. By then it has sunk in, well and truly sunk in.

Oh. So there was all of that to look forward to.

We were meeting in a church. She had put out a notice announcing a support group for parents in mourning.

Someone had told us about it and here we were. The only attendees.

The woman was a counsellor.

In India perhaps this kind of gathering will not be so successful, she observed. People already have family, friends whom they rely on. But I was part of such a group in the US and it really helped. (Her daughter had died in an American hospital.)

We talk about marriage break-ups. Couples separate—they can't take the burden of grief—their own and their partner's. They want to get on with life.

It is not as though I am averse to getting on. I only wonder how you can do it when your spirits are so weighed down you cannot move. And what was the use of splitting up with your partner? For who else in the world could this particular loss be as significant?

◆

Some time after the event, I walk hesitatingly to my study. Hesitation because with each step I move towards a life that no longer contains her and that wrongs every moment.

On the way I notice that the gladioli I had planted earlier have begun to bloom. The gay red tips hurt me with their insouciance.

It shows how stupid I have become. I feel personally aggrieved by the way everything continues. I long for a day when flowers can flourish, birds can sing and I not be offended.

I unlock my study door and enter.

I stare at my computer, squat black, the morning light reflected off its thick layer of dust. How can I do the same things when everything is changed? It seems morally reprehensible.

The before time, the after time.

There are some things we never do again. I have never since stuck a photo in an album, never put mehendi on my hands. My husband stopped pursuing his development plans, abandoning a project that had been his dream for over twenty years. There are places we don't visit because they are associated with her, songs we don't listen to, books we don't open, drawers that remain shut. Unbeknownst to anybody, we continue with our pointless statements.

I turn the machine on and dredge up the novel I am working on. I scroll down page after page. I can barely understand what I have written, let alone relate to the characters. I feel as weak before the narrative as a baby in a grown-up world.

I close the file.

Writing had once meant a lot to me, and now I wonder whether this too has collapsed along with so much else. My hands move over the keys. Uncertainly, I begin to jot down a bit of what I have been going through.

It is useless. Words cannot do justice to what I feel. I switch the computer off. In the now blank screen I can see my dim reflection. The reflection of a fifty-three-year-old woman.

I make a list of authors who have lost their children:

William Shakespeare, Rabindranath Tagore, Roald Dahl, Mary

Shelley, Goethe, Isabel Allende, Carlos Fuentes, J. M. Coetzee, Mridula Garg.

This is a list I find soothing. I cling to Shakespeare & Co and continue switching on my computer and gazing at the screen.

Pebbles in a Tin Drum

Translated from the Hindi by Masooma Ali

Kajjan and I spent the whole day sitting in the deserted lobby of that fortress of a hospital. We were allowed to 'visit' Candy for five minutes at nine o'clock in the morning and five minutes in the evening. From a distance, across the glass wall, over the phone.

'Did you have dinner? Was your bed comfortable? Have you brought your woollens?' Candy made several queries in a row.

I didn't have the heart to ask her anything such as, 'How did it happen, my child? How did your clothes catch fire, my Candlou? Where does it hurt? What do they give you to eat? Are you in pain?' I did not want to remind her of the traumatic accident. She should not think of those terrible flames at least during the brief moments she was sharing with me.

Candy's composure and smiling manner gave no indication of her pain and suffering. It seemed as if she had just scalded her foot or knee after which she was resting and she would recover in a day or two. Then we would go and tour Europe, chat over cups of coffee, sit in the sun; listen to music and go home to Arpana. My head buzzed with a million thoughts, like bats blinded by floodlight, striking helplessly against each other. But a strange invisible control made me speak in platitudes—lies that I desperately wanted to believe in. 'We'll go sightseeing and return home to Dolly,' I said. Dolly is Arpana's pet name.

'No, Ammi. We'll ask Dolly to come here and then we'll tour together. How can she stay alone for so long?' Candy said. Was she also playing the game, mouthing soothing lies?

During the 'visit' in the evening, she said, 'You have been wearing this sari since yesterday. Haven't you brought any luggage?'

Controlling my tears with difficulty, I answered, 'Oh, oh. I did not remember to change.' How could I tell her that I had neither washed nor changed nor eaten anything since I had arrived.

I had only been saying to God, 'Look, I have not committed any sins all these years. To my knowledge, I have not even hurt a fly. But if I have unknowingly caused pain to anybody, please do not avenge it by punishing my child. Please let me suffer for my sins. Please be just. Have mercy on me if you can. Forgive me, Friend. I have been punished enough. Please forgive the rest. Bless my daughter and help her get well. She is going to be nineteen on the twenty-sixth of November. This is no age to go through such suffering. At this age she should enjoy herself. You know fully well how she has spent her childhood sharing her mother's poverty and how she had to face her father's temper and hatred. Things have just started getting a little better. It is only now that we can afford to relax in the evenings and listen to music and discuss books. Our greatest strength is that we have each other as friends.

'The friendship I enjoy with my two daughters has given warmth to my life and dispelled the pain from my existence. Please, God, do not take us away from each other. If ever I have done a good deed, please bless me for it by helping my child get well. You are benevolent. Please show compassion to me.'

At such moments I would hear the voices of my inner samskaras. With God's grace, the lame can scale the peaks of the mountains and the blind can not only see but have the knowledge of the whole universe illuminate their eyes. God's will can create land in the middle of the sea and inundate the land with deep waters.

Then Candy said wistfully, 'I think it'll take two months for me to recover completely. I asked the nurse and she said so. Where will you stay for two months? How would you arrange for so much foreign exchange?'

'Don't tax yourself with these niggling worries,' I answered, 'I have made all arrangements. Your Uncle Jasbir has written to all his friends in London, the US and other places. They'll send us as much money as we need. Then our embassy has assured me that they'll arrange for the foreign exchange.'

'Okay. Let me talk to Kajjan.'

I handed the receiver to Kajjan. He talked to her in French so I could not follow what he was saying.

She looked at the nurse with a smile and said something. The nurse also smiled. I asked Kajjan what she was telling the nurse. He said she was telling her that she had beautiful eyes and so did her mother.

Controlling our tears, we came out. Five minutes were gone all too soon. We saw the doctor standing behind the window opening into the corridor. He looked cross. He said something in French to Kajjan. His tone was harsh and impatient. Kajjan seemed to be appeasing him or maybe he was apologizing.

'What is the matter?' I asked softly.

'He is asking why we are hurting her so much. Talking is bad for her. Excitement, too, is bad.'

'But why? She is getting better, isn't she?' I asked. Kajjan conveyed my question to the doctor. In response he protested vehemently, and kept saying something over and over again.

'What is it?' I asked Kajjan.

'He says that she suffers much pain when she speaks. She keeps talking to you bravely and does not let you know it but the effort of talking hurts her very badly.'

'But…' I was surprised and upset at the same time. 'How come she looks so relaxed? She seems all right. Tell me how badly is she burnt?' I was really scared.

Kajjan was the interpreter between me and the doctor. Quietly, he told me, 'She is burnt completely neck down and her injuries are grievous. The doctor says all that skin simply cannot form back.'

Stricken, I implored, 'Please graft my skin on her body. Can't plastic surgery be performed?' The doctor smiled at me as if I were an ignorant child, I persisted and said, 'Tell me why it can't. I promise I'll lie down quietly and you can remove the skin from my legs, arms, back and belly and graft it on her body gradually. I am sure her body will accept my skin. After all she is my flesh and blood. Of course she will accept my skin. How long will it take? Two, four or six months? I don't care how long—I'll keep lying quietly.' I could not hold back my tears. Folding my hands in entreaty, I placed my forehead on the window in front of the doctor.

The doctor left. Kajjan told me, 'He was saying that he'd have to wait for her burns to heal. Then he would see.'

I may not have followed what the doctor was saying but I clearly understood the message his expression conveyed. In simple terms he was saying, 'We'll see if she survives.'

I sank on the same bench as before and cried, feeling utterly helpless. My child was right there—just a few feet away, but all the doors were closed—doors that were white like shrouds.

PADMA SACHDEV

Translated from the Dogri by Shivanath

An Infant's Dream

The Sun
Before going down into the sea
Has spread a sheet
Drenched with its own blood
On the sky where it touches the waters.
Someone
Has placed on its dye
A screen freshly woven with colourful
     strands of jute
Its rose red is rather faint but deep
And a golden streak cuts through it.
Like some saw
Behind this screen.

In the warm glow of the Sun
Several fairies
Are bathing
And washing their bodies, covering them
With the muslin of the last rays of the Sun.

These fairies
Will open the vanity boxes
Make up their faces and see them in the mirrors.

Will then loosen their hair
Tuck raat-ki-rani flowers in them
Will put on stolen wings of some birds
And then set out
To appear in the dream of that infant.

Who has gone to sleep
Suck the breast of its mother
Burning like a hot plate
And has missed
To tell her the story
It had been memorizing throughout the day.

Mother Tongue

I approached a stem
Swinging on a reed
And asked him
To give me a quill.
Irritated, he said
I gave you one only the other day
A new one, what have you done with it?
are you some sort of an accountant
With some *Shah*
Writing account books
Where you need a new pen
Every other day he asked.
No, I don't work for a *Shah*
I said, but for a *Shahni,* very kind,
    very well off
And I am not the only one
Working for her
She has many servants
Ever ready to do her bidding
That *Shahni* is my mother tongue
Dogri
Give me, a quill, quickly
She must be looking for me
The reed cut off its hand
Gave it to me and said
Take it
I too am her servant.

LILA MAJUMDAR

The Yellow Bird

Translated from the Bengali by Kamala Chatterjee

Behind the kitchen was Jhogru's quarters and next to the kitchen was the hot-water room. Here three large stones made up a stove, and water was heated in large kerosene tins placed over this.

For the stove, wood was used instead of coal and such a variety of woods, each with its distinctive colour and smell. Sometimes, the burning woods would release a sloughing sound and fill the room with a sweet aroma.

Jhogru said, 'Naturally, that is the smell of the hair of wood-nymphs.'

'There are no wood-nymphs, Jhogru.'

'What sort of talk is that, Bogey Dada?'

'There are no fairies or even wood-nymphs.'

'Then why is it written in your book? Yesterday Grandma read out of a book about them.'

'They are all make-believe stories, Jhogru; fairies do not exist.'

'So you say, even if it is written in a book! And I have seen one.'

'Have you seen one with your own eyes?'

'No, not exactly; but my father had seen one. Was my father telling a lie then?'

'Where and when did he see a fairy?'

'Many years ago, Rumu Didi, he saw one in the hills of Dumka. But I know you are not going to believe it!'

'No, no, Jhogru, do tell us how your father saw a wood-nymph.'

Jhogru shoved a light green twig into the stone stove where the water was boiling, and said, 'Nymphs live in this type of wood and not in the dried-up dead wood.' Instantly, the whole room was filled with an incense-like scent.

'Now look properly into the fire, Bogey Dada; not where it is just starting to burn, but at the very centre where the fire is burning fiercely. Can't you see something—houses, trees?'

Immediately, Rumu and Bogey felt they could indeed see houses and trees made of fire, red and blue ones. The roofs, walls and branches constantly moving, quivering, breaking and being rebuilt again! It was as if they were watching a whole city made of fire.

Bogey covered his eyes and said, 'Not only in wood-fire, but in coal-fire too I have seen wars being fought, towns getting burnt down and huge palaces collapsing.'

'That may be true, but in Dumka we burn wood only, so I can't say much about coal.'

'Dada, why do you talk so much? Now do tell, Jhogru, how your father saw a fairy.'

'My father was quite old at that time. The chill in his old bones lingered all the time. He spent the whole day sitting near the round-shaped iron furnace. A pile of wood was always there beside him. Once in a while, he took a piece of wood and pushed it into the fire. Smoke filled the room, making the eyes of his visitors sting. They asked my father, 'Don't your eyes burn, old man?' And he replied, 'Arrey, I don't even feel the burning of my heart, let alone that of my eyes!'

'He used to spend the whole day sitting by the fire and eating sweet potatoes which he roasted on the fire with the help of a long twig. He offered them to people who came to visit him. They often asked, 'Old man, there are rat-bites on the potatoes, have they entered your potato fields?' My father's eyesight was poor and he would reply in anger, 'If you don't feel like it, don't eat them.'

'One day, as he placed a sweet potato in the fire, he felt there were people inside those fire-houses. Somebody picked up the potato and started roasting it by rotating it in the fire. It was an old man with a long beard, who started to eat the sweet potato. My father quickly pulled out the roasting-stick and with the potato out came the old bearded man! Father saw him for an instant, before he disappeared like dust in the air. Now do you still want to say these are made-up stories, Bogey Dada? And not only my father, but the woodcutters too knew of many things found in the forests that are never mentioned in any book. What would people living within the four walls throughout their lives know about trees and plants found in the forests?'

'But human beings love animals; shouldn't they know all about them?'

'Who said humans love animals? Once I went to watch the kheda operation, where wild elephants are caught by men using magnificent tame elephants as decoys to lure them. I saw free-spirited animals, who rejoice in going down the green hillsides with their herd, being shackled and taken away. Do you call that love for animals?

'Baby elephants feel very ticklish if one touches their soft skin. Do you know, men use rough scrubbing brushes on them to get rid of that ticklish feeling, so they could put the howdah on them? Otherwise, at the slightest touch the little ones would roll on the ground laughing their heads off! Do you call these methods acts of love?'

Rumu said, 'But we love dogs, don't we, Dada? We love Bhulo. You also said that people in Dumka love all animals except cats.'

'People in Dumka are different. Once there was a forest fire. Hordes of scared animals came running out of the forest. The villagers were busy trying to save their own homes, so they said nothing to the animals.

'There was a strange-looking bear, the like of which nobody had seen before. There was a band of white fur round its neck that looked like it was wearing a garland of white flowers. The bear was a very powerful and fearless animal and terrorized the villagers by eating honey from their beehives and injuring or wounding the local people. But being a very cunning animal, nobody could catch or kill it.

'During the forest fire, the bear too came out with the others; there was a cub with it, who was limping from an injury. The little one fell down right in front of our sardar, the village chief. A year ago, this bear had chewed to pieces the foot bones of the sardar's son, so now he was ready with deadly bow and arrows in his hands.'

'He killed the bear?'

'When the sardar raised his bow, the bear clasped the cub to its breast and stood staring at him. And our sardar lowered his bow, turned and walked away. It is not an easy thing to love animals, Didi. It is not enough to keep a dog or a cat in the house and pet and caress them.'

Food

Food, for many women, translates to work. The kitchen and larder have been female domains for centuries, and it is not surprising that a lot of women's writing about food is heavy with the subtext of power. In traditional homes, women are encouraged to eat last, after the men have had their fill. Ashapurna Devi's story (from *Snakebite and the Distant Window*) illustrates how dependent people are on those who prepare their meals. She appears to be using food as a metaphor for human vulnerability. In another novel (not included here), she has a scene where a little girl exhibits an early streak of rebellion by—and is rebuked for—asking for a bigger helping of dessert.

Widows in some parts of the nation were denied salt as well as all tasty, rich dishes. There was an obvious attempt to break women's spirits by suppressing their appetites. Bulbul Sharma's story 'Mushroom Madness' picks up on this conflation of appetites and gives us a protagonist who longs not only for good, diverse food but also refuses to limit herself to one man.

There is more to food, of course, than just the preparation and consumption of it. Even in this endless business of preparation, there are clues to power and hierarchy. Food has deep, twisted links to caste and class in India—what can and cannot be eaten, by whom, when, and what happens to those who break the norm. Nilanjana Roy's essay on eating meat plunges directly into the heart of these difficult questions.

Our food norms involve both indulgence and self-denial. Prathibha Nandakumar's poem spans the whole cycle—from feasts to fasts. There are also hunger strikes, which are steeped in politics as well. Rarely do you see writing as politically sharp and as centred on hunger as the extract included here from the novel *Mistaken Identity* by Nayantara Sahgal.

Shivani's *Apradhini*, an intensely sympathetic set of essays about women in prison, begins with the description of a feast that has been prepared by the prisoners. The writer, a special guest, is served not just a rich meal but also a delicious anecdote about a male admirer who came to visit one of the inmates and how that led to a rather unexpected outcome.

NAYANTARA SAHGAL

Mistaken Identity

Bhaiji reopens the question of a protest fast. This time there's no argument, but the comrades get into a huddle at their end of the barrack to discuss it. Before lights out Iyer announces their decision. They are prepared to go on a fast provided it is called a hungerstrike. They don't want the issue confused with puritanical twaddle. My remark, that I will get just as hungry whether I go on a fast or a hungerstrike, is coldly received by all eight. I have never seen them so united. With all eyes on me I haven't a hope of refusing. I'm not sure it would be wise to refuse. One never knows how a conspiracy trial may go. The way this one is stretching out, I may need a reprieve as badly as any of them, never mind Vacha. I can't be the only one to forfeit public sympathy, always supposing the public hears about us. But my companions are determined the public shall hear.

Bhaiji sends for his lawyer and briefs him, and I've never seen a lawyer look so thrilled. The project fills him with ghoulish satisfaction. He says he understands the issue perfectly and will draft a statement for the press the minute he gets to his office. Two days later we read it. In solidarity with other political prisoners, it informs us, and in memory of the martyr who gave his life in jail, we, too, are prepared to make the ultimate sacrifice for our sacred motherland. It is too late to back out of the rendezvous with suicide he's landed us with, and the comrades launch their hungerstrike in a rage. I feel extremely nervous myself. On the other hand Bhaiji and the twins already have a sacrificial glow about them.

The rest of us are in a foul temper and giddy with hunger when we return from court the first evening. We are forbidden exercise in the yard, our newspaper has been stopped, and we have absolutely nothing to do. Comrade Pillai says reasonably enough it's silly to take it out on each other when the fault is that nincompoop lawyer's. He suggests we form a circle and play a game. He has it from a slimming expert that concentrating on food works on the subconscious to substitute for food and stave off hunger pangs, so let's take turns describing the most memorable meal we've ever eaten.

'We'll proceed clockwise, shall we?' He points to Bhaiji.

'Cornflakes,' says Bhaiji.

We wait, but this is it. Bhaiji has found this English foodstuff most unusual, chiefly because it is completely tasteless. Most food has taste.

Dey, the force-fed comrade, comes next, and I learn he is well-travelled. He says he's going to tell us about a meal he ate on his visit to Moscow two years ago. He made a tour of restaurants, among other places, and is pleased to report that the famous Yar, where the bourgeoisie used to blow up fortunes on drunken gypsy entertainments, has been converted into a motorcycle garage. He came across several restaurants that have been turned into old people's homes and young people's communal parlours. Finally he discovered a restaurant that was still a restaurant. Here he had crayfish soup, salmon à la monastery, cauliflower à la Polonnaise, lamb-filled pirozhki, boiled potatoes, sour-cream pancakes, butter, cheese, tea and a bottle of wine. The menu glides off his tongue with the fluency of hours of mental practice. His face is alight with memory. We are all too desperate to utter, except Bhaiji who beams as he waits for the game to continue and is disappointed it has ended so soon.

Comrade Dey offers to relieve the gloom by enlightening us about the non-culinary aspects of his Moscow trip. We listen—there's nothing else to do—but the various celebrations in honour of the Revolution's tenth anniversary leave our stomachs growling. Only Sen responds with pleasure. He's still at the stage where a story is as good as food. The dullest driest facts delight this boy. I am certain it wouldn't have made me leap up and slap my thigh if, at nineteen, I had been told the west had boycotted the tenth anniversary, but fraternal delegations from Persia, Turkey, Afghanistan and Mongolia had hailed it. Sen is such an ideal audience that Dey goes on to tell him the story of a film he saw about mutiny in the Tsar's Black Sea fleet. Sen is enthralled. The ratings' revolt, their enthusiastic reception at the port, the spectacle of Cossacks pouring down the great flight of steps and firing volleys into crowds of people who scatter and flee, keep him engrossed after the rest of us have gone to bed. I'm so hungry, I'm the only one who hears the happy ending. The Tsar's ships sail by with sailors waving from the rigging, a sign that they have joined the Revolution.

By the third day of our hungerstrike we aren't talking to each other. We could be two rows of newly caught fish gaping at each other all the way to court and back in the lorry, and eight cooked fish laid out on our cots on our return. Bhaiji, compared with the rest of us, is cheerful if not spry. He slyly admits he's used to fasting once a week and eating lightly the rest of the week. On his tours to convert the population to khaddar and sexual abstinence, he's used to getting by for days on a handful of peanuts, so he hasn't felt the strain. Comrade Iyer glares at him and controls his wrath with an effort.

'At least when Gandhi goes on a fast he doesn't trick his associates into going to death's door with him,' he says curtly.

On the fourth day we have no more sense of solidarity left than famine victims. There's no such thing as a communal yawning chasm, and Bhaiji does not win the comrades' hearts by pointing out we are now one with the hungry peasants. The twins slump against a wall when they are not lying limp on their cots, content to be led to the last gasp and too far gone to raise an eyelid. The hairy twin manages to raise his, nudges dumpy, and asks him to watch him cantilever his right arm up listlessly a few inches and let it drop again—to demonstrate, I suppose, how feeble he has become. We have suspended our food orders but tin plates of gritty jail mishmash keep arriving at mealtimes. Nothing would prevent me from swallowing the mess if the other eight weren't there. I've made up my mind to do so if the jailer decides to force-feed us. He has been round to say the government doesn't want us to think it can't discriminate between respectable middle-class people and ordinary low-class persons. If there's any lack in our lives we should tell him, and our social position will be taken into consideration. He's met with silence and goes away.

I try concentrating on the hollow of my throat. I try thinking of Sylla instead of food but a smoked haunch of lamb intervenes. My Afghan host plucks out its eyes and offers me, his guest of honour, this delicacy for a starter. Before I fall asleep I train my mind sternly on Sylla.

Being a Parsi she wears frocks, swims in a bathing costume, and has bobbed hair, all of which account for the informality between us from the start and the ease with which we became friends. Outside of foreign parts, Sylla's Bombay was the most foreign city I had seen. It had trams and a few taxis. Half the people in it were English and the Indians might as well have been. I had never seen so many short-haired, dog-owning women. They gave their dogs names like Bonzo and Mr St Clair, and said 'woopsie-daisy' when they spilled ice cream on their blouses. Their saris were made of English crepe and French chiffon, and I heard about ice blue and tango orange for the first time. Sylla had a chic older friend, a leader of fashion who smoked through a foot-long holder, wore tango orange saris whipped twice around her tightly instead of once loosely, and looked like a better brand of cigar. She had that brown wizened look, too, from sunning, which I thought rather a shame as I liked her, till I heard it was dreadfully smart.

Mushroom Madness

Rain dripped from the deodar branches and formed a pool near his feet. Nath moved further into the shade of the tree but the rain still caught him, drenching his back and head.

'I will catch rain fever and die. Then they can live together happily in my house, sleep in my bed,' he thought, taking a long pull at his bidi and, as his heart filled with a rush of self pity, he suddenly felt much better. He looked up and saw that the sky was slowly clearing. Just a few grey-white clouds remained in one corner and he could see the rain moving beyond the mountain peak. A faint patch of pink sunlight now touched the treetops further up the hillside. Nath tucked his half-smoked bidi carefully behind his ears and began climbing up the path. The rain had made the stones slippery as glass and he had to walk slowly, taking shorter steps.

'I will reach home late today with nothing in my bag except for a few early plums. He must have gone to the other side of the forest and with his luck, would have found black mushrooms today,' Nath said to himself with a sigh. 'They will sit together in the kitchen. Chinta will fry the mushrooms in til oil and then she will eat them one at a time as he watches her.' Nath could taste the slippery, spongy, fried black mushrooms in his mouth. He took out his bidi and lit it again. The tobacco mingled with the mushrooms as he exhaled clouds of smoke. He stood and watched the trail of smoke as it disappeared into the branches. He could make out the faint shape of Chinta's face in the cloud of smoke, just her eyes shaded by heavy eyebrows; and her nose. She followed him everywhere but always in fragments. Sometimes it was her face that peered at him from behind trees; sometimes her arms reached out to him, covered with her favourite green glass bangles. One day, when he was out ploughing, he met just her feet clad in the red plastic slippers he had bought her from the Renuka fair. They followed him for a while, flip-flopping in the wet mud and then disappeared. Nath wondered why Chinta tormented him, piecemeal, like this. He could have understood it if she was dead and her ghost was floating around divided into various parts. But Chinta was alive and living, in fact much more alive than anyone else he knew. She sang louder, walked faster, talked, laughed and ate more than any other woman in the village. Like a heavenly golden swan she shone amongst the drab she-sparrows at village gatherings.

Nath had met her at his aunt's funeral feast in her village which was at the other end of the valley. Chinta was sixteen years old, plump and glowing with health like a pregnant cow. Her large, firm hips and her breasts promised many sons. Though she was ripe for marriage, Nath was amazed that no offers had yet been made for her.

'Her eyebrows join in the middle. It means she will always cause strife wherever she goes,' a village elder told him, as Chinta walked past them carrying a plate loaded with besan laddoos. Nath's eyes followed her till she reached the end of the courtyard and then he saw her furtively crushing a laddoo in her mouth before she placed the plate on the floor. She turned around and saw Nath staring at her in amazement. Instead of looking ashamed at being caught red-handed, eating before the men had been served, Chinta giggled and, from far away, offered him a laddoo hidden in her soft palm, moist with sweat and sugar dust.

They were married as soon as the next auspicious day was available because Chinta's father was worried Nath might change his mind.

'Fortunately, his parents are both dead and his uncles can be silenced with a bottle, maybe two, of rice wine. But I'm afraid some interfering relative might break up the match. Then we will have this girl on our hands all our life. Let him feed her from now,' he said to Chinta's mother when she objected to the unseemly haste.

Nath brought Chinta to his village, which was a day's walk away along a narrow, tree-covered ridge leading to the other side of the hill. All along the way she sang in a loud, broken voice and laughed and skipped over rivulets, behaving like a carefree girl instead of walking quietly, at least five steps behind him like a new bride should.

'You will get lost if I let you walk ahead. I know this path better than you,' she said when Nath tried to overtake her. The village women called out to Chinta. 'Caught yourself a murga at last, eh? See you don't eat him up.' Chinta laughed and turning towards them, spat out the seeds of blackberries she had been eating all along the way. When they stopped to drink water at a spring, she forced a handful of wild blackberries into his mouth, and the juice dripped down to mark a purple trail on his new wedding clothes.

He should have asserted himself on that very first day. Stood firm or given her a beating. Now all was lost. He was a slave to her demands. Both of them were her slaves, Nath and Mohan. The villagers laughed and jeered when they both tried to carry the grass she had cut, raced each other to fetch water for her, fought over ploughing her fields, giving her presents. Nath had given her all his land but Mohan had built a new house for her with carved pillars.

Though it was three years ago, Nath clearly remembered the first day Mohan had walked into the house asking for a bottle of lamp oil.

'You are Kanta Mausi's nephew from Rajgarh, aren't you?' Nath had asked, giving him not only the oil, but a new box of matches and a bidi. How did he know then that he was allowing a serpent into his house? Worse than a serpent, because this man did not slither off as a snake would have done, after biting him.

Mohan now lived with them as Chinta's co-husband. He had to share her with him like the pradhan's wives in the village shared a husband. The women were used to it, in fact they even liked each other's company, but for a man it was torture. The joint eyebrows had brought strife just as the old man had predicted. Her breasts had fooled him with false promises—Chinta had still not given him a son. Maybe it was god's wisdom, else how would they know whose child it was? But he loved her more than ever, everything about her—her strange demands for food, her quick temper, her lazy ways had brought him joy till this man arrived and divided her in half.

Nath hardly spoke to Mohan now, but earlier they had fought every night when Chinta began to prepare for bed. Like cocks fighting in the village fair they had circled each other with clenched fists, and once Mohan had scratched his face with a wooden lice comb. But ever since the day she had picked up a burning log from the kitchen fire and chased them out of the house during one of the quarrels, they kept away from each other.

'She will tire of him, he is a simple-minded lout. They are not even married properly. He hasn't paid her father any bride money,' Nath would reassure himself every night. As the first husband, he had the right to sleep in the same bed as Chinta but he often woke up and found her in Mohan's room which was a loft above the kitchen.

Tonight she would be there again because Mohan must have found the black mushrooms which she was so greedy for. Fresh green ferns, out-of-season vegetables, rare fruits from the plains, black mushrooms, rhododendron flowers, blackberries were some of her favourite foods. While the other women in the village were happy with dal and five thick chapattis with a lump of fresh white butter, Chinta would only eat these rare fruits.

PRATHIBHA NANDAKUMAR

Salvation

Translated from the Kannada by the poet

Remembering can be the means of salvation
~ A.K. Ramanujan

1. The Salad Days

Oh, they were tender, green, leafy and raw.
Fresh cut, as in the breaking in of a colt
Wild, as in first flight of a nameless bird
floating about the narrow dark alleys
searching for a parking spot to
land and indulge in some peeling, slicing and
sucking of juices with matching exclamations.
Everything got soaked and sprouted.
They were the days of talking and taking.

2. The Fasting Days

Everything resembled a dish.
Denial was the mantra.
Do not, the anthem.
Pangs hit diaphragm.
Aching heart, intestines and mouth drying,
To chew was a curse, to swallow a punishment.
Hungry forever, thirsty every minute,
Vastness taking over dilated pupils,
To fast was to preserve.
To consume was to serve.
We were on diet and we meant to quiet
the heart, the intestine, lungs, legs and
the unmentionables in anticipation of
the next feast.

3. The Dessert Days

And then, there was pudding

of all sorts.
Creams, cakes, nuts, fruits,
Exotic, ethnic sweets
It was time to indulge.
How many poems make a day?
How many dreams make an hour?
How does the metaphor bird build nests on railings?
Who needs to sanction these constructions?
They were days of extravaganza and
A phone call away, a filling pizza.

4. Salvation

And it happened one day.
It was getting crowded.
His elusive multiple beings engulfed
in that one single second, he
the lord of the blue waters,
lost his every appetite and left.
The jain monks call it sallekhan.

If to remember is to find salvation
To forget is to be cursed to return to life.

ASHAPURNA DEVI

Snakebite and the Distant Window

Translated from the Bengali by Anima Bose

The windows were all shut to keep out the hot midday sun. He heard a knock on the window as though someone was signalling. It continued, so the gentleman had to divert his attention from the book and get up from the bed. He opened a window and was surprised. He said, 'Yes, what is it now?'

Parvati looked hot and bothered. Her sari, clinging to her breast, was moving up and down with her heaving and panting. She looked very excited. No doubt, she was nervous, but she mustered courage to blurt out, 'Sir, I beg you not to eat the meat curry that Dasarath will serve you for lunch.'

Needless to say, the gentleman was more than surprised. This was evident from the tone of his voice 'What are you referring to?'

'I'm saying...' Parvati took a deep breath and repeated, 'Please don't eat the meat curry that Dasarath will serve you for lunch.'

The repetition did not seem to have enlightened the gentleman. He asked, still more surprised, 'Why not?'

'That is rotten meat, sir. You'll be sick if you eat it.'

The gentleman felt quite amused and thought it to be her new trick in order to become friendly with him. This type of woman knows many tricks. She might be one of them. But he couldn't help noticing that the woman showed deep anxiety. And then she had come back all the way in this terrible sun, only to play up to him? he wondered. It all seemed so strange! Why didn't she tell him before she had left, in the first place?

The gentleman voiced his thought with these words, 'Why did you come back all the way to say just this?'

'Well, had I said this in Dasarath's hearing, wouldn't he have quarrelled with me? He has bought that already-cooked meat curry to economize on cooking time. It's rotten meat.'

The gentleman enquired amusedly, 'Why, is it beef? I'm used to beef.'

Parvati didn't faint at hearing this bit of information, despite the fact that a person like him, born in the Mukherji family could have uttered such profane words (being born in the Mukherji family meant he was from an orthodox Brahmin family!) Gravely she said, 'I know. You've been to England, to America, I know. But the situation here happens to be quite different. He really has bought something utterly rotten from the tea shop. They say meat curry cooked there contains the flesh of rats.'

This time the gentleman looked concerned, and a shudder seemed to pass through his body. But, with a frown, he asked, 'The flesh of, what did you say?'

'Rats. Those that run round the fields. The low-class villagers enjoy rat meat with toddy.'

The gentleman was visibly upset this time. 'How do you know all this?'

Parvati replied calmly, 'I've seen this with my own eyes. I recognized it as soon as I saw that curry. Many eat it in our locality...' Many of her husband's pals ate it, she knew. Whether her husband also did so behind her back, she wasn't quite sure. So she did not mention it.

'Alright,' the gentleman said gravely, 'you may go. I will take care of all this.'

Parvati then urged him with a touching concern in her voice, 'Please don't tell Dasarath that I have drawn your attention to this, sahib, please. He'll be upset. He calls me didi after all.'

The gentleman cut her short, 'How do I know that you are telling the truth?'

Parvati was surprised, 'Why should I come all the way to tell you a deliberate lie?'

The gentleman seemed a little uncomfortable by the angry tone of her voice, and decided to keep calm. He said with a smile, 'What's so strange about that? People do worse things if there is a hostility.'

'What hostility can I have towards Dasarath?'

'How would I know?' he responded in rather a harsh voice. 'You have no responsibility as regards my meal. Why should you be so concerned?'

'That curry will act as poison for you, sir,' she added. 'What the lower class people can stomach, can you stomach that?'

The gentleman replied expansively, 'The lower class people are also human beings. We are all made of the same stuff. We are all human beings, aren't we?'

Does the gentleman really believe in what he said just now? Parvati thought, stunned. She had never heard anything like this before. Rather, she had always heard the opposite from the memsahibs she worked for. 'You people can stand all this, but goodness me, it frightens me! Such coarse rice? Only the poor people can stomach it. If we eat this coarse rice, we would have to visit the hospital in no time!' The memsahib then gave a discourse on the delicacy of her children's appetite and enlightened Parvati by an analysis of a comparative situation under similar circumstances vis-a-vis their children, and those of the poor, lower class people. That's why the egalitarian declaration of the gentleman surprised Parvati. She had heard nothing to the effect all her life. So, almost unknowingly, she had let her hand go from the window-grill. The sahib also let go of his hand from the grill because both of them were holding on to the same grill at the window. Parvati was standing below; the sahib, on a higher level, inside the room. She stood outside; he inside. The rubble under her feet hurt Parvati; the sahib had a thick carpet under his feet.

Yet the words the sahib had uttered were noble words, words of equality and fraternity. So Parvati lowered her head and said softly, 'Alright, sir, do as you think best.'

The gentleman remonstrated, 'I shall not eat that curry, rest assured. After all, you took all the trouble in this hot sun to come and warn me. Yes, and I promise I shall not say anything to Dasarath about this matter Will that be alright?'

Parvati turned away and started to walk towards her house. The sahib watched her for a while as she walked away and then said to himself, 'Must be rather whimsical, or else why should she bother about me so much?'

One does not come across such women every day. The ones who generally come the sahib's way are the Dasaraths. They can do everything for their self-interest, or out of fear, or maybe, just to harm another person unwittingly. This woman did seem uncommon, strange indeed!

In the Flesh

Here is a partial list of animals I have eaten over the last three decades.

Goat (legs, stomach, brain, sweetbreads, kidney, liver, yes; eyes and head, never); cow (usually in the form of steaks, but also the tail in soups, the tongue, the parts inside—liver, kidneys, even heart, brain, intestines; but of the head only a small portion of a calf's head, to be sociable), the feet in a glutinous soup somewhat like nihari; pig (the legs, roasted, the cheeks, the flesh in diverse forms, from pork chops to sausages, the blood in black pudding, the stomach and several organs in the form of haggis, the liver, deliciously, in a sorpotel); rabbit, twice or thrice, liking and repelled by its strong tang and dark, earthy taste; snake, if I am to believe the lady who fed me this rich, musty stew at a street stall in Kuala Lumpur, but I fear she was lying and it was only, after all, chicken; deer, presumably an illegally hunted specimen, in my youth at the home of a friend whose family was gun-happy and uncaring of the country's laws; ants, in a spicy, fiery chutney; crickets, fried.

This list is heavy on feet, innards and offal, but low on eyeballs and faces.

Fish (the back, the stomach, the tail, always when available, caviar or humble but equally welcome fish roe, and in loyalty to my Bengali heritage, if reluctantly, the head, often—all of it, in fact); prawns, oysters, mussels, lobsters, crabs, with and without the shells, always with relish; baby jellyfish, sea urchins and the like, on occasion, but never sea horse. I don't know if anyone actually eats sea horses; dried sea horse is used in some alternative medicine therapies, but I found no recipes for sea horse entrées on the Net. Snails, which should show up once in the meat section for their slight resemblance to marrow and once here for the oysterish texture, I've eaten whenever I can get them, their taste enhanced by those tiny, doll's house forks you use to extract the flesh.

Chickens, entire, and severally: the feet in Malaysian and Chinese soup, the beak, once and never again, the comb of a rooster, once and ditto, the breast and legs and wings, too often to count; ostrich, as steaks, three or four times, as eggs, three or four times; duck, often, in tired orange sauce and equally tired Peking duck pancake specials, once, memorably, after a shoot, in curries and sandwiches, the taste of it robust, gamey, but marred by the memory of the dying light in the shot bird's eyes; goose and turkey at Calcutta Christmases, often but not of late, once in Canada, once in the US; pheasant, once, an unpleasant experience for an

Indian unused to the practice of hanging meat until it turns ripe, gamey, rotted to our senses; partridge, several times; tiny birds whose name I have forgotten but that were served whole on toast—it would be nice to speculate that these were ortolans, but they were probably just snipe; quail, often, despite those fidgety bones; frogs, legs of (I suppose these belong with the fish, but everyone insists that frogs' legs taste of chicken, so they're here), a few times, without either pleasure or repulsion.

Here is a partial list of animals I have never eaten and that I would be reluctant to taste: dogs (especially puppies), horses, cats (especially kittens), guinea pigs, budgerigars, humans (perhaps one might make an exception for babies, the kind that cry at high volume), monkeys, chimpanzees, apes and orangutans, elephants, owls, nightingales, whales and dolphins, ibexes, penguins (and especially puffins, with their comically sweet faces), lizards, from the ordinary house-and-garden variety to iguanas and monitor lizards (though crocodile steak I might eat), white mice, vultures, hoopoes, ocelots, lynxes, foxes and wolves, albatrosses, jaguars, panthers, tigers (and cubs), lions, sharks, duck-billed platypuses, kingfishers, hummingbirds and sparrows.

These lists. How arbitrary they are, how illogical in their implicit acceptance of what I will allow into my body and what I will forbid.

For thirty-one of my thirty-four years, I have been the perfect omnivore, the harassed hostess's best friend—I will eat anything. (Almost anything—see lists—but then, very few Indians serve hummingbird, orangutans, puffins or iguanas to their guests; I have seldom been tested on my taboos.) My strongest dislikes are vegetable, not animal—stewed tomatoes, waterlogged bhindi, frozen American corn—and these were relatively few.

Of all the members of the animal kingdom, it was the mosquito that did me in. Like many Indians, and like the stereotypical army colonels of the British Raj, I have an admirable malarial tendency—the year I turned thirty-one, I had my thirtieth bout of malaria, a source of perverse pride for me. I emerged from episode number 30 in the long-running Malaria and Me soap opera, thinner, marginally more prone to the very Victorian complaint of fatigue—and with a changed palate.

It took me a while to realize that I couldn't stomach meat any more. For the sake of my family, emphatically carnivorous, I hid this bizarre side-effect, politely attempting to eat the fried chicken, the mutton curries, the lightly steamed fish in mustard, the robust home-made kababs that were staples of my mother's table. For the sake of my husband and a host of cheerfully flesh-eating friends, I continued to cook meat and fish long after both had turned to ashes on my palate. I went to great lengths to conceal this inadvertent vegetarianism at first, and I waited, patiently, for my palate to cease its apostasy. I found I could eat a little bit of flesh—fish, fowl, animal—through an effort of will, though I would throw up afterwards; for some reason, my appetite for prawns remained unaffected.

India is an easy country for a vegetarian. The European or American table holds meat in pride of place, vegetables as adjuncts, and it shows in the number of meat substitutes available for vegetarians—poor imitations made in soy protein or wheat gluten. The Far Eastern table gives fruits and vegetables the respect they deserve, but is unconcerned with vegan purity. Fish sauce will lace Thai meals, Japanese 'vegetable' dishes will often contain a smidgeon of pork or fish for flavouring, the light stocks that Chinese vegetables favour are often simmered in or are usually prepared from fish or meat bases. Here, we place rice and dal, or rotis and dal, at the heart of the meal. Even the classic Bengali non-vegetarian feast will have a strong line-up of vegetable fries and mashes, vegetable stews, vegetable chutneys. To stay away from meat is easy in the practical sense—it's only on the social front that drifting towards meatlessness creates problems.

So, I became an equal opportunity offender.

My carnivore friends saw the shift towards meatlessness as apostasy, even betrayal; many of them mentioned one of the world's most prominent vegetarians, A. Hitler, as the classic counter-example to that other prominent vegetarian, M. Gandhi. The good or evil that men do may be interred with their bones, they implied, but it certainly wasn't to be inferred in the flesh they abstained from.

Carnivores attempted cunningly to turn me back to the path of flesh, offering Lucknow's tundey kababs, tender cuts of lamb cooked Chettinad style, fragrant biryanis richly layered with beef, pabda maach cooked with whole black cumin, Goan pomfret fried in aromatic spice pastes—in extremis, they would smuggle home-made chicken stock into the dal and declare an underhanded victory.

Vegetarians were annoyed by me, as true believers are by the half-hearted convert. Some were tolerant; they saw dietary preferences as a private, very personal choice, and if they disapproved of what was on your plate, that disapproval rarely took the form of interference, or moral judgement. Others had arrived at intolerance after years of fighting for animal rights or having to defend their own dislike of meat, which didn't make their righteousness any more palatable.

In the first few months of turning away from meat, I faced a battery of Purity Tests. So I didn't eat meat? How about eggs, cheese, milk? (Eggs and milk I can take or leave, but anyone who takes my Gorgonzola or Reblochon away from me will die, I promise.) Did I understand that prawns suffer (yes, but I don't like prawns as creatures, so I don't care), that fish die in agony (yes, and I like fish as creatures, so I do care), do I wear fur (no), silk (yes), use leather (if I can't find another option), use products that weren't tested on animals (as far as possible, yes), campaign against slaughterhouses (no), support chicken battery farming (no), use insecticide (yes, though it's a home-made herbal concoction)?

I accepted my own inconsistencies, and found them mildly fascinating, as fascinating as the question of what dead flesh I would eat and what I would eschew. But after a while, every passionate vegetarian argument, every fine-tuned query, began to sound like the tired chorus of a worn-out song: Was I pure enough, good enough, clean enough? Was I pure or tainted, righteous or sainted? Was I slightly pure, mostly pure, potentially pure?

SHIVANI

Apradhini

Translated from the Hindi by Ira Pande

The kind-hearted doctor had brought about several changes in these drab lives. From time to time, she would invite guests to meet the prisoners. And her research work was dedicated to studying their behaviour. She had mingled her heartbeat with those of the hundred and eighty prisoners that she monitored. By now, she knew their bodies as well as she knew their minds and had the histories of each one at her fingertips. Their lives were like well-thumbed books that she read and re-read almost every day.

'The one who is fanning you,' she said, 'her name is Heera. She must be about fifty-eight or so, but if you had seen her dance last year at the Independence Day function, you would have been amazed. She could put to shame any twenty-year-old!' I looked up to see this Salome, and her lined and withered face broke into a sweet smile. When she was not fanning me, she ran to fetch me hot puris from the kitchen and, no matter how much I dissuaded her from piling more on my thali, she would slip another hot one in. When I finished my meal, she ran to fetch a basin and jug of water and made me wash my hands as if I were a child. Then, before I knew what she was up to, she drank the water from the basin.

'Stop!' I cried in horror. 'What are you doing?'

'Bahuji'—she looked into my eyes—'my burden of sins is so heavy that I can hardly hold my head upright. This water from the hands of good women like yourself is not dirty water, bahuji, it is like gangajal to sinners like us. It may wash my past away.'

I returned to the table and asked the doctor to tell me more about Heera; I was stunned by what I heard. The woman who had drunk 'gangajal' today had helped her son burn alive his young wife. The son had been sent to the gallows, but she had been given a life sentence and left alone to be forever haunted by the noose that had killed her son.

The doctor next pointed out a dark young girl with sad eyes. She was innocent in the sense that she had committed no heinous crime herself, but she was guilty of assisting her three brothers in committing armed robberies. Now, she was the unofficial seamstress of the jail and would be sorely missed by her fellow inmates when her term came to an end, the doctor went on. Her nimble fingers crocheted complicated roses and flowers and her knack for transforming the drab prison uniform into something else was widely appreciated. Give her a shapeless vest, and she would add a tuck there and a pleat here to make it into a sexy body stocking.

I knew that the minute a woman enters a prison she is stripped of all her jewellery and personal clothing and issued a coarse dhoti-kurti. Yet, these women had devised all kinds of ways of adding a touch of individuality to their uniform. I had been struck earlier by the absence of any mirrors—for most women this must be a fate worse than death. Yet, every woman had neatly parted hair, some had a black bindi on their foreheads and even a hint of kajal in their eyes. How had they managed this without a mirror, I wondered. Then the secret was revealed to me. I saw a tall, strapping woman bent over a pail of water. She looked at her reflection in the water and patted her hair. Obviously, not even the grim confines of a prison can quash a woman's vanity! The doctor told me how they made kajal from burnt wood, crushed coals to make missi to fill the spaces between their teeth and cut rose petals to fashion a bindi.

After the meal, I went with the doctor on a round of the cells. The sun was shining outside, but a pall of silence and suffocating darkness seemed to envelop the rooms. The windows had thick iron bars and the sky had shrunk so far that it was just a hint of blue-grey. I could well imagine how they must crane their necks to see more of it before their eyes, tired of squinting, gave up the effort. The large dormitory had a long, depressing row of cement slabs, not unlike those that you see in a morgue. Each one had neatly rolled-up bedding of rough blankets. The walls had 'Raghu Pati Raghav Raja Ram, Patit Pavan Sita Ram'painted in bold lettering all along the room. Did these lines provide solace to souls tossing restlessly at night? Or did these words strike out like a hooded snake to remind them of all they had done? The neck of a husband severed for a lover, a daughter-in-law burnt alive, the rape and pillage of a dacoity, the selling of young girls to pimps and prostitutes, the killing of newborn girls...

Until a few months ago, two sisters-in-law were incarcerated together in this jail, I was told. Both were serving life sentences, but their visceral hatred of each other became so hard to handle that one had to be packed off to Naini Jail near Allahabad. 'I was afraid they would kill each other one day,' the doctor said. And then I was told of the strange saga of their feud. For years, the older one had watched her brother-in-law lavish attention on his young wife. He was prosperous and she loved clothes and jewellery. Each time he gave her a new gift, she came to her older sister-in-law and showed it off. Finally, the older one could take it no more. She decided to hack off the neck that was draped with the jewels that she coveted; she would have been given the death sentence were it not for the infant at her breast. The mother and baby were sent here.

According to the rules of the time, a child could stay with its mother until the age of six. In the meantime, her brother-in-law married his dead wife's sister. When the son turned six, he was sent back to his father's house. The child became very attached to his new aunt, who loved him in turn.

Then, one day, the child's mother arrived home on parole. The son refused to go to her and clung to his aunt's sari. Burning with rage, the mother felt as if her new sister-in-law had grown another head to replace the one she had hacked all those years ago. As the time for her return to jail drew nearer, she felt more and more enraged and helpless. Her frustration had added a wicked edge to her tongue and her family began to dread the lashings they received from her. She turned to her new enemy one day.

'I'll hack your neck just as I hacked your sister's off, understand? I'll come from jail if I have to,' she spat. 'Don't you dare charm my little Nanku away from me! You think I haven't seen you slyly feeding him milk and jalebis to wean him away from me? I know you will kill him one day.' The child, who was listening to this exchange, blanched when he heard his mother. From that day, he wouldn't go close to his aunt. His mother had barely reached jail after her parole when she was told that her son had been hacked to death by her sister-in-law.

This is how they both found themselves in the same jail, serving life sentences. Forced to see each other every day was a predicament harder than the sentence itself. Finally, the older one was packed off to Naini Jail. With her arch enemy gone, the younger one began to be haunted by the crime she had committed.

'Why didn't they send me to the gallows instead?' she would wail. 'Every night, the little one comes to my ears and calls out: 'Chachi, O Chachi!'

I was told that the room where she killed her little nephew was so dark that the police had to carry burning torches to collect the pieces of the child's body.

Yet, the same jail also housed those who were completely unrepentant. The doctor took me to a cell where a tall woman, Najmati, stood proudly alone. Her arms were decorously crossed in front of her and she looked briefly at us as we entered, then turned her gaze away. What glowing skin she had, and what a nose! Perhaps her haughty and irreverent attitude was responsible for her being excluded from this morning's feast. That brief glance she had cast at us had shaken me—she looked like a barely controlled lioness at a circus, who could jump and trap you between her jaws if the ringmaster lost control. Her tawny eyes burnt with an anger that sent a shiver down my spine. I stood hesitantly at the door of her cell as if she were a maharani and I had dared to intrude into her private chamber.

At first glance, she appeared to be about twenty or so, but when I looked closely, I realized she was older. I saw her look slyly at us and assess me exactly as I was assessing her. 'So,' she seemed to say silently, 'seen enough, have you? Are you satisfied with the specimens you've seen at this zoo?' She flashed a defiant grin my way, dazzling me with her missi-laced teeth and tawny eyes. Then, she rudely turned her back on us and withdrew to her own world.

'What a beauty she must have been in her youth!' I told the doctor as we moved on.

'I wish her life had been half as beautiful,' the doctor replied. 'God knows how many lives she helped extinguish, how many happy families she destroyed—she was the moll of a gang of dacoits. You should see the visitors she gets! One of them is a young Thakur boy: he had come the other day with a basket full of dry fruits for her. No one is allowed to keep so many, I said. You can only bring her as much as she can eat while sitting here. So he flashed me a wicked grin and fed her the whole lot in one go!' The doctor laughed. I was reminded suddenly of a story I was once told of a Pathan who was travelling on a train with his ram: when he was asked to buy a ticket for the ram, he cut it up and ate it there and then!

Work

There is much history and politics contained in the phrase 'women's work'. It holds the implication that some work which was traditionally undertaken by women must be done only by women. As a corollary, there was disapproval for women who chose to do any other kind of work. As an additional corollary, there was a long list of fairly arduous, time-sapping tasks that was never recognized as 'work' at all because it was being done by women who were not being paid for it.

Times have changed, especially over the last century, with women entering a wider range of professions—from mountain-climbing to the police and armed forces, and from rocket science research to sport. But there still remains a great deal of resistance to the idea that ability is not defined by gender.

This section is given over to literature that describes people's work experiences, and to the professional challenges they face.

Vaidehi's 'Gulabi Talkies' gives us a protagonist who decides to stop working as a midwife in favour of working the entrance of a local cinema hall, and manages to change the social behaviour of the housewives in the village. Bama's story 'Chilli Powder' is actually about landlessness and caste dynamics, but it presents a picture of landless village women as resourceful workers who keep pressing forward with their sense of humour and adventure intact. On the opposite side, it offers up a picture of a landowning woman, one who guards her land and its produce with eagle eyes.

The extract from P. Sivakami's novel *The Taming of Women* is a scene describing the labour of women on farms, including the landowner's wives and children. Though it is non-household work, women who bear more than their share of responsibility are rarely classified as 'farmers' since they are not owners. Kamala Markandaya's novel *Nectar in a Seive* is also set in a rural household. The extract included here describes nature's impact on a farming family and the tragedy of tenant farmers who fall into debt after a bad season.

Sarah Joseph's *Gift in Green* is a novel about an unfolding ecological disaster in a quiet part of the country and the brutality with which voices of protest are crushed. This particular extract picks up on some of the brutal aspects of hospital work, and a nurse's first brush with the ugly truth.

The extract from Mridula Garg's *Country of Goodbyes* is about a scholar whose husband steals her research, her imagination and her storytelling ability; it also references Zelda Fitzgerald, raising questions of authorship and ownership of women's creative input in the work that their husbands claim as their own.

VAIDEHI

Gulabi Talkies

Translated from the Kannada by Tejaswini Niranjana

That day Lillibai entered Rangarao's house with more than her usual force. She had brought the newborn child's diapers which she had taken home to wash, neatly folded in a basket. 'From tomorrow I'm not coming here late in the evening. I'll come at four-four-thirty and help the mother have a wash. Then I'll come back only in the morning. If this is my only hope, how can my cart move ahead?' Lillibai spoke to the walls, the door and the cot as she put away the diaper cloths, and then went on her way. What had happened to her?

'Have you had a drop too much or what?' asked Vanajakshi, the child's mother. 'Not at all,' said Lillibai. You know the new talkies opens tomorrow? They've given me the gatekeeper's job at the women's entrance.'

When all the older women came to investigate, Lilli went on to say that she had to stay there until the second show was over. That she could go home only when the doors were finally shut. That she might be late coming to work in the morning. That people should adjust to her new routine. She had got the job because of Gulabi. Anyway her house was right behind the talkies. Luck had come looking for her.

The talkies!

And Lilli in the talkies!

When they went to the gate, there was Lillibai! This fact had its own excitement for the women. Because of the talkies, the town had lost a midwife. Saying that one month's salary as gatekeeper was more than three months' earnings as midwife, Lillibai had trashed her earlier occupation. How long she had waited to do just that! Not having imagined that this sort of relationship would emerge between the talkies and Lillibai, people had to shake themselves awake. The town's doctor shop, marginalized all these years because of the reluctance to involve a man in childbirth, now began to glow with a new coat of paint.

Talking films came to the new theatre.

◆

Day by day the bangle shop began to stock various kinds of face powder and other cosmetics as its business began to soar; the seamstress struggled to tune her skills to the new fashions, and her creations were passed off as fashionable, causing a commotion in the world of clothing which crossed over into the speech and gait of women; the ornaments of brides and the other women at weddings were touched by the breeze of the cinema; the cook in Rangarao's house started to be possessed by the ghost in the deodar tree, which would go away only when the price of a cinema ticket was placed before the creature; women waited to get their period so that they could be relieved from their daily duties and go off to the talkies, thus creating a problem for rules of pollution; they all put on the airs of playback singers and began to sing whenever they felt like it; in the School Day a competition for film songs was introduced; in bhajans too film tunes and styles crept in; even in love-making, words from the cinema came in, making all that was wordless seem worthless; and above all, mothers who composed little lullabies as they swung their infants to sleep now began to hum cinema lullabies. At another level, the cinema had begun to influence another sort of behaviour, and that too was through Lillibai.

◆

Lillibai now had many things to talk about. Look out of the window this evening, you'll see the boxes of reels being taken out of the bus, she would say—and how true that would turn out to be! Boxes carrying the worlds of magic. Then Lilli was to be found leaning against the outer gate of the talkies, her ankles crossed, her hand feeling in the little bag strung round her neck for a piece of arecanut, looking for all the world as though both the theatre and the reels of film belonged to her.

The day after the latest film arrived, Lilli had her review ready. If someone said loudly—'Here's the newspaper!'—it meant that Lilli had come, and every woman and child immediately appeared. 'This is a useless cinema. Issi. Made by some prostitutes no doubt. All they do is dance around in dresses showing their entire bodice,' Lilli would declaim as she sat on the narrow verandah of Rangarao's house. Those who heard her would go and see the film anyway, to find out if what she said was true. There were some who, after hearing her, decided to wait for the next film which was mythological. Lilli, who could even tell with her eyes shut what the 'next change' was going to be, began to seem like a woman who knew the entire world of the cinema.

And this wasn't all. As the days passed, Lillibai had spicier things to talk about than the cinema. The talkies manager, who looked so respectable, has slept with the sweeper woman. Imagine dragging away the creature who was washing the bathrooms...a real womanizer. No one says anything because he's such a tiger.

Relating everything as she had seen it, Lilli would say at the end that there was nothing she had not seen. The women of the house, engaged in their never-ending tasks, saw the new worlds Lilli opened for them, and always came out to listen to her. They asked her questions over and over again and laughed at her stories. Now wherever Lillibai went she was assured of a cup of coffee. If there was anything to eat, she would get a little of that too. Even the women from the Konkani grain merchant's house, who knew how to cook so that not even a morsel remained after dinner, said to themselves that there was no harm giving something to Lilli, since they always got their money's worth.

And if the women of the Big House went to the cinema, next day the paper would be out. 'Amma, O Amma, you know who came to the cinema yesterday? Both mother-in-law and daughter-in-law! It was *Santa Sakhoo* they were watching. As they watched, both of them sobbed and sobbed. I stopped seeing the film and watched them instead!'

When it became known that such and such watched a film, it would be decided that it must be worth seeing. To the men of the house, the women would say: The Big House women had gone. Nothing bad about this film, Lilli says. We hear that they cried and cried... This made it easier for them to get permission to go to the talkies. The men who decide on seeing the film poster whether or not their wives and daughters could go, who loudly declare that the cinema was not meant for women at all, such men pay attention when a petition of this kind is submitted. If the Big House women cried so much, the film may not have any scenes not meant for women's eyes. And now that Lillibai herself is at the gate, the men don't have to escort the women to the entrance. Even the timidest women went out into the street on the assurance that Lilli was at the talkies. Slowly they got accustomed to going out by themselves.

But what about money for the tickets?

Without knowing that she had increased the number of women spectators, Lillibai was also responsible for introducing another practice. She would let in four people for the price of two tickets, pushing them quickly in, one after the other. Then she would go to them in the dark after the film began and take half the amount they were to have paid for the two extra tickets, putting it away in the bunch made by her sari pleats where she tucked them in at the waist.

This was quite unexpected. It caused a small commotion in the minds of the women, making them squirm. They had to go to the cinema. But just one or two of them couldn't go by themselves. The house was full of people, full of children. If one person set out for the talkies, a horde followed her. And money for all this? Did the situation warrant their acceptance of Lilli's collection practice?

Till then none of them had done such a thing. They were after all from respectable families. Unable to resolve the problem, they sought to put the whole matter on the shoulders of the men. When the man said, 'What! So many people going to the cinema? You think money is like tamarind seeds?' a small voice would answer fearfully, the eyes brimming over with tears: 'We needn't pay the entire amount. Lillibai...'

Chilli Powder

Translated from the Tamil by N. Ravi Shanker

After two or three days Pachayamma, along with two other women, went to Gangamma's fields again to cut grass. While they were busy cutting, Gangamma crept up to them. Moving like a cat, she quietly returned to her house and came back with chilli powder rolled in a sheet of paper. It suited her that the field was near her house. She came straight to the ridge where Pachayamma was cutting grass and said, 'You thieving wretch, is it because you have no other place to go to that you come here and slit my throat? Your own colony women say that you are shameless! Looks like they're right. Everyone else does a detour when they come upon Gangamma's fields—but you, you have to show off, eh?' Hardly had she finished saying this than she threw the chilli powder into Pachayamma's eyes.

As soon as the chilli hit her eyes, Pachayamma went wild with rage. Wiping her burning eyes with the end of her munthani she began shouting, 'Chi, can you be called a woman? Throwing chilli powder in my eyes just for cutting grass that grows on its own? Is there such a harvest of fruits and vegetables here that we will come and steal them? Look at her face, swollen like a huge big gourd! And look at the shameless widow's belly, bulging as if she is perpetually ten months pregnant! Your husband popped off after just one child because of your character, di!'

Still hurling abuses, she bundled up the grass and called out to the two women who had accompanied her, 'Better gather up your grass quickly. Oh, my eyes! Whore-widow! May you be taken around like a corpse in procession!! I can't open my eyes at all! May you have a leper's hands! Look at the dead bitch standing there like a fat pot of grain.' So saying, she left along with the women who ran back with her, glad to have got off lightly.

Gangamma wasn't keeping mum either. She matched abuse for abuse. Even after she left her fields Pachayamma continued her haranguing, 'Don't get a swollen head just because you threw chilli powder into my eyes today! Slut! Evil eye! Has a nice name, too...Gangamma Nolliyamma... not even a shitting dog will look up when you pass... Look at her...swinging her hair like a rat's tail!'

This incident was the only topic of discussion that day in the streets. Everyone had a different version.

'Knowing that woman so well, why did these women go there to cut grass? Why such arrogance?'

'But how could she be so crafty? She took all the trouble to go home and bring the chilli powder to throw into Pachayamma's eyes! What if she had gone blind? If this is what she does just for cutting grass, what will she do if someone touches her harvest? She wouldn't hesitate to kill!'

'And where else can we go and cut grass if not in the fields and orchards of landowners? Where else do we go for grass to feed the cattle we survive on? As if she owns some special kind of fields that no one else in the world has!'

'Ei, it's not right to speak about her like this. It's this Pachayamma who has developed such a swollen head that she keeps going only to that woman's fields. Like a fat crab that can't stay in its hole. No one else goes to her fields—why should Pachayamma alone go there as if she is the governor's wife?'

After this, everyone began referring to Gangamma as molagappodi—chilli powder. The woman would get so furious at just a mention of the word, but Pachayamma and the other women enjoyed themselves by repeatedly saying molagappodi in her presence.

It was thus that, one day, Pachayamma and four or five women were returning home after working in the mustard fields. Seeing Gangamma approaching from a distance Pachayamma said provocatively, 'Heard that a chilli powder machine has come to our village, too. The wife of that teacher who lives in the street below us isn't grinding chilli paste any more—she's using chilli powder, just like the landowners.'

'Is that so, mathini? Must be so convenient to store chilli powder like that. We can use it to cook and also to throw into people's eyes.' Gangamma drew abreast just as Chittamma finished speaking.

Walking a few steps ahead of them Gangamma began yelling furiously, 'Endi, stinking whore-widow! How dare you talk like this? She's so poor she has next to nothing to wear, but look how the donkey speaks! Brazen bitch!'

When she heard this, Pachayamma's anger exploded and she made as if to strike Gangamma with her vessel of koozh. The other women also joined in. Trapped, Gangamma did not stop to reply. She took to her heels, huffing and puffing all the way.

Two weeks later, ten or twelve women who had gone to cut weeds near the forest in the upper reaches of the village were returning home after finding there was no work for them. Pachayamma said, 'No work, no wages! Don't know what I'm going to cook the meal with today. What kind of life is this! You get kanji only if you work! Otherwise, you just drink some water and go to sleep.'

'Ei...what's your problem? Your man would have earned enough when he returns...'

'Be quiet! Are you talking about that useless fellow? For two whole months he was without work. Then last month he left, saying there is well-digging work somewhere and he has to stay there. I don't know whether he'll stay and finish the work or leave it halfway and come back. The fellow's heart is not in his work and you are counting on him?' Pachayamma plucked some full-grown pods from the cotton plants there and tucked them into her waist. Seeing her, the other women followed suit and in no time, each had collected a nice pile of pods. On the way they didn't hesitate to lay their hands on Gangamma's plantation, too. As if on cue, Gangamma made her appearance right then. Seeing Pachayamma, she swore she would teach the women a lesson one way or another, and went back to her house.

Meanwhile, a police inspector and two policemen had come to Gangamma's street on work. She immediately took them to her plantation. The inspector was their own man—he used to stay in Gangamma's elder brother Chinnachami Naicker's house, on the top floor. Gangamma lost no time in using this connection.

Pachayamma and the other women who were still plucking the cotton pods were taken aback when Gangamma suddenly appeared with the policemen. Immediately, they lifted their bundles and started running for it. But even as she ran, Pachayamma said, 'See what that molagappodi has done? Brought policemen with her! Done it purposely to create problems for us. Everyone listens to money.'

'Ei...keep quiet, Akka. For once, don't spoil everything by talking too much! Compromise, think of how to get home now. See, finally we got caught today!' complained Madathi.

'How long have you been making a living stealing things from someone else's fields?' demanded the policeman. 'Everyone, drop the pods and come with us to the station!'

Pachayamma immediately retorted, 'Why should we? All this cotton is not from this plantation only—we have picked most of it from what was lying around in the wasteland to the west. We only picked this much from here.' Saying this, she dumped the pods from her waist-band on the ground.

'Open up all the bundles! Let's see if they are from the wasteland or not,' demanded Gangamma.

Since the policemen also insisted, all the bundles were opened up and the pods heaped on the ground. Finding that they were good quality cotton, the policeman said, 'Does this look like cotton from the wasteland? How will the farmers make a profit if you steal like this? To the station, everyone!' And so all the women were loaded onto Gangamma's tractor and taken to the police station.

On the way, in the tractor itself, each one started blaming the other or swearing at her. Only Pachayamma finally made them keep quiet.

'Why are you quarrelling with each other now? Are they going to cut our heads off at the station? Take it easy, women! As for me, I'm dying to pee.'

As she finished, Veerayi said, 'Isn't it bad enough that we have been caught stealing like this? This has never happened before, we have never been taken to the police station. We are in this mess because of you. Don't be so shameless.'

'Ei...what's shameless about this? Are we stealing so we can build tiled houses for ourselves? Are we going to make some jewellery for our necks and ears? We steal because that is the only way we will not starve—even though we need only a little bit of kanji. Tell me, with prices so high, can we afford to have our fill of kanji with the wages we get? We don't have a single coin on us today. Even when there is work and we get paid, we can have only broken-rice kanji and rasam. Today I thought I would sell the cotton and buy some dried fish for a curry, but that sinner's daughter came and spoiled it all.' Pachayamma turned her attention to the policeman. 'Ayya, just let me get down for a second. I'll pee and come running back.'

'We can't let you down anywhere, you'll get down only at the station. Now keep your mouth shut,' said the policeman.

'Who is this fellow, talking to us as if he's telling schoolchildren to shut their mouths? Have our mouths been open till now?' Pachayamma laughed as she said this. Immediately, all the women began laughing, too, and were in high spirits, taunting and mimicking each other till they reached the station.

Old woman Kalathi was disapproving, 'How can one sit in this and travel? Up-down, up-down, it keeps tossing us up and down. What kind of stupid vehicle is this? And look at these women, laughing as if they are on their way to some holy festival. Keep quiet, you!'

Pachayamma said in reply, 'You keep quiet, perimme. The way this vehicle is swaying, I'm unable to control my bladder. These fellows won't even let us pee. If it takes any longer I will be forced to squat right here, it's getting so bad!'

When they reached the station the policemen ordered them to get down. As soon as she did, Pachayamma quickly lifted her clothes and

Unbound

peed right there, standing up. The other women, too, did the same. Seeing this the policeman grumbled, 'Chi, arrogant donkeys! They'll make the whole station stink!'

Pachayamma said, 'Ayya, one can hold back one's anger, but not one's piss. That's why we asked you to let us down on the way. It's you who said we could pee only after reaching the station,' she laughed.

P. SIVAKAMI

The Taming of Women

Translated from the Tamil by Pritham K. Chakravarthy

After several days Anandhayi set off for the fields. Arul accompanied her to join the labourers harvesting coriander.

'That's a scorpion, Amma, with its tail coiled up!'

'Well, it's minding its business on the palm tree. How is it troubling you?'

Arul had screamed in fear on seeing the scorpion on the short palm tree, its tail stiff, but was surprised at her mother's casual remark. She followed Anandhayi silently along the mud path.

The child rested its face on Anandhayi's shoulder, gazing at the green field with its bright, shining eyes. The vast blue sky, the ragged scarecrow, the tall green crop, the field sparrows retreating into the bushes after feeding on the ripe grains...the child's eyes drank in everything without making any sense of it.

Arul walked on, playing with the dripping dewdrops that were warming in the hot sun's rays. On seeing the white cacti flowers amidst the bushes, she murmured without realizing, 'New flowers, new cactus, new air, new crop...'

'Mad child, what are you mumbling to yourself?'

Arul bit her tongue in shame.

After a while seeing the red sunrays, the yellow horizon, the scurrying garden lizard, and smelling the fresh moong crop Arul sang, *'New sky, new smell, new garden lizard.'* This time Anandhayi did not have the heart to chide her joyous girl. She simply smiled.

After some time, unable to find new words, Arul fell silent, tired after a long trek.

At the fork where the three mud roads met, twenty labourers gathered.

'Is this your youngest child, Anandhayi?'

'Yes, Akka.'

'He looks exactly like his father.' She pinched the child's cheek. He burst into tears.

The field workers dug under the vanni tree, buried their lunch in the pit and split into groups. Chinnasami began to demonstrate to the groups, drawing on the ground with a long stick.

'She's very young,' argued Vadakathiyaal softly for Poongavanam. 'Don't task her too hard.' Poongavanam had been taken out of school and brought along to work in the fields.

Chinnasami divided the work equally. The field had to be weeded. Vadakathiyaal kept Poongavanam by her side.

Arul sat with the child under the vanni tree, muttering to herself. Crazy girl, what could she be telling herself? On the field Chinnasami was bossing around.

'Hey, Vadakathiyaal, why has your daughter dug up all that soil? Tell her to just cut the weed, not the plant.'

'Look at that, are you a woman?'

'What's wrong with the manner in which I cut it?' demanded Pasudhi in her screechy tone.

'You did not chop the weed next to the plants; instead, you covered it up with soil.'

Pasudhi returned to the coriander patch, gently bunched away the plant like a tender chicken and plucked off the weed.

'Bring your daughter and come up. Why are you lingering behind?' Anandhayi urged Vadakathiyaal.

'You go ahead. I'll finish the weeding. It is not as if these grasses were born before me.'

'Does Iyyakannu need to come to weed with his wife?' Pasudhi asked aloud.

'Oh yes,' replied Angamma, Iyyakannu's wife. 'I have a granary full of rice grains at home that I can sit around and eat. Cross-Eyed Jack and his wife are refusing to water the fields and threatening us with a knife. Who would say we belong to the same caste! This is such a shame, for crying out loud. But I swear on this field of coriander that Ponnusami is not paying our coolie wages.'

'I hear that Manickam, the younger brother of Cross-Eyed Jack, is romping around with all the women in town.'

'It's not as if he can take every woman for a ride. Only the crazy ones are going to fall for his words.'

'Every time I see him with a curly cowlick on his forehead, flicking it as he walks, I feel like I am on fire.'

Anandhayi had not worked in the fields after her delivery, so she began to tire very fast in the heat. When she saw young Poongavanam slogging away, her hands cracking with the hard toil, she comforted herself, thanking her luck. She sent Poongavanam with a bucket to fetch water to give her a brief rest.

Arul sat curled up under the vanni tree. The creepy-crawlies and tiny ants were making it difficult for her to sit comfortably. She kept singing and chatting to herself. Even though Anandhayi had told her not to, she had thrown a tantrum and insisted on coming with her mother to the fields. How she now feared these ants. She looked up at the vanni tree. Fluffs of clouds in the shape of a jackal were passing by.

It was almost two when Anandhayi came up to the tree, having done with her weeding and collecting her wages. Arul was fast asleep. Anandhayi had breastfed the child just once in the morning and it was sleeping too.

Anandhayi felt faint. Kala would come of age by the end of this year. She looked almost ready. Maybe Anandhayi should make her a pair of jumkas. She should harvest two sackloads of coriander, and then she could buy the jumkas and two goat kids besides. Of course she had to make sure her husband did not come to know about it. Half of what he earned went to his women. He must have set up something in the place where he had got the contract. After all, he came home only once in three days.

Anandhayi could not help feeling bitter. She was fed up with this life. She was reduced to being just a mother to her children. As she breastfed the child, she wiped away her tears. When a drop fell on the baby's cheek, it looked at her and smiled.

Already a year has gone by. This one must have its ears bored, head tonsured. I must also offer pongal to Ponnusami. Balan looks as if he is anaemic. He is very pale. He is constantly chewing rice and never seems to listen to me.

Suddenly she felt heavy and soon thought of all the work she had to do.

'Amma, have you finished eating? Can I have some rice water?' Chinnasami broke into her thoughts.

KAMALA MARKANDAYA

Nectar in a Sieve

That year the rains failed. A week went by, two. We stared at the cruel sky, calm, blue, indifferent to our need. We threw ourselves on the earth and we prayed. I took a pumpkin and a few grains of rice to my goddess and I wept at her feet. I thought she looked at me with compassion and I went away comforted, but no rain came.

'Perhaps tomorrow,' my husband said. 'It is not too late.'

We went out and scanned the heavens, clear and beautiful, deadly beautiful, not one cloud to mar its serenity. Others did so too, coming out, as we did, to gaze at the sky and murmur, 'Perhaps tomorrow.'

Tomorrows came and went and there was no rain. Nathan no longer said perhaps; only a faint spark of hope, obstinately refusing to die, brought him out each dawn to scour the heavens for a sign.

Each day the level of the water dropped and the heads of the paddy hung lower. The river had shrunk to a trickle, the well was as dry as a bone. Before long the shoots of the paddy were tipped with brown; even as we watched, the stain spread like some terrible disease, choking out the green that meant life to us.

Harvesting time, and nothing to reap. The paddy had taken all our labour and lay now before us in faded useless heaps.

Sivaji came to collect his master's dues and his face fell when he saw how much was lost, for he was a good man and he felt for us.

'There is nothing this year,' Nathan said to him. 'Not even gleanings, for the grain was but little advanced.'

'You have had the land,' Sivaji said, 'for which you have contracted to pay: so much money, so much rice. These are just dues, I must have them. Would you have me return empty-handed?'

Nathan's shoulders sagged. He looked tired and dispirited. I came and stood beside him, Ira and the boys crouched near us, defensively.

'There is nothing,' Nathan repeated. 'Do you not see the crops are dead? There has been no rain and the river is dry.'

'Yet such was the contract, else the land would not have been rented to you.'

'What would you have me do? The last harvest was meagre; we have nothing saved.'

Sivaji looked away. 'I do not know. It is your concern. I must do as I am bid.'

'What then?'

'The land is to be given to another if you cannot make payment.'

'Go from the land after all these years? Where would we go? How would we live?'

'It is your concern. I have my orders and must obey them.'

Nathan stood there sweating and trembling.

'Give me time,' he said at last humbly, 'until the next crop. I will pay then, somehow.'

'Pay half now,' Sivaji said, 'and I will try and do as you wish.' He spoke quickly, as if to give himself no time to repent of his offer, and hurried away even before my husband had assented.

'No easy job for him,' I said. 'He is answerable, even as we are.'

'That is why he and his kind are employed,' Nathan said bitterly. 'To protect their overlords from such unpleasant tasks. Now the landlord can wring from us his monies and care not for the misery he evokes, for indeed it would be difficult for any man to see another starve and his wife and children as well; or to enjoy the profits born of such travail.'

He went into the hut and I followed. A few mud pots and two brass vessels, the tin trunk I had brought with me as a bride, the two shirts my eldest sons had left behind, two ollocks of dal and a handful of dried chillies left over from better times: these we put together to sell.

'Rather these should go,' said Nathan, 'than that the land should be taken from us; we can do without these but if the land is gone our livelihood is gone, and we must thenceforth wander like jackals.' He stared awhile at what we had to sell, and made an effort to say something and tried again and at last he said, choking. 'The bullocks must go. Otherwise we shall not have enough.'

But when we had added them and reckoned and re-reckoned, there was still not enough. 'There are the saris left,' I said. 'Good ones and hardly worn, and these we must sell.'

I brought out the red sari that had served for both my wedding and my daughter's, and the sari and dhoti I had bought when Thambi worked at the tannery, made a parcel of them and set out.

'Ah, Rukmani,' said Biswas with false welcome. 'What brings you here? I have not seen you for a long time, not had any of your succulent fruit. Would that be what you bear with you?'

'No indeed,' I answered shortly, his voice grating on me as always. 'For the earth is parched to dust and all that I grew is dead. The rains failed, as you know.'

'Yes, yes, yes,' he said, looking at me with his cunning eyes. 'These are hard times for us.'

Not for you, I thought. You thrive on others' misfortunes.

'We need money for the land,' I said. 'I have brought the two shirts my sons no longer need, being away, two saris I never wear and my husband's dhoti to sell to you. The saris are very finely worked, and worn but a few times.' I took them out and laid them before him.

He fingered the rich stuff, and measured the borders between outstretched thumb and little finger, and lifted up the silver threads to examine them the closer, and held up the shirts to the light for sign of wear.

'How much do you want for these?'

'It is for you to make the offer.'

'Tell me first how much you want and I will see what can do.'

'Enough to pay the land dues.'

'How much is that?'

'It is my business.'

He was silent for a while, and I said to him exasperated. 'Tell me if you are not prepared to buy and I will go elsewhere.'

'Always in haste,' he rebuked me in that gentle, oily voice of his. 'Yet I think this time you will have to await my pleasure, Rukmani.'

'What do you mean?' I said, ruffled. 'There are many who would be pleased to buy such good material.'

'I think not,' he said. 'I think not. For, you see, the wives of other men have come to me, even as you have, and have gone away as you threaten, yet they have to come back to me because nobody else can afford to buy in these hard times.'

'As no doubt you can,' I said with contempt, and then an inspiration came to me and I went on: 'Unless you pay a fair price I shall take these saris elsewhere. There is the Muslim wife of a tannery official whom I know, and she will buy from me as she has done before.'

'Indeed,' he said, a little disconcerted. 'Well, Rukmani, since we have done business for a long time, and because you are a woman of spirit whom I have long admired, I will give you thirty rupees. Nobody could be fairer.'

'Fairer by far,' I retorted. 'I will not take one pie under seventy-five rupees. Take it or not as you please.' I put the clothes away, making a pretence of going to the door. I hoped he would call me back, for in truth I did not know where else to turn, but if not—well, thirty rupees was too far from our needs to be of use, and if I did not get what I asked I might as well keep the saris. As I got to the door he called to me. 'Very well, Rukmani. I will pay you what you ask, since it will help you.'

I waited. He disappeared into another room and came back in a few minutes with a sour face and a small leather pouch full of money. He pulled the drawstrings and took from it notes and silver, counting them twice over to make sure.

'A very rare price,' he said, handing me the money. 'Remember always the good turn I have done you.'

I tucked the money away, making no reply, and I went back with a lighter step than I had come out.

Nathan had returned too, having sold the pots and pans, the food and the bullocks. We pooled the money and counted it, and there was in all 125 rupees, not even the half we had to pay.

'There is still the seed,' Nathan said. 'We must sell that.'

'What of the next crop?' I said. 'If we sell the seeds we may as well give up the land too, for how shall we raise a new crop?'

'It is better to be without the seed than bereft of the land in which to plant it. Seed is cheap, it can be bought. I can earn a few rupees, or perhaps my sons...'

How? I cried to myself. How? Is not my son every day at the tannery, and no one will look at him because of his brothers! And you, my husband, what chance have you when so many young men are festering in idleness.

'It will mean only a few rupees,' I said. 'Let us not sacrifice the future to our immediate need.'

'What is the alternative?' he shouted. 'Do you think I am blind and do not see, or so stupid as to believe that crops are raised without seed? Do you take me for a fool that...'

He was not shouting at me but at the terrible choice forced upon us; this I knew, yet could not prevent my throat contracting, or force the tears back into their well.

MRIDULA GARG

Country of Goodbyes

Translated from the Hindi by Manisha Choudhry

'My partner,' he said as he hugged me tightly and rained kisses all over my face.

I heard, 'My partner, this novel has been written by both of us, it will be published in both our names.'

But there was still something that kept me from speaking about Ruth. Many days passed. Every night Irving would repeat his plea that the novel was our soul's offspring, a child created from our joint consciousness. Every night I heard him say that the novel would be published in both our names. Even so, I stood my ground and refused to be checkmated.

Then one night...he finally said, check; he thought up such an infallible move, it must have sprung from the passion buried in the pages of my journal. How else could he have figured out just what to say so that I would surrender? Caught in his web of clever words I read consent in coercion. I don't know whether it was the depth of my pain or his piercing eye—whatever it was it was enough to checkmate me.

'Listen to me, Marianne,' he said as he caressed my satiated, sleepy body, 'as soon as the novel is printed we will make another baby. Won't you give me a real baby, in flesh and blood, a symbol of our union, of body and soul? You also want one, don't you, your own child, flesh of your flesh, born of your body? Our very own, sprung from our blood and sinews?'

The next day I handed over Ruth's diary to Irving.

The novel was published. *Woman of the Earth*. I picked it up reverentially as I would my own child. A wave of awe and excitement rose in my body, then crashed into an abyss. What popped out of my mouth was, 'But this has been published in your name only.'

'Naturally—what else?' said Irving.

'You said it would be published jointly, in both our names.'

'When did I say that? You must be mad.'

'Didn't you say this was the child of our joint consciousness? Then my name...'

'A child is known by its father's name,' he said, delighted with his repartee.

But I couldn't let go. Still in denial, I repeated stupidly, 'You said that I had sowed the seed and you were carrying the baby. Didn't you say that?'

'Maybe I did,' he replied carelessly, 'when you are in the throes of creation all manner of images float across your mind.'

The illusion shattered and anger replaced the dream.

'It was all lies! You were just using me.'

'Using you? What use could I make of you?'

'I collected all the material...'

'Gratitude!' he said with sarcasm. 'You cannot write a novel simply by collecting facts, my dear. There is a difference between sociological research and creative writing. I haven't stopped you from writing your thesis.'

But I wanted creation. You led me to believe that I was creating, that I had already created and you were just there with me. Why did you lie to me? Why did you say again and again that this was our joint creation, our spirit child, and that it would be known as such? I gave you everything, all my work, those detailed diaries of the four women in whom you saw my image. No. I kept Ruth's diary hidden from you for a long time. So then...was this elaborate charade played out just to get your hands on that? You say you cannot write a novel only by collecting facts. But you had all the facts about Ruth, didn't you? Only her emotional journey remained with me. Which means that this work is mine, far more than it is yours.

As I turned the pages listlessly and all this welled up inside me, I raised my head to spit at Irving but he had left already. As I burned in rage I turned the pages, looking for any hint of salve to soothe the wound. Nowhere in the entire book, neither in the beginning nor the end was there any acknowledgement of my contribution to it. Even the dedication was in the name of Everywoman. I recalled that I had said we would dedicate our novel to Everywoman. All I had known then was that it was *our* novel, born of the two of us.

I had lived a long time with the energy generated from creating the novel, I couldn't bear it when that illusion was shattered. I fell into an abyss of depression. As I struggled to keep afloat I started to read the novel.

I must have reached the halfway mark when I felt Virginia's arrogance and rage creep up my ankles till it reached my head. Fraud! Incompetent fool! Thief! There was not a single meaningful page in the novel which had not been taken in its entirety from my journal. Irving had only played around with the language. In this creation, I had not only sowed the seed, I had carried it in my womb and birthed it. Irving had merely swaddled it and stolen it. This was my child which he had kidnapped.

When Irving returned I hissed at him with rage and contempt. I hadn't known I could hurl so much vile abuse with such force—I was Virginia's daughter after all.

'You Cunning, Sly, Impotent Bastard,' I hissed, 'You lifted my entire journal and had it published. This is out and out theft, I will never forgive you, you sleazy bastard, never let you get away with this.'

'Don't shout,' he said calmly,' I haven't committed a crime. You gave me your journal of your own free will, no more than that. D. H. Lawrence, Scott Fitzgerald and many others used their wives' journals when they wrote their novels. Zelda Fitzgerald didn't even give hers willingly. She went to court to register her protest, but then she was half-mad. And what happened? The court granted Fitzgerald legal permission to use her journal. You know the history of literature but you're still railing and protesting.'

'You son of a bitch! You impotent bastard!' I seized the collar of his shirt and shook him, 'So you think you will have me committed to the asylum like Zelda! That was then, this is now. I'm going to get you for this! I will have you in prison on charges of plagiarism. This novel will be sold only when it has my name on it. Get that into your head.'

'What proof do you have of your contribution to it?' he asked me dispassionately.

'My journal, what else?'

'What journal?'

'The one that...I gave...you,' but before I could complete my sentence I knew that he had destroyed it.

As my head spun I steadied myself by twisting his shirt in my fists. It tore and I drew blood from his chest and shoulders with my sharp nails and teeth.

Irving freed himself with great difficulty. He managed to push me to the ground but didn't lay a finger on me otherwise.

My anger passed. The tiredness which follows violence sat heavily on my body. Zelda Fitzgerald's words rose from my subconscious and burned my ears. Women are so adept at bearing injustice that the most sophisticated of them behave like peasant women—weeping and wailing but unwilling to fight. What else could she have said? She was even more helpless than Roxanne, Susan, Elena and Ruth. The salt of tears, the smell of coffee, the magic of embroidery and relentless work were not options she would exercise; all that she had as a basis for her identity was her journal. As soon as that was stolen from her she lost her mental balance. She had already suffered a nervous breakdown; now she spent her last days in an asylum. My journal had been taken away from me, I hadn't even made a copy. Irving first committed rape, then murder. He murdered my child. He killed Susan, Roxanne, Elena and Ruth. But I didn't want to go to the madhouse. An intense sadness descended on me. Darkness before my eyes. Why was I not able to cry? My hands and feet grew numb, I lay on the earth, twisted and tortured like a wounded animal. Irving stood at my head. I looked up at him with difficulty. Blood was dripping from his torn shirt, the blood of my unborn child. I tried to scream but fell down unconscious. When I came to, Irving had vanished. Surprise, surprise. He had departed without a fuss. Despite my spitting and scratching Irving hadn't lifted a finger against me. Was he ashamed of what he had done?

Fool! What was the point of displaying Virginia's arrogance for a brief moment when I was so worked up by the attack on my identity? When had I ever acquired her mastery of technique? I wasn't Virginia at all, I was Zelda, cowering in the margins. No, not even Zelda, Marianne. Oscillating between protest and tears, whining and complaining, unable to get past betrayal, unwilling to acquire feminine wiles. A mere woman.

After freeing himself from me Irving had gone straight to the police station. He had his abrasions photographed and filed a petition in court to the effect that his wife was subject to hysteria and fits of mental disturbance, and consequently grew violent. Therefore he wanted a divorce.

Abhijatri

Translated from the Assamese by Sajal Dey

'Oyee, just look at that! Look, look at that female riding a bicycle!'

'O no, now I've seen everything. A female creature on a bike! Of course, this female is abandoned—what else do you expect from her?'

Seeing a big peepul tree, Chandraprabha got down from the cycle and after wiping her sweaty face with her chadar, squatted on a big root which seemed to have forced its way above ground. Then she soliloquized: 'One gets used to everything in time. These snide remarks will lose their sting after some time—of course they will!'

Then she got up on her cycle again, but not before fondly caressing it. Without this conveyance, there was no way she could take those narrow, looping roads of the villages where she was trying to organize the womenfolk. Usually people did not have occasion to travel from one village to another. When they did have to travel, the men walked, except for a few who had cycles. A few lucky women—those from affluent households—travelled by bullock carts. The rest men and women tramped the good earth.

Chandraprabha would not walk. She had to flit from place to place, organizing, educating, holding meetings. She had initiated moves to form a women's organization at Nagaon, but the effort was aborted because of a man named Bidyadhar Barua, a well-known lawyer who actually broke up the meeting when the subject was mooted.

But there was a resurrection of such activities, blessed by the president of the next Sahitya Sabha at Dhubri, Benudhar Rajkhowa. Chandraprabha remembered his plangent words with some emotion: 'Peace and prosperity to the Bengalis, and I hope they feel similarly about us. Let all races in India thrive and progress. Let the Brahmaputra follow its own course, and let the Ganga, the Jamuna, the Kaveri, and the Indus do likewise. Finally they'll all flow into the Indian Ocean and that's our Indian nation.'

A lot of things fermented at Dhubri: it was awash with triumphant, glad memories for Chandraprabha, struggling to initiate something like a women's movement in the state. Many of the luminaries of the land lent their voices and supporting arms to Chandraprabha's cause. With the backing of people like the zamindar-literateur Nagendra Narayan Chaudhuri, a fabulous meeting was held at 'Bijni' Hall. People made a beeline for this meeting, often coming in cars with jubilant women inside them. Even a police officer named Bhuban Datta raised their spirits with his benign and cooperative presence.

The scintillating memories of those days spurred Chandraprabha on, enabling her to stoically bear the curses and abuses slung at her, and the rain and the sun that alternatively tested her physical endurance. Chandraprabha and her trusty bicycle kept going, on and on.

◆

Gangapriya was peering into a bowl of vegetables—which she had collected from the small garden at the back—as if looking for some answer to the painful conundrum of her life. She had laboured with clenched teeth to deliver more than ten children, yet there was not a single one by her side. Lonesome drudgery in the twilight of her life was bending her back, dimming her eyes. Entering the house, she almost stumbled with surprise. Boxes and cases were strewn all over the frontyard, and Atul was rampaging through those, with his grandfather making feeble attempts to check him. As she stood gaping, Chandraprabha entered, dragging her bicycle.

'I'm back, Mother, Father. I've resigned from Kaljirapara School.'

The reason for this stunning decision was kept in abeyance while the mother and the child got refreshed. Then her father pressed her for an explanation.

Chandraprabha, who had finished her last gulp of rice, said: 'I begged for leave to attend the Congress conference, but it was not granted. The chairman thundered that he would not permit any karamchari of his to attend any function that was inimical to the British interests. He also made digs at the Congress, saying—if only it was so easy to become independent, just by holding these meetings and conference! I could not stand it, my blood started boiling. I just quit.'

Ratiram Majumdar started to absorb all this, somehow lonely and empty with his grief and bewilderment. As it had happened with his wife a few moments ago, sad thoughts about his progeny speared his tired consciousness.

A few of his offspring had already kissed the dust, Dharma was a no-good, footloose wanderer, and then there were Chandraprabha and Rajani. The last two did not seem destined to lead normal lives. But as he thought about them, the cockles of the old man's heart started warming. These two were sterling creatures, bursting with talent, energy and yes, humanity.

'Father? Why are you so silent? Are you angry with what I did?'

'No, child, it's not that at all. You must go to the great gathering. But I fear you and Atul will face poverty.'

Chandraprabha thought about Dandinath who kept sending money.

But these gifts were accompanied by reprimands. Why did Chandraprabha keep on forming new attachments with male friends? Why couldn't she keep a rein on her expenses? Didn't she realize that he was not getting a pittance from his publications?

Darkness shrouded Chandraprabha as she thought about those accusatory paper missiles.

◆

It was another day of December 1926. The entire Pandu region was cloaked in chilly fog. Two women who emerged from women's camp were wraithlike figures in the murky light. One of them asked: 'Baideu, is it really necessary to see the Brahmaputra in this cold?' The other, obviously older woman, replied with a smile: 'Indu, I feel for you. You have not gone through the grind while growing up, as we did. But you have to take troubles and hardships in your stride, now that you have joined the movement.'

A look of determination appeared on the young woman's face: 'I'll follow where you lead, baideu. Even my husband has encouraged me to do that. Now I am so proud that I'll be part of this great Congress conference.'

'You should be. To be a part of this event I resigned from my job.'

Indu darted a look of admiration at the old soldier by her side. Talking about the conference, they reached the river bank. In the nearness of the great river, Chandraprabha felt the tug of long dormant emotions.

'You know, Indu, when I first confronted the Brahmaputra at Tezpur, I had difficulty in accommodating the greatness of the river because of being used to the petty, slender streams of the villages. And I thought, I'll make my life as broad and generous as this river. But fate ordained differently. I've been swept away to some deep, gloomy dungeon.'

Induprabha knew a little about Chandraprabha's life. But although her heart went out to the long-suffering woman, she said in a voice that dripped admiration rather than pity: 'Baideu, I've rarely seen lives as fulfilling and generous as yours. My husband and others say that if Assam had a few more women like you, new horizons would have opened up.'

Praise always buoyed Chandraprabha. Clutching Induprabha's hand, she asked excitedly: 'Really? Someone like your husband, Dr Bhubaneswar Barua, stakes so much faith in me? Now, if I start organizing women's activities, will you help me?'

The quiet, compliant Indu said with a smile: 'I will, indeed.'

With her gaze transfixed on the Brahmaputra, Chandraprabha said: 'See, Indu, the blanket of fog is lifting. The sun is piercing the fog and lighting up the waves of the river.'

RAJALAKSHMI

The Apology

Translated from the Malayalam by R. K. Jayasree

'So the most disgusting of pronouns is...'

She paused.

'She!'

It came from a bench in the back.

The class fell silent.

The young teacher turned pale.

The most hated pronoun in the language.

'She!'

The class consisted of only twenty students. There was only one girl in the class. And she happened to be absent that day.

The only female of the species present in the small room among the nineteen boys was the young teacher herself.

The most disgusting word—'she'. The voice was only too familiar.

And she also knew only too well that she ought to haul him up and take him to task.

She stood before the students for a moment, her face pale as paper. Then she walked out of the class, not even bothering to pick up her book lying on the table.

When she returned to the staff room right in the middle of a period, all the other teachers were there.

'Ah! Let off classes whenever you feel like it! Well, well, not bad. Lucky the principal didn't see you.' Mr Kartha said, half in earnest, half in jest.

She couldn't hold out any longer. She rested her head on the table and burst into tears—tears which simply couldn't be held in check.

'Oh! What's wrong?'

Everyone rose to their feet.

'What did you say to her, Kartha Mash?'

Everyone was getting to be chivalrous.

This is a great shame, she told herself, it's so degrading, breaking into tears like this before all these men. They are all nice people but still they're strangers.

She thought all this, but she couldn't hold her tears back.

Somebody went over to another department and fetched a woman lecturer.

The men trooped out.

The lady—a nice woman, the mother of three kids—didn't ask her any questions, but drew up a chair and sat beside her, patting her head gently.

Gradually the sobs subsided. She brought her a glass of water. 'Wash your face.'

Going over to the window she washed her face. She made a pretence of wiping her face dry with her colleague's dainty handkerchief.

'May I go? I don't feel like taking any more classes.'

'Yes of course, Rema. I'll tell them. Go and sleep it off. You need come only tomorrow. I'll get someone to take your classes.' She accompanied her to the gate.

People who were on the verandah or out in the yard at the time noticed her as she left, hiding her face behind her umbrella.

What really happened?

There was a furore on the campus. Mr Kartha himself called one of the students and spoke to him, to learn about the affair.

The news spread like wildfire. It was an unprecedented event in the history of the college.

A teacher having to leave a class and bursting into tears! And poor Miss Rema at that.

As for her teaching, there had never been any complaints.

The incident grew more dramatic in the telling.

She had been crying when she left the class.

A boy stood up in the class and said something obscene.

And she walked out, crying.

Poor Miss Rema who wouldn't hurt a fly. And the person who made the comment was Paul Verghese, the President of the College Union.

Complaints against Paul Verghese, which no one had heard before, began to surface.

He's something of a rogue. Now that he's become the president, he's getting too big for his boots.

Someone came up with the discovery that he was hanging around the girls' waiting room all the time.

There were others who had seen him enter a liquor shop through the back door.

It took only twenty-four hours to make a villain out of Paul Verghese. What really transpired in the class? Only this? Were the other students lying to shield him? If this was all that had happened, why should the teacher have taken it to heart—well, nobody comes to the staff room and breaks down just like that, do they?

What really did happen for her to take it so much to heart—that was what Rema too had been wondering about.

Why did she have to break down like that? Just because the boy said that? Was she really so ineffectual? If she couldn't even handle just one student—or was it Mr Kartha's teasing that did it? Oh, no! She wasn't that touchy.

Okay, she was fond of Paul Verghese. A smart boy, so bright and smart. When she heard that in his voice—still, did she have to—

Could it be that she was reminded of something she'd lost—lost irrevocably—

Or could it be that she glimpsed the emptiness of what she called life as it stood unveiled in the unkindly glare of the moment?

The anguish of yesterdays, the emptiness of today and the futility of tomorrows—did she glimpse them all, in that moment?

Was that why she wept?

The next day she walked into the department without raising her head.

Everybody was considerate. The professor came to tell her that she need no longer take the Final main class.

No longer take the class?

It ought to have made her happy. It was there she was insulted. She ought to be happy that she didn't have to go there or meet them any more.

Paul Verghese—

He would never have imagined that this affair would become so controversial.

What will he be thinking of her now? Will he think she brought on all this trouble by bursting into tears?

Why did the boy have to say that? Did he mean to insult her? In Strachey's essay the phrase 'most disgusting pronoun' stands for the first person singular.

And she had been teaching the essay. A predilection for the word—'I'

The most disgusting pronoun—

Being saddled with a big 'I'—hadn't that always been her trouble?

'Let me not, oh Lord, be troubled by the feeling of 'I'

She'd been to the class, thinking how akin Strachey's thought was to Vedanta.

And there, after the introductory remarks, she'd been warming up to the topic, when—

Paul Verghese—

The tall, slender, handsome boy, what did he hope to gain by insulting her?

The issue was becoming serious.

She was told it had reached the principal. And that he was said to have taken the whole thing seriously.

Paul had been asked to bring his guardian.

Oh, that'll be the end of it, Rema consoled herself. The guardian will come, chat with the principal and leave. The case will be closed. What a relief it will be!

If only the whole thing would be over and done with—

It did not turn out the way she expected it to. Paul didn't fetch his parent.

The principal was getting more and more incensed. Paul was barred from attending classes.

SARAH JOSEPH

Gift in Green

Translated from the Malayalam by Valson Thampu

SHAILAJA SUSPECTS SWEEPER MARY

Every delivery means a bucket full of blood. Shailaja dumps into a massive toilet bowl and flushes away, besides the blood, leftovers like placenta, severed umbilical cords, sanitary napkins, blood-soaked rags and cotton packs. At once, a whirlwind rises from beneath and carries it all away with a clamorous slurp, leaving behind not even a touch of moisture. How marvellous!

'Where does this stuff go?' Shailaja asked.

'To the bottom of the earth,' replied sweeper Mary mechanically.

None of this holds any unease or surprise for Mary. Shailaja is, however, new on the staff. She abhors the labour room, enters it hesitantly and walks about fearfully. Whatever she sees, hears and handles there upsets her. The subhuman scream that breaks out of a woman at the tearing climax of her labour makes her drop the bucket and run out of the labour room. In front of an open vagina on fire with pain, she stands paralyzed. Repulsed by the sight of the pallid sliminess of the umbilical cord, she turns her face away from the newborn.

Mary is immune to all this.

'Wipe that floor, girl. Can't you see the blood?'

'Don't stand there whimpering, take away that bedpan.'

'Change the bed sheet, it's soaked in the stuff from that ruptured placenta.'

On the strength of her seniority, Mary keeps issuing orders. These are peppered with warnings when Shailaja begins her work.

'It won't do to pass tenth class, drape yourself in a white sari and stray into a hospital. You must learn to *do* the work.'

A terrible silence invades the room after each delivery. Watching the beads of sweat on the forehead of the women impaled on pain and lying exhausted on the delivery table, Shailaja mops the pools of blood from underneath their legs. She goes to the toilet bowl when blood fills the bucket. Each time, it amazes her: how does the earth suck in so much, so fast? And, that, too, without leaving a stain or a trace!

'It is not the earth,' attendant Vasu whispered.

'Then?'

'There are pages here that you have not read. Girl, you can't understand them.'

Because of what attendant Vasu told her, Shailaja began to distrust sweeper Mary's words. The placenta does not get absorbed into the womb of the earth. It only gets cast out as flesh once again, through a large pipe, back to the bosom of the primal waters.

One day, unbearably intrigued, Shailaja began to climb the steps of the massive granite fortification that separated the hospital from the lake of death behind it. Halfway up the steps, her legs and hands began to tremble. A strong headwind beat against her. The steps were narrow and steep. A security guard noticed her when she had some twenty steps more to climb.

He mistook her, at first, for a huge white heron among the rocks. The next moment, he raised an alarm, hollering at her and blowing his whistle frantically.

Shailaja was in the vortex of a gale. Stamping down the clamour of the security guards, she clawed her way up to the top of the rocky structure.

The sky alone was above her now. Beneath her lay an endless stretch of water. The gale lifted her clothes, tousled her hair, shook her body, and made her stagger. How right was the surmise of the security guard! Shailaja was only a white heron with its wings poised to fly. She could fly down any time now. The security guards ran helter-skelter.

'Who are you? Come down, you daughter of a bitch. What do you think you are doing? Come down!' one of the guards shouted at the top of his voice. The gale snatched and scattered his words, so Shailaja did not hear any of it. Even otherwise, neither the security guards nor their whistles, nor the crowd gathering below, nor the hospital authorities, mattered to Shailaja at that point in time. She was searching for a mirror in the heart of the water to settle her suspicions and misgivings. Oh god! Nothing was clear, No sky. No clouds. No sun in full blaze. Only a dark stretch of water.

'Shailajaaa...' It was sweeper Mary who had yelled. 'The wind is too strong. You will fall down. What drama do you hope to see by climbing over there? Come down! Right now!'

Liar! I distrust her every word, every warning. Placentas were putrefying in the water. They were not buried in the earth. Nor did they decompose to become manure for trees. Besides placentas, there were aborted foetuses. Shailaja had carried such foetuses in buckets in the past.

'Mother, I want to touch the earth,' the foetuses begged of Shailaja before they were emptied into the large closet.

'I am not your mother.'

In one desperate inversion of the bucket, Shailaja cast them to the whirlwind. In a flash, they were sucked out of sight, carrying with them every trace of the sins that stained their mothers' wombs. Each time a woman, her womb cleaned up, left her bed in peace, Shailaja went to the large toilet bowl, peered in and asked in a thunderous voice: 'That woman who is leaving: whose mother is she?'

To Shailaja, waves were born when the fingers of god tapped a rhythm on the surface of the water. May the faith of sweeper Mary save her! God had already withdrawn his fingers, which once moved over the water. It shocked Shailaja to contemplate the calamities that were in the offing.

Laden with the stench, the wind was heavy. Besides placentas and murdered foetuses, Shailaja saw, emerging from innumerable cracks and crevices, severed limbs, swabs oozing with pus, blood clots, decomposed phlegm, chemical agents, plastic bottles and bags, garbage. A terrible thirst afflicted Shailaja. Her throat was dry, her lips parched. She sweated profusely.

The security guards laboured up the stone steps. They were struggling, the steps being steep and narrow.

'Mind you, she could leap down to her death. She looks determined, the way she is standing.' Shailaja could hear the shouts from the crowd below her. The warning seemed to come not so much from individuals as from the mouth of a roaring crowd: the multitudinous responses to a woman standing on a rocky wall, determined to leap to her death.

Her belief that the resources for human survival rested in water, for generations to come was shattered to smithereens. She sank to her knees and collapsed on that stony fortification.

The people standing below shouted in relief that she had given up.

Identity

India is a country of deeply entrenched and highly layered social identity. We are defined not only by gender and class but also caste, gotra, tribe, race, religion, food habits, political affiliation and skin colour. Women writers have examined the politics of 'being' from every perspective. There are stories about caste power equations and how this destroys lives.

Maitreyi Pushpa's *Alma Kabutari* is a novel that seeks to tell the history and oppressive contemporary reality of the Kabutra tribe. It is about caste, land, corruption, violence and the inevitable failure of justice when accompanied by prejudice. The extract from Chandrakanta's novel *A Street in Srinagar* takes on the false moral code and cowardice of religious people who insist on strict segregation along caste lines but do not step forward to help someone who is part of their caste and community.

The extract from Rashid Jahan's short story 'One of my Journeys' is a hilarious account of a catfight in a moving train between two groups of women from different communities. Romila Thapar's essay ('Somanatha and Mahmud'), a small portion of which is included here, examines the role of Mahmud Ghazni in destroying the Somnath temple and the effect this has had on community relations down the centuries.

An extract from Shama Futehally's *Tara Lane* takes us through a young girl's painful awareness of class. There is oppression and fear embedded at all levels of the heirarchy as the wealthy fear a loss of integrity, respect and love along with their privileges. Mrinal Pande's 'Bibbo' looks at class from a sexual lens, with the middle and upper classes living in fear of the sensuality and sexual freedom of their servants.

Nirupama Dutt's Punjabi poems reflect on how women are judged on their appearance and their refusal to conform to social norms. Someone with dark skin bears the brunt of society's obsession with fair skin, and a woman who refuses to follow the rules is labelled a 'bad woman'.

Finally, Nivedita Menon's essay speaks of identity in the context of professional sport, given that gender is a spectrum rather than a binary.

RASHID JAHAN

One of my Journeys

Translated from the Urdu by Rakhshanda Jalil

The Muslim women who were sitting on their benches and chomping paan after paan, seemed just as illiterate. Moreover, they seemed to belong to one particular biradari. The Hindu women, though uneducated, looked as though they belonged to different castes such as Bania, Thakur and Brahmin. But I have always found that, while travelling, everyone becomes a Brahmin, and in all my travels I have never found anyone belonging to a caste lower than a Thakur, at the very least!

A Muslim woman, wearing tight black pyjamas, a pink dupatta and laden with silver jewellery, got up from her seat.

Her nose ring, worn as it was on her septum and not her nostril was so large that it hid her paan-stained lips and teeth darkened with missi. I am sure that, once upon a time, some man, fed up with a talkative woman, must have invented the nose ring so that a woman's voice would remain trapped in her mouth. And women are such silly creatures that they turned this invention into tradition. No wonder then that every religion teaches that women have feeble minds.

Anyhow, listen! The Muslim woman picked up her lota and began to move towards the toilet. Hindu women quickly huddled away. One poor woman, who was sitting on her luggage, got onto her suitcase with her shoes on in her haste to get out of the way. The Muslim woman passed blithely on—her dupatta trailing behind her like a blanket of benevolence passing over the Hindu woman on the suitcase and another who sat beside her.

The two Hindu women squealed with rage and turned to the others: 'Did you see? Did you see how odd she is? She went past us with her clothes touching us.'

'How else could she go to the toilet? Why are you sitting in the way?' a middle-aged woman spoke up.

'Who has stopped anyone from going? But she could at least draw her dupatta tight around herself when she walks past us.'

'Why must she touch us with her clothes?' my neighbour asked with a crackle in her voice. She was holding a Hindi newspaper in her hand.

'If you sit in the way this is bound to happen,' another Muslim woman said with deliberate carelessness.

'If we don't "sit in the way", where should we sit? On your head? Look at you, sitting there with your legs sprawled while we are so cramped. And, still, this bothers you! As though the train belongs to your father and you are the only ones who have bought tickets.' Turning around and gesturing with her hands, a Hindu woman spoke to the Muslim woman.

'Yes! The train belongs to our father. And we will sit with our legs sprawled like this. Do what you can. And, one more thing, if you speak any more rubbish, it won't be good for you.' The middle-aged Muslim woman spat a stream of paan juice in the middle of the compartment and scolded the Hindu women.

'Won't be good for us? What will it be, then? Are you a collector that you will have us tied to cannons?' the Hindu woman retorted and, turning towards her own 'party', she asked me, 'Are you listening, Behenji? Ever since these Musalmaniyan have entered this compartment, they have been creating havoc.'

By now I had understood why these two 'camps' were sitting separately. A battle between Hindus and Muslims was raging inside this compartment. These women from poor households seldom got a chance to fight on the streets. Now, by a stroke of good fortune, they found themselves confined together in a third-class railway carriage; and so had decided to make the most of this rare opportunity to vent their spleen at each other.

I sat up and began to listen more carefully to what was going on around me. A young Muslim woman spoke loudly, obviously for the benefit of her Hindu audience: 'Ai Chachi, why are you bandying words with these low-born types? These people are not fit to be spoken to.'

'What did you say? Low-born? Mind your tongue, or are you bent on spilling blood?'

The woman who was sitting next to me spoke up haughtily, 'Do you know who I am? If you utter another word, I will have you witches taken off the train right now.'

The Muslim girls let out a raucous peal of laughter. 'Did you hear that? There sits the Latsaheb's wife!'

My neighbour pushed me aside and got up in a flurry of excitement. Just then the door of the toilet opened and the woman with the enormous nose ring came out. She was still standing by the door when the woman atop her suitcase called out, 'Look here, you, watch where your clothes go when you walk.'

'I will walk as I please,' she said as she sauntered back carelessly with her dupatta trailing behind her. Again, her dupatta touched the woman sitting atop her suitcase. Gritting her teeth, the woman with the luggage tugged the dupatta sharply so that the woman with the nose ring fell down. Her lota tumbled away; most of the water inside it splashed on

Unbound

two Hindu women and drops fell on many more. All the Hindu women shouted in unison: 'Ram! Ram!' The woman who had pulled the dupatta let it go and began to examine her own dhoti for signs of pollution. Meanwhile, the woman with the nose ring picked herself off the floor. The entire episode had happened so suddenly and quickly that her companions were still getting to their feet when she flung her dupatta aside and stood straight. Then, looking neither this way nor that, she planted a sharp blow on her enemy's bent head. 'Haramzadi! What do you think of yourself?'

A strange wave of frenzy and fury coursed through the compartment. Each woman glared at the women of the other party, eyes popping with rage. I bent my head to peer out of the window to see if a station was approaching, so that it might serve to distract these women. But this was an express train; it left behind all the small stations and had a long way to go before it came to a halt.

After being assaulted and drenched, was it possible for these women to remain silent? Those who were in wet clothes were willing to fight till the death. Now, they fell upon the woman with the nose ring with combined fury. Help came from the other side too. Four or five women grappled with each other in that cramped space. One grabbed a tuft of the other's hair while her own earring was being yanked.

They fell on their luggage, got up quickly, only to fall down once again. As the Hindu women lunged for the nose rings and ear loops, the Muslims yanked their braids. They dug their teeth into whatever piece of flesh they found on their enemies' bodies. And if they managed to land one punch, they followed it with a flurry of blows and kicks. In other words, kicking-scratching-biting-punching Furies were writhing over the luggage and the floor of the compartment.

The lady who sat next to me shifted her luggage to one side so that she too could get into the thick of the battle, but she couldn't find an inch of space to stand in. Maddened beyond control, she stooped and landed a couple of blows on an eight or ten year old Muslim girl. At this, a couple of Muslim women who had so far been content with indulging in verbal warfare, jumped into the fray and landed plumb into the enemy's territory. On this side too, Hindu women who had so far been on the fringes of the battle, got to their feet. The wrestling bouts, so far confined to one side, now began on both sides. I shrank further into my corner. My neighbour saw my fainteheartedness and invited me to join the fray with the following exhortation: 'Behenji, why are you sitting there and watching? Will you get beaten by these malech women?'

A middle-aged Muslim woman glowered at me with her terrifying eyes. I quickly averted my gaze and began to look out of the window to convince her that I had no desire to be a party to this slaughter and mayhem. I noticed that some children were cowering in a corner and taking in the scene with terrified eyes, and others were bawling at the top of their lungs. And the mothers... such was their inflamed communal frenzy that they were oblivious even to their offspring. The only thing missing here were cries of 'Allah-o-Akbar!' and 'Sri Krishan Maharaj ki Jai!' Instead, cries of 'Whore!', 'Slut!', 'Bitch!', and such other words rent the air. I cannot even write some of those words; you must imagine the rest.

An old Muslim woman who had so far been sitting in a corner and shaking her head came up with a new ploy. Perhaps her intentions were good; the outcome was disastrous. She opened her packet of food and began to shower pieces of meat and dollops of mince on the other party. The Hindu women paused for a minute then changed tack. One picked up the lota that had fallen on the floor and threw it out the window. The Muslim women lunged for the luggage of the Hindus and in the blink of an eye, each side was sticking to the other's luggage like glue. If one party was trying to prise it away, the other was hell bent upon saving it. This snatching and pulling of luggage assumed monstrous proportions. Already, a few small items had been flung out and were lying somewhere in the fields yonder. By now I was scared that after they were done with the luggage they might start hurling the children.

MAITREYI PUSHPA

Alma Kabutari

Translated from the Hindi by Raji Narasimhan

It's a beginning yet, and the place is steadily growing, steadily coming up.
Kadambai looks at her life from all sides. And she lends her ear to Kehar's
crystal-gazing, playing the oracle: 'The government is now going to come
into the hands of us people, because we are the only ones who can make
and save it. Don't you see our boys being noticed by the people? It's not
just liquor that's here, but people of substance. The days are gone when
our enemies bashed us up. Now our liquor contract gives us a platform
of power. We have not bought or sold women. Nor killed anyone. We
have proclaimed a new tenet that shows how the hidden strength of a
man considered worthless becomes a means of creating wealth—and how,
for the lack of such wealth he and his kind had been made faceless. This
theka of Mansaram and Kehar is no slaughterhouse like a police station.
Out there the only thought in their heads is how to stir up trouble, how
to kill and pillage and reap the benefits.'

Kadambai recalls the early days, when, along with Bheekham, Gomta,
Dhan Singh and Roop Singh, some other boys too had come. Kehar
Singh arranged for their food and massage as if they were ace wrestlers.

The people said Kehar was raising hooligans, rearing goondas. The
rumour spread so thick, that an old oil-presser woman turned up; her
two bighas of land had been taken over by the sons of her elder brother-
in-law. The sons tilled it, kept the produce and the old woman starved.
Kehar set his boys on the job: Go and throw out the plough from the
old woman's field.

That done, a kachchi came next, whose backyard was being laid
waste by a fellow kachchi. If this one said anything, the other just beat
him up. The boys of the theka went over, flexing their muscles, and the
predatory kachchi folded his hands.

The third incident involved a peasant. The bania stopped his crops
from leaving the threshing floor. The children cried, what would they
eat? Bheekham and Gomta went at night time, twisted the arms of the
bania and put the fear of god into him.

Now two show-offs came to Kehar. Smooth skinned, neta-type boys.

Kehar Singh, weathered and made astute by his profession, studied
them. Had they come to ogle at the kabutara girls? The fourteen-year-old
Gorki was in the theka at the time. But the poor boys didn't so much

as throw a glance at the girl. Then Kehar thought—they are afraid of the kabutari women.

Mansaram treated them like gods and offered them water to drink, which they didn't drink. Then he offered drink. They turned it down without a word. Not water. Not liquor, not a pretty face or form did they seem to want. Then why had they come?

Drawing Kehar aside, they said, 'We want two kabutaras.'

'For?'

'For robbing someone.'

A chance to make money! Kehar rubbed his hands. The boys would eat good food, build their physiques. He'd probe a bit.

'Eight thousand.'

'We'll give sixteen thousand.'

'And why this bounty?'

'To destroy evidence, as after the robbery, we shall shoot the kabutaras.'

'Then why don't you do the robbing yourself?'

'Take thirty-two thousand, come along.'

'Kunwar sahib, we are talking of selling our prowess for eight thousand. We are not talking of selling our lives for thirty-two thousand or sixty-four thousand. You don't know the stuff of bravery, why have you come here? And talking lightly of shooting down our children!'

The men looked at each other, exchanged foolish glances.

Kehar said: 'I give you my full guarantee that my boys will swoop like arrows on the treasure that you want robbed, and swoop back to their quiver, treasure in hand. There won't be so much as a scratch on the body of the man robbed.'

'Kehar Singhji, we've come to you precisely because of your reputation.'

'Look, this money will help with the food and upkeep of the men. I personally am in no need of money.'

'Try to understand our problem. Tell us the price of the kabutaras, not the price of renting them.'

'By price you mean death! You listen carefully. Our boys are not even to be injured. Got it?'

'If they are caught, who will they name? Us? The names of our fathers will become mud before ours. The least bit of carelessness and it'll be the jail for us.'

'How much do you want robbed?'

'Two lakhs.'

'Ten per cent ours. These boys have stomachs to fill too.'

'No, the terms will be the same.'

'Look, your condition comes into force only if they are caught, or will you be shooting them down anyway? I am telling you, even if they are caught, they won't talk, won't rat. Won't get into the newspapers. We'll give a little to everyone. Everyone will hide all they know. And the good work of finishing off scoundrels from the face of the earth will go on.'

Kadambai remembers—for all that Kehar Singh talked and harangued, he kept awake the whole night circling round like a bat. God knows what he thought, he simply put into hiding all the boys along with Bheekham and Gomta. He sent Mansaram home, locked up the theka, and went away himself too. Leaving, he said, 'Don't be distressed at this closure. We have to save our lives now. What kind of faith can you have in people who come looking for goons to rent? The bastards think their fathers' pride is worth more than the lives of our boys. If their fathers' pride is so dear to them let them live like decent folks. Must have money to live it up, and also keep alive the myth of family. These are the rulers of the world.'

Then he said, 'But, Mansa, whatever they were, they were honest. Honest because they were new to the job. What if they had killed without telling us? But I also do not understand why those ready for shooting down kabutaras couldn't kill the rich bastard themselves? And rob him at leisure?'

And he recalled an old incident when a son had wanted his father looted. Kehar said, 'Was it some such relationship which looks light compared to money?'

Kehar Singh didn't sleep for two nights. His eyes would droop and he would wake up with a start. The thought nagged him—these richies can do anything. What if they simply do away with the boys?

On the third night another worry came up. That if he wasn't present at the theka the boys he'd fed and nurtured would go thin without food. Wouldn't be able to work for months. Suppose somebody raided the theka while it was closed?

Kehar came back. And he said to Kadambai, 'There's something else we'll have to now arrange for.'

'What?'

'Start retaining Gorki, and Gomta's wife Machchla in the theka at daytime. Bheekham's wife Mundra comes along anyway for bringing in the liquor. If she stays on a bit longer what'll it matter? Kadambai, I have dealt with women for full six years, I haven't seen women like Machchla and Mundra. High cheekbones, pert nose, full lips. Their gaze kills.'

Kadambai burst out laughing. 'Kehar Singh, you proper badmash! Is it because of these two lassies that you're overflowing with sympathy for Bheekham and Gomta? You watch out, the boys will cut off your dick in sleep. Bachelor boy you've been till now, as a eunuch...'

'You needn't tell me, Kadam. They keep smiling at me, drowning in gratitude, but have I ever looked at them with *those eyes?* No, even though woman is the greatest weakness of man. Forget about all this Kadam. Listen to me. Our boys are not meant to be shot down by these richies. If they'd been in the army they'd have been heroes. But here…'

Kehar went quiet, drawing a deep breath.

CHANDRAKANTA

A Street in Srinagar

Translated from the Hindi by Manisha Chaudhry

Bapu had given him permission to go but he fell silent in the face of Mai's opposition. More than Rupa, Mai disapproved of Ratni, 'Such women in this neighbourhood...if you see their face in the morning you might have to fast in penance.'

Sansarchand tried to placate his wife, 'Bhagwanti! She is a woman who fasts and prays, she is religious and worships in the way she is supposed to. Why do you get upset with her for no reason...'

'Upset with her, indeed!' Arundhati reacted to praise for Ratni as if someone had touched her with a pair of hot tongs, 'I know what she is like! Please limit your admiration for her piety to her house. Don't talk about her over here! You ruin my day, I feel I will go up in smoke...'

Mai was angry with Ratni. If somebody aggravated her sore temper, the wart on her cheek that had two long hairs sprouting from it, quivered strangely and her face turned a fiery red.

Ratni was an extremely beautiful woman. The veteran of forty springs, her body was still shapely. She had light brown hair and her eyes held an enormous attraction. Her presence in the gali was a continuous challenge for the men. She carried herself with such haughty grandeur that people nearly bowed before her. What chance did poor Sansarchand have? No sooner did he hear Ratni approaching he was like Majnu-Farhad with eyes only for his beloved.

But for Arundhati, Ratni was a mere female and that too a widow. Such shamelessness in how she lifted her face to the men and laughed— hee-hee, thi-thi! Were these signs of respectability?

Sansarchand said to his wife, 'Fate has been really unkind to her.' She retorted, 'Her fate has turned her into a shameless hussy. If she had a husband, wouldn't he have held her by the hair and locked her up in the basement?' Whatever you might say, fate had been unkind to Ratni and she had kept her head held high.

Little Rupa was four when typhus struck and killed four members of the family. Rupa's grandmother, then her father and then two of her brothers were felled by the disease.

People from the gali shudder as they recall those times. Sansarchand says that the neighbourhood reeled under the furious onslaught of the disease. People would seal their eyes and ears and scuttle into their houses as soon as they heard that somebody had been struck down by the illness. How could anybody go to Ratni's house to help pick up the corpses? Nobody showed up until there were two deaths in the family. It was terribly contagious. She was a young woman then and covered her face with a ghoonghat. But when her husband's corpse lay unattended for twelve hours with not a neighbour in sight, this demure bahu ripped off her veil. She stepped out into her courtyard and screamed at the top of her voice—as if she were drunk, 'Respectable neighbours, I am calling the chamars for the last rites of my husband. Can you hear me, I'm letting you know so that you don't make it impossible for me to live here because your religion has been sullied.'

Four men from the chamar toli had actually come to take away the corpse of Ratni's husband. Ratni cast off her mourning and got them to clean and disinfect the house. She went to the municipal corporation office to inform them. They came to spray the area with disinfectant.

People were stunned. They had thought this woman would fall at their feet and implore them to act; at least they might have gone to the municipal office. But she who had been only seen occasionally, hidden behind a veil, shrinking and delicate, suddenly turned into a Chandi, the devouring goddess, who now sat astride their chests. Her neighbours were culpable, they had violated the code of neighbourly dharma, but it was the fear of death that had caused them to lapse from grace.

Ratni was faced with a tiny but difficult question in the form of little Rupa. Everything in her life was over; but she was like a determined small sunflower growing among the ruins of Ratni's world. She needed light and it was Ratni's dharma to ensure that she got it. Ratni defined dharma in her own way. When Avatara came on a clandestine visit to take lessons from Rupa, Ratni needled him sometimes, 'Ave, do you know the meaning of dharma?'

Avatara stared at her blankly with his mouth bunched up like a string purse. 'Now look here, Avatare, there is one religion that your Mai practises and another which your Chachi follows, can you see any difference between the two?'

Ratni Chachi would laugh as Avatara looked at Rupa di helplessly.

'You don't understand, do you?' Ratni Chachi continued to laugh without any reason.

'Oh, let it go, Ma!' Rupa di would remonstrate gently, 'Why do you say all this to him! Poor thing, he is so young...'

Poor little Avatara! He was a real runt even though he was in Class VI. He understood some things but did not understand many others. But he was always keen to learn. It was this curiosity that led him to peep into Ratni Chachi's house at midnight, or sometimes early in the morning. Their windows touched in any case. If you just went up on your toes you could see their kitchen. On the other side was the open courtyard with its screen with square frets and next to it was Ratni's bedroom.

Tempting aromas wafted across from Ratni Chachi's kitchen. One day Avatara asked her, 'Chachi, what do you cook everyday? I begin to feel hungry as soon as I smell something cooking in your kitchen.'

Ratni Chachi was overwhelmed by just a few words of praise. She immediately offered, 'Oh my little Krishna Kanhaiya, I'm cooking what Sudama brought along with him! You come over, I'll feed you with my own hands. Such delicious food that your mouth will water with its memory!'

Avatara could not restrain himself that day. When he was sure that Mai and Jawa Makhna were not looking, he went off to Chachi's house. Chachi put a bowl full of rice and hot kanul greens cooked with vari and spices in front of him. Avatara swallowed one mouthful and loved it. He said to her, 'Really Chachi! This is so tasty...'

'Come another day and I'll cook onions and potatoes for you. They will taste so good you will forget about meat and fish.'

Avatara went back home, his tongue tingling with new flavours. He went up the steps on bare feet. He was afraid of making any sound that might alert Mai to the fact that he had been to Ratni Chachi's house. He knew he would be scolded for nothing.

Mai was busy in the kitchen cooking shalgam-nadru and draining the starch from the rice but Jawa Bhaiya had been lying in wait for him.

He held Avatara by his ear and presented him before Mai, 'Here Mai, he's back from his little tryst with that woman—the kanjri.'

Jawa's eyes glowed red with anger and his voice shook. Avatara stared at Mai, stunned. He was shocked by Jawa's choice of words. But perhaps this was the right choice according to Mai because she did not rebuke him. Instead she nodded as if this was appropriate.

'And why did you go there? Tell me!' She shot at him threateningly.

'Oh, just like that, Mai,' muttered Avatara.

'What do you mean, "just like that"? You don't get food at home? Or have you developed a taste for onion and garlic?'

Scared, Avatara said truthfully, 'Ratni Chachi said she cooks what Sudama used to bring home. I was tempted to taste that. And she called me Krishna Kanhaiya...'

'Quiet!' Mai cut him short and Avatara held his tongue. 'Don't you tell me stories about that witch! Sudama's greens, Krishna Kanhaiya's devotee indeed! As if I don't know this sorceress! Heaven knows what potions she uses on children. She knows all kinds of charms and chants, I'm sure!

You, who haven't even lost your milk teeth. What chance do you have... even a learned man like your Bapu turns into a lamb...'

After this Mai twisted his ears twice and he had to rub his nose on the ground and repeat three times, 'I will never go to Ratni Chachi's house again, I will never go to Ratni Chachi's house again, I will never go to Ratni Chachi's house again.'

Somanatha and Mahmud

Mahmud's raid on the temple of Somanatha and the destruction of the idol has become an event of immense significance in the writing of Indian history for the last couple of centuries. According to some writers, it has been seminal to antagonistic Hindu-Muslim relations over the last thousand years. Yet a careful investigation of the representation of this event and related matters in various sources of this thousand-year period suggests that this conventional view is in itself a misrepresentation of the reading of the event in terms of Hindu-Muslim relations.

In 1026, Mahmud of Ghazni raided the temple of Somanatha and broke the idol. Reference is made to this in various sources, or reference is omitted where one expects to find it. Some of the references contradict each other. Some lead to our asking questions which do not conform to what we have accepted so far in terms of the meaning and the aftermath of the event. An event can get encrusted with interpretations from century to century and this changes the perception of the event. As historians, therefore, we have to be aware not just of the event and how we look upon it today, but also the ways in which the event was interpreted through the intervening centuries. An analysis of these sources and the priorities in explanation stem, of course, from the historian's interpretation.

I would like to place before you five representations of this and other events at Somanatha, keeping in mind the historical question of how Mahmud's raid was viewed. They cover a wide span and are major representations. The five are the Turko-Persian chronicles, Jaina texts of the period, Sanskrit inscriptions from Somanatha, the debate in the British House of Commons, and what is often described as a nationalist reading of the event.

Let me begin with a brief background to Somanatha itself. It is referred to in the Mahabharata as Prabhas, and although it had no temple until later, it was a place of pilgrimage.

As was common to many parts of the subcontinent there were a variety of religious sects established in the area—Buddhist, Jaina, Shaiva and Muslim. Some existed in succession and some conjointly. The Shaiva temple, known as the Somanatha temple at Prabhas, dates to about the ninth or tenth century CE. The Chaulukyas or Solankis were the ruling dynasty in Gujarat during the eleventh to thirteenth centuries. Kathiawar was administered by lesser rajas, some of whom were subordinates of the Chaulukyas.

Saurashtra was agriculturally fertile, but even more than that, its prosperity came from trade, particularly maritime trade. The port at Somanatha, known as Veraval, was one of the three major ports of Gujarat. During this period western India had a conspicuously wealthy trade with ports along the Arabian Peninsula and the Persian Gulf. The antecedents of this trade go back many centuries.

Arab raids on Sind were less indelible than the more permanent contacts based on trade. Arab traders and shippers settled along the west coast married locally and were ancestral to many communities existing to the present. Some Arabs took employment with local rulers and Rashtrakuta inscriptions speak of Tajika administrators and governors in the coastal areas. The counterparts to these Arab traders were Indian merchants based at Hormuz and at Ghazni, who, even after the eleventh century, are described as extremely prosperous.

The trade focused on the importing of horses from West Asia and to a lesser extent on wine, metal, textiles and spices. By far the most lucrative was the trade in horses. And in this funds from temples formed a sizable investment, according to some sources. Port towns such as Somanatha-Veraval and Cambay derived a handsome income from this trade, much of it doubtless being ploughed back to enlarge the profits. Apart from trade, another source of local income was the large sums of money collected in pilgrim taxes by the administration in Somanatha. This was a fairly common source of revenue for the same is mentioned in connection with the temple at Multan.

We are also told that the local rajas—the Chudasamas, Abhiras, Yadhavas and others—attacked the pilgrims and looted them of their donations intended for the Somanatha temple. In addition, there was heavy piracy in the coastal areas indulged in by the local Chavda rajas and a variety of sea brigands referred to as the Bawarij. As with many areas generating wealth in earlier times, this part of Gujarat was also subject to unrest and the Chaulukya administration spent much time and energy policing attacks on pilgrims and traders.

Despite all this, trade flourished. Gujarat in this period experienced what can perhaps be called a renaissance culture of the Jaina mercantile community. Rich merchant families were in political office, controlled state finances, were patrons of culture, were scholars of the highest order, were liberal donors to the Jaina sangha and builders of magnificent temples.

This is the backdrop, as it were, to the Somanatha temple which by many accounts suffered a raid by Mahmud in 1026. There is one sober, contemporary reference and this comes, not surprisingly, from Alberuni, a Central Asian scholar deeply interested in India, writing extensively on what he observed and learnt. He tells us that there was a stone fortress built about a hundred years before Mahmud's raid within which the lingam was located, presumably to safeguard the wealth of the temple. The idol was especially venerated by sailors and traders, not surprising considering the importance of the port at Veraval, trading as far as Zanzibar and China. He comments in a general way on the economic devastation caused by the many raids of Mahmud. Alberuni also mentions that Durlabha of Multan, presumably a mathematician, used a roundabout way involving various eras to compute the year of the raid on Somanatha as Shaka 947 (equivalent to 1025-26 CE). The raid therefore was known to local sources.

Not unexpectedly, the Turko-Persian chronicles indulge in elaborate myth-making around the event, some of which I shall now relate. A major poet of the eastern Islamic world, Farrukhi Sistani, who claims that he accompanied Mahmud to Somanatha, provides a fascinating explanation for the breaking of the idol. This explanation has been largely dismissed by modern historians as too fanciful, but it has a significance for the assessment of iconoclasm. According to him, the idol was not of a Hindu deity but of a pre-Islamic Arabian goddess. He tells us that the name Somnat (as it was often written in Persian) is actually Su-manat, the place of Manat. We know from the Koran that Lat, Uzza and Manat were the three pre-Islamic goddesses widely worshipped, and the destruction of their shrines and images, it was said, had been ordered by the Prophet Mohammad. Two were destroyed, but Manat was believed to have been secreted away to Gujarat and installed in a place of worship. According to some descriptions, Manat was an aniconic block of black stone, so the form could be similar to a lingam. This story hovers over many of the Turko-Persian accounts, some taking it seriously, others being less emphatic and insisting instead that the icon was of a Hindu deity.

The identification of the Somanatha idol with that of Manat has little historical credibility. There is no evidence to suggest that the temple housed an image of Manat. Nevertheless, the story is significant to the reconstruction of the aftermath of the event since it is closely tied to the kind of legitimation which was being projected for Mahmud.

The link with Manat added to the acclaim for Mahmud. Not only was he the prize iconoclast in breaking Hindu idols, but in destroying Manat he had carried out what were said to be the very orders of the Prophet. He was therefore doubly a champion of Islam. Other temples were raided by him and their idols broken, but Somanatha receives special attention in all the accounts of his activities. Writing of his victories to the caliphate, Mahmud presents them as major accomplishments in the cause of Islam. And not surprisingly, Mahmud becomes the recipient of grandiose titles. This establishes his legitimacy in the politics of the Islamic world, a dimension which is overlooked by those who see his activities only in the context of northern India.

But his legitimacy also derives from the fact that he was a Sunni and he attacked Isma'ilis and Shias whom the Sunnis regarded as heretics.

It was ironic that the Isma'ilis attacked the temple of Multan and were, in turn, attacked by Mahmud in the eleventh century and their mosque was shut down. The fear of the heretic was due to the popularity of heresies against orthodox Islam and political hostility to the caliphate in the previous couple of centuries, none of which would be surprising given that Islam in these areas was a relatively new religion.

Mahmud is said to have desecrated their places of worship at Multan and Mansura. His claims to having killed 50,000 kafirs (infidels) is matched by similar claims to his having killed 50,000 Muslim heretics. The figure appears to be notional. Mahmud's attacks on the Hindus and on the Shias and Isma'ilis was a religious crusade against the infidel and the heretic.

But interestingly, there were also the places and peoples involved in the highly profitable horse trade with the Arabs and the Gulf. Both the Muslim heretics of Multan and the Hindu traders of Somanatha had substantial commercial investments. Is it possible then that Mahmud, in addition to religious iconoclasm, was also trying to terminate the import of horses into India via Sind and Gujarat? This would have curtailed the Arab monopoly over the trade. Given the fact that there was a competitive horse trade with Afghanistan through northwestern India, which was crucial to the wealth of the state of Ghazni, Mahmud may well have been combining iconoclasm with trying to obtain a commercial advantage.

In the subsequent and multiple accounts—and there are many in each century—the contradictions and exaggerations increase. There is no agreement on the form of the image. Some say that it is a lingam, others reverse this and describe it as anthropomorphic—a human form. But even with this there is no consistency as to whether it is a female Manat or a male Shiva. There seems to have been almost a lingering wish that it might be Manat. Was the icon, if identified with Manat, more important perhaps to Muslim sentiment?

SHAMA FUTEHALLY

Tara Lane

'Salaam, Tahera, salaam. A holiday from school, eh? Or have you run away? Why are you going to the factory? Your old uncle dares to ask.'

'No real reason,' I said.

'Come, come, tell me. Don't be shy. Do you need something? We will get it together. What is your uncle for?' And he turned me back.

'Do you need cash or some such thing?' he said, adult to adult.

'No, no!' Even a brief meeting with my uncle seemed to take me outside the world I knew. 'I only need tracing paper. For my homework.'

'Is that all?' he said. 'And such a fuss! You are just like my revered brother, your father.'

He took me to a large room in the basement which I had never seen before. As typists and draughtsmen and office-boys studiously kept their eyes averted, he opened a cupboard fitted into a far wall. And there I saw row upon row of foolscap paper, tracing paper, typing paper, copy paper, carbon paper, pencil rubbers, ink rubbers, paint rubbers, paper clips, drawing-pins, tackboard pins, pens, ball-pens, sketch-pens, signature pens. I looked up at my uncle with a faint fear that my parents would somehow not like it.

'How many sheets can I have?' I said.

He only smiled.

So I took four instead of two. As he was closing the cupboard he said, 'Do you want anything else?'

There were sketch-pens and tracing-pens as well, and those American magic markers which only very few of my classmates had.

'Can I really take them, Imran Chacha?' I said.

'No one will say anything', he smiled.

'But is it...' I was a little shy of asking my question, which was, 'Is it right?' So I said instead, 'To whom does it belong?'

'My god!' Imran Chacha guffawed. 'The whole damn thing belongs to all of us!'

This reassured me much more than hearing that no one would say anything; and so, with a properly clear conscience, but very aware of the studiously silent typists, I took two sketch-pens and went home.

That summer even water was being fetched from the factory. The rains had failed; it was nearly July, and in place of the thunderstorm which should announce the monsoon there was only an evil yellow evening when dust, not rain, swirled into the house. The well in our backyard was dry;

you could see the glistening black rocks right at the bottom, and Ayah told us you would soon be able to see the tortoise as big as a waterpot, which lived inside the well. Soon we grew used to seeing our mali moving between the factory and the house with a bucket in either hand, and to our great delight the bathwater was restricted to half a bucket per person.

'Oy, you grandfather of malis!' I heard Sutli shouting one day in the backyard. 'Do you go to sleep there in the factory? Here are all my clothes waiting to be washed for the last hour. And where are you?'

'What to do?' said the mali. 'Those women there don't let me get to the pump. Fill two small buckets, and they start grumbling. Fight, fight, that's all they do.'

'Grumbling?' Were we taking away someone else's water, then? I had assumed that the buckets were only part of the smooth flow from the factory. Again I felt a little worm pricking its way across my mind. I despaired of this worm—whatever you did it was there—crawling or turning or still, but it was there. And then I had to do something drastic to make it go.

'Samuel?' I said to him timidly that evening. 'Is it wrong to get water from the factory?'

'Eh?' Samuel, wiping the windscreen of the Ambassador, looked bewildered as he often did at my questions.

'Is it wrong to get water from the factory pump?'

'Why, little one! Do you want to stop having even half a bath?'

'But there isn't enough water for the people at the factory.'

'What to do?' said Samuel. 'This son-of-a-gun rain is late by a month. It is another gorement, this rain.'

'The people in the factory don't like it.'

'They don't like anything,' said Samuel.

'The pump is for them, after all,' I said, despairingly. Samuel was forever missing the point.

'Good-for-nothings,' said Samuel. 'Who do they think they are? Who put in the pump if not your father? Just trouble makers, the whole lot of them. I tell you, when that Irshadullah or anyone says anything to me, I just turn around and...'

But Samuel had answered my question, just as Imran Chacha had in the office, and in a flood of relief I had stopped listening. My father could be trusted. As I moved away from Samuel I felt a deep, peaceful gratitude that he could, after all, always be trusted. When I saw the children in the workers' slum and asked troubled questions, I was told that my father was having swings put up for them, or that there was going to be a Sports Day at the factory, and for whom was that if not for them, or that he had instituted a scholarship for any child who wanted to study. If Ayah told me that her hut leaked and I mentioned this cautiously to my parents, I would learn that my father had already given her the asbestos to repair it. It was surprising, really, considering how entirely he could be trusted, that I was so very nervous of our being collectively and unwittingly in the wrong. Perhaps I felt an unconscious fear because the source of all good seemed to be so entirely my father; Mushtaq saab has put up tube-lights in the slum; Mushtaq saab has ordered that an extra bore-well be dug. It would have been reassuring to learn that other people were capable of putting up lights; or rather, that a whole lot of people did what they were supposed to do, whether it was putting up lights or anything else.

In the meantime the drought continued. Ayah told us exciting and terrible stories about the drought in her village. If our parents were out in the evening, she would get us ready for bed and then settle down on the mat nearby. 'Sit down', she would say, 'I will tell you such a story as you have never heard.' She crossed her legs comfortably. 'When I was small like you there was just such a drought. No water in the river. No water in the wells. They were dry, like this mat.' Ayah thumped the mat impressively. 'Every day we had only so much water to drink,' holding up two fingers. 'Then,' said Ayah, taking her time, 'my cousin-brother began to die of thirst. He was seven years old. How many?' said Ayah sternly.

'Seven,' we breathed.

'Seven. And everyone thought, this time god will surely take him away. For five days his mother did not eat. Then one day the gorement sent a tanker of water to the village. As soon as he heard it coming he jumped up from the mat and drank three drums full. And then,' said Ayah solemnly, 'there was so much water in his stomach that he never drank another drop for the rest of his life. Such are the miracles of god,' said Ayah, crossing herself reverently. And we went bewildered to bed.

When the drought got worse Pandit Nehru came to Bombay. We heard the grown-ups talking about it and learnt that we would be taken to see him. I was unsure exactly what he would be like—whether he would be the white-clad figure who featured in the newspapers or a 'Panditji' with a dhoti and a shaven head.

'Why is he coming?' I asked.

'He is going to the villages,' said my mother. 'The villagers are rioting for water, and he has to tell them to be patient, and allow the government to help.'

And on the appointed day, dressed in our best by Ayah, we squeezed into the Ambassador to go to Shivaji Park. It was a blazing afternoon;

shimmering points in the tar were picked up and spread rainbow-thin by the sun. Tara Lane was deserted, and the Ambassador grunted its way to the main road in solitary state.

Shivaji Park was a sea of people. The orange and green of the Congress flag was everywhere; paper flags and Congress stickers were being handed to all comers; croaky loudspeakers were being tested. 'Hullo, hullo,' they called from time to time. In the parking area, large aggrieved Ambassadors like ours glowered at each other and honked their horns. Then a shining purple Ambassador came face to face with us and refused to move. We could go neither to the left nor right—Ambassadors stood everywhere. On such occasions Samuel became the upholder of the family's honour. He raised himself higher in the driving seat.

'Eh, you! Does your father own the road?'

But did the purple Ambassador not have an honour of its own? Immediately a head shot out of a window to defend it.

'Yes he does. Go and tell him.' And there was laughter from within the purple Ambassador. More heads appeared at the window. One of them, wearing dark glasses, began to hum a film song. Delighted urchins collected around us. The policeman at the corner came interestedly to watch.

'Please move,' said my father, quietly. And there was a sudden embarrassed look on the faces in the Ambassador; as though they had been hit below the belt. The Ambassador backed quietly away.

MRINAL PANDE

Bibbo

Translated from the Hindi by the author

First, the luggage arrived. Several truckloads of it, piled high. Then came the flowerpots, all aglow with exotic flowers and leafy greens, then the dog, then the cockatoo in a gilded cage, then came those two—the husband and the wife. Last of all came Bibbo.

The husband was a tall and genial fellow, friendly, youthful and easy-going. His beautifully spun woollen kurta and Aligarhi pyjamas sat on his athletic frame with a feudal carelessness. Yes, these two did not 'wear' their clothes as the fat and paunchy offspring of the nouveau riche lalas in our small town did. Their priceless robes 'sat' on their graceful forms, as they do upon those priceless statues in ancient temples. The husband might not have a princely angavastram upon his shoulders, yet such was his presence, that as he stretched out his long aristocratic arms in a telling gesture, you could almost see the folds of the fabric rippling behind him rhythmically.

The pretty wife was diminutive, fragile and doll-like. And in spite of her severe bun, her gold-rimmed granny glasses and brows plucked into thin supercilious arches, she had a girlish air about her. Her jaw was square and had a set to it, which bespoke centuries of feudal authority. Her voice was soft and polite though and flavoured with gentle English sibilants, with ever such cute flecks of a darling ethnic Punjabi accent. She spoke in short crisp sentences that curled at the edges with a musical lilt, and her hands, those little doll's hands, fluttered around in attractive ethnic mudras as she spoke. Her fingers were short, plump and square-tipped.

Bibbo was different. She had come, or been brought along as a personal maid for the little doll-wife. Her physique matched her name. Her well-rounded body had the typical Punjabi fullness of a very satisfying sort. Dressed usually in her mistress's cast-offs from yesteryears of fashion, she nevertheless lent a personal touch to each garment. She had slashed the necks of all the kurtas into deep V-shapes, wherein her well-moulded cleavage could be seen trembling like two soft and fragrant shapes of jello. Her waist was broad, her hips full, firm, and somewhat protruding. Her eyes were like two large vacant holes in an expressionless face. But her gait was another matter. Strangely hypnotic, it was the unbalanced gait of a young wheat-eating peasant, drunk with the nectar of a short-lived youth. She teetered from side to side when she walked, and made each viewer feel that she would perhaps not be able to walk without his support. Faces turned her way automatically as she passed, holding wonder like a cup, and arms ached with a desire to touch her, to support those thighs.

Since all the bathrooms in the house had marble floors, Bibbo did her laundry outside, at the little tap at the corner of the lawn. She first hung her dupatta upon the shrubs, hitched her salwar up, pushed her sleeves up to her elbows, and set about battering the clothes with the wooden mallet, slowly, but with a careless regularity. As soon as the sound began, all the servants from the surrounding houses would abandon the pots and pans upon the gas fire, and huddle around the hedges drooling and whining gleefully. She never exchanged either a look or a word with any of them. After she had finished the laundry, she would extend a muscular arm and pick up the dupatta from the shrub, lift the bucket with its load of well-wrung clothes and walk back into the house, teetering drunkenly. Thereafter the colony felt those pendulous buttocks undulating all afternoon long.

Every day the husband would leave for work in his car, and the wife would see him to the door. They kissed like the English people do when they bid goodbyes, and then the wife would go in, calling out to Bibbo in her soft lisp. At exactly half past eleven, Bibbo would come out with an attractive plastic shopping bag, and go waddling towards the market place. As soon as Ramanaresh, the launderer, raised the volume of his Vividh Bharati songs, one knew she was descending the slope around the corner. Then the laughter at Chaurasia Pan House would grow suddenly loud, little plastic combs emerged out of oily hip pockets, and hair was puffed upon foreheads like cock's combs.

Slowly the master and the mistress began to make friends locally. This was the poshest colony in the town, and all the inhabitants of the area were sons or grandsons, or great-grandsons of big shots. Going to work was a sort of hobby for them. They had so much that they had no need to say how much they had. These bungalows had their own world, their own parties and picnics, their special sly and subtle in-jokes. People here were allergic to anything new or glittering. Inside the long cool living rooms within these bungalows, old priceless antiques, slightly faded velvet upholstered furniture, and gee-gaws had lain around undisturbed for generations. The refrigerators in these houses were in the kitchens or pantries, and the music systems were hidden in dens within. Men and women who lived here ate, walked and talked with a somnolent lassitude that takes everything for granted. A simplicity of soul that comes straight out of fairy tales, and belongs to princes and princesses alone.

The wife often told her friends in her simple girlish tones how Bibbo was a beautiful experiment in democratic relationships for them. If you treat servants like humans, there is no reason why they would not work beautifully for you like humans. After all, they too have their vibes, their ambiences, don't they?

Bibbo ate what they ate. Butter, eggs, fruits, milk, cheese, everything. Each month she was given a new set of cast-offs, each fortnight she was given a good brand-name soap, and occasionally half a bottle of shampoo and a can of talcum powder were also made available to her. 'What she does with them is her own headache. We want to treat her on a beautiful human level. We communicate, not as master to servant, but as one human to another.' The mistress would soften her already soft tones some more, and call out musically, 'Bibbo, may we have two nimbu panis, please!' At this, Bibbo Rani would emerge with her expressionless mien, waddling her favourite waddle, like a sexy robot, holding a heavy family silver salver, 'Nimbu pani with salt or sugar?' Her brassy voice like her body, was gutter bred, but also strangely inviting in its total lack of a cultivated grace. The mistress would immediately apologize, and ask the guests what they would like to have. She herself had salt, but sugar was no problem! The order would be duly given and Bibbo rani would waddle back leaving the little tribal bells jangling upon the pelmets.

At that point, once the husband and wife told their friends that they had had Bibbo trained at a beautician's so that she may master an art... She did not want to learn typing or go in for those nice adult-education courses—but now she gave such excellent facials that your face just glowed. 'See, how well she defuzzes my arms?' So saying the doll-wife would extend her smooth fair arms towards the audience.

'Does she give facials only to women?'

'No, no!'

'Do women have the sole right to a glowing face?'

'Well, if you like, you too...'

Ha, ha, ha—jokes become leery—you first, no, no you! Then a man delightfully pierced through with jokes with double meaning followed Bibbo into her little room, giggling self-consciously. After half an hour he emerged with his face all flushed and glowing, 'Well, what do you know, the fatso does have magic hands!'

'This is what really amazes me,' the doll-wife would chirp. 'When she is working in the house, she is all thumbs. Honestly, if we didn't have the cook, we'd probably never sit down for a proper meal in this house. I can't even count how many cups and glasses she smashes in a week, but yes, she's perfect in the art of giving facials.'

'Well, each to her kind of art, ha, ha, ha.'

Then suddenly the numbers of people dropping by casually at their house began to grow. As it is, the men in this area were not the nine-to-five types. The offices they worked in belonged to them as also the buildings which housed half the offices in town. Often now when the husband came home for lunch, the wife would be muttering grumpily that lunch was half-cooked and Bibbo was again giving a facial to someone.

Well, things were rather delicate at this point, since it was a neighbourhood matter. After all, the beautiful speeches they had made about democratizing the lumpen, how could they retract their words and begin yelling at Bibbo and her clients like those desi cheapies who live in janta colonies? Goodness is its own whip!

Translated from the Punjabi by the poet

The Black Woman

The dreams of a black woman
are very fair
and her truth pitch dark
She is born with a pain
to which no colour
can be assigned
It borrows the colour of water
To fill her eyes
to swim in the red wounds
of her dark body
She suppresses on her lips
the silent screams of
every dark person and turns
darker still
The dreams of a black woman
fly away like white birds
to pick bits of moonlight
and scatter them in her lap
A black woman longs for
a fair child...

Wicked Woman

If you come to my city
you are bound to find
my name in the roster
of wicked women
I have all that it takes
to be as wicked
as they come
I have a goblet
brimming over
in my hand
My laughter is known
for its abandon
Flames find a home

in my mouth
My heart beats and
every nerve does
a little dance
The road is at my feet
And just the sky above
I have the courage to bear
and express myself without fear.

Seeing like a Feminist

Ifi Amadiume's work on the Igbo of Nigeria, too, establishes that, in pre-colonial Igbo society, daughters could assume male roles and become sons, and wealthy women could obtain 'wives'. The linguistic system of the Igbo had few gender distinctions, and terms for roles such as 'head of household' were un-gendered, while the 'master' or 'husband' role did not necessitate a male classification. Amadiume terms this 'gender flexibility'. However, we can go further with the framework that Oyewumi provides us, for it enables us to radically interrogate whether the category of 'gender' existed in any recognizable way in pre-colonial Igbo society. Oyewumi insists that the African ways of understanding the world were radically different from the Western, but have been continually translated, even by African scholars, into Western categories and languages already loaded with gendered and patriarchal assumptions. Was 'gender', then, invented in Africa through the processes by which colonial interventions made African societies legible to Europe in its own terms (Amadiume 1987)?

Similarly, in Native American culture, before the Europeans came to the Americas, 'two-spirit' referred to people who were considered gifted because they carried two spirits, male and female. It is told in ancient artefacts that women engaged in tribal warfare and married other women, and there were men who married other men. These individuals were looked upon as a third and a fourth gender, and in almost all cultures they were honoured and revered. Two-spirit people were often the visionaries, the healers, the medicine people, the nannies of orphans, the care-givers. This type of identity has been documented in over 155 tribes across Native North America (Roscoe 1988).

Consider now the poets of the Bhakti movement in the land mass we now call India—this movement originated in the southern part, in the Tamil region in the sixth century CE and flourished in the north from the fifteenth to the seventeenth centuries. These mystics expressed a kind of desire for god that travels through the body and reconfigures it. Their desire was to attain the loss of maleness as power and the loss of femaleness as sexualized powerlessness. A. K. Ramanujan suggests that 'the lines between male and female are continuously crossed and recrossed' in the lives of the Bhakti saints. They demystified the body and sexuality by dismantling the codes and conventions that 'sex' the body. Bhakti saints turned away from sex in this world—not from fear or hatred of sexuality, but because their sexual passion was invested entirely and in a disembodied manner, in the chosen deity as lover.

A tenth-century devotee of Shiva, Devara Dasimayya, wrote:

If they see breasts and long hair coming,
They call it woman,
If beard and whiskers
They call it man.
But look, the self that hovers in between
Is neither man nor woman...

Ramanujan points out that when women saints like Lal Ded of Kashmir and Akka Mahadevi of Karnataka threw away their clothes, they were making us see that 'modesty'—which is invested in hiding the body with clothes—is 'a way of resisting and enhancing sexual curiosity, not of curbing it. It is this paradox that is exposed when clothes are thrown away. By exposing the difference between male and female, by becoming indifferent to that difference, [they are] liberated from it.'

This is how the female saint Akka Mahadevi, who clothed herself only in her own long hair, perceives the body:

You can confiscate
Money in hand;
Can you confiscate
the body's glory?
Or peel away every strip
you wear,
but can you peel
the Nothing, the Nakedness
that covers and veils?

Clearly even by the time of the Bhakti movement, normative notions of masculinity/femininity and appropriate/ inappropriate sex had come into being, against which the Bhakti saints were in rebellion. But considerable fluidity still existed even till the mid- to late-nineteenth century, when the processes of colonial modernity, in alliance with the modernizing nationalist elite began the process of disciplining it.

WOULD YOU PASS A GENDER TEST?
'Gender verification' tests for the Olympic Games were suspended in 2000 after enough evidence had emerged that 'atypical chromosomal variations' are not atypical at all, but rather, so common that it is impossible to judge 'femininity' and 'masculinity' on the basis of chromosomal pattern alone. Maleness and femaleness are not only culturally different, they are

not even biologically stable features at all times.

But in sports, as in all other spheres of life, despite evidence to the contrary, it continues to be assumed that every human being can be assigned to one of two sex categories. Thus, the Olympic Committee retained a policy of 'suspicion based testing' on a case-by-case basis, as did other sports bodies. This policy at different times resulted in two women athletes—South African Caster Semenya and Indian Santhi Soundarajan— being disqualified after winning their events, for failing 'gender tests'. Their experiences raise a host of questions about this biological body that is considered to be simply available in nature.

Three sets of characteristics are held to determine sexual identity:

a) genetic—the XX female and XY male chromosomal pattern;
b) hormonal—estrogen (female), androgen/testosterone (male); and
c) genital—the visible physical characteristics of penis/vagina.

However, feminist scholars of science studies have directed our attention to developments in biology that show that the three are not necessarily linked. Thus, if a body has female genitals it is not necessarily the case that it would have preponderantly female chromosomes and female hormones. Moreover, sex chromosomes themselves often defy the pattern of XX (women) and XY (men) and have been known to exhibit other patterns, such as XO (females with only one X chromosome), XXY, XYY, XXX, or a 'mosaic condition', in which different cells in the same individual's body have different sex chromosomes (Buzuvis 2010).

Most bodies (including yours and mine) marked male and female in this world would not pass 'gender tests' if the perfect congruence of these three factors were being examined. The point is that in everyday life, gender tests are not routine because once a sex has been assigned at birth, one lives one's life accordingly.

It is mainly in sex-segregated activities like competitive sports that the question arises, and only for women, because it is assumed that having male characteristics is an advantage in physical activities. Thus, 'real' women would face the unfair advantages that 'not women' have on the field. Of course, women athletes who are disqualified for some chromosomal, hormonal or physical variation that casts doubt on their 'femaleness', do not get categorized as 'men'. They are still excluded from men's sports events and professions reserved for men.

At least two questions arise here. First, how fair are competitive events that assume male bodies to be the norm, so that to have male features is an advantage? This only reflects the general understanding that any quality associated with men is superior and must set the norm for all humanity.

In whichever ways women are different, their difference is considered to be an *inferior* difference, not *just* a difference, or a *superior* difference.

But the second more fundamental question here arises from the fact that not all natural advantages are considered illegitimate in sports. For instance, height in basketball is an accepted natural advantage, while American Olympian swimmer Michael Phelps's particular body proportions that enable him to cut through water more easily than 'normal' men may, in fact, be a disease called Marfan Syndrome. Different ethnic groups have different physical characteristics, such as height and build. The point is, really, that competitive sport does not sort out competitors on the basis of comparable physical features and athletic ability—there is no level playing field. Men of different physical attributes, levels of training and differential natural advantages such as height and strength, compete against one another, as do women. Is it not important to ask why the only standard of difference applied is that of an assumed gender bipolarity? To put it in the striking words of one scholar:

Saying that no one can use natural advantage is antithetical to sport. The average individual does not become a world-class or Olympic athlete... [Those who excel in sport have genetically acquired physiological advantages whose potential has been realized fortuitously through cultural and environmental factors]. Yet, for conditions other than those related to sex, such variation is not challenged as beyond the bounds of fair play (Buzuvis 2010).

Consider an intriguing story from the war zone of the sports field. In the 1936 Olympics, Polish sprinter Stella Walsh, known as the fastest woman in the world, was beaten by American Helen Stephens, who set a world record. After the race, a Polish journalist protested that no real woman could run so fast, and Olympic officials performed a 'sex test' on Helen, in which it was established that she was a woman. Forty-four years later, Stella Walsh, who had become an American citizen, was shot to death in a parking lot. The autopsy of her body revealed that Stella, who had run slower than Helen, had in fact 'been a man' (Boylan 2008). Another strange story from the same Berlin Olympics—twenty years afterwards, a Hitler Youth member who had competed as a woman and ranked fourth in the women's high jump event, confessed he was a man who had been forced by the Nazis to compete as a woman. This 'real man' came fourth, behind three women (Buzuvis 2010).

Battles

This section represents two strands of conflict: one refers to political movements or battles against an oppressive administration; the other strand includes texts that reflect on violence against women. I had initially thought to treat the two as separate themes but how does one ignore the fact that much of the violence visited upon women is not in retaliation to their struggle for gender equality but as punishment for activism linked to land, water, forests?

Though the battles women fight can be bloody, the violence they face is most insidious when it takes the shape of ingrained fear, economic deprivation, religious constraints, and marginalization in public life. I have attempted to organize the section as a web of connections between struggles violent and non-violent. Starting with fantasy, we have a cheeky yet direct challenge to patriarchy from Rokeya Sakhawat Hossain in 'Sultana's Dream', which sits quite well beside K. Saraswathi Amma's *A World Without Men*. Sarojini Naidu is well known for writing romantic poems but the extract included here is from a speech that was really a battle cry for equal citizenship, delicately positioned at a moment in Indian history when women's participation in the freedom movement was critical.

Easterine Kire's account of four generations of a family in Nagaland describes the political bungling that followed India's independence and the violence that followed. The extract from *Bitter Wormwood* captures the relatively innocent early days that ended soon after Gandhi's assassination. Temsula Ao in her story from *These Hills Called Home* writes about the tragedy that unfolded after armed forces were deployed in northeastern states to deal with political disagreements.

The extract from Qurratulain Hyder's *Fireflies in the Mist* describes the shadowy resistance of students plotting against British rulers. The same chord, student politics, is touched upon by Bani Basu in *The Enemy Within* as she describes how the 'Naxalbari' generation turned towards armed revolution in Bengal. Joya Mitra was one of these young women and her memoir *Killing Days* is a gripping account of her years in prison. It paints a heartbreaking picture of women on the fringes of society, broken until they can be broken no more. The extract there also offers a dash of humour through the prison authorities' fear of books. It is both ironic and the best testimonial a writer can hope for—that their work is both useful and powerful.

Amrita Pritam's iconic poem addressing Waris Shah describes the suffering of Punjabi women during Partition in 1947. Urvashi Butalia's

The Other Side of Silence documents them too, but in the extract reproduced here, she describes an attempt to seek closure or reconciliation. Jyotirmoyee Devi's novel *The River Churning* describes Bengali women's struggle to be accepted by their own families after having survived communal violence.

Aruna's Story by Pinki Virani is an investigator's look at the aftermath of a brutal rape, attendant with all the horrors—the violence itself, family apathy, and laws that are loaded against women. The extract from Arundhati Roy's *The God of Small Things* describes the harassment women face, even at the hands of those who are assigned to protect them.

Some people say that all stories can be found within the Mahabharata. The story of oppression, especially of forest-dwelling tribes, is certainly part of the epic, and 'The Palace of Maya' from Irawati Karve's *Yuganta* describes a genocide in the context of Aryans and Adivasis. It is an important reminder of the roots of the conflict, and it sits well beside Anita Agnihotri's *Forest Interludes*. Agnihotri writes of the hardships endured by tribal communities, and the power (or powerlessness) of smaller cogs in the development machinery.

Rajni Bakshi, in *Bapu Kuti*, talks about a different sort of development carried on by post-independence Gandhians. The book is as much about science and architecture as about pro-worker ideologies. It describes small, peaceful revolutions in places where oppression has deep roots, and is a wonderful counterview to the militant revolutions unfolding elsewhere.

ROKEYA SAKHAWAT HOSSAIN

Sultana's Dream

One evening I was lounging in an easy chair in my bedroom and thinking lazily of the condition of Indian womanhood. I am not sure whether I dozed off or not. But, as far as I remember, I was wide awake. I saw the moonlit sky sparkling with thousands of diamond-like stars, very distinctly.

All of a sudden a lady stood before me; how she came in, I do not know. I took her for my friend, Sister Sara.

'Good morning,' said Sister Sara. I smiled inwardly as I knew it was not morning, but starry night. However, I replied, 'How do you do?'

'I am all right, thank you. Will you please come out and have a look at our garden?'

I looked again at the moon through the open window, and thought there was no harm in going out at that time. The men-servants outside were fast asleep just then, and I could have a pleasant walk with Sister Sara.

I used to have my walks with Sister Sara when we were at Darjeeling. Many a time did we walk hand in hand and talk light-heartedly in the Botanical Gardens there. I fancied Sister Sara had probably come to take me to some such garden and I readily accepted her offer and went out with her.

When walking I found to my surprise that it was a fine morning. The town was fully awake and the streets alive with bustling crowds. I was feeling very shy, thinking I was walking in the street in broad daylight, but there was not a single man visible.

Some of the passersby made jokes at me. Though I could not understand their language, yet I felt sure they were joking. I asked my friend, 'What do they say?'

'The women say that you look very mannish.'

'Mannish?' said I, 'what do they mean by that?'

'They mean that you are shy and timid like men.'

'Shy and timid like men?' It was really a joke. I became very nervous when I found that my companion was not Sister Sara, but a stranger. Oh, what a fool I had been to mistake this lady for my dear old friend, Sister Sara.

She felt my fingers tremble in her hand, as we were walking hand in hand.

'What is the matter, dear?' she said affectionately.

'I feel somewhat awkward,' I said rather apologetically, 'as being a purdahnashin woman I am not accustomed to walking about unveiled.'

'You need not be afraid of coming across a man here. This is Ladyland, free from sin and harm. Virtue herself reigns here.'

By and by I was enjoying the scenery. Really it was very grand. I mistook a patch of green grass for a velvet cushion. Feeling as if I was walking on a soft carpet, I looked down and found the path covered with moss and flowers.

'How nice it is,' said I.

'Do you like it?' asked Sister Sara. (I continued calling her 'Sister Sara' and she kept calling me by my name.)

'Yes, very much; but I do not like to tread on the tender and sweet flowers.'

'Never mind, dear Sultana. Your treading will not harm them; they are street flowers.'

'The whole place looks like a garden,' said I admiringly. 'You have arranged every plant so skilfully.'

'Your Calcutta could become a nicer garden than this if only your countrymen wanted to make it so.'

'They would think it useless to give so much attention to horticulture, while they have so many other things to do.'

'They could not find a better excuse,' said she with smile.

I became very curious to know where the men were. I met more than a hundred women while walking there, but not a single man.

'Where are the men?' I asked her.

'In their proper places, where they ought to be.'

'Pray let me know what you mean by "their proper places".'

'Oh, I see my mistake, you cannot know our customs, as you have never been here before. We shut our men indoors.'

'Just as we are kept in the zenana?'

'Exactly so.'

'How funny.' I burst into a laugh. Sister Sara laughed too.

'But dear Sultana, how unfair it is to shut in the harmless women and let loose the men.'

'Why? It is not safe for us to come out of the zenana, as we are naturally weak.'

'Yes, it is not safe so long as there are men about on the streets, nor is it so when a wild animal enters a marketplace.'

'Of course not.'

'Suppose some lunatics escape from the asylum and begin to do all sorts of mischief to men, horses and other creatures. In that case what will your countrymen do?'

'They will try to capture them and put them back in their asylum.'

'Thank you! And you do not think it wise to keep sane people inside an asylum and let loose the insane?'

'Of course not!' said I, laughing lightly.

'As a matter of fact, in your country this very thing is done! Men, who do or at least are capable of doing no end of mischief, are let loose and the innocent women are shut up in the zenana! How can you trust those untrained men out of doors?'

'We have no hand or voice in the management of our social affairs. In India man is lord and master. He has taken to himself all powers and privileges and shut up the women in the zenana.'

'Why do you allow yourselves to be shut up?'

'Because it cannot be helped, as they are stronger than women.'

'A lion is stronger than a man, but it does not enable him to dominate the human race. You have neglected the duty you owe to yourselves and you have lost your natural rights by shutting your eyes to your own interests.'

'But, my dear sister Sara, if we do everything by ourselves, what will the men do then?'

'They should not do anything, excuse me; they are fit for nothing. Only catch them and put them into the zenana.'

'But would it be very easy to catch and put them inside the four walls?' said I. 'And even if this were done, would all their business, political and commercial, also go with them into the zenana?'

Sister Sara made no reply. She only smiled sweetly. Perhaps she thought it useless to argue with one who was no better than a frog in a well.

K. SARASWATHI AMMA

A World Without Men

Translated from the Malayalam by Dr Lakshmi Devi Menon

If after reading the title 'A World without Men', you are reminded of the titles of some poems you learnt in primary school, it is only natural. I mean, titles like 'A Time without Yama', 'An Earth without Air'. Just because I mention this, it doesn't mean I am going to establish that man is cruel like Yama or that he is insignificant like the breeze; don't take up cudgels against me thinking so. But I have no arguments with those who have such an opinion based on their own experience.

Can there be a time without Yama? If there is no air, what will be the state of the earth? Similarly, is it likely that there can be a world without men? A great man has said that children are the fragrant flowers in the garden of life; another has said that a world without women is like a desert without a garden. (Though the second mentioned has no other claim to greatness, he deserves such a position for this single opinion.)

In continuation of the two remarks that children are flowers and that women are gardens, do you know what I feel like saying about men? Not that they are the guards of the garden, but that they are the shady trees in the life's journey of the above mentioned two groups. That is my well-thought-out opinion. What do you say? Do you accept it? Will you kindly give me a respectable place among the great luminaries? Or do you have any objection?

Just think for a while. After creating the earth and the sky, the birds in the sky, the fish in the water, the animals on the shores, and other creatures, whom did god select to be the ruler to enjoy all these? A man—made in the image of god himself. (Even if we agree that man created god in his image, remember that man's importance does not diminish.) And then to relieve the boredom of this epitome of god's affection and to give him pleasure, for this alone, woman was created. This creature made for man by the supreme being was not made from a combination of special things like lotus petals, lentil flowers, 'thondi' fruit and elephant head, but from a piece of bone taken from man himself, which was given shape and life; and thus was formed a woman—a pleasurable item that would give man no peace; good at persuasive temptation. (Here a logical doubt arises, doesn't it? We, women, can keep it a secret amongst ourselves. Let not the men hear. Even if they do hear, it is okay, but some women should not hear it at all. More than the enemy on the opposite side, what we need to fear are the members of the fifth column on our own side. Well, I haven't said what the doubt is. Haven't you noticed that even today, many men, after they get a life partner, seem to have some defect in their backbone? Does that mean that what the supreme Creator did to the first man has its repercussions even after thousands of generations? What is the reason for that? What do you think? Don't say the answer aloud, keep it to yourselves. But remember one thing. If the defect didn't provide enjoyment—if the operation did not give pleasure to the body and through the body to the mind—it would not be repeated like this. The race of mankind continues to prevail only because they pass through that operation table—the wedding mandap.)

Okay, then, where were we? Yes, right from her origin, the woman is subservient to man; his happiness is the aim of her life; separated from him, she is a non-entity. And just look at women today, clamouring and fighting for equality with men, and raising slogans! Have they become the snake that bites the hand that feeds it milk? Isn't there a limit to ingratitude? Won't the patience of those on the opposite side be shaken?

Once there was a girl; she established a kingdom without men. Not an ordinary girl, but a queen, a great queen; a bold person. And what happened eventually? Haven't you heard that story? Well! There will only be a few who do not have at least a faint idea of the story of Allirani. Isn't it a well-known story? You do know, don't you, what finally happened to that war-strategist queen? There is no need to go into the details of how her arrogance had to bow down and surrender before the valiant archer Arjunan. In short, it can be said that this story was written by some do-gooder with noble intentions, who wanted this to be a moral lesson to prevent girls in the future from straying away from the right path.

Even after hearing all this, are you going to argue that this story was deliberately made to end that way only because it was written by a man? It is quite possible for such a transformation to happen to a woman in a world without men. You might be taking comfort in the thought that if there were no men at all, anywhere in the world, such situations would not occur in real life or in books. But you must take note of one thing. That relief will lead to unremediable lack of happiness and perpetual boredom in your life. Do I need to explain how in detail? There will be no one to sing to you in love, no one to speak in contempt, no one to praise you disproportionately. Many find it essential to be either praised or humiliated with a lot of fanfare. What will those women do, who consider the blows from a male hand and kicks from stout legs to be more enjoyable than the Thandava dance? There is some comfort in the thought that one will not have to hear contemptuous aphorisms like 'women do not deserve freedom', 'women are capricious and uninhibited', 'women are a necessary evil' and so on, but there is another problem. What will be the situation of those who will feel that life is not worth living if they cannot be thrilled hearing laudatory phrases like, 'as fragrant as a flower, 'as beautiful as the moonlight', 'as lovely as a bridal chamber', 'as sweet as honey' and so on?

Indian Women and the Franchise

Not without a due sense of my great privilege do I venture to lay before this committee, in briefest outline, some of the reasons on which the women of India base their claim to equal franchise in the scheme of reforms to inaugurate responsible self-government for India.

I may observe that my sole title to be regarded as an all-India representative of my sex on a question of such far-reaching importance lies in the fact that I am intimately aware of every shade of orthodox and progressive opinion alike, throughout the country, and I am closely associated with all the larger public movements of the day, especially in relation to the vital and delicate problem of Hindu-Muslim unity.

There are two reasons why I desire to dwell for a moment on the ancient and historic Indian tradition of woman's place and purpose in the civic and spiritual life of the nation, and to recall the versatile and illustrious record of her contribution to the national achievement by her wit and wisdom, her valour, devotion and self-sacrifice, as scholar and statesman, soldier, saint, queen of her own social kingdom and compassionate servant of suffering humanity.

Firstly, to refute the reiterated argument of the illiberal or uninstructed opponent of women's suffrage as being too premature or too novel and radical a departure from accepted custom likely to offend or alarm a sensitive and stationary prejudice.

Secondly, to demonstrate that the Indian woman is essentially conservative in her impulse and inspiration, and so far from demanding an alien standard of emancipation, she desires that her evolution should be no more than an ample and authentic efflorescence of an age-long ideal of dedicated service whose roots are deep hidden in the past.

I do not for one instant deny that the story of her progressive development has suffered severe interruption and shared in that general decline—I had almost said decadence—that befalls a nation with so continuous a chronicle of subjection to foreign rules but of recent years the woman of the Indian renaissance, largely owing to the stimulus of invigorating Western ideas and influences, has once more vindicated herself as not wholly unworthy of her own high social and spiritual inheritance. And already she is beginning to recover her natural place and establish her prerogative as an integral part of the national life.

It is, indeed, a curious and startling irony of fate that the trend of a doubtless conscientious, but over-cautious official decision is to refuse her a formal legislative sanction for a privilege which is already hers in spirit and substance, tacitly acknowledged and widely exercised; for the power of the Indian woman is supreme and her influence incalculable in the inner life of her own people. I do not exaggerate when I assert that there is no summit to which she might not aspire or attain in any sphere of our national energy or enterprise unhampered save by the limitations of her own personal ambition and ability.

Wherein has her sex disqualified the Indian woman, or disinherited her, from the rich honours she has earned in equal emulation and comradeship with her brother in every field of intellectual or patriotic endeavour?

In our universities she has won brilliant distinction in the arts and sciences, medicine, law and oriental learning. She holds office in the courts and senates of universities, like Bombay University, the Hindu University of Benares and the Women's University of Poona and the National University.

She has evinced her creative talent in literature and music. She has proved her consummate tact and resource in administering vast properties and intricate affairs, and demonstrated beyond all question her marvellous capacity to organize and sustain great educational institutions and large philanthropic missions for social service. She has been pre-eminently associated with the political life of the country, uplifting the voice of her indignation against all measures of unjust and oppressive legislation, like the Partition of Bengal, the Press Act, the Defence of India Bill and the Rowlatt Bill, she has accorded her cordial support to all beneficent, social and economic measures, like Gokhale's Bill for free and compulsory education, the Civil Marriage Bill of Mr Basu, the Inter-Caste Marriage Bill of Mr Patel and the Swadeshi movement inaugurated by my friend and leader, Mahatma Gandhi, and all efforts to ameliorate the condition of the depressed and afflicted members of our society.

Moreover, not only has she participated in the programmes of our great periodic national assemblies, like the National Congress, the Muslim League, the Social Reform and Social Service Conferences but has not infrequently been called upon to guide their deliberations, direct their policies, harmonize their differences, and unite their ideals towards a common goal of self-realization.

Where then lies the logic of their refusal of a franchise to Pundita Ramabai, or Swarna Kumari Ghosal? To Ramabai Ranade or Kamala Sathianadhan, Kamini Sen or Shireenbai Cursetji? To Nagutai Joshi or Anasuya Sarabhai? To Abola Bose or Cornelia Sorabji? To Indira Devi or Sarala Devi? To Sarala Ray, Faiji Patel, Uma Nehru or Vidya Ramanbhai? To Mrs Chandrasekhara Aiyar of Mysore or Mrs Sadasiva Aiyar of Madras?

And what of that group of women in the seclusion of the purdah, whose culture and accomplishments rival the golden age of the Saracens? Sultan Jehan of Bhopal and Nazli Raffia of Janjira? Abru Begum, Tyaba Begum, Khujista Sultana Begum; Abadi Banu, the iron-hearted mother of the Ali brothers: to the courageous young wife of the poet Hasrat Mohani; the late Suhaiwardja Begum, who from her sequestered corner set papers in oriental classics for the Calcutta University and Amina Hydari who won the Kaiser-i-Hind decoration for her selfless services in a time of tragic distress in the Hyderabad state?

But it is the purdah which constitutes the chief weapon in the armoury of opposition against franchise for Indian women. I readily concede that it might in its initial stages seriously inconvenience and complicate the electoral system, and perhaps even be attended with temporary danger of fraudulent votes.

Although it is no part of either my mandate or my mission to ask for any concession or preferential treatment for women, I am still constrained to say that I fail to understand, when the interests of small political minorities of men are safeguarded with a scrupulous care, why it might not be possible in course of time to extend a similar chivalrous consideration to the purdahnashin in those local and limited areas where this custom is rigidly enforced, for I am sure that her vote would usually be exercised with intelligence and discretion and prove a valuable acquisition to the country.

Without discussing the merits or demerits of this old social custom, I am convinced that, like the other all time-honoured but already obsolete social observances and usages, the purdah system can no longer remain immutable, but must read just itself to the needs and demands of a widespread national re-awakening. And after all, the terrors of the polling booth would scarcely daunt the purdahnashin who in the course of her religious pilgrimages habitually encounters immense multitudes and becomes no more than casual unit of a heterogeneous pilgrim-democracy.

What, however, of the unsequestered women of Malabar and Madras, Maharashtra and Gujarat and the Central Provinces? Of the enlightened women of the Parsi, Sikh and Christian communities, of the Arya Samaj of Punjab and the Brahmo Samaj of Bengal? Whether the franchise be one of literacy or of property, their inclusion would in no way disturb or deflect the normal electoral arrangements.

In the name of the women of India, I make my appeal to the statesmen of a glorious country whose cherished freedom is broadbased upon the people's will. There is not one citadel of Hindu civilization, or one centre of Islamic culture, where I have not scattered broadcast my message of India's duty and destiny among the free nations of the world. I have spoken to the youths in their academies, to the women in their walled gardens, to the merchants in the marketplace, to the peasants in the shade of their fig and banyan trees, but how shall my prophecy be realized and how shall my country take her predestined place worthily in the noble world federation of liberated peoples, until the women of India are themselves free and enfranchised, and stand as the guardians of her national honour and the symbols of her national righteousness?

Fireflies in the Mist

Translated from the Urdu by the author

In Calcutta, as their sister Bhavtarni Debi put it, the boys had got into bad company and taken to violent and non-violent politics. Dinesh, the younger one, became a terrorist. He was tried and hanged in Alipur Jail. As further punishment, the remaining Sarkar lands in Mymensingh were confiscated. Older brother Benoy had qualified as a doctor. He became a follower of Gandhiji, took part in the non-cooperation movement in the 1920s and courted arrest. After he came out of jail, his practice did not pick up. His wife died of cancer.

By 1939, the once resplendent Chandrakunj had turned into a semi-ruin. Its expensive furniture had long been sold off. The ceiling leaked during the rains. The venetians had sagged. The garden had gradually turned into a dense jungle. Thieves and intruders sneaked in and out at will through the surrounding foliage and half-broken doors and windows. The house had been burgled several times, while there were still some valuables left in its dank and gloomy rooms.

Benoy Chandra, elder son of Romesh Chandra Sarkar, treated the poor free of charge and made his family live in penury. The fact that the Sarkars of Chandrakunj had come down rather badly in the world was well known in Dacca. Now they had very few friends.

The good doctor had converted part of the colonnaded front verandah into his clinic and used his wife's old saris as its curtains. The drawing room was almost bare. A folding harmonium stood in a corner. The walls were also bare, except for two large portraits. Adorned with garlands of tarnished, artificial gold ribbon, they gave the sunless room the air of an unfrequented shrine. Half-hidden behind the garlands, a woman and a man faced each other across the brick floor. The lady was dressed in the fashion of the 1920s and looked a bit like Pola Negri, as she dreamily gazed into the camera. The young man sat by a vase full of roses and solemnly read a book. The same volume was placed on the cornice underneath. The strange, ghostly chemistry, which fades the photographs of the dead, had already worked on these portraits.

The ballroom once served as Romesh Baboo's jalsaghar. It had become roofless and turned into a quadrangle. Kali had been transferred to a side-room. Part of the dining hall was now used as a dormitory. It was cluttered with three string cots, ink-stained desks, tin trunks, canvas shoes and school books.

A small room facing the courtyard contained a brass bedstead and a cane stool. A hand mirror, a bottle of coconut hair oil and a chocolate box, full of glass bangles and trinkets, stood in a neat row on a broad windowsill. College books lay scattered over a reed mat. A trunk covered with a printed bedcover served as a chair.

Songbirds lived in a broken-down carriage which stood in Chandrakunj's little jungle. On moonlit nights it looked like Cinderella's coach lying abandoned in an enchanted forest.

The coachman had died long ago. His son, Abdul Qadir, lived in the servant quarters with his wife and seven half-starved children. The stable now housed his own horses and rickety carriage which he plied as a gharry-wallah.

Chandrakunj's desolation and decay was quite incredible.

◆

It was heart-rending, therefore, that such a miserable household should be burgled again. For, that December evening of 1939, the last of the rare heirlooms were stolen from Chandrakunj's storeroom.

The burglar was Dr Benoy Chandra Sarkar's nineteen-year-old daughter, Deepali.

Dr Sarkar had closed his clinic at six o'clock in the evening and gone out for his long walk by the river. His three sons, nicknamed Khoku, Tonu and Shonu, had not returned from the football grounds. The sound of running water emanating from one of the cave-like bathrooms indicated that the doctor's widowed sister, Bhavtarni Debi, was getting ready for her evening devotions.

Dr Sarkar's talented daughter Deepali used to practise her singing in a lonely turret upstairs. At 6.30 she peeped down through a skylight and saw her aunt shuffling out of the bathroom. Deepali picked up her lantern and came down. There was no one in the courtyard except a crow sitting on the clothesline. It eyed her balefully and flew away. Deepali went inside and posted herself behind the half-open door of the puja room.

Bhavtarni Debi had finished burning her joss sticks. She closed her eyes, and mumbled her shlokas. Presently, she got herself into a trance. She had her plump, broad back towards the door.

Deepali picked up the lantern and hurried across to the storeroom. In the evenings aunt and niece were always alone in the house. They were too poor to employ servants and hardly had any visitors. The coast was clear for at least another hour. The girl unlocked the box-room and went in. Bolting the door behind her, she straightened her back and felt suffocated. Nervously, she opened the Chinese camphor box. It contained the Sarkar 'leftovers'. Twice a year Bhavtarni Debi took out the expensive clothes, aired them, lined them with fresh neem leaves and put them back, sighing.

Gingerly Deepali took out a pair of Kashmere shawls and Banares silks. At last she found the proudest of the Sarkar possessions—three 'Balucher bootedar' saris. They were a hundred years old but looked as though they had just come off the handlooms of Murshidabad. Despite the extreme precariousness of the situation, Deepali gaped at the woven designs. The broad end of a purple sari had a row of stylized profiles of a Nawab-Nazim. He sat in a howdah on an elephant. A John Company Englishman in a canoe was repeated on the end of a sunset-orange sari. The turqoise sari displayed a nawab begum of Bengal delicately smelling a rose. Time seemed to have stood still as it got entangled in the rich silks woven by the Muslim craftsmen of old Bengal.

Deepali wrapped the three saris in a yellowing piece of Dacca muslin. A cat jumped off a woodapple tree near the stairs. A hansom clip-clopped past the front gate. Deepali came out with her 'loot' and locked the godown.

Bhavtarni Debi continued to pray.

◆

A young man with a bicycle lurked in the thicket outside waiting for Deepali Sarkar.

In the backroom of a house in the old city, a group of young men huddled together, talking in undertones. Deepali came in and reverently placed the bundle in front of them. 'Sorry,' she whispered apologetically, 'I didn't have anything more expensive than this.'

One of the boys opened the package. 'Balucher saris!' he exclaimed. The others craned their necks and stared at the rare antiques. 'I told you about these,' she said modestly.

'Yes,' answered one of them. 'But how did your aunt give them to you? Did you say you wanted them for a fancy-dress party or something?'

'I stole them.'

'Did I hear right?'

'First I pinched the keys.'

'You did what?'

'My aunt was fast asleep, in the afternoon. I untied the keys from the corner of her sari.'

'Nimble-fingered, aren't you?'

'I do a lot of petit point embroidery and cross-stitch.'

'Look, I didn't mean that you steal your own heirlooms.'

'I should have stolen somebody else's?'

There was a short silence.

The girl began to cry. 'You said it was absolutely imperative that you get five hundred rupees by this evening, that it was a matter of life and death.'

There was another silence.

'I know a person who might purchase these for Calcutta Museum. Thank you, Deepali.' Their leader picked up the bundle.

EASTERINE KIRE

Bitter Wormwood

AN UNFINISHED LIFE

In the winter holidays, Mose accompanied his mother to the fields. At the edge of the field, he plucked a bitter wormwood leaf and stuck it behind his ear.

'Grandmother says it keeps the spirits away. Well, actually she said that it kept away those bad spirits that caused you to do bad things,' he said to his mother by way of explanation. She laughed, but plucked a leaf as well and placed it in her basket. It was common to rub it on cuts and insect bites.

There wasn't much work to do now. The boy enjoyed being outdoors. Occasionally they took a pumpkin home for their dinner. Mose always had his slingshot with him, but he had only got a couple of birds.

'That squirrel must have been a fluke,' he said in a disappointed tone.

'Don't say that, son; never say such things without thinking. Not if you want to be a great hunter.'

'Why, Mother?' he asked.

'Because our words destroy or make our destiny. The wives of hunters say, 'We are not satiated with the food you brought. You must bring more.'

'How odd!' said Mose, 'It almost sounds rude.'

'Yes, but it makes the men get more game when their women say that.'

'We want to eat more meat!' Mose shouted.

'I shall say it when we are at home,' said his mother, stifling a giggle.

On the days that they stayed in the village, Vilaü and Khrienuo dried the paddy and ran in and out shooing chickens away. They took turns pounding the paddy in the long mortar that stood inside Vilaü's house. Except for these activities, the winter months were not as hectic as the summer months. The days were shorter and colder. The winter vegetables needed regular watering, especially mustard leaves and garlic.

Every evening, they sat after dinner and religiously listened to the news on the radio. On 30 January, when Mose turned on the radio, he immediately raised his hand, indicating that everyone should be quiet. He gasped as he listened to the news and put his ear close to the speaker. He then tried putting up the volume but there was a crackling sound as he did this, so he lowered it again. After the long broadcast, readings from the Hindu scriptures accompanied by the harmonium could be heard on the radio.

Mose sat down and stated, 'Gandhi was shot dead today!'

'Who is that? Gandhi. Gandhi. Isn't that the old man who is the leader of the Indians?' Khrienuo asked.

Mose nodded yes.

'Why would anyone do that? He looks so harmless,' Vilaü stated.

'The radio says that they have caught the killer. We were studying about Gandhi in school last year. They call him the Father of the Nation. Our teacher said he was the man who brought Indian independence. How sad that he should be killed!'

'Who was it that shot him? A white soldier?' Vilaü asked.

'No, they say it was a Hindu. A brown man.'

'His own countryman? That is terrible.'

They were all quiet for some time.

'He is not the leader of India, is he? That is some other man, isn't it?' Vilaü wanted to know.

'No, he is not the Prime Minister of India. That is Nehru.'

'Are they brothers?' Khrienuo asked.

'No, of course not,' was Mose's reply.

'Oh, I always thought they were brothers. At the big meetings, the men always use their names together—Nehru-Gandhi, Gandhi-Nehru, like that. Hmm, nothing good can come out of killing a good man. That is for sure.'

A week after the assassination of Gandhi school reopened. At the assembly, the headmaster talked briefly about Gandhi and his life. Then he added, 'Before he died, this great man met a group of Nagas. He asked how he could help them. The men said they wanted independence from India. Gandhi told them they had every right to it. This was truly a great man who understood the rights of all human beings. Gandhi's death is a loss not only to India but to the Nagas and to the whole world.' They stood in silence for two minutes and prayed for his soul. Everyone looked solemn as they did this.

In the new school year, Mose and Neituo had both been promoted to the fourth grade. At first, the students were shy with the new teacher but in a week's time they had grown almost as boisterous as the year before. Some of the weaker students had not passed. Though there were still ten of them, two were students who had failed in the fourth grade. Their class teacher was much stricter than the previous one had been. He insisted that they buy all their books within four days. They were not allowed to come to class if they did not have books.

Soon, Mose's class was learning to write essays on different subjects. The reason for the rapid progress in teaching was the stipend exam they would take at the end of the next year. Those who passed the exam would receive a stipend to help them with their school fees.

'What a lot to study! Don't your teachers think it's too much?' Vilaü asked when Mose was home.

He had sat for two hours poring over his books by the light of the lantern.

'No, Mother, this is what they learn in the fourth grade every year.'

'If you ask me, it's a great deal for a small boy.'

'I'm a big boy now, Mother, I'm eleven.'

'That's right. Still, it seems a lot of work to me. I'm glad I never went to school.'

'Oh, Mother!' Mose laughed.

TEMSULA AO

The Last Song

One particular year, the villagers were in an especially expectant mood because there was a big event coming up in the village church in about six months time: the dedication of the new church building. Every member of the church had contributed towards the building fund by donating in cash and kind and it had taken them nearly three years to complete the new structure of tin roof and wooden frames to replace the old one of bamboo and thatch. In every household the womenfolk were planning new clothes for the family, brand-new shawls for the men and new skirts or 'lungis' for the women. The whole village was being spruced up for the occasion as some eminent pastors from neighbouring villages were being invited for the dedication service. Pigs earmarked for the feast were given special food to fatten them up. The service was planned for the first week of December, which would ensure that harvesting of the fields would be over and the special celebration would not interfere with the normal Christmas celebrations of the church. The villagers began the preparations with great enthusiasm, often joking among themselves that this year they would have a double Christmas!

These were, however, troubled times for the Nagas. The Independence movement was gaining momentum by the day and even the remotest villages were getting involved, if not directly in terms of their members joining the underground army, then certainly by paying 'taxes' to the underground 'government'. This particular village was no different. They had been compelled to pay their dues every year, the amount calculated on the number of households in the village. Curiously enough, the collections would be made just before the Christmas holidays, perhaps because travel for the collectors was easier through the winter forests or perhaps they too wanted to celebrate Christmas! In any case, the villagers were prepared for the annual visit from their brethren of the forests and the transaction was carried out without a hitch.

But this year, it was not as simple as in previous years. A recent raid of an underground hideout yielded records of all such collections of the area and the government forces were determined to 'teach' all those villages the consequences of 'supporting' the rebel cause by paying the 'taxes'. Unknown to them, a sinister plan was being hatched by the forces to demonstrate to the entire Naga people what happens when you 'betray' your own government. It was decided that the army would go to this particular village on the day when they were dedicating the new church building and arrest all the leaders for their 'crime' of paying taxes to the underground forces.

In the meanwhile, the villagers caught up in the hectic activities prior to the appointed day, a Sunday, were happily busy in tidying up their own households, especially the ones where the guests would be lodged. The dedication Sunday dawned bright and cool, it was December after all, and every villager, attired in his or her best, assembled in front of the new church, which was on the same site as the old one. The villagers were undecided about what to do with the old one still standing near the new one. They had postponed any decision until after the dedication. That morning the choir was standing together in the front porch of the new church to lead the congregation in the singing before the formal inauguration, after which they would enter the new building. Apenyo, the lead singer, was standing in the middle of the front row, looking resplendent in her new lungi and shawl. She was going to perform solo on the occasion after the group song of the choir. As the pastor led the congregation in the invocatory prayer, a hush fell on the crowd as though in great expectation: the choir would sing their first number after the prayer. As the song the crowd was waiting to hear began, there was the sound of gunfire in the distance; it was an ominous sound which meant that the army would certainly disrupt the festivities. But the choir sang on unfazed, though uneasy snuffles could be heard from among the crowd. The pastor too began to look worried; he turned to a deacon and seemed to be consulting with him about something. Just as the singing subsided, another sound reverberated throughout the length and breath of the village: a frightened Dobashi, with fear and trembling in his voice was telling the people to stay where they were and not to attempt to run away or fight. There was a stunned silence and the congregation froze in their places unable to believe that their dedication Sunday was going to be desecrated by the arrogant Indian army.

Very soon the approaching soldiers surrounded the crowd, and the pastor was commanded to come forward and identify himself along with the gaonburas. But before they could do anything, Apenyo burst into her solo number, and not to be outdone by the bravery or foolishness of this young girl, and not wishing to leave her thus exposed, the entire choir burst into song. The soldiers were incensed; it was an act of open defiance and proper retaliation had to be made. They pushed and shoved the pastor and the gaonburas, prodding them with the butts of their guns towards the waiting jeeps below the steps of the church. Some of the villagers tried to argue with the soldiers and they too were kicked and assaulted. There was a feeble attempt by the accompanying Dobashi to restore some semblance of order but no one was listening to him and the crowd, by now overcome by fear and anger, began to disperse in every direction. Some members of the choir left their singing and were seen trying to run away to safety. Only Apenyo stood her ground. She sang on, oblivious of the situation as if an unseen presence was guiding her. Her mother, standing with the congregation, saw her daughter singing her heart out as if to withstand the might of the guns with her voice raised to god in heaven. She called out to her to stop but Apenyo did not seem to hear or see anything. In desperation, Libeni rushed forward to pull her daughter away but the leader of the army was quicker. He grabbed Apenyo by the hair and with a bemused look on his face dragged her away from the crowd towards the old church building. All this while, the girl was heard singing the chorus of her song over and over again.

OKKUR MACATTIYAR

Translated from the Tamil by George L. Hart III

Purananuru 279

HER PURPOSE IS FRIGHTENING, HER SPIRIT CRUEL

Her purpose is frightening, her spirit cruel.
That she comes from an ancient house is fitting, surely.
In the battle the day before yesterday,
her father attacked an elephant and died there on the field
In the battle yesterday,
her husband faced a row of troops and fell.
And today,
She hears the battle drum,
and, eager beyond reason, gives him a spear in his hand,
wraps a white garment around him,
smears his dry tuft with oil,
and, having nothing but her one son,
'Go!' she says sending him to battle.

BANI BASU

The Enemy Within

Translated from the Bengali by Jayanti Datta

The year 1967 is an astonishing year in the political history of West Bengal. In the February general elections of that year, twenty years of Congress Party rule in that state came to an end. An unprecedented fourteen-party coalition government came into power among whose members were the Moscow-following CPI (Communist Party of India) and the China-oriented CPM (Communist Party of India, Marxist). The general public of West Bengal shed tears of joy at this extraordinary turn of events. To the public at large still believing in the joint family system, perhaps this union appeared to be a happy reconciliation among brothers after a long dispute. Though even his enemy will not accuse the Bengali of political naivete, an exaggerated romantic ardour and emotionalism is both a bane and a blessing to the Bengali character.

After the first tide of expectation had ebbed and the waters receded to reveal the barren sand-banks of idealistic differences, it was no longer possible to conceal the differences in opinion among the allies. Altercations began between the Marxist and the non-Marxist groups over the role of the police, labourers and land policy, causing the government to split and reconstitute repeatedly.

After the mid-term elections of 1969, the state now had its second United Left Front government. Right from 1967, the people of the state had swung between hope and despair like the lower middle-classes do when they buy lottery tickets. People continued to daydream in trams and buses. The habit of talking big persisted despite the regulatory experience of a year of President's Rule.

In a bus bound for Alipur a plump man with a heaving paunch tilted his cheek towards the passenger sitting next to him—'What do you think, brother, will it last this time?'

The person so addressed replied solemnly—'Only god knows. But it's getting a shake-up, that's for sure.'

In the seat behind there was an enthusiastic person who seemed to keep in touch with all the news.

He said loudly, 'There is no difference left between West Bengal and France. Kolkata will also become another Paris. How much of Moulin Rouge do you want?'

A somewhat thin, irritable looking old man was perhaps a bit offended at the mention of Moulin Rouge. He made a gesture of warding off a fly from before his nose and quavered in a voice sounding tinny with snuff—'Will Ajoy Mukherjee be able to cope? He doesn't have Profulla Sen's clout, does he?'

'What makes you think Jyoti Basu will?' came a ready rejoinder from the other side. 'Having grown up being beaten black and blue by the police, now they're in charge of the police ministry. What do you make of that? Have the mongoose and the snake ever lived together?'

Munni and Bibi, as they listened to this standardized bus conversation, glanced at each other from time to time. They were two friends of disparate ages. Munni was older. Her glowing appearance caught the eye. In an attractive printed sari and matching handbag she was quite modern as well. Bibi was thin and tall, very young yet with a serious face. Munni said under her breath—'These people will never grow up. They will be their Mama's boys, go to office late chewing paan, lunch-boxes in their hands packed by dutiful wives, having talked big in the tram or bus.'

Bibi said, 'What else can they do? Perhaps they can do nothing more.'

Munni said in a soft but agitated voice, 'These petty bourgeois people are the real class enemies. Just because of their passive, negative attitude. They're responsible for the status quo all around us.'

They were going to a girls' hostel on the outskirts of Kolkata. Past the National Library, the Alipur Zoo, on both sides of the road huge trees stood at regular intervals, holding hands, shadow merging into shadow. If one were to come here suddenly, one would not think of Kolkata as a city of grime, of beggars and of processions. Here it seemed as though Kolkata were a shaded city of tree-lined avenues. When spring arrived the coral trees and the silk cotton trees caught fire. Yellow sprigs of laburnum blossom brushed against rustling blade-green leaves. Bunches of red oleander raised their heads beside the gates of large residences. Red and yellow wherever you looked. Red like blood and yellow like fire. These are the colours of spring. Tender green is also a spring colour. Red and yellow were splashed on various shades of green in some reckless Holi festival. Only youth has the daring to match this clash of colours. What at any other age would have seemed foolhardy appears to the young as boundless bravery, invincible courage.

On this April noon the sun had been directly overhead. Now it dipped slightly to the west. The nip in the morning air had vanished as soon as the dewdrops dried. The two girls walked up to the front of their hostel. The watchman was not at the gate. He may have gone to his own quarters to cook while humming a Tulsidas song. The tune came floating out together with the smell of chapatis, like the smell of earth soaked in the first rain. In the afternoon, the hostel appeared to be absolutely deserted. Even after crossing the front compound and entering the building they could not hear any human activity. The matron, most probably, was sunk deep in her afternoon nap. All the students were at the university, or had gone somewhere else making the university an excuse. Even if anyone was present, no sound could be heard.

Munni opened the door of her room and said, 'Wait a bit. I'll go and see whether they've kept some food for me. I'm famished. I didn't eat anything this morning'.

Bibi sat down in the chair by the side of the bed. It was only April, but already very warm. The fan kept whirring but did not give much breeze. Perhaps all hostel fans are like that. It was a dry heat. There was a long crack along one side of the ceiling beam, and a thin film of cobweb at the other end. The room for two postgraduate students. Both beds were made neatly. But the cover on Munni's bed was made of some expensive material like velvet, with a silky sheen. It looked very soft and comfortable! On the back of the metal chair provided by the hostel was an embroidered cover and a dunlopillo cushion on the seat. On the table there was a beautiful cut-work tablecloth. All the text books and exercise books were covered with the same kind of brown paper. They were arranged in a row in a book stand supported by a wooden elephant on either side. In the middle of the stand was a fat porcelain vase filled with pens, pencils, dot-pens and a paper knife.

Bibi opened the windows. The breeze swept in and ruffled the cover with printed squares on Munni's room-mate's bed. Bibi tucked in the end of her sari at the waist and quickly placed a large dictionary-like book on the heap of papers on the table. Right then Munni entered the room.

'Finished so soon, Munni di?' Bibi asked.

'No,' said Munni. 'You know what they've left for me in the meat-safe? Cold rice and some pumpkin hash. We were supposed to be given fish today. We get those tiny ones, full of bones. The others have eaten most of the fish and left me only the heads. Who's going to eat that? Come, let's try something else'.

Munni lit the stove in one corner of the room and had the coffee ready in minutes. She poured in condensed milk with a generous hand. From various pretty boxes and tins she brought out little tiny biscuits, cashew nuts, raisins, almonds.

'Come, Bibi. Let's start. You must be pretty hungry too by now'.

Bibi smiled and replied, 'I've come straight from home after a full meal cooked by Mother. I can't get hungry again so soon. What I actually need is a bath.'

Munni widened her eyes, 'Again?'

Bibi laughed, saying, 'Again!'

'You're quite a bath-freak, aren't you? Will you have a bath every time you come here? Wait, finish the coffee first. It's ready. Then we'll both go and have baths. We'll have another round afterwards. What do you say?'

She took a fistful of dry fruits and tossed them into her mouth. Chewing on them she said, 'This stuff is really for soldiers. We should all get used to it. It's both nutritious and filling.' Pulling out a suitcase from under the bed, she took two clean towels from it and some soap from her desk-drawer, then said, 'Come on, let's see how much bathing you can do today.'

There was a wall between the two bathrooms, with a gap of about three feet from the ceiling. The noise of water spraying from the two showers seemed to echo like some unheard melody. From time to time a pair of soapy hands could be seen gleaming from the other side.

'Here, catch!' Munni's voice was thin, a bit sharp, but full of life.

Bibi caught the flung soap skilfully, saying at the same time, 'Munni-di, this bathroom is the best room in your hostel. I would give anything for a shower like this.'

Killing Days

Translated from the Bengali by Shampa Banerjee

They carry the stretcher out of the gate. I can't remember whether this is the police station or the hospital or the little town jail. In the morning, on our way to court, one of the officers told me, 'Don't forget, we didn't treat you badly at all while you were in the lock-up.' I spat next to the car; the phlegm still had flecks of blood in it.

I learned much later that it was customary to make that remark—somewhat like the hangman's apology before slipping the noose round your neck.

But that was in the morning. Since then I have spent the whole day sitting in the black car surrounded by them. That's what they mean by making an appearance in court. Sometime in the middle of it all, my eyes encounter darkness. I hear a voice from somewhere: '…may have to give her oxygen.' Strange how I keep losing consciousness all the time—at least it takes away some of the tediousness of sitting here.

By now they have taken me out on the stretcher and dumped me on the floor of a higher and larger vehicle. Where is this? Who knows? I've heard the clicking sound of boots so often in the last ten days that I can no longer make out if it is real or just in my head. In the dark I hear a disgruntled voice: 'What if she dies on the way? Who will take the blame for it?' My eyes are open. I can see in the dark, just inches from my face, pairs of feet in boots, and at one end of the floor instead of a solid wall, a strip of emptiness, and fleeting light. In time I realize this is an army truck, covered with tarpaulin. I am lying at the feet of those sitting on the benches on either side. I'm very thirsty. Maybe I make a sound—a woman's voice asks: 'Did you say something?' A female warder. I don't know why they have to be with me.

'Where am I going?'

'Medinipur.'

'When do we reach there?'

'About two-thirty.'

Somebody speaks sharply, probably asking the warder to shut up. Incidentally, people have asked me, their eyes wide with wonder, 'So it's the men who beat the women too?' And immediately, in place of the raging, hysterical male officers, I would try to imagine a rotund, angry woman. What would she have in her hand? A ruler? A baton? No.

Nothing suits a middle-aged, fat and furious female with the mentality of a policewoman better than a broom. But, is it okay to use a broom to chastise suspects in a police lock-up?

The truck is moving in darkness most of the time, some of it outside, and some in my mind. Occasional brief flashes of light announce the presence of human habitation. My body and my mind seem to be quite independent of each other. The body keeps hurting itself at will, tossing around with every jolt of the truck, losing consciousness, then coming back to life again. Through the narrow slit at one end of the tarpaulin, the cold night air brushes my face and head. None of this has any relationship with the mind. As if the body is not connected to it at all. The mind keeps thinking away, as best it can: if I reach Medinipur in the middle of the night, I'll see nothing, and no one will know.

I keep telling the warder, 'Tell them to drive slowly; I'm feeling sick.' Afraid that I may throw up on their feet, my captors slow the truck down. Somebody nudges me with his boot. Are they taking me there to shoot me? At the lock-up they had said: 'Shoot her and throw her into the Kansai. She'll float straight to her holy land, Medinipur.' But then, they had said so many other things. Also, there's not enough water in the Kansai to hold in the palm of my hand. How can I float in it? I laugh suddenly at the thought, disconcerting the officers in the police station. In any case, why should they bother to waste petrol and take me so far away just to shoot me?

The moving emptiness at the bottom of the tarpaulin reveals that the darkness outside is fading. Just a trace of light, trees and shrubs on the run, a forest in silhouette, and then a hint of dwellings. The truck stops with a jolt. There are voices, the sound of boots, the loud metallic noise of a steel door being opened. I am dragged out like a sack of grain. I sit up on the floor and look around me. Two rooms, untidy, and dimly lit. They look like offices. Between them, in the porch, the truck. The sound of voices on the other side. A rough looking man says: 'It'll take time to get a stretcher. Don't worry; they have the lifespan of a turtle. How about it? You can walk, can't you?'

Although I look at the man with cold eyes and collapse in the courtyard, I feel comforted. At least I can see more if I walk. Now I notice the black signboard high up on the gate, and on it written in white letters: MIDNAPORE CENTRAL JAIL. I come to another huge door, with a smaller door cut into it. The lock opens noisily, and finally I'm inside the prison. I come to a shuddering stop. The overpowering sound of slogans shatter the early morning sky. Far and near, red walls, and windows with people standing clutching the bars. So many! So many of them! Whoever is with me almost drags me by the hand and pushes me through a door. Sinking into darkness once again, I hear a man's voice: 'Write down! 21/9, first transfer of the day.' I remember in a flash, it's my birthday, the beginning of my twenty-first year...

◆

...Krishna says the water of the green coconut is good for bronchitis, it brings out the phlegm. After talking to the doctor, we manage to get the girls a green coconut and a lemon everyday. The lemon will give them Vitamin C. The first day we are a little taken aback when a hospital warder walks up with a whole green coconut and an uncut lemon. But not for long. We realize this is intentional: they want us to beg them to cut the fruits for us. So we discover a way around this problem. Those who have once been to prison develop limitless inventive powers. Using a safety pin to slice a lemon, and taking off the impenetrable top of the coconut by knocking it just so against the bars of the cell are pretty ordinary achievements. They say the boys in Dum Dum jail, given inedible okra, chew the vegetables to pulp, dry the pulp, and use it as fuel to make tea!

When Swati was arrested, she was three months pregnant. She had a miscarriage in police custody. She also suffers from high blood pressure and rheumatism. Snigdha's fever has been so high from time to time that it's hard to even touch her. Her breath is so hot, we feel it will scald us. Usually her fever rises at night. But neither Krishna nor I are allowed to be with her then. We failed to convince the authorities that we can't teach the girls to be any worse than they already are. So when the fever rises at night, we try to bathe her head from outside the cell. When we asked for a container to keep some water inside the cell, we were sent a small basin covered with paan stains.

We don't know if the girls will recover. Finally, one day, in response to the repeated worried inquiries from the ward, we can say that the fever has gone down. Both of them, of course, feel extremely weak, with about the strength of a mouse. These days all five of us have our afternoon meals together. Do they sometimes secretly think of their daughters as I do? They've appointed me the 'commune mother'. I mix the rice for them, and hand them the food as mothers would. Unsure whether Swati and Snigdha can digest anything other than the simplest food, I give them mashed potatoes and rice, and say, 'Here, have some fried cauliflower,' or 'The fish curry is not too hot, is it?' And we finish our meal with much laughter. This way everybody feels a little more enthusiastic about the food.

After this, to 'stay spic and span' and to 'do enough physical labour', we mop our cells and the corridor clean. We scrub our metal plates for a long time until they shine. Maya tells us stories that make us laugh. Also, she is our only link with our friends in the ward. She couldn't understand at first why a small piece of paper should be exchanged between the ward and us with so much secrecy. But she knew it was something important. So whenever she found a little piece of paper anywhere, she would run to us to ask: 'Should I take this to the sisters in the ward?'

The tumblers and plates used in the ward are made by prisoners in Dum Dum Jail. For those who use them, these utensils have personalities of their own. The plates that were at one time with Santhal tribal prisoners have beautiful designs engraved on them. The engravings were done with a nail or a sharp piece of metal bit by bit, with infinite care. The designs reveal the unconquerable and mysterious human passion for creating beauty. These unexpected symbols of human inspiration, and ability to confront life in the inhumane, unclean, and vitiated atmosphere of a prison, carry their own unique message to others.

At the other end of the spectrum are the plates and bowls used by prisoners suffering from tuberculosis. These utensils are marked by a hole at the edge made with a nail. According to prison regulations, they are supposed to go back to Dum Dum where they are to be melted down and made anew. In reality none of this happens. If someone happens to get one of them, maybe it is a little scary. Who knows whom it belonged to? What were her thoughts when she sat within these friendless, uncaring walls, and ate off this plate? Alone in my cell, when I think of all this, I feel sad for this unknown woman.

Swati and Snigdha's illness was a blessing in disguise, as apart from two hours in the afternoon, our cell doors are now kept open all day. Instead, the door at the bottom of the stairs is kept locked. Of course at night we are in our individual cells, but we spend the whole day together. We know that this can change any day. So we decide to spend our time together in a planned way. Getting the books we want is always a problem. It's hard to believe, but books sold in the open market may be unavailable to us. We had to take recourse to much subterfuge to bring in books like Bertrand Russell's *War Crimes in Vietnam,* or a history of the Russo-German war, or even Gorky's *The Mother.* The authorities couldn't understand our logic when we tried to explain that these books are not only sold openly outside, but also have nothing to do with our politics. They have always felt scared and mystified by the printed word.

In this context, I remember old Anantada in Baharampur, who has been in and out of jail since 1942. The first time was when he was in school and was caught selling *Swadhinata.* Well, this is the story he told us. They had just been transferred from Baksa to Presidency Jail. The moment they were inside the gate, there were orders to search them. They refused, and settled down on the ground. 'We've come here from another jail. Why should we be searched here? They searched us before we left.' The jail authorities were equally obstinate. Eventually the prisoners were searched on condition that whatever they had brought with them would not be confiscated. The prisoners were carrying a large number of books. There was a list from the Intelligence Branch against which the books were being checked. All the books 'passed', except *Tabla Tarangini*.

'The name is not on the list. You can't take it in.'

'But...! But this isn't a regular book! It just helps you learn to play the tabla!'

'I don't know about that. This book is not allowed.'

The prisoners were determined to get their way, so they stayed where they were. Many telephone conversations took place between the jail office and Writers Building. In the evening came the final decision: 'Tabla allowed, Tarangini not.'

Yuganta

Translated from the Marathi by the author

THE PALACE OF MAYA

Khandava was a great forest on the banks of the Yamuna and its small tributary, the Ikshumati. The name 'Khandava' means 'made of rock candy'. Ikshumati means 'full of sugar cane'. The Madhu forest, which was also supposed to be on the banks of the Yamuna and is described in a later Purana, also means 'a sweet forest' or 'a honeyed forest'. From all these names it is clear that the forests contained something sweet. Was it madhu (honey)? Was it ikshu (cane)? Was it something else? Today the central Indian forests contain a large beautiful tree called mahuva. This tree, called madhukain Sanskrit, is a source of bounty for the tribal people. From its leaves they make plates; from its fragrant honey-filled flowers they make wine. The dried blossoms are eaten as a delicacy, and from the sticky juice of the flowers all kinds of sweetmeats are made. Perhaps it was because it was filled with such trees that the Khandava forest was called 'sweet'. The sweetness of the forest, however, could be valued only by the people living in it, and not by the Aryans.

Like the other kingdoms, the Pandavas' kingdom was a capital surrounded by villages and fields, but it was comparatively small and the brothers were trying to expand it. Dharmaraja was making the small town into a great capital. Perhaps Krishna and Arjuna burned the forest to provide more land for cultivation. This was the duty of a ruling king. In this way he could expand his realm without encroaching upon other Kshatriyas—something forbidden by the Kshatriya code.

Krishna and Arjuna were great warriors. They had fought and won many battles. But in none of these battles did they gain any land by conquest. The Kshatriya life as presented in the Mahabharata had a certain definite pattern. Each known house had its small territory which passed from father to son. Wars were fought, tribute was demanded, but no Kshatriya house was deprived of its kingdom. An enemy was spared if he asked for mercy. If he fought and was killed, his son was put on the throne. A Kshatriya never killed women and children. Nor was he supposed to put to the sword any defenceless person. His most sacred duty was to defend the helpless. The charge that he had not done so was the worst that could be made against him.

The need for expansion explains the burning of the forest, but the question still remains: why was it burned so mercilessly? There is a very curious contradiction in the narration. When Agni first appeared, he said he wanted to burn the forest. No specific mention is made of his wanting to feed on the creatures in it. But when we come to the end of the narration, we are told that Agni went away satisfied with all the flesh and fat he had devoured.

Moreover, this forest was not merely a forest with birds and animals in it. We are told that Takshaka, the king of the Nagas, lived there. But who were the Nagas? The word naga is generally used for serpents. However, in the Mahabharata, the Nagas seem to be human beings. The Mahabharata also mentions a bird-woman, who had children from a Brahman, living in the same forest. The bird might be the clan name of certain people living there. In the same way, many of the animals may not have been animals at all but people belonging to clans having animal names. But only regarding the Nagas is the word raja used. Apparently the Nagas represented the ruling class. The Mahabharata has given the names of the various Naga rajas belonging to different regions.

From the western Himalayas up to the middle reaches of the Ganga and to the south of the Narmada, the country was shared by the Aryans and the Nagas. The Nagas apparently lived along the rivers in the forests, while the Aryans preferred a more open country. The house of the Nagaraja, Airavata, was on the banks of the river Iravati. The house of Takshaka was apparently in the Khandava forest on the banks of the Yamuna. Many an Aryan king must have acquired new lands by burning or cutting parts of a virgin forest not owned by anyone. However, in the Khandava fire it appears that Krishna and Arjuna had a more audacious plan—to possess an entire forest, part of which happened to be the kingdom of the Takshakas.

This plan, it seems, did not go counter to the Kshatriya code. The code applied only to the Aryan Kshatriyas and not to outsiders. At least a part of the forest was Takshaka's domain and obviously the Pandavas wanted to possess it to distribute it to their own subjects. The land was usurped after a massacre, a massacre which is praised as a valorous deed. This was because the victims were not Kshatriyas or their Aryan subjects. All the high-sounding morality of the Kshatriya code was limited to their own group. Here again Krishna and Arjuna played the familiar role of the conquering settler. The Spaniards and Portuguese in South America, the English in North America and Australia are but later historical examples of the same process. Did Krishna and Arjuna feel that they had to kill every creature in order to establish unchallenged ownership over the land?

The Mahabharata narration is very curious in that the human qualities of the Nagas are played down, and the other inhabitants of the forest are described purely as birds and animals. The whole story sounds like a week-long hunt of animals. Even granting that there were only animals, this type of killing still went contrary to the Kshatriya code. There were explicit rules of hunting. Mating animals, females carrying their young, and very young animals could not be killed. Pandu was supposed to have been cursed with impotence because while hunting he had killed a mating animal. The Ramayana opens with the curse of Valmiki on a hunter who had killed one of a pair of mating birds. Nor could the animals be killed in such measure that they would become extinct. We can see this clearly in the following story: During their exile, the Pandavas were living in a forest. To feed their retinue they hunted and killed many animals every day. One night, a stag appeared to Dharmaraja in a dream and said, 'King, you are killing so many of us that we are on the way to extinction. Go into some other forest; give us respite. When we have multiplied enough, you may come back.' The next day Dharmaraja went to another forest with his brother.

There were rules which applied to all animals, but apparently no rules which applied to all human beings. If you spared an animal today, you could always kill it tomorrow. But if you spared a human being—even to make a slave out of him—he would in the course of time acquire certain rights. There was indeed great danger in sparing the lives of those who owned the land. Krishna and Arjuna, therefore, must have felt the necessity of completely wiping out the enemy.

The people who were killed in the Khandava forest belonged to the clan of Takshaka Naga. Not all the Takshakas, however, were eliminated. Nor could they forget the wrong done to them by the Pandavas. Takshaka himself is said to have taken the shape of an arrow or ridden on the tip of an arrow in order to kill Arjuna. He was cleverly foiled in the attempt by Krishna. Either the same Takshaka or his son succeeded in killing Parikshita, Arjuna's grandson, who ruled Hastinapura after the Pandavas. Janamejaya, the son of Parikshita, in turn massacred half the Nagas. The Mahabharata starts with this Janamejaya who is told the story of his forefathers. We thus see that the main Mahabharata plot has woven into it a subsidiary theme—the feud between the Pandavas and the Takshakas—which incidentally tells us of the colonization of the land by the Aryans. Apparently, during this period, the country around the river Yamuna was made free of Nagas. This conjecture is supported by an incident of Krishna's life described in the *Harivamsha*. Krishna is supposed to have subdued a Naga chieftain in a particular area of the Yamuna. In return for his life the chieftain promised that he would leave the area.

The burning of Khandava starts with the request of Agni who had come in the form of a Brahman. It is implied that being Kshatriyas, Krishna and Arjuna could not refuse. Even this excuse is flimsy. Not every request of a Brahman was fulfilled by the Kshatriyas. The Brahman Parashurama had ordered Bhishma to marry Amba; Bhishma had refused. In the burning of Khandava no rules of conduct seem to have been observed. The sole aim was the acquisition of land and the liquidation of the Nagas. But the cruel objective was defeated. Just as Hitler found it impossible to wipe out a whole people, so did the Pandavas. All that they gained through this cruelty were the curses of hundreds of victims, and three generations of enmity.

ANITA AGNIHOTRI

Why Does That Girl Trudge Across?

Translated from the Bengali by Kalpana Bardhan

Siddhartha is a young civil engineer. The position he holds is that of an assistant engineer in terms of prestige and rank, but he has an uncertain future and a rather tenuous present. In this state there are about two thousand civil engineers like him, who are 'employed' on an ad hoc basis and get paid a small amount as stipend each month instead of a salary. Today, Siddhartha has started out very early in the morning. This day he has been assigned to the top end of the barrage bridge, at the new checkpost for collecting toll-tax. Those working in this project have one advantage that is not available to everyone. Because of the distance from town, not all the houses in the staff colony are occupied. Siddhartha has somehow managed to settle down with his family in a second-class wobbly kind of house. His father has retired from his job, but his father-in-law has a position for two more years, and that is a major help. Otherwise, Siddhartha would never have managed even the expenses of just the paper and stamps, let alone the costs of the canvassing, the legwork, the legal recourse through the courts, all the things involved in seeking a permanent post. His parents-in-law came the day before yesterday for a visit, and are staying with them. Living in that two-room lodging is managed with difficulty. Still, Siddhartha at least sees a bit of fish curry on his plate of rice at this time of the month. Shortly before his father-in-law prepares to go food shopping, Siddhartha absents himself from home on vague excuses and returns when his wife is expressing happiness and surprise at the contents of the shopping bag. Siddhartha then asks for a cup of tea, simply to beat the weariness in his mind.

Today his tour duty is for the whole day, but he has to go quite close to his home and office. Only three stops by the local bus. Quietly opening the latch of the front door to leave for the 6 a.m. bus, Siddhartha notices his father-in-law is also up. He comes up to him and holds out two hundred-rupee notes, saying, 'Keep this.' Siddhartha watches with some surprise how mechanically, automatically, his right hand takes the money and puts it in his pocket. There's not the least doubt in his mind that it is his increasing number of debts in the marketplace over the past one year that have made him so helplessly shameless. These days, even if the office jeep is available, Siddhartha takes the train or the bus, even on distant tours. He has adjusted to the fact that the driver and many of

Unbound

the 'Group-D' officers earn more than he does, but still the knowledge hurts from time to time like a long-embedded thorn.

The barrage bridge was inaugurated with great fanfare about six months ago. On its right, lies the riverbed, on its left the reservoir. Submerged under the water are three villages. Two more are counting the hours before getting inundated. Counting the hours because the barrage is still not fully functional. The gate is in place, the paint-and-varnish too has been laid on. An important reason for the barrage not functioning is, surprise of surprises, the canals to carry water haven't been constructed yet. This fact was, of course, skilfully hidden from visitors on the day of the inauguration. The ordinary people, who had gathered there to agitate about their grievances, were kept away by commando and police forces. The barrage has water coming up to two-thirds of its full level. For now, a hydroelectricity corporation, also under a government department, is contracted to use the water for its own residential and commercial purposes. More on this later. For now let us go back to the toll post.

The problem here began the day after the post was opened. In this country, once a part of the infrastructure as expensive as a bridge or a road is ready and the red ribbon has been cut, the drive begins to recover the costs of investment from the pockets of ordinary people. Those who will use this facility must bear the burden of this cost, at least a major part of it, the argument goes. That's exactly what has happened with this bridge, the one Siddhartha and his colleagues worked on. But, since few projects of this size have been completed in recent times, the toll in this case is set at very stiff rates. To cross the bridge a truck must pay a hundred rupees per trip; similarly, a bus sixty rupees, a car thirty-five, a two-wheeler ten—separate rates for different modes of transport. Within fifteen days, the truck owners' association, all the bus companies, the car owners, all petition the government variously in voices loud and thin, protesting the excessive rates. This will force them to jack up the prices of the fresh próduce and coal they transport, to raise bus fares, and cars will just have to stay inside garages. Of course, it's true that after opening the bridge the distance between the capital and the steel-town of Rourkela is reduced by almost a hundred kilometres. So on balance, the high rates of toll tax should not really hurt anyone. But the inside story is this. Even though by the laws of economics, prices go up when the cost of production increases, they do not go down correspondingly if the cost is reduced. So, what if the distance goods have to be transported is reduced, traders aren't going to lower prices because of that! The truck owners still insist on higher charges on account of the toll tax. Bus drivers commuting over short distances argue that the bridge hasn't lowered their cost of operation, they could ply other routes if they weren't plying this one! 'Here we're paying sixty rupees per trip at the toll post. If we don't recover that from the passengers, how are we going to recover it?'

Siddhartha has been asked to sit at the toll station for one whole day and collect information. How many trucks or motor vehicles cross every day, which kinds are they, how much is collected, who does not pay tax, which vehicles make multiple trips on this route, etc. With all this information Siddhartha will have to write a lengthy report; this will then go to the headquarters. There, they'll discuss whether reducing the toll rates is justified. Perhaps the report Siddhartha prepares will never be read by anyone at all, and in time dust will settle on it, but why should Siddhartha neglect his duty on account of that?

He has managed to reach there quite early, but after he's been there for a while, he gets up and moves around a bit. If people, especially the bus and truck people, realize that he's sitting there continuously taking note of things, then all sorts of stray incidents may 'happen' just to get attention from the 'government'—some stone-throwing, even small-scale barricading wouldn't be a surprise. This is a day in August. The morning began with some slight clouds. After ten, the sun is sharp, the temperature steadily up. Not a sign of rain anywhere for several days now. Siddhartha is returning, head bent low against the sun, around 2 p.m. after a lunch of bread and omelette at a hole of a shop about a quarter of a mile to the south. The meal over, he wipes his lips with the kerchief, on his way to the check post. He has just started up the steep dust track that joins the paved road, when this little scene goes through his heart.

A young woman is crossing the bridge on foot. A passenger bus has just arrived at the toll point. It will head north after touching the little hamlet on the other side. After paying the toll, the bus emits a scraping sound on the molten tarmac along with a small puff of dust and speeds away to the other side. Siddhartha notices the girl just as the bus leaves. One look at the figure and he knows she's in an advanced state of pregnancy. She has a load on her head, a child on her hip. Perhaps it's asleep or can't walk yet. She walks slowly, stepping carefully through molten patches of pitch. Yes, today the temperature is about 47 degrees centigrade. Why else would the baby be lifeless like that?

He sees that the girl walks in the same direction as the bus; why, then, is she walking? She could have crossed over in the bus, couldn't she?

Bapu Kuti

BIRTH OF AN ANDOLAN

For generations, the fishermen of Kahelgaon have risen halfway through the night, long before the first rays of light shimmer over the horizon, and set out in their small wooden boats to harvest the river. But for over two decades now, many have not been able to make an adequate living as the quantum of fish in the river has steadily declined. Thus, they have joined the countless, faceless people who live on the pavements or slums of some large city, breaking stones or lifting bricks at a construction site as casual labourers.

The fisherfolk of Kahelgaon regard themselves as the descendants of the malaha who carried the exiled Prince Rama across the Ganga. That Puranic boatman has been remembered and revered over centuries as a blessed one. But his descendants feel they are a cursed people, poor of mind and perennially victims of circumstance.

Even the practice of jalkar zamindari was unique to this eighty-kilometre stretch of the Ganga in the region of Bhagalpur. The zamindars charged an average tax of about Rs 5,000 per year on every boat. With five thousand boats in the area, the total income came to about Rs 2.5 crore annually. The system was ruthlessly administered through kachheris run by the armed henchmen of the zamindars.

By the 1980s, the zamindars were not the only problem of the fisherfolk. The once-bountiful Ganga, the veritable cradle of north-Indian civilization, had become an open sewer. All the towns along the Ganga's 2,290 km journey, from Gangotri to the Bay of Bengal, dump their sewage and industrial effluents, virtually untreated, into the river. The falling catch of fish was a consequence of this slow death of the river, a tragedy seemingly beyond the fisherfolks' realm of action.

A struggle against the atrocities of the zamindars seemed more feasible. But even this latent desire to challenge the oppressors was overlaid by a strong sense of helplessness. The fisherfolk believed that they were suffering the consequences of an ancient curse which has forever condemned the community to suffer the indignities of poverty and social oppression. So how did the same people come to even dream of liberating themselves *and* their mother, the river?

The genesis of the Ganga Mukti Andolan was in the revolutionary excitement of Bihar in the mid-seventies. In 1974, the veteran Sarvodaya leader, Jayaprakash Narayan, led a students' movement against corruption and for a comprehensive social-political renewal which he called Sampoorn Kranti, Total Revolution. This wave of idealistic energy swept through Bhagalpur carrying on its crest hundreds of young men and women. One of them came from that old mansion in the narrow Girdharishah Lane at Sujaganj, in Bhagalpur.

Ram Saran was born shortly after Independence into a prosperous zamindar family. The family's ancestral haveli has spacious inner courtyards and a private temple. Women of the house are still rarely seen in the outer rooms. Ram Saran grew into a tall, soft-spoken youth with an intense interest in the world around him.

By the time he graduated from college, with an MA degree in 1972, the movement led by Jayaprakash Narayan (JP) was just gathering force. Ram Saran was swept along, in spite of opposition from his family. In January 1975, when JP formed the Chattra Yuva Sangharsh Vahini, Ram Saran became an active worker. The Vahini was meant to be a youth force that would work for the interests of the most oppressed or antim jan, last person, by peaceful means. The Vahini's age limit was thirty years and its members were prohibited from contesting elections.

The JP Movement momentarily built up an active challenge to the status quo. It helped to create the atmosphere which led Prime Minister Indira Gandhi to react by imposing the Emergency and suspending democratic rights. Thousands of political leaders and activists were arrested. Ram Saran did not go to jail but remained active in the 'underground' work of the Vahini. When the Emergency was lifted in 1977, Ram Saran was working on an adult education programme with the Gandhi Peace Foundation's unit in Bhagalpur. Some of the people in this programme were the fisherfolk from Kagzi-tola.

The fisherfolk would often tell friends like Ram Saran about the cruel ways of the jalkar zamindars, water landlords. The henchmen of the landlords were known to slash a man's body and leave him half immersed in the river to slowly bleed to death. The fisherfolk and landless labourers around Bhagalpur had lived with such atrocities for years. Thus, many people supported the blinding of undertrials because they had lost faith in the courts to deliver justice. The same criminal elements were linked with the 'mafia' which robbed the fishermen.

While the blindings of the undertrials had made national headlines, a successful land struggle in Bodhgaya District, led by the Vahini, was virtually unknown outside Bihar.

Two thousand and five hundred years earlier, Gautama Buddha had attained enlightenment under a peepul tree beside a stream. That place has since been known as Bodhgaya, today a bustling little town polluted by exhaust fumes of autorickshaws and tempos. Since the sixteenth century a Hindu muth has controlled about 9,575 acres of land in Gaya district. Most landless peasants of that area laboured for a wage on the muth's lands.

In January 1978, scores of Vahini activists went to live among the landless of Bodhgaya, eating the same food and living as members of the community. There followed a string of protest actions challenging the power of the muth. By 1981, the movement had succeeded in getting land out of the muth's control for the tillers.

There were many, more ambitious, land struggles all over Bihar at that time. But most of them were led by groups either formally linked with the Naxalite stream, or ideologically inspired by it. Big landlords had created their own 'armies' to crush these armed land struggles. The Vahini activists look pride in the fact that since they did not use armed methods, no counter-army was created in Bodhgaya. The emerging 'star' activist of this movement was Anil Prakash.

Anil Prakash was born into a middle-class family of Muzaffarpur, a night's train journey away from Bhagalpur. By the time he was in college, two types of slogans were common in Bihar. One kind was popular with the Naxalite groups: 'Blood, Blood…The Blood of Capitalists'; 'One spark can burn an entire jungle'. The other kind of slogans was raised by Jayaprakash Narayan: 'Neither do injustice nor tolerate injustice'.

While he studied for a Bachelor's degree in physics Anil also read the works of Karl Marx. But he was more drawn to Jayaprakash Narayan and plunged full-time into the students' movement. This landed him in jail for six and a half months during the Emergency. There he read Mahatma Gandhi's autobiography. This got him thinking about the importance of seeking goodness within and acting on its strength. But Gandhi didn't seem to offer any answers on how to change the social system. And Anil was restless about doing some thing to bring about Total Revolution. The Vahini answered this need for action and Anil flung himself into the Bodhgaya struggle.

The Bodhgaya movement taught him that non-violence was essential for the success of any such struggle. The Marxist-Leninist (ML) groups, he decided, were not likely to succeed because landlords were instead becoming more powerful. But, 'by our means his [landlord's] weapons are dropped. The ML groups created the Senas. Even the Bodhgaya Mahant tried to build a Kisan Suraksha Samiti (Farmer Protection Committee) but it could not be built… We have not learnt non-violence from books but from experience. We have come full circle from doubt to reaffirmation. And none of us have read Gandhi's full set.'

Some of the fisherfolk of Kagzi-tola had watched the Bodhgaya movement with hope and were now keen to launch a similar struggle of their own. So Ram Saran and other friends in Bhagalpur urged Anil to shift to the banks of the Ganga to confront the problem of jalkar zamindari.

AMRITA PRITAM

To Waris Shah

Translated from the Punjabi by Khushwant Singh

To Waris Shah I turn today!
Speak up from the graves midst which you lie!
In our book of love, turn the next leaf.
When one daughter of the Punjab did cry
You filled pages with songs of lamentation,
Today a hundred daughters cry
O Waris to speak to you.

O friend of the sorrowing, rise and see your Punjab
Corpses are strewn on the pasture,
Blood runs in the Chenab.
Some hand hath mixed poison in our five rivers
The rivers in turn had irrigated the land.
From the rich land have sprouted venomous weeds
How high the red has spread
How much the curse has bled!

The poisoned air blew into every wood
And turned the flute bamboo into snakes
They first stung the charmers who lost their antidotes
Then stung all that came their way
Their lips were bit, fangs everywhere.
The poison spread to all the lines
All of the Punjab turned blue.

Song was crushed in every throat;
Every spinning wheel's thread was snapped;
Friends parted from one another;
The hum of spinning wheels fell silent.

All boats lost the moorings
And float rudderless on the stream
The swings on the peepuls' branches
I lave crashed with the peepul tree.

Where the windpipe trilled songs of love
That flute has been lost
Ranjha and his brothers have lost their art.

Blood keeps falling upon the earth
Oozing out drop by drop from graves.
The queens of love
Weep in tombs.

It seems all people have become Qaidos,
Thieves of beauty and love
Where should I search out
Another Waris Shah.

Waris Shah
Open your grave;
Write a new page
In the book of love.

JYOTIRMOYEE DEVI

The River Churning

Translated from the Bengali by Enakshi Chatterjee

Tamijuddin sahib came up to the kitchen door where Sakina's mother was chopping vegetables and Sakina was washing the rice. He had some letters in his hand.

'Who has written?' Sakina's mother wanted to know. Tamij sahib perched on a stool and said, 'Gopal babu's eldest son, Sanat, and his son-in-law, Bimal, are worried because they have not heard from him. There was some bad news in the paper, so they have written to Gopal Babu at the school address. They have also written to me.'

'What do they say, Ba-jaan?' asked the two sons, Aziz and Moinuddin. Their father handed them the letters. One was for Sujata—her husband Bimal wrote to ask all of them to come to Calcutta. He said the same to his father-in-law, everybody here seems to think it advisable.

That was also what Sanat had written to his father and Tamijuddin sahib.

Sutara was in the room as usual.

For some time no words were exchanged. Sakina's mother broke the silence. 'What is to be done now? You must reply, because they have written to you as well.'

'Yes, I suppose I will have to,' replied Tamij sahib.

'They must have heard everything if news from this part is getting there.'

'Well, obviously they got some news but not all the details, names and so on. It's difficult for anybody to believe the news though we've been neighbours for generations. A bloody massacre without a reason, without a dispute.'

'If only the men had confined the killing to themselves...' Sakina's mother could not go on, her voice grew husky.

Aziz stared at the ground. Sakina could not look up. Only Moinuddin gave his mother an uncomprehending stare and went into his room. Sakina's mother glanced at her daughter once, then continued, 'You want to partition the country, go ahead; you want to fight over it—do it by all means. But why don't you leave the women alone? Does your religion allow you to dishonour women the way they are doing? Does the Koran approve of it? You are the educated section of the community—teachers, lawyers, mukhteers—why are you keeping quiet? Shame on you!'

Tears choked her voice, she couldn't go on.

Tamijuddin sahib replied, 'It's not that we haven't said anything, in fact many of us did. Do you know what they told us? We know you have kept a Hindu girl in your house—why? To do the Hindus a good turn? Then they laughed and said things that I can't repeat. One of them said, "Let's set fire to their house, they must realize what it means to be nice to Hindus." Rahamatulla sahib has also sheltered some Hindus. The mullas warned him too, but because he is a zamindar they couldn't do more than that.'

Bewildered, Aziz's mother did not know what to say. Tamij sahib went on, 'I appealed to them, said leave the girls alone, don't we too have women in our homes? Do you know what they said? They said, "Can you tell us of a single instance when women have not been molested, pushed about? Look at the stories in their Puranas—what about the abduction of Sita? What about Draupadi?" I tried to tell them that these are not good examples. They scoffed at me, saying these things happen. We know. Aziz, you would be surprised to hear that the people who argued in this way were all educated, religious. They do their namaz, go to the mosque, observe roza.'

Sutara had slipped out of her room and stood behind them. 'Why did you come out, my girl,' complained Sakina's mother. 'If you needed something you could have called Sakina.'

'No, I don't need anything. I overheard Moinu and Fakir say that Kaka has got some letters—that's why I came out.'

Tamij sahib gave her all the letters including the one to Sujata. Sutara's hands trembled as she took them. She flopped down on the porch but did not try to open the letters.

After a while she asked, 'Kaka, whose letters are these?'

'Your dada's and jamai babu's.'

'Do they know what has happened here?'

'I don't think so. But they are anxious to know.'

The atmosphere was heavy with unspoken agony. What could they tell this girl? How would she take it?

How, within the flicker of an eyelid, the ruffled life of a quiet village was spun into turmoil and the lives of men, the honour of women, lost. How ancestral homes were defiled and destroyed. Why? Was it the decree of god? Who could answer this question. Some were gone for ever, killed at the hands of men they had known as friends and neighbours for generations. How could Tamijuddin sahib utter such a shameful truth? How could he admit that inspite of their deepest desire they had not been able to save any of them?

The Other Side of Silence

I often wonder what kind of silent twilight world my grandmother lived in for those nine years after Partition. Did she not wonder where her children had gone? Did she think they had all abandoned her? Did she even understand what had happened? Dayawanti, the merciful one, had indeed been fortunately named. Blessed with a large family—her surviving children numbered nine, six daughters and three sons—and a husband whose medical practice was enormously successful, she had good reason to be happy. Then, suddenly, tragedy struck and her elder son, Vikram, died in an air crash on a practice flight. As my mother tells it, Dayawanti retreated into some kind of shell from then on, although cooking and caring for the children would occasionally pull her out of this. Then, the second tragedy happened: her husband took ill and died and Dayawanti again sought solace in an inner world. When Partition came, the chances are that Dayawanti did not know what was happening. But the journey in and out of her twilight world must have left her with long moments of what one might call 'sanity'. What must she have wondered about her family. Who could she have asked? What must she have felt about her new identity? My mother has often described her mother as a 'kattar Hindu'—not a rabid, flame-spouting type, but a strong believer who derived comfort from her daily routine of prayer and fasting. What must it have cost her to convert overnight to a different faith, a different routine? Did it, I wonder, bring on an even more intense alienation, a further recoil into herself, or did it bring on the reverse, a kind of cold, clear sanity and understanding of the lie she had to live till she died? Who was with her these nine years? Will history be answerable for Dayawanti's life and death?

◆

Twelve million people were displaced as a result of Partition. Nearly one million died. Some 75,000 women were raped, kidnapped, abducted, forcibly impregnated by men of the 'other' religion, thousands of families were split apart, homes burnt down and destroyed, villages abandoned. Refugee camps became part of the landscape of most major cities in the north, but, a half century later, there is still no memorial, no memory, no recall, except what is guarded, and now rapidly dying, in families and collective memory.

Some of the tales I heard when I began my research seemed so fantastic, they were difficult to believe. We had heard time and again that in many villages on both sides of the border hundreds of women had jumped—or were forced to jump—into wells because they feared that they would be taken away, raped, abducted, forced to convert to the other religion. This seemed bizarre: could the pull of religion be so strong that people—more specifically women—would actually kill themselves? And then I met Bir Bahadur Singh's mother, Basant Kaur. Basant Kaur, a tall strapping woman in her mid-sixties, had been present in her village, Thoa Khalsa in March 1947 when the decision was taken that women would jump into a well. She watched more than ninety women throw themselves into a well for fear of the Muslims. She too jumped in, but survived because there was not enough water in the well to drown them all. She said: 'It's like when you put rotis into a tandoor and if it is too full, the ones near the top, they don't cook, they have to be taken out. So the well filled up, and we could not drown... Those who died, died, and those who were alive, they pulled out...'

And Bir Bahadur Singh, her son, had watched his father kill his sister. He described the incident with pride in his voice, pride at his sister's courage and her 'martyrdom' for she could now be placed alongside other martyrs of the Sikh religion. The first time I had been alerted to family deaths, that is, men of families killing off their women and children, was when I had met an old man, Mangal Singh, in Amritsar during the course of the film *A Division of Hearts*. Mangal Singh told me how he and his two brothers had taken the decision to kill—he used the word martyr—seventeen members of their family. 'We had to do this,' he told me, 'because otherwise they would have been converted.' Having done this 'duty' Mangal Singh crossed over into Amritsar where he began a new life. When I met him, he was the only one left of the three. He had a new family, a wife, children, grandchildren, all of whom had heard, and dismissed, his stories. Why do you want to know all this, he kept asking me, what is the use? I told him that I wanted to know how he had coped with the grief, the sense of loss, the guilt. He said: 'Hunger drives all sorrow and grief away. You understand? When you don't have anything, then what's the point of having sorrow and grief?'

◆

Why do you want to know this? This is a question I have been asked again and again—by the people I have wanted to interview, or those to whom I have tried to present my work. Two or three times, having begun work on Partition, I gathered my courage and read a couple of papers in academic gatherings. I wanted to share some questions that had been bothering me: why, for example, had straight historical accounts not been able to really address this underside of the history of Partition, to gather together the experiences of people, to see what role they had played in shaping the India we know today? Was it that they knew they would have to deal with a story so riven with pain and grief, a story that was so close to many people—for in many ways, several of our families were Partition refugees—that some time had to elapse before this work actually began? I wanted to understand how to read the many stories I was now hearing: I knew, without being a historian, that I could not look at these unproblematically. Could I, for example, rely on the 'truth' of the stories I was hearing? How much could one trust memory after all these years? For many of those who chose to tell me their stories, I must have been just another listener, the experience perhaps just another telling. I knew that my being middle class, a woman, a Punjabi, perhaps half a Sikh, would have dictated the way people actually responded. What value then ought I to place on their memory, their recall? Often, what emerged from the interviews was so bitter, so full of rage, resentment, communal feeling, that it frightened me. What was I to do with such material? Was it incumbent on me, as a might-have-been historian, to try to be true to this material, or should I, as a secular Indian, actually exercise some care about what I made visible and what I did not? A question that has dogged me constantly has been: is it fair to make these interviews public if they relate (as mine do) to only one side of the story? Doesn't that sort of material lend itself to misuse by one side or another? To this day, I have not solved this dilemma: I am torn between the desire to be honest and to be careful. And all the time, I was asked: why, why are you doing this? The question became important for another reason: the way borders were drawn between our two countries, it was virtually impossible for me to travel to Pakistan to do research, or even to carry out interviews. With the result that my work remained—and still does—very one-sided. I knew that this was not right. I didn't know—I still don't—what I should be doing. Ought I to have given up the work? There are no easy answers. But in the end, I decided that if this search meant so much to me, I simply had to go on with it. I could not abandon it.

Aruna's Story

7.45 a.m. Inder is looking towards the duty room door in the basement; it is slightly open. He is not sure of what he should do. The light is on in that room. Suppose he goes in there and the sisters are changing their clothes? Obviously someone is in there, the basement's main door was unlocked when he came down with the keys from Ward 31, perhaps one of the sisters arrived very early today. But by now she should have come out of the duty room, he has been sweeping and swabbing the basement for the last twenty minutes. He is certain it is only one of the nurses who can be in there, there is no third key. Maybe there is only one sister in there, the other one may be on leave like yesterday, but why so long inside? Inder is worried now, should he knock on the open duty room door? He does, the door swings open a little more, but there is no response.

A sound from the main door. Inder is relieved to see Sohanlal at the end of the corridor, entering the basement. Sohanlal comes from a village called Dadupur, which is also in Bulandshahr district, Inder's native place. He is a little hotheaded, says things he should not, but he is young and has come only three years back to Bombay, he will learn. Inder quickly explains his concern to Sohanlal who says, 'We will go inside.' They slowly push open the door completely. Nobody. A big purse, some other things lying on the table but nobody in the duty room. The dog surgery door is closed. Inder looks at Sohanlal, walks up, knocks on it. No response. He knocks again, louder, 'Sister! Nurseji!' He cocks his head for any sound. Silence within.

Inder tries the knob, finds the dog surgery door unlocked, swings it open.

The light from the duty room falls on a naked leg stretched out on the floor of the dog surgery. Two naked legs, a sari with its petticoat rolled up, on it inky blackness which looks like blood...Inder slams the door shut.

'What is there, let me see.' Sohanlal is behind him, trying to open the door. Inder shakes his head, don't touch that door. He grabs Sohanlal by the arm, come on we have to call somebody.

◆

8.25 a.m. Sister Sulochana Beechi, forty-six, has just finished setting up her table at the CVTC out-patient department on the ground floor of the building. She is in charge of the OPD, her duty will run till 4.30 p.m.

Soon the crowding will start, more and more people suffer from heart problems in Bombay. It's not so much the Indian diet, it is the amount people eat, that too non-stop. However, Indian women seem to have stronger hearts although they cope with much more, there are more men to be seen in the CVTC OPD. Sister Beechi's thoughts come to a halt as a panting sweeper, followed by another one, run up to her duty desk.

'Sister, Sister, there is a problem downstairs in the basement.'

'What problem?'

'I don't know. There's a nurse who is not coming out from the dog surgery.'

'Which nurse is not coming out from the dog surgery?'

'I don't know, but she is not coming out.'

'Why not? Did you look to see?'

'She's sleeping inside, or lying down.'

'What? Why didn't you look properly?'

'She... she... I think she might not be wearing any clothes, so I did not want to see.'

'Come on!'

Sister Beechi hurries down the basement stairs, almost runs down the corridor, bursts into the duty room, looks around. On one corner of the duty table is an open brown hand bag; a small cane change purse lies next to it. There is a glass almirah with surgical instruments, and an open wooden cupboard with a key in its keyhole. Partially obscured by the open cupboard door is a red chappal. The other red chappal is halfway across the duty room, pointing towards the dog's operation theatre. Sister Beechi looks at Inder, he gestures towards the door.

She pushes it open. It is dark in there. 'Is there a light here?' Inder nods, puts his hand inside, on the other side of the door jamb and flicks on the switch.

A low 'Hey Bhagwaan!' from Sister Beechi.

There's a young, small-boned, fair woman crouched on the floor. She is face down, her forehead touching the floor, her hair tangled and covering her face. Her elbows and the back of her hands touch the floor, the rest of her body isn't completely in contact with the ground till her knees, calves and ankles. She is on all fours. Her brown sari is bunched up near her waist along with her petticoat which has rolled up with it. Her legs are bare and slightly apart. There is blood everywhere, on her clothes, on her skin, on the ground. Her panties are soaking with blood, a rivulet of it runs down her inner thigh to form a small pool on the floor beneath.

The woman grunts.

Sister Beechi's hand flies to her mouth, 'Hey Bhagwaan!' She turns, sweeper Sohanlal wants to know who the woman is. She pushes out the sweepers from the room, bangs the door shut, screams at the sweepers that they should quickly bring a stretcher and runs up to the OPD. Staff nurses Chinamma and Amod Kutti have reported on duty at the OPD. 'Hurry,' she instructs them, 'go down quickly to the dog surgery with the first-aid kit.' From the door of the OPD she sees Dr Uday Gadgil, near the lift, on his way to Ward 9. She runs up to him, 'Doctor, please come immediately, there is an emergency in the basement.' He follows her, they both break into a run.

◆

8.40 a.m. Dr Gadgil gently turns the woman over. Her eyes are wide open. Her hair is matted with blood, vomit and mucus. There is blood on her face, from her nose, her mouth. Her lower lip is hideously swollen. Dr Gadgil swiftly does a check. 'Rush her to the Casualty, I will phone them from upstairs that she will need intensive care immediately. Also inform neurosurgery to reach Casualty rightaway.' Sister Beechi's lips move silently, she has begun praying, as she recognizes the unfortunate woman: staff nurse Aruna Shanbaug.

There is a hiss, a sharp intake of breath as the other nurses recognize staff nurse Aruna Shanbaug. Sweepers Inder and Sohanlal place her on the stretcher. Sister Beechi leans forward and covers Aruna's exposed breasts and body with a sheet. She finds herself holding her breath as she watches the sweepers run across the by now busy road with the stretcher, dodging the morning traffic with its buses, taxis, cars and curious humans. Still praying she moves to the phone in the OPD and telephones matron Belimal. Sister Premila Kushe answers the phone. 'Staff nurse Aruna Shanbaug has been attacked in the basement, she's being carried to the Casualty. Something has gone terribly wrong for that child.' She puts the receiver down on its cradle to find tears in her eyes.

The God of Small Things

The government never paid for Sophie Mol's funeral because she wasn't killed on a zebra crossing. She had hers in Ayemenem in the old church with the new paint. She was Estha and Rahel's cousin, their uncle Chacko's daughter. She was visiting from England. Estha and Rahel were seven years old when she died. Sophie Mol was almost nine. She had a special child-sized coffin.

Satin-lined.

Brass handle shined.

She lay in it in her yellow Crimplene bell-bottoms with her hair in a ribbon and her Made-in-England go-go bag that she loved. Her face was pale and as wrinkled as a dhobi's thumb from being in water for too long. The congregation gathered around the coffin, and the yellow church swelled like a throat with the sound of sad singing. The priests with curly beards swung pots of frankincense on chains and never smiled at babies the way they did on usual Sundays.

The long candles on the altar were bent. The short ones weren't.

An old lady masquerading as a distant relative (whom nobody recognized), but who often surfaced next to bodies at funerals (a funeral junkie? a latent necrophiliac?) put cologne on a wad of cotton wool and with a devout and gently challenging air, dabbed it on Sophie Mol's forehead. Sophie Mol smelled of cologne and coffinwood.

Margaret Kochamma, Sophie Mol's English mother, wouldn't let Chacko, Sophie Mol's biological father, put his arm around her to comfort her.

The family stood huddled together. Margaret Kochamma, Chacko, Baby Kochamma, and next to her, her sister-in-law, Mammachi—Estha and Rahel's (and Sophie Mol's) grandmother. Mammachi was almost blind and always wore dark glasses when she went out of the house. Her tears trickled down from behind them and trembled along her jaw like raindrops on the edge of a roof. She looked small and ill in her crisp off-white sari. Chacko was Mammachi's only son. Her own grief grieved her. His devastated her.

Though Ammu, Estha and Rahel were allowed to attend the funeral, they were made to stand separately, not with the rest of the family. Nobody would look at them.

It was hot in the church, and the white edges of the arum lilies crisped and curled. A bee died in a coffin flower. Ammu's hands shook and her hymnbook with it. Her skin was cold. Estha stood close to her, barely awake, his aching eyes glittering like glass, his burning cheek against the bare skin of Ammu's trembling, hymnbook-holding arm.

Rahel, on the other hand, was wide awake, fiercely vigilant and brittle with exhaustion from her battle against Real Life.

She noticed that Sophie Mol was awake for her funeral. She showed Rahel Two Things.

Thing One was the newly painted high dome of the yellow church that Rahel hadn't ever looked at from the inside. It was painted blue like the sky, with drifting clouds and tiny whizzing jet planes with white trails that crisscrossed in the clouds. It's true (and must be said) that it would have been easier to notice these things lying in a coffin looking up than standing in the pews, hemmed in by sad hips and hymnbooks.

Rahel thought of the someone who had taken the trouble to go up there with cans of paint, white for the clouds, blue for the sky, silver for the jets, and brushes, and thinner. She imagined him up there, someone like Velutha, bare bodied and shining, sitting on a plank, swinging from the scaffolding in the high dome of the church, painting silver jets in a blue church sky.

She thought of what would happen if the rope snapped. She imagined him dropping like a dark star out of the sky that he had made. Lying broken on the hot church floor, dark blood spilling from his skull like a secret.

By then Esthappen and Rahel had learned that the world had other ways of breaking men. They were already familiar with the smell. Sicksweet. Like old roses on a breeze.

Thing Two that Sophie Mol showed Rahel was the bat baby.

During the funeral service, Rahel watched a small black bat climb up Baby Kochamma's expensive funeral sari with gently clinging curled claws. When it reached the place between her sari and her blouse, her roll of sadness, her bare midriff, Baby Kochamma screamed and hit the air with her hymnbook. The singing stopped for a 'Whatisit? Whathappened?' and for a furrywhirring and a sariflapping.

The sad priests dusted out their curly beards with goldringed fingers as though hidden spiders had spun sudden cobwebs in them.

The baby bat flew up into the sky and turned into a jet plane without a crisscrossed trail.

Only Rahel noticed Sophie Mol's secret cartwheel in her coffin.

The sad singing started again and they sang the same sad verse twice. And once more the yellow church swelled like a throat with voices.

When they lowered Sophie Mol's coffin into the ground in the little cemetery behind the church, Rahel knew that she still wasn't dead. She heard (on Sophie Mol's behalf), the softsounds of the red mud and the hardsounds of the orange laterite that spoiled the shining coffin polish. She heard the dullthudding through the polished coffin wood, through the satin coffin lining. The sad priests' voices muffled by mud and wood.

> We entrust into thy hands, most merciful Father,
> The soul of this our child departed,
> And we commit her body to the ground,
> Earth to earth, ashes to ashes, dust to dust.

Inside the earth Sophie Mol screamed, and shredded satin with her teeth. But you can't hear screams through earth and stone.

Sophie Mol died because she couldn't breathe.

Her funeral killed her. *Dus to dus to dus to dus to dus.* On her tombstone it said *A Sunbeam Lent To Us Too Briefly.*

Ammu explained later that Too Briefly meant For Too Short a While.

◆

After the funeral Ammu took the twins back to the Kottayam police station. They were familiar with the place. They had spent a good part of the previous day there. Anticipating the sharp, smoky stink of old urine that permeated the walls and furniture, they clamped their nostrils shut well before the smell began.

Ammu asked for the Station House Officer and when she was shown into his office, she told him that there had been a terrible mistake and that she wanted to make a statement. She asked to see Velutha.

Inspector Thomas Mathew's moustaches bustled like the friendly Air India Maharaja's, but his eyes were sly and greedy.

'It's a little too late for all this, don't you think?' he said. He spoke the coarse Kottayam dialect of Malayalam. He stared at Ammu's breasts as he spoke. He said the police knew all they needed to know and that the Kottayam Police didn't take statements from veshyas or their illegitimate children. Ammu said she'd see about that. Inspector Thomas Mathew came around his desk and approached Ammu with his baton.

'If I were you,' he said, 'I'd go home quietly.' Then he tapped her breasts with his baton. Gently. *Tap, tap.* As though he was choosing mangoes from a basket. Pointing out the ones he wanted packed and delivered. Inspector Thomas Mathew seemed to know whom he could pick on and whom he couldn't. Policemen have that instinct.

Behind him a red and blue board said:

Politeness
Obedience
Loyalty
Intelligence
Courtesy
Efficiency

When they left the police station Ammu was crying, so Estha and Rahel didn't ask her what veshya meant. Or for that matter, illegitimate. It was the first time they'd seen their mother cry. She wasn't sobbing. Her face was set like stone, but the tears welled up in her eyes and ran down her rigid cheeks. It made the twins sick with fear. Ammu's tears made everything that had so far seemed unreal, real. They went back to Ayemenem by bus. The conductor, narrow man in khaki, slid towards them on the bus rails. He balanced his bony hips against the back of a seat and clicked his ticket-puncher at Ammu. *Where to?* the click was meant to mean. Rahel could smell the sheaf of bus tickets and the sourness of the steel bus-rails on the conductor's hands. 'He's dead,' Ammu whispered to him. 'I've killed him.'

'Ayemenem,' Estha said quickly, before the conductor lost his temper. He took the money out of Ammu's purse. The conductor gave him the tickets. Estha folded them carefully and put them in his pocket. Then he put his little arms around his rigid, weeping mother.

Unbound

Myth &
Fable

All writing builds on writing from the past. Many of our ideas about ourselves are drawn from mythology, fable, fairy tales, legends and epics. Society seeks to prescribe and proscribe behaviours based on these older narratives. Gender rules draw legitimacy from them too. No wonder then that women writers often seem to argue with the stories they have inherited. This section is devoted to literature that seems to reach back to these myths and fables for new conversations and references events from the epics in newer contexts.

Malathi Maithri's poems are charged with the feminine reclamation of mythology. One poem refers to Karaikkal Ammaiyar, the poet-mystic who was deserted by her husband. Another refers to a half-goddess and half-Sivan; building on the idea of ardhnariswar, she poses the difficult question of blood—after all, if a goddess has a woman's body, then a goddess must bleed. And so must a god, if he is half-woman.

Rukmini Bhaya Nair invokes the 'mayamriga' (the illusory deer that appeared to Sita in Ramayana) in her poem 'Mayamriga, California', and articulates the loneliness of a powerful goddess in 'Kali'. Mallika Sengupta harks back to the roots of our anti-girl child sentiment in her poem 'Pandu's Desire for Sons', and the obliteration of women's lives in official histories in 'While Teaching My Son History'.

Pratibha Ray's landmark Oriya novel *Yajnaseni* looks at the Mahabharata and its principal protagonists from Draupadi's perspective. The extract included here gives voice to her suspicion that, suddenly being saddled with five husbands, she is being used as a pawn in a complicated game of balancing power within the Pandava family.

Suniti Namjoshi's brief, delightful investigations into myths and fables are stunning in their revelation of how gender bias and cruelty is handed down the generations in the guise of tradition. The fables included here involve the story of the monkey and the crocodile and the Panchatantra fable about the Brahmin who prayed for a son.

Kumudini's wry retellings of episodes from the Ramayana and Mahabharata are well known. The extract included here is a scene from the play *Viswamitra*, which invokes the legend of Raja Harischandra. However, in her narrative, Harischandra's wife does not follow him unquestioningly into exile and poverty. The women use their wits to undermine the great sage Viswamitra, and drive him off the throne.

Saudamini Devi's *Adbhuta Ramayana* is a fascinating version of the epic, wherein Sita reveals herself as an avatar of the Goddess Kali. While she warns her abductor of the rage and power of her husband, ultimately she herself must kill Ravana, cheered on by all the other gods.

SAUDAMINI DEVI

Adbhuta Ramayana

Translated from the Bengali by Arjun Choudhuri

21ST SARGA

Tripadi

Thus did the battle, unceasing, terrible,
continue long, with both sides equal
in their strength or glory of arms.

A thousand eyes watch in wonder
the battle day and night,
neither victory nor defeat
comes to either side.

I who have conquered all,
master of the three worlds,
now have to battle these
monkeys and men.

To speak of this means ridicule,
if people know an insult too,
the fire of infamy shall rage
through the whole world.

Musing thus the great-bodied one,
mounting a wind-speed chariot,
enters the battle fray like
a fish enters the sea.

Inside the armies of Rāma,
the valiant one muses then,
I will not slay these monkeys or men.

Thinking thus the clever one,
called on the Wind Missile,
unleashing it thus in anger

on the armies there.

Twisting thus to and fro,
the armies rose in the wind,
and were taken away
to their respective homes.

Jāmbuvān, Vibhīṣaṇa, Sugrīva
and all the other monkeys
were all taken away
to the places whence they came.

Everyone stands amazed,
almost as if it were a dream,
all the gods tremble thus
in abject fear.

In the ether the gods and sages,
so that Rāma the battle wins,
begin then chanting aloud
the sacred Vedic texts.

They shower their blessings then,
'Be victorious, scion of Raghu's clan,
save the three worlds now
by destroying your foe.'

Blessed by Śaṅkara
the proud night-walker
alights from his chariot
onto the ground.

Angered beyond compare,
he brings four mountain peaks there
and roars aloud then leonine.

At that terrible sound, the four brothers
in each chariot, faint away in sheer terror.
Rāvaṇa then captures each of them
from their stands in their chariots.

Heaving each mountain peak,
he places each brother beneath,
and thinks that the battle has been
won at last by him.

Great joy suffuses him,
lion roars he then emits,
and dances in glee
with his armies on the grounds.

Seeing this then did Jānakī,
furious, fiery in her wrath,
tie her veil around
her slender waist.

The daughter of Janaka,
devoted to her lord-husband,
in her sorrow for her master
could no longer charioted remain.

With bow and arrow easy in hand,
before the foe she took her stand,
and showered abuse on Rāvaṇa then.

'You, O corrupted one, through cunning
have this battle won, and yet you rejoice
in your victory then, but today will I
surely slay you and your life thus end.

Hear me, O evil one,
Śrī Rāma is my lord,
him you have under
a mountain's weight.

Your death thus has neared,
give me battle now and here,
no one can save you today
from my wrath.

Hearing Jānakī thus speak,
the thousand-faced one startled,
and saw ahead of him

that peerless Jānakī-jewel.

Her beauty aroused the great-bodied one,
and he swooned nearly with awe,
thinking, amazed, of that fascinating form.

Such a beautiful maiden,
I have never seen nor heard of,
her slave I will be
for ever and ever then.

Thus did Rāvaṇa, as his thousand faces shone,
laughingly spoke to the daughter of Mithilā.
'Come, come, O beloved mine, come to me now,
I will take you with me and destroy your sorrow.

You, dear, are worthy of my pleasure, not
for this mere man, I will make you chief
among all my queens. I will give you all
you want; I will serve you as a slave,
if you but come away with me this soonest.'

Hearing this, the angry Sītā, trembling soon,
picked her bow, and fixed a sharp barb to the string.
That fiery arrow did the chaste one fling
towards Rāvaṇa the demon king,
and yet the evil one, aroused,
would think not of fighting.

Over and over to Sītā
he would address his words foolish,
come away with me, O moon faced one.
Soft bodied you are indeed,
newly churned butter like,
is it your place to fight this war?

I am worshipped in three worlds,
all creatures are my followers,
what will your arrow then do to me?
With folded hands I say to you,
beautiful one, now come to me,

come away with me to my abode.

I will be a devoted slave,
and you my mistress of all,
enslaved by you thus I will remain.

Shining like the lightning then,
Sītā said to the demon,
your life has now come to an end.
She who is mother to all three worlds,
you say such things to her in your lust,
I do not see how you will survive.

Payāra

The gods gaze down from the firmament
and watch Sītā with the bow in her hands.
They ask each other in great amazement
how will Janaka's daughter fight this battle.
The evil one through Śaṅkara's boon
has won the three worlds so soon.
How will Jānakī now slay him then?
Riding on Garuḍa when Hari came to fight,
the Discus-wielder did the demon put to flight.
Viṣṇu with his mount did he fling to the seas even.
Who would then be brave to face this demon!
And since then none of us gods do dare to go
even nearer to the place where the demon resides.
As the jackal flees on the lion's arrival,
so do we fear him like all consuming Time!
That Hari is incarnate in Daśaratha's home,
him the demon has subdued under that mountain.
Golden-creeper-soft-bodied is Janaka's daughter,
how will she ever be the demon's victor?
Thus do the gods converse amongst them,
wondering ceaseless about Jānakī's victory.
The sages say 'Janaka's daughter, victorious be!'
Chanting Vedic metres they bless her then.
In order that her strength may increase manifold,
one thunder-sound uttered the King of the Gods.
Hearing that sound did Śrī Rāma's wife

thinking of Rāvaṇa was angered further.
More did she thirst for battle of late,
jittering the demons then did pullulate.
Bow in hand, Sītā then entered the fray,
the transcendent one in her embodied form,
Sītā burns fierce like fire in her dire anger.
Saudāminī begs for place at her lotus feet.

23RD SARGA

Payāra

And thus did the battle rage for long
yet Jānakī could not the night-walker slay.
Then did she assume the fierce Kālī form,
emaciated, hollow eyes, terrible to behold.
In anger do her eyes wheel ceaselessly,
her third eye blazes with a fiery fury.
A necklace of heads swings around her neck,
on her waist she sports a girdle of hands.
Terrifying, speeding forth, loudly roaring one,
horrifying, deformed bodied, terrible yon.
Lolling tongued, four-armed, pendulous belly,
large-lipped, dark as Pralaya clouds.
Matted hair, cleaver in hand, and a skull cup,
large bodied, large hair covering it all.
Sītā thus changing form turned Asitā.
With a stroke then she cleaved Rāvaṇa's heads.
Yet by Śiva's boon the brave one did not die.
Over and over did she cut off his heads.
By Śaṅkara's boon they were restored again.
Seeing how she couldn't slay the valiant demon,
worry thus entered the heart of the goddess.
A single drop of blood when it touched the earth,
the heads would spring back onto their place.
Seeing this the great goddess extended her tongue
and covered the whole battlefield with its girth.
On it she lifted the evil night-walker,
and then cleft his thousand heads off on her tongue.
All the blood that burst forth she drank to her fill,
and thus did the evil demon part with his life.

Seeing Rāvaṇa dead all the gods above
showered blossoms on the goddess' head.
The sages extolled her with paeans and hymns.
The night-walker's death pleased thus all that lives.
'Hail Kālī, Kālī' sang the ḍākinī-yoginī hordes,
and dancing naked feasted on flesh and gore.
From her hair follicles did the Mātṛkā countless
issue forth then to sport with the dark goddess.
Listen, O sage, they do permeate this world,
fear-giving to the evil, kind to the good.
I have spoken briefly, sage, about all of this.
The one who listens will have no fear of death.
Prabhāvatī, Viśālākṣī, Gomatī, Pālikā,
Śrimatī, Bahulā, Apsujātā, Ambālikā,
Putrī, Dhumāvatī, Dhruva, Ratnā, Bhayankarī,
Vasudāmā, Sudāmā, Viśokā, Jaleśvarī, Mattajānī, Jayā, Senā, Kālākhyā,
Śobhanā,
Śatrunjayā, Mahācūḍā, Romānvitānanā,
Meghasvanā, Amitākṣī, Jayā, Kopavatī,
Padmāvatī, Sunetrā, Karajā, Bhogavatī,
Santālikā, Kālapatnī, Kalā, Mahābalā,
Nityapriyā, Mahānandā, Saṃvid-mekhalā,
Śataghaṇṭā, Śatānandā, Suprabhā-bhāvinī,
Vidyujjihvā, Candrasītā, Mangaldāyinī,
Kankālī, Bhadrakālikā, Sphatikā, Cāmarī,
Kapālamālinī, Kumbhākṣa, Śatodarī,
Mandodarī, Manoramā, Putanā, Suprabhā,
Krośanā, Kotarā, Śokanāśā, Ravinibhā,
Utkrāmvinī, Taḍitākṣī, Krośanā, Kankaṇā,
Vetālajananī, Irāvatī, Citrasenā,
Namramukhī, Ketakī, Kukkutī, Ūrdhvaveṇī,
Dīrghajihvā, Valotkatā, Mukutī, Kāñcanī,
Lohitākṣī, Mahāmāyā, Medhā, Sukumārī,
Gokarṇā, Mahiṣananā, Jāyā, Lambodarī,
Anuṇābhā, Mahābhāgā, Dīrghakeśyutā,
Bhutitīrtha, Agocarā, Trilokaprasutā,
Kharasparṣā, Lambodarā, Kankanā, Śobhanā
and countless other nāyikā one barely could count.
Śrī Rāma-Jānakī's lotus feet do I bear in my heart.
Thus does the poor slave Saudāminī compose this.

Mayamriga, California

Light knives slice   redwood tops
Falling liquid   on leaves below

Crunch of adidas feet   and barbecue
Smoke-signs   whose woods are these

Oldest tree traps   resinous prisons
Catching life   precisely as it was

Ten thousand years ago   amber flies
Lucent winged   fixed compound eyes

Gazing at eternity   unflinching
Whose woods are these imagination's

Spotted deer at the creek   alert
Listening for   a treacherous crackle

Would know   the cars on the highway
Whizzing by   rifles loaded with buckshot

Seek her she is conquest, shimmering in
Shadow and these are deer hunter's woods

Or, some queen in exile wants a golden deer
That makes these the woods of royal caprice

Calendar artists camp out nights   waiting
To get her on paper   a poet describes her

She is all things to all men   the sport
Of gods   so these are woods of wild desire

But at times   tired of the feverish chase
Bothered by all the attention   deer goes

Berserk   changes herself to a *rakshasa*
Devouring   these become her killing woods

Queens carried off, hunters dead   blood-red
Woods whose woods are they   whose woods

Kali

A goddess chews on myth
As other women might on paan
Red juices stain her mouth.

Bored by her own powers
Immense and spectral, Kali broods
About Shiva, she is perverse.

She will not plead with him
Nor reveal Ganesha's birth
She will not ask him home.

Shiva loves her, but absences
And apsaras are natural to him
No god is hampered by his sins.

Kali desires a mortal, whose day
Begins with her, ends at nightfall
In her arms, a man who will die

Without her, whose love is fallible
But secure, she wants to be held
Like a warm creature, not a fable.

Loneliness drives this goddess mad
She is vagrant, her limbs askew
She begs a mate, her hair unmade.

Fickle as Shiva, memory deserts her
Chandi or Durga or Parvati, which
Is she, which of her selves weeps here?

Even Ganesha, for whom she feels
Only tenderness, excludes her, even he
Seems impatient with her flaws.

Where should such a goddess turn?
Kali, mistress of the temporal world
Wants bliss defined in human terms.

Staid Ganesha knows this wildness
Must be curbed, Shiva, peripatetic
Agrees, and across the wilderness

Both gift Kali a companion eagle, hurt
By no arrow, fed on nothing, it returns
Each night to its eyrie in her heart.

MALLIKA SENGUPTA

Translated from the Bengali by Arunava Sinha

Pandu's Desire For Sons

[Two and a half thousand years later
Sex will be determined on earth
Its name, amniocentesis.
~So astrologers said]

We want only sons
Let the infant smell of sons pervade the green earth

Pandu said, sons are of many kinds
My own son will be of my own seed
But if not, I depend on you, my partner in duty
Lie with the man I choose, create a son for me
Or I can buy the rare sperm of a man
A son will be conceived in your body

The woman's womb-soil seeks a plough
If I am impotent, I shall hire, or employ
Or by any other means bring you seed, Kunti, grain-goddess
Fill my arms with your harvest

Kingly joys or wealth and fame, I want none of it
I do not want the birth of a daughter, we want only sons

While Teaching My Son History

'History is nothing but man's activity
In pursuing his aims'
~Karl Marx, *The Holy Family*

From history we have come to know all this
The first human was Java Man, Cro-Magnon
Neanderthal Man, all of them barbarians
Surviving by battling with nature
Killing bears with blunt stone weapons
Blowing into reeds to play the flute
They created this man-made civilization
Shadow women by their sides, or not

When Paleolithic Man stepped aside
All humans were Stone Age men
Iron Age men moulding the hard metal
All these ancient people were men
From history we have come to know all this

The forefathers were alone, mankind too
We have no womankind, nor foremothers
History is his story of sperm and valour
Because it makes no reference to women
We know women did not exist then

Man was born in the womb of Java Man
Neanderthal Man fed children at his breast
Java and Neanderthal Men were only male
The man alone was both god and goddess

The male mother was the male father
The male was both melody and flute
The male was both penis and uterus
From history we have come to know all this

The historian was in fact a eunuch

KUMUDINI

Viswamitra

Translated from the Tamil by Ahana Lakshmi

Scene 2

Two days later in the garden of the Inner Palace
(CHANDRAMATI and Minister SATYAKIRTI are seen talking)

CHANDRAMATI:	Has the King given away his entire kingdom?
SATYAKIRTI:	Yes. Not only that. Earlier the sage had bought materials for the sacrifice and left them with the king. Now he is demanding that they be returned, after taking away the kingdom and all the treasures.
CHANDRAMATI:	What did the king say?
SATYAKIRTI:	He said that he would go to Benaras, somehow locate the things and give the amount due. Don't we know the king's obstinate nature!
CHANDRAMATI:	Where is he now?
SATYAKIRTI:	He is going to leave after taking off his ornaments. He sent me here to give you this information.
CHANDRAMATI:	Um...who is going to look after Ayodhya here?
SATYAKIRTI:	I don't know. Maharishi is the one who must supervise that.
CHANDRAMATI:	What are you going to do?
SATYAKIRTI:	After eating the king's salt all these years, is there any doubt about what I am going to do? Of course I am going to follow the king. You are also going to do the same, aren't you?
CHANDRAMATI:	*(apparently in deep thought)* Um...what?
SATYAKIRTI:	You are also going to follow the king, aren't you?
CHANDRAMATI:	Why should you follow him? Send some trustworthy person with him. You have other work here. Your duty is to put the king back on his throne as soon as possible. Instead of that, what purpose is gained by us tagging along with him? That is a crazy thing to do!
SATYAKIRTI:	*(taken aback)* But aren't you going with him?
CHANDRAMATI:	No, and neither are you going. There is no need to repeat things to smart people like you who understand things

Unbound

even before they are told. There is a lot of difference between Viswamitra formerly reigning in Kanyakubja and our king reigning over Ayodhya now. The rishi does not know all the current rules and regulations. It will be exhausting just to understand them. Also, he has become a Brahmarishi. It must be so arranged that he goes away saying that he does not want to shoulder the responsibilities of the kingdom.

SATYAKIRTI: Then, shall I discuss this with the other ministers and with my father, and make appropriate arrangements?

CHANDRAMATI: Yes, do so. *(She whispers something to him)*

(Chandramati's aunt and some of her sons and daughters enter.)

CHANDRAMATI: *(sends away the minister and runs towards the aunt, falls at her feet and clutches them)* Aunt! Aunt!

AUNT: May you live a long happy wedded life! You are sitting around with just one son. Time you had four more! Anyway, at least he should keep well!

CHANDRAMATI: I don't know what is going to happen! Only you have to save me, Aunt. The kingdom is all gone. He has also gone away to Benaras.

AUNT: What! What farce is this?

CHANDRAMATI: I don't know what is happening. Viswamitra came, demanded this and that, demanded money, the kingdom... and has taken everything away. One falsehood has to be uttered, and all that will come back to us. But Harishchandra will never utter a lie. The rishi is chasing us out of the kingdom. Maybe he wants to demean us because of being Vasishta's disciples!

AUNT: What a ridiculous situation!

CHANDRAMATI: The women's quarters are filled with all kinds of comforts. You must stay here to give me support and company. Navamalika, take Aunt inside, give her something to eat and take care of her properly. Aunt! Why have you lost so much weight?

AUNT: Some losing of weight, this! I am unable to carry my body around; I have become so fat. And you say I have become thin! Huh!

(As the AUNT and her children exit, the companion enters)

NAVAMALIKA: Amma, Nakshatreyan wants to meet you.

CHANDRAMATI: Maharishi's disciple? Fine. First undo my hair and leave it loose. Here, take these ornaments and put them away, I am going inside. Bring him in after a few moments.

(exits)

Scene 3
The Inner Palace.
CHANDRAMATI is seen lying down with her hair loose and dishevelled, sobbing uncontrollably. NAKSHATREYAN enters looking uneasy.

NAKSHATREYAN: *(clearing his throat)* Muni...
CHANDRAMATI: *(closing her eyes tightly)* O Prananatha!,O Giver of life...!
NAKSHATREYAN: *(clearing his throat a little more loudly).* I have come here under orders from the most eminent of sages.
CHANDRAMATI: *(with great difficulty raising her head and opening her eyes very slowly)* Oh. Looks like it is the foremost of disciples, Nakshatreyan. Salutations!
NAKSHATREYAN: I have come as ordered by the sage.
CHANDRAMATI: The good fortune of having a disciple like you must be admired. Navamalika, where have you gone? Perform the requisite hospitality to the guest. *(looking inside)* What? Is there nothing available? O how wretched I feel! I did not have the occasion to extend a welcome to you in my better-off days—now—O Prananatha—why do you keep deserting me?—God!—
NAKSHATREYAN: I have come as ordered by the sage. He...
CHANDRAMATI: What has he ordered?
NAKSHATREYAN: Nothing. If you plan to follow your husband, you will not be impeded. You...
CHANDRAMATI: That's all is it? That's only if I were planning to follow him, isn't it? Right now, I am not going to go after him.
NAKSHATREYAN: *(surprised)* Oh...

(AUNT enters)

CHANDRAMATI: *(sits up)* Aunt, I was thinking only of you. Drowned in misery, I am unable to be properly hospitable to a guest. You were searching for a proper bridegroom for your youngest daughter, Lalita. Here he is, a very suitable boy. A disciple of Sage Viswamitra. He has exceptional qualities.
AUNT: Is that so? Looks like Manmatha himself! What is your gotram?

NAKSHATREYAN:	*(in surprise)* Shadamarshana.
AUNT:	Very good. What else does one need? Would you like to see the girl? I have no objections. Chandramati, your uncle was wont to say, 'Why do you worry about your daughter? She has taken after you. They will compete to marry her. *(a little shyly)* For some reason, that man used to think that I was very beautiful. What do you say? Is it alright if my daughter is like me? Would you like to get married?
CHANDRAMATI:	Why would he not like it, Aunt? Is it not because he is interested that he immediately revealed his gotram? Otherwise, would he tell us this?

(Two of AUNT's daughters enter)

AUNT:	Bhami, Dhima. Here is the new son-in-law of our house. He is going to marry Lalita.
BHAMI:	What! Mother! Is our Lalita going to get married? Wait! Let me call my elder brother.

(She exits)

DHIMA:	Mapillai, if you harass the daughter of our house, we will be very unhappy. Will you take loving care of her?
NAKSHATREYAN:	*(falteringly)* Without giving me a chance to speak, you are saying everything. I am a brahmachari. ...marriage...
AUNT:	Why are you feeling sorry that you are a brahmachari? I shall tell our Vasishta and ask him to set a date as soon as the Chitrai month begins.
NAKSHATREYAN:	Ayyayo! I don't know anything about this! To send Chandramati to the forest...
AUNT:	What is there to know? Is it a big accomplishment to know how to exchange garlands and swing on the marriage swing? Maharishi will teach you all the requisite mantras.
DHIMA:	Does it matter if you don't know? When we all got married, Lalita was observing everything carefully. She knows it all. She will teach you.
AUNT:	I should not praise my own daughter. But she is very intelligent. If she sees anything just once, she never forgets.

(Two of AUNT's sons enter)

FIRST SON:	Is this our mapillai? Very good *(pats him on the back)*. A man should be like this! It is not even a couple of hours since we came here. In that short space of time, you have cajoled Mother and settled the marriage!
NAKSHATREYAN:	*(pulling his hair)* No, not at all.
SECOND SON:	Mother was saying that she was going to keep her youngest daughter with her and not going to get her married!
AUNT:	What could I do? On seeing him, I could not refuse his request!
BHAMI:	Mother, why are you worried? He assures us that he will take good care of her.
FIRST SON:	Excellent, mapillai. That's the way to settle things. Some people feel shy about these things. I don't like that!
NAKSHATREYAN:	*(jumping, beating his head)* Ayyo, I did not say anything like that!
SECOND SON:	Mapillai saar, be careful! You may have some claims over your wife. However, if you hurt her in any way, we are there, see? Don't be under the impression that a husband can get away with anything.
DHIMA:	Here, please partake of these snacks. Lalita has made them all by herself.

(NAKSHATREYAN tries to run away. Everyone surrounds him preventing this.)

Scene 4
The King's Court

(On one side, Minister SATYAKIRTI is talking to some people. Brahmins, pundits, poets, physicians, all are seated in state. VISWAMITRA enters. Everyone stands up to greet him.)

ASSEMBLY:	Jaya vijayi bhava! May you be victorious! Hail Kusika's son! Long live Kaathi's son.
VISWAMITRA:	Your king...
ASSEMBLY:	Yourself!
VISWAMITRA:	*(sounding alarmed)* Ha! What!
ASSEMBLY:	Your ascending the throne to govern Ayodhya brings good fortune to this city and is a result of the tapasya of its people.
VISWAMITRA:	I did not take the kingdom with the idea of ruling it. Your king...
ASSEMBLY:	It is our good fortune that an esteemed person, full of

prowess, radiant in character, able to hold his own against Vasishta can reign over us. It has to be you! Please seat yourself on the throne.

(Satyakirti leads Viswamitra by hand to the throne and makes him sit there. The maid servants of the palace come forward and begin massaging his feet.)

VISWAMITRA: *(startled, shakes them off his feet)* I am an ascetic. You should not touch me.

KANCHUKI: Aryaputra! These people are hereditary masseuses of the king's feet. If you reject them, they will be upset. Yearning to do their duty, they will give up their life. This sin against womanhood will be on your head.

(The women wipe their streaming eyes with great show of suffering and massage his feet with greater fervour and touch their eyes to his feet)

SATYAKIRTI: Customary practices should not be abandoned. It is said in the Niti Shastras...

VISWAMITRA: What! Are you going to teach me about the Shastras?

SATYAKIRTI: No, esteemed sage, forgive me.

VISWAMITRA: Then shut up! *(deep in thought)*

POET: Lord who performed fiery penance
In the terrible forest;
You helped the shivering Trisanku
Stay in mid-air;
You have the complexion of molten gold
This is an auspicious time.
Do ascend the throne
In a trice!

VISWAMITRA: *(closing his ears)* What? What is this?

SATYAKIRTI: Merely that the poet of this assembly is reading out his composition. He has also written it in prose form. Oh Poet, please read that out too.

VISWAMITRA: There is no need.

POET: It won't take long. It is very short. Just about 400 lines. But in some places I may have to explain it in detail for it cannot be understood that easily.

VISWAMITRA: *(strongly)* There is no need for that.

(The Poet sits down looking downcast)

HERALD ANNOUNCER: O King, the messenger from the Anga Kingdom has arrived.

VISWAMITRA: Alright, let him come.

(The messenger from Anga enters, places several gifts in front of the king and salutes him)

MESSENGER: O King of Kings! Pride of Kings! Kosala and Anga enjoy the best of relations. Renowned for bravery and never fatigued in war, our sovereign, the King of Anga, has heard frequently from his messengers much about the progress of Kosala, its trade, its industry and the beauty of its capital city, Ayodhya; all these have gladdened his heart. Anga is in no way inferior in valour or wealth. Hence, the King of Anga, our sovereign has sent me forth on this mission. He has decided to give in marriage his daughters to you. He has asked us to inform you of this matter, and request that you, with your family grace our country.

VISWAMITRA: Narayana! I am an ascetic! Why should I get married?

SATYAKIRTI: *(in the sage's ear)* The King of Anga is very powerful. We don't have the capability now to wage war with him. It is better to agree to their request.

ARMY CHIEF: *(secretly)* Ignoring everything I advised him to do, Harishchandra foolishly sent away half the army to work in the fields. Now we have no capacity to fight any country. Our plight will be utterly miserable if the Anga army comes here. The king's duty is to safeguard the country. It is now upto you. There is nothing more that I can do. I am prepared to hand in my resignation.

VISWAMITRA: *(controlling his anger)* How many daughters does your king have?

MESSENGER: There are twenty-seven stunning princesses; equal to the twenty-seven celestial stars!

VISWAMITRA: Which of these does he want to offer to me?

MESSENGER: All of them. Our King, resplendent like the shining sun, is never mean-spirited or miserly.

VISWAMITRA: *(with disquiet)* I am an ageing ascetic. How can I marry twenty-seven young maidens?

(One servant enters, whispers into SATYAKIRTI's ear that MENAKA has arrived. SATYAKIRTI asks that she be sent in. MENAKA enters)

MENAKA: Ah, Aryaputra! It has been such a long time since I've seen you. I came running when I heard that you had left the forest and ascended the throne of Kosala. Beloved! Do you remember once on the banks of the River Malini, on the night of the fourth day of the waxing moon in the autumn, we were talking all by ourselves? You said sadly, 'My Queen! I do not even have a kingdom to offer you! Now, you will surely give me a place in your kingdom, won't you?'

Yajnaseni

Translated from the Oriya by Pradip Bhattacharya

With bowed head my husband spoke out clearly, 'The command that has issued from Mother's lips and which you have accepted, is my dharma. I would have been happy to have Krishnaa to myself. But that will violate dharma for I would have to defy Mother's command as well as yours. You, too, have already said that we shall all marry Krishnaa. I do not wish to disagree with this and incur sin. With you, the elder brother, yet unmarried, how can I marry first? I would rather my happiness be less than my dharma suffer. Destroying dharma, violating the commands of my mother and elder brother, the happiness that will accrue to me will not really be happiness. This will not bring pure contentment to my mind. Therefore, we shall all enjoy the princess equally. She will be the wife, according to dharma, of us all.'

Hearing my husband's words, I flared up. I wished I could turn into a searing flame of the sacrificial fire and destroy the world and in it these five brothers too. If my husband were to turn into a fistful of ashes I would not be sorry. He, who with undisturbed heart, could hand over his wife to another man for fear of his own dharma being destroyed, might be the most virtuous soul in the world, but he could never be a proper husband for any woman of discrimination.

I burnt in inner anguish. But not a word came through my lips. Perhaps Mother understood my inner turmoil. After all, she was a woman and therefore it was natural for her to sense a woman's feelings.

In a soft, sympathetic tone she began speaking, 'I have heard that princess Krishnaa is wise, intelligent, learned in scriptures. In this situation of perilous distress let her resolve the dilemma herself. We cannot forcibly impose our wishes on her.'

Exactly then scripture-learned Lord Vyas arrived. I thought: 'What link does Vyasdev have with this Brahmin family? How did he happen to land up here? Anyhow, as he has arrived by god's grace it will be appropriate for him to resolve this dilemma. By leaving the responsibility of the solution to me, Mother wants to keep herself free of all blame. The elder brother, right from the beginning, has been speaking of how to keep both sides happy. My husband, too, is anxious to be free from blame. Then what shall I do?'

Hearing everything, Vyasdev became grave and was lost in thought.

Softly, Mother said, 'Had they announced right from the beginning that having won Krishnaa they had brought her, all this difficulty would not have arisen. Now please find a way so that my words remain true, my sons honour their mother's command, and yet no sin touches princess Krishnaa.'

I wondered how these two conflicting statements could be reconciled. It seemed to me that the elder brother had deliberately uttered such equivocating sentences to convey the news of my arrival to Mother. The elder brother knew that every day the food and money obtained as alms was divided equally amongst themselves. Then why did he not say, 'Mother, your third son, having won princess Krishnaa in the svayamvar, has brought her here and your third daughter-in-law is waiting at the door for your blessings?' Therefore, if he did not state this openly, clearly there was an ulterior motive behind his words. Mother was bound to say before opening the door that the beautiful object should be enjoyed equally by all the five brothers. That was why he had used such words. Perhaps, like others, he too had been infatuated with my beauty and had conspired in this fashion to obtain me! The other brothers would also have been attracted to me. Therefore, why would they let such an opportunity slip from their grasp?

My mind was whirling with such thoughts. Vyasdev was speaking to Mother—'You know that I had sent you word to send all the five brothers to the svayamvar of the princess of Panchal. You knew that the conditions of the svayamvar could not be fulfilled by anyone other than your third son. Therefore, despite knowing everything if you gave such a directive to your sons then what is there left for thinking? You knew this too that even if the earth should dissolve your sons would not violate your directive. What was to happen has happened. No amount of regret will call back the words that have been uttered. Therefore, let the entire decision be left to princess Krishnaa. Aryan virgins have been vested with the freedom to choose their husbands. How can we intervene in this?'

I was not pained by the words of Gurudev Dvaipayan. I was astonished, taken aback. I thought in this world no one invited blame upon himself. Everyone was busily shifting the responsibility onto others to remain blameless. What the mother wanted, the elder brother wanted, Gurudev wanted, I knew. I wanted to make it abundantly clear that I had only one husband. It was he who had won me. Him alone I had chosen. But then the mother's words would not be honoured. The brothers would be guilty of violating the mother's command. My husband, too. In fact, his sin would be greater. In such circumstances would I be able to found a household of joy with my husband? From the very beginning I would become the target of everyone's aversion for not honouring the mother's and the elder brother's words. Ultimately my husband, too, would blame me for turning him into a rebel against his mother. In such a situation, how could I speak out my mind openly?

If this was not possible, how could I accept the alternative? There was no precedent for one woman marrying five men. This would not add to the fame of woman as a species.

For all future time Draupadi would remain condemned in the history of the world as a woman of despicable and stained character. So much so that in the Kaliyuga people would call fallen women having many men 'Draupadis of this era', making me the butt of scorn. What would they understand of the situation in which Panchali became the wife of five men? I was angry with the mother. Animosity against her rose in me. But the moment I looked at her I forgot the sorrow of leaving my mother. Knowing everything, why did she utter such a sentence? She had sent her sons to Panchal. She knew that her third son would surely win me. Then, why did she say that?

Every mother wants that her daughter-in-law should be beautiful and, if not wise, full of discrimination and knowledge, be of blameless character, chaste and virtuous, spending her entire life concentrating lotus-like on one husband. But how contrary was this situation! For the sake of her own word how she was hinting to her daughter-in-law to take five husbands!

It seemed to me that the matter was not that simple. There was surely some deep mystery behind this. There might, perhaps, be some greater design. But, however noble the intention, how could I marry five men? I had already chosen one husband.

In my heart the memory of Krishna arose. I poured out all my heart's anguish before him. I thought, if he had been present he would have rescued me from this perilous distress. All of them wanted to accomplish their own aims by using me, but were chary of acknowledging it. Krishna was not like that. By a mere gesture he would have conveyed to me what ought to be done. Was it the integrity of my womanhood that was of greater moment to me or the mother's word, the protection of my husband's and his brothers' dharma? To sacrifice myself for safeguarding the dharma of others—was that my duty, or was it my duty to choose one husband for the sake of my self-respect and happiness? This I could not make out! In the secrecy of my heart I cried, 'O Govind! I have accepted you as sakha. I have offered myself before you. In all Aryavart it is you who are the most wise, qualified and discriminating. Did you not know that these Brahmins would enact such a play for sacrificing Krishnaa in their dharma-yajna? Then why did you not give me a hint? Now what am I to do?'

Then, suddenly, it happened. I had just thought of him and Krishna and Balaram appeared at the door!

SUNITI NAMJOSHI

The Fabulous Feminist

THE PANCHATANTRA

In the holy city of Benares there lived a Brahmin, who, as he walked by the riverbank, watching the crows floating downstream, feeding on the remains of half-burnt corpses, consoled himself thus: 'It is true that I am poor, but I am a Brahmin, it is true that I have no sons, but I, myself, am indisputably a male. I shall return to the temple and pray to Lord Vishnu to grant me a son.' He went off to the temple and Lord Vishnu listened and Lord Vishnu complied, but whether through absent-mindedness or whether for some other more abstruse reason, he gave him a daughter. The Brahmin was disappointed. When the child was old enough, he called her to him and delivered himself thus: 'I am a Brahmin. You are my daughter. I had hoped for a son. No matter. I will teach you what I know, and when you are able, we will both meditate and seek guidance.' Though only a woman, she was a Brahmin, so she learned very fast, and then, they both sat down and meditated hard. In a very short time Lord Vishnu appeared. 'What do you want?' he said. The Brahmin couldn't stop himself. He blurted out quickly, 'I want a son.' 'Very well,' said the god, 'Next time around.' In his next incarnation the Brahmin was a woman and bore eight sons. 'And what do you want?' he said to the girl. 'I want human status.' 'Ah, that is much harder,' and the god hedged and appointed a commission.

THE MONKEY AND THE CROCODILES

A monkey used to live in a large jambu tree which grew along the banks of the river Yamuna. The fruit of this tree was unusually delicious and a bit like plum. At the foot of the tree lived two crocodiles. The monkey and the crocodiles were very good friends. The monkey would feed the crocodiles plums and the crocodiles in return would make conversation. They also protected her—though she did not know it—by keeping a watchful eye on her. The day came when the monkey began to feel more and more restless. 'I'm off,' she said, 'to explore the world.' 'Here, jump on my back,' said one of the crocodiles, 'and I'll ferry you over.' 'No,' she said, 'I don't want to go to the other river bank. I want to follow this river to its ultimate source.' 'That's dangerous,' said the crocodiles. 'Why?' said the monkey. 'There are beasts along the way. They'll eat you up.' 'What sorts of beasts?' asked the monkey suspiciously. 'Well, they are long and narrow with scaly hides and powerful jaws.' 'I don't understand,' said the monkey. 'Don't go,' said the crocodiles. 'But I want to find out and see for myself.' 'Beware of the beasts,' said her friends the crocodiles. The monkey set off. Seven years later she hobbled back. She had lost her tail, six of her teeth, and one eye. 'Did you find the source of the river Yamuna?' 'No,' said the monkey. 'Did you encounter the beasts?' 'Yes,' said the monkey. 'What did they look like?' 'They looked like you,' she answered slowly. 'When you warned me long ago, did you know that?' 'Yes,' said her friends and avoided her eye.

THE GIANTESS

Thousands of years ago in far away India, which is so far away that anything is possible, before the advent of the inevitable Aryans, a giantess was in charge of a little kingdom. It was small by her standards, but perhaps not by our own. Three oceans converged on its triangular tip, and in the north there were mountains, the tallest in the world, which would perhaps account for this singular kingdom. It was not a kingdom, but the word has been lost and I could find no other. There wasn't any king. The giantess governed and there were no other women. The men were innocent and happy and carefree. If they were hurt, they were quickly consoled. For the giantess was kind, and would set them on her knee and tell them they were brave and strong and noble. And if they were hungry, the giantess would feed them. The milk from her breasts was sweeter than honey and more nutritious than mangoes. If they grew fractious, the giantess would sing, and they would clamber up her legs and onto her lap and sleep unruffled. They were a happy people and things might have gone on in this way forever, were it not for the fact that the giantess grew tired. Her knees felt more bony, her voice rasped, and on one or two occasions she showed irritation. They were greatly distressed. 'We love you,' they said to the tired giantess, 'Why won't you sing? Are you angry with us? What have we done?' 'You are dear little children,' the giantess replied, 'but I have grown very tired and it's time for me to go.' 'Don't you love us anymore? We'll do what you want. We will make you happy. Only please don't go.' 'Do you know what I want?' the giantess asked. They were silent for a bit, then one of them said, 'We'll make you our queen.' And another one said, 'We'll write you a poem.' And a third one shouted (while turning cartwheels), 'We'll bring you many gifts of oysters and pearls and pebbles and stones.' 'No,' said the giantess, 'No.' She turned her back and crossed the mountains.

MALATHI MAITHRI

Proscribed Blood—1

Translated from the Tamil by N. Kalyan Raman

In the sanctum's dark stands
Our half-female Goddess,
Waiting on her one aching foot
Inside her stone prison,
Bolted shut and baking
In April's stifling heat

With his lone right eye, Sivan
Glares askance at Shakti
As she wriggles in discomfort,
Caused by the sticky trickle of ooze
In her vagina from her bursting eggs

As the blood scent spreads, causing
One half of the snake to slither down,
Bearing the other half in its memory,
She grabs and pulls the snake
Towards her to wipe the blood
Before flinging it away

Feeling extremely worn today
From the more copious than
Normal discharge of blood,
She asks Sivan to move away
To offer some relief to her body
The one who is one half
Of her feels upset:
How can I survive with this half-body
For three whole days?
Our contract must not be breached, he says

Without you, I don't exist,
He declares, as he folds her
In a tight embrace with his right hand
I need to sit with legs stretched out

I must sleep with my own body
She rips and throws Sivan away
With her left hand, and sits down
Once again in the vacant space
Of her age-old throne

All along the pathway around
The temple's perimeter are found
The bloodied tracks of a lone foot

Proscribed Blood—2

Translated from the Tamil by N. Kalyan Raman

On this rainy night
The full moon hangs precariously
From the temple's sacred mast
The radiance dripping
Into her nose ring slips
Away and flies out
To catch her pecking parrot

Meenakshi follows the light, giving chase
As the moon pours down with the chill wind
As cold mist on the stone plinth,
Her soles sting and her body thrills
Wiping the trickle descending
Hotly between her thighs
With her long skirt, she runs

After flying through the thousand-
pillared hall on the outer perimeter,
Her darling parrot alights and perches
On the moon afloat on the surface
Of the Golden Lotus pond

Removing her undergarment,
She rinses it in the pond's water
Impelled by the blood scent,
Fish swarm to her feet

And peck at her hands
She sets out to catch them
As in the days of yore,
Casting wide her sari's end

Seeing the marvel
Of the pond's moon
Turning red, little by little,
The parrot calls her, shrieking:
Meenakshi! Meenakshi!

Demon Language

Translated from the Tamil by Lakshmi Holmström

The demon's features are all
woman
woman's features are all
demon

Demon language
is poetry

Poetry's features are all
saint
become woman
become poet
become demon

Demon language
is liberty

Outside Earth
she stands:
niili, wicked woman.

Journeys

The pieces represented in this section have one thing in common—a journey. However, this does not make them travel writing. What I have looked for is writing that communicates a sense of discovering a new place, be it rural or urban, cosmopolitan or provincial. It could even be an internal journey to a place inside one's own head.

There are places that exist but which you cannot return to, as described by Popati Hiranandani's poem. It travels though history and geography, describing the pain of cultural exile and lost homelands. Mahadevi Varma's *A Pilgrimage to the Himalayas* is full of pen sketches of people she met during her travels, and essays on lives lived in her villages or hometown. The piece included here, 'The Chinese Pedlar' is a story of larger travels that come to you through meeting another traveller who has journeyed much further and has brought his story to your doorstep.

Ismat Chughtai's essay is an account of her brush with the law when she was tried for 'obscenity' in Lahore. It illustrates the writer's famous sense of fun and adventure but, despite the breezy tone, this essay also makes evident the price writers sometimes pay, socially or legally, for truth-telling.

Prabha Khaitan's memoir *A Life Apart* describes the year she spent in the USA during which she had to learn to fend for herself, tolerate differences in lifestyle and diet, and learnt to recognize the depths of loneliness as well as love. It is a suitable companion to Sailabala Das's older work, *Bilat Prabas*, which describes a rare journey undertaken by a group of young Indian women travelling to England during the colonial era. The extract included here describes their experience of being on a ship, getting seasick, and mingling with co-passengers of another race.

Arundhathi Subramaniam's poems capture the shorter, equally intense, journeys that occur within a city. This journey could be a movement through time as one moves into or out of a city. Or it could be a sense of homecoming—the reader discovers a metropolis through the poet's experience of leaving and then returning. Mamang Dai's poems travel in the same way, with the hills and a remote landscape being the place we are headed to. Eunice de Souza's five-part poem 'Travelling' does precisely what it sets out to do—it travels.

ARUNDHATHI SUBRAMANIAM

Where I Live

(for Anders who wants to know)

I live on a wedge of land
reclaimed from a tired ocean
somewhere at the edge of the universe.

Greetings from this city
of L'Oreal sunsets
and diesel afternoons,
deciduous with concrete,
botoxed with vanity.

City of septic magenta hair-clips,
of garrulous sewers and tight-lipped taps,
of '80s film tunes buzzing near the left temple,
of ranting TV soaps and monsoon melodramas.

City wracked by hope and bulimia.
City uncontained
by movie screen and epigram.
City condemned to unspool
in an eternal hysteria
of lurid nylon dream.

City where you can drop off
a swollen local
and never be noticed.
City where you're a part
of every imli-soaked bhelpuri.

City of the Mahalaxmi beggar
peering up through
a gorse-bush of splayed limbs.

City of dark alleys,
city of mistrust,
city of forsaken tube-lit rooms.

City that coats the lungs
stiffens the spine
chills the gut
with memory

City suspended between
flesh
    and mortar
        and foam leather
            and delirium

where it is perfectly historical
to be looking out
on a sooty handkerchief of ocean,
searching for God.

5.46, Andheri Local

In the women's compartment
of a Bombay local
we search
for no personal epiphanies.
Like metal licked by relentless acetylene
we are welded—
dreams, disasters,
germs, destinies,
flesh and organza,
odours and ovaries.
A thousand-limbed
million-tongued, multi-spoused
Kali on wheels.

When I descend
I could choose
to dice carrots
or dice a lover.

I postpone the latter.

The City and I
(returning to Bombay after 26 November 2008)

This time we didn't circle each other
hackles raised,
fur bristling.

This time there was space
between us—
and we weren't competing.

Space enough and more

for the nose-digging librarian
and her stainless steel tiffin box,

for the Little Theatre peon to read me
his Marathi poems
on rainy afternoons

for the woman on the 7.10 Bhayandar slow
with green combs in her hair
to say
and say again,
He's coming to get me.
He's coming

This time
the city surged
towards me

mangy
bruised-eyed
non-vaccinated

suddenly
mine.

MAMANG DAI

Prayer Flags—2

The wet mountain road.
This is where we spent all our time
wondering if we would get across.

Someone planted a prayer flag in my heart.
Green living, white clouds, and juniper incense
mingled with the blue
left by a sea that once owned this land.

Perhaps the storm will blow it down
someday, after it has halted the wind
a thousand times.

We found each other yesterday,
after they told us the past is over.
Now we are floating smudges of colour
flying high over the mountain barrier.

Small Towns and the River

Small towns always remind me of death.
My hometown lies calmly amidst the trees,
it is always the same,
in summer or winter,
with the dust flying,
or the wind howling down the gorge.

Just the other day someone died.
In the dreadful silence we wept
looking at the sad wreath of tuberoses.
Life and death, life and death,
only the rituals are permanent.

The river has a soul.
In the summer it cuts through the land
like a torrent of grief. Sometimes,

sometimes, I think it holds its breath
seeking a land of fish and stars

The river has a soul.
It knows, stretching past the town,
from the first drop of rain to dry earth
and mist on the mountaintops,
the river knows
the immortality of water.

A shrine of happy pictures
marks the days of childhood.
Small towns grow with anxiety
for the future.
The dead are placed pointing west.
When the soul rises
it will walk into the golden east,
into the house of the sun.

In the cool bamboo,
restored in sunlight,
life matters, like this.

In small towns by the river
we all want to walk with the gods.

In the Name of those Married Women

Translated from the Urdu by M. Asaduddin

It was about four or half past four in the afternoon when the doorbell rang loudly. The servant opened the door, then drew back in fear.

'Who's there?'

'Police!' Whenever a theft took place in the mohalla, all the servants were interrogated.

'Police?' Shahid got up in a huff.

'Yes, sir.' The servant was shaking with fear. 'I haven't done anything, sahib. I swear by god.'

'What's the matter?' Shahid went up to the door and asked.

'Summons.'

'Summons? But...well, where is it?'

'Sorry. I can't give it to you.'

'Summons for what? ...For whom?'

'For Ismat Chughtai. Please call her.' The servant heaved a sigh of relief.

'But tell me this...'

'Please call her. The summons is from Lahore.'

I had prepared milk for my two-month-old daughter, Seema, and was waiting for it to cool. 'Summons from Lahore?' I asked as I held the feeding bottle in cold water.

'Yes, from Lahore.' Shahid had lost his cool by then. Holding the bottle in my hand, I came out barefoot.

'What is the summons about?'

'Read it out,' said the police inspector dourly.

As I read the heading—*Ismat Chughtai vs The Crown*—I broke into laughter. 'Good god, what complaint does the exalted king have against me that he has filed the suit?'

'It's no joke,' the inspector said severely. 'Read it first, and sign it.' I read through the summons but could barely make out the sense. My story 'Lihaaf' had been accused of obscenity. The government had brought a suit against me, and I had to appear before the Lahore High Court in January. Otherwise the government would penalize me severely.

'Well, I won't take the summons.'

'You have to.'

'Why?' I began to argue, as usual.

'What's up?' This was Mohsin Abdullah sprinting up the stairs. He was returning from some unknown destination, and his whole body was covered with dust.

'Just see, these people want to inflict this summons on me. Why should I take it?' Mohsin had already passed his law exams and obtained a first class.

'I see, which story is this?' he asked after reading the summons.

'It's an ill-fated story that has become a source of torment for me.'

'You'll have to take the summons.'

'Why?'

'Don't be stubborn,' Shahid flared up.

'I won't take it.'

'If you don't, you'll be arrested,' Mohsin growled.

'Let them arrest me. I won't take the summons.'

'You'll be put in prison.'

'In prison? Good. I've a great desire to see a prison house. I've urged Yusuf umpteen times to take me to a prison, but he just smiles. Inspector sahib, please take me to the jail. Have you brought handcuffs?' I asked him endearingly.

The inspector was flustered. Barely restraining his anger he said, 'Don't joke. Just sign it.'

Shahid and Mohsin railed at me. I was chattering merrily. 'When my father was a judge in Sambhar, the court used to be held in the mardana, the part of the house meant for menfolk. We would watch through the window thieves and robbers being brought in handcuffs and chains. Once a band of fearsome robbers was brought in. They had a beautiful woman among them. A stately figure in coat and breeches, she had the eyes of an eagle, her waist was supple as a leopard's, and she had a luxuriant crop of long, black hair on her head. I was greatly impressed by he...'

Shahid and Mohsin made me thoroughly confused. I wanted the inspector to hold the feeding bottle so that I could sign, but he retreated with shock as though I had held a gun to him. Mohsin quickly snatched away the bottle from me, and I signed.

'Come down to the police station to sign the surety document. The surety is for five hundred rupees.'

'I don't have five hundred rupees with me now.'

'Not you. Someone else must stand surety for you.'

'I don't want to implicate anyone. If I don't present myself in court, the money will be lost.' I tried to show off my knowledge of the law. 'Please arrest me.'

The inspector didn't get angry this time. He smiled and looked at Shahid, who was sitting on the sofa holding his head in his hands. Then he said to me gently, 'Please come along. It'll take a couple of minutes.'

'But the surety?' I asked, pacified. I was ashamed of my stupid behaviour.

'I'll stand surety for you,' said Mohsin.

'But my child is hungry. Her ayah is young and inexperienced.'

'Feed the child,' said the inspector.

'Then please come in,' Mohsin invited the policeman. The inspector turned out to be one of Shahid's fans and flattered him so much that he forgot his irritation and began to talk pleasantly.

Mohsin, Shahid and I went to the Mahim police station. Having completed the formalities, I asked, 'Where are the prisoners?'

'Want to see them?'

'Of course.'

There were ten or twelve men lying in a huddle behind the railings.

'These are the accused, not prisoners,' said the inspector.

'What crime have they committed?'

'Brawls, violence, pickpocketing, drunken fights...'

'What will be the punishment for them?'

'They'll be fined or imprisoned for a few days.' I felt sorry that I got to see only petty thieves. A couple of murderers or highwaymen would have made the visit more exciting.

'Where would you have put me up?'

'We do not have arrangements to house women prisoners here. They are taken either to Grant Road or Matunga.'

After returning from the police station, Shahid and Mohsin chided me severely. In fact, Shahid fought with me the whole night, even threatened to divorce me. I silenced Mohsin by saying that if he made too much fuss I would disappear and he would lose his five hundred rupees. Shahid could not bear the disgrace and humiliation of a public suit. His parents and elder brother would be terribly upset if they heard of it.

When newspapers published the news, Shahid received a touching letter from my father-in-law, which ran thus: 'Try to reason with Dulhan. Tell her to chant the names of Allah and the Prophet. A lawsuit is bad enough. That, too, on obscenity. We are very worried. May god help you.'

Manto phoned us to say that a suit had been filed against him, too. He had to appear in the same court on the same day. He and Safiya landed up at our place. Manto was looking very happy, as though he had been awarded the Victoria Cross. Though I put up a courageous front, I felt quite embarrassed...I was quite nervous, but Manto encouraged me so much that I forgot all my qualms.

'Come on, it's the only great story you've written. Shahid, be a man and come to Lahore with us... The winter in Lahore is very severe. Aha! Fried fish with whisky...fire in the fireplace like the burning flame in a lover's heart...the blood-red maltas are like a lover's kiss.'

'Be quiet, Manto sahib,' Safiya reprimanded him.

Then, filthy letters began to arrive. They were filled with such inventive and convoluted obscenities that had they been uttered before a corpse, it would have got up and run for cover. Not only me, but my whole family including Shahid and my two-month-old child were dragged in the muck...

I am scared of mud, muck and lizards. Many people pretend to be courageous, but they are scared of dead mice. I got scared of my mail as though the envelopes contained snakes, scorpions and dragons. I would read the first few words and then burn the letters. However, if they fell into Shahid's hands, he would repeat his threat of divorce.

Besides these letters, there were articles published in newspapers and debates in literary and cultural gatherings. Only a hard-hearted person like me could put up with them. I never retaliated, nor did I refuse to admit my mistake. I was aware of my fault. Manto was the only person who would get furious at my cowardice. I was against my own self, and he supported me. None of my friends or Shahid's friends attached much importance to it. I am quite sure, but probably Abbas got the English translation of 'Lihaaf' published somewhere. The Progressives neither appreciated nor found fault with me. This suited me well.

I was staying with my brother when I wrote 'Lihaaf'. I had completed the story at night. In the morning I read it out to my sister-in-law. She didn't think it was vulgar, though she recognized the characters portrayed in it. Then I read it out to my aunt's daughter who was fourteen years old. She didn't understand what the story was about. I sent it to *Adab-e-Lateef* where it was published immediately. Shahid Ahmad Dehlavi was getting a collection of my short stories published and included it in the volume. The story was published in 1942 when Shahid and I were fast friends and were thinking of marriage. Shahid didn't like the story, and we had a fight. But the controversies surrounding 'Lihaaf' had not reached Bombay yet. Among journals, I subscribed only to *Saaqi* and *Adab-e-Lateef*. Shahid was not too angry, and we got married.

We received the summons in December 1944 to appear before the court in January. Everyone said that we would just be fined, not imprisoned. So we were quite excited and began to get warm clothes stitched for our stay in Lahore.

Seema was a small baby. She was weak and whimpered in a shrill voice. We showed her to a child specialist who declared that she was in good health. Nevertheless, it was not wise to expose her to the severe cold in Lahore. So I left her with Sultana Jafri's mother at Aligarh and set out for Lahore. From Delhi, Shahid Ahmad Dehlavi and the calligrapher who 'copied' the manuscript joined me. The Crown had made him one of the accused as well. The suit was brought not against *Adab-e-Lateef* but against the book published by Shahid Ahmad Dehlavi.

Sultana had come to the station to pick us up. She worked in the Lahore radio station and was staying at Luqman sahib's place. It was a gorgeous mansion. Luqman sahib's wife had gone to visit her parents along with her children. Thus the entire place was at our disposal.

Manto had also reached Lahore, and soon we were flooded with invitations. Most of the callers were Manto's friends, but many also wanted to have a look at a strange creature like me. We appeared before the court one day. The judge only asked my name and wanted to know if I had written the story. I admitted to the crime. That was all!

We were greatly disappointed. Our lawyer kept on talking all the time. We couldn't make much of it as we were whispering among ourselves. Then the date for the next hearing was announced, and we were free to freak out. Manto, Shahid and I roamed around in a tonga, shopping. We bought Kashmiri shawls and shoes. When we were buying shoes, the sight of Manto's delicate feet filled me with envy. I almost broke into tears looking at my rough and graceless feet.

'I hate my feet,' said Manto.

'Why? They're so graceful.'

'They are absolutely womanly.'

'So? I thought you have an abiding interest in women.'

'You always argue from the wrong angle. I love women as a man. This does not mean that I want to be a woman myself.'

'Come on, forget this man-woman controversy. Let's talk about human beings. But, do you know, people with delicate feet are very sensitive and intelligent. My brother Azim Beg Chughtai, too, had very delicate feet. But...'

And I was reminded of how his feet had swelled up before he died and become a detestable sight. And Lahore, decked like a newly wedded bride with apples and flowers, was transformed into the sandy graveyard in Jodhpur where my brother was sleeping in his grave under tons of earth. Thorny bushes were planted on his grave so that hyenas did not dig out the corpse. Those thorns began to stab me, and I left the fine pashmina shawl on the counter.

Lahore was beautiful, lush and lively. It greeted everyone with open arms. It was a city of people who were amiable and who loved life. It was the heart of Punjab.

We wandered about the streets of Lahore, our pockets stuffed with pistachios. We popped them into our mouths one after another as we walked along, deep in conversation. Standing in a lane we gorged on fried fish. My appetite was wonderful. In the salubrious climate of Lahore, whatever one ate was digested easily. We entered a hotel. My mouth began to water at the sight of hot dogs and hamburgers.

'Hamburgers contain "ham", that is, pig meat. We can have hot dogs,' Shahid said, and we, like good Muslims, stuck to the religious prohibition and abstained from eating hamburgers. We stuffed ourselves with hot dogs, washing them down with the juice of Qandhari pomegranate.

However, we soon realized how crafty the white race is. If hamburgers contain pork, hot dogs contain pork sausages. When he heard this, Shahid felt like vomiting although it was two days since we had eaten the hot dogs. It was only when a Maulvi sahib expressed the view that if one ate it unwittingly one may be forgiven that Shahid felt somewhat relieved of his emetic fits.

In the evening when Shahid and Manto got themselves drunk, the hamburger-hot dog controversy was revived and raged on for some time. Eventually, it was decided that one should abstain from both because it was impossible to prove conclusively which was halal and which was haram. Under the circumstances, they settled for chicken tikka.

We made the rounds of Anarkali and Shalimar, and saw Noor Jahan's mausoleum. Then followed endless rounds of invitations, mushairas and gossip.

And suddenly, my heart sent up a thanksgiving prayer to the Crown of England for providing us this unique opportunity of enjoying ourselves in Lahore. I began to look forward eagerly to the second hearing. I did not even care if the verdict was that I be hanged. If it occurred in Lahore, I would certainly achieve the status of a martyr. The people of Lahore would give me a befitting funeral.

POPATI HIRANANDANI

A Homeless Sindhi Woman

Translated from the Sindhi by Anju Makhija and
Menka Shivdasani, with Arjan Shad

In Akbar the Great's durbar,
Anarkali, Queen of Beauty, reigned.
      Yet
even she was buried alive.

Delhi, India's pride, and I,
inheritor of the marvels of Indus architecture.
      Yet
even I have been buried alive

homeless in history's graveyard.

EUNICE DE SOUZA

Travelling

I

We walk to the shrine of the diamond-eyed god
This is the hour he's in green and gold
The women moan

He looks a little camp to me
upturned palm with rose
joss sticks burning

but oh the black granite thighs

II

Green roses on a terrace
lemon grass, golden moon
a golden oriole chases a crow

Mine host waxeth sentimental.

Not a lover in sight.

III

The tattered balladeers invoke the
sun, the moon, the stars,
sing of kings who rode a night of sand
to plant a flag
on yet another sand dune,
of women who died when the sands shifted
in the wind.
A bulbul sings in the thorn tree.

IV

Wedged between houses, a sliver of sea,
casuarinas, clean sand,
infinity.

V

This town boasts a one-armed postal clerk
always drunk
a dog named Dumpy who can't stand the smell of drink
a street with three war widows and two light-eyed girls
who went astray
seven hen-pecked husbands
Copernicus who likes to treat his friends
and disappear when the bill appears...

Never underestimate a dishevelled town
the Colonel says
reaching for the rum.

MAHADEVI VARMA

The Chinese Pedlar

Translated from the Hindi by Lillian Srivastava and Radhika Srivastava

It is difficult for me to discover distinct and memorable features which will distinguish one Chinese from another. Their identical flat faces seem to have been turned out of the same mould, and the pleat-like noses which break the monotony of their faces can hardly be differentiated. The neat outline of their slightly slanted, half-opened eyes, fringed with strange brown eyelashes, makes one wonder whether all these eyes have been cut out by a sharp-edged instrument according to the same fixed pattern. Their natural yellow complexion takes on the colour of dried red leaves lying covered with dust in the footsteps of the sun. Physiognomy, deportment and dress all combine to make these inhabitants of a distant land look like mechanically controlled puppets. That explains why, although I had seen a Chinese pedlar several times, it was difficult for me to distinguish him from others and remember him.

But today one Chinese with liquid blue eyes stands out in my memory from a maze of almost similar faces; his silent expression says to me, 'We are *not* carbon. I, too, have a life story and if your eyes are not ignorant of the alphabet of life, why don't you try to read it?'

It was many years ago. Alighting from a tonga I entered my yard and there saw a Chinese pedlar with a brown bundle of cloth hanging from his left shoulder. He was coming out of the gate, twirling a metal yardstick in his right hand. Perhaps, having found my house locked, he was going away.

'Will you buy something, memsahib?' asked the unfortunate Chinese.

How could he know that this manner of address instantly arouses my ire. I have been called 'mother', 'elder sister', 'daughter', and so on, and I am familiar with all of these and like them. But this foreign mode of address makes me feel as if I have been shorn of my identity and as though; my sari has been replaced by a dress. After having called me 'memsahib' it would be positively difficult if not impossible for him not to go away disappointed. With contempt I replied, 'I don't buy foreign cloth.'

'Me a foreigner? But I come from China.' There was not only surprise but also pain in his voice at my slight. This time I paused, wanting to have a closer look at the man. Hiding his small feet in dirty white canvas shoes, wearing a lower garment which seemed a strange blend of trousers and pyjamas, and a jacket fashioned like a combination of coat and shirt, his hat half covering his forehead, with its frayed brim proclaiming its age, this thin, short-statured man without moustache or beard was the eternal Chinese. To see him as an individual entity—this was the problem that arose for me for the first time.

Thinking that my apathy had pained the foreigner, I tried to soften my negative answer by saying, 'I don't want anything, brother.'

The pedlar turned out to be a strange person.

'You call me brother. Then you buy—you buy, yes!'

Finding myself out of the frying pan and into the fire reluctantly I had to say, 'All right, show me what you have.'

Putting his bundle on the porch the pedlar said, 'Very fine silk I brought, sister, Chinese silk-crepe.'

It became necessary, after much interchange, for me to buy two table napkins. I thought it was good riddance, for with such a minimal sale it wouldn't be worth his while to come back again. But after a fortnight I once again found him seated on his cloth bundle on the porch, humming and tapping the yardstick on the floor. In order not to give him a chance to speak, I said in a peremptory tone, 'Now I absolutely will not buy anything, do you understand?'

Rising, taking something from this pocket and beaming with pleasure, the Chinese said. 'For sister I brought hankie-very best-all rest sold-hid in pocket.'

He had out a few handkerchiefs. Every corner crocheted with lilac thread, and every petal of the dainty flowers in the corners embroidered with the same colour, expressed not only the nimbleness of Chinese women's fingers but also the pathetic story of life's deprivations. Seeing my disinclination, blinking his blue, slit-like eyes, he began repeating in one breath, 'For sister I brought-for sister I brought.'

I thought to myself that I had acquired a peculiar brother. As a child people had often teased me by calling me Chinese. Now I wondered whether there had been some truth to their jibes. Otherwise how did it happen that this real Chinese had come to establish brotherly relations with me, ignoring the rest of the population of Allahabad? From that day on the Chinese pedlar acquired the special right to visit my place from time to time.

Through the refined tastes of this pedlar, I began to realize that even an average Chinese has a special affinity for art. Which colour painting would look well on a white curtain–in all these the Chinaman had the same perceptiveness which can be found in any good artist. His intimate familiarity with colour made me believe that even blindfolded he would be able to identify a colour by mere touch.

Seeing the colourful cloth and paintings of China I began to wonder whether every atom of Chinese earth was not soaked in these variegated hues. Whenever I expressed the desire to see China he would begin shouting, 'I go, too, sister.' And the azure of his eyes would gleam with joy.

He was eager to tell me his life's story, but there was a considerable communication gap between the narrator and the listener. He knew Burmese and Chinese only, of which I was ignorant despite my learning. In the curious mixed language he used, of English nouns without its verbs and verbs of Hindustani without its nouns, the full pathos of the story could not be conveyed. But stories which flow out of the heart, bursting its barriers in order to express themselves, are invariably pathetic and the spirit of pathos communicates itself despite inarticulateness. The Chinese pedlar's story was no exception to this universal truth.

He was born after his parents had moved to Mandalay where they had opened up a small tea shop. He had great reverence towards the mother whom he had never seen: she had died giving birth to him, leaving him in the care of his seven-year-old sister. Perhaps a mother is the only being whom a person can remember as if there were nothing more to know, even if he has never actually seen her. This is but natural, for mother is the goddess who connects man with the world. By not acknowledging her it is possible to deny the world, but it is impossible to acknowledge the world and then to deny the mother.

Unbound

PRABHA KHAITAN

A Life Apart

Translated from the Hindi by Ira Pande

One day, Greta Garbo came to our health club and I was asked to fill
in for Nancy, who was Diana Trotsky's usual assistant on such important
occasions. I watched for hours as expensive creams and lotions were rubbed
onto Garbo's face. Then, a watermelon was cut in half, a triangular vent
for breathing made before it was placed over Garbo's face. I was instructed
to stay and watch that nothing untoward happened. At the end of that
complicated facial, Garbo got up to leave and extended a $50 tip towards
me. My face flamed in embarrassment and I babbled that I was an Indian
and did not accept tips. Her eyes widened and then she smiled (Garbo
smiled with her eyes) and went off. When Trotsky heard of this, she was
livid. 'How dare you insult Garbo?' she screeched. 'She is one of our
greatest Hollywood stars!'

I did not know who she was, I offered as an explanation.

'You mean you have never seen any of her films?' she asked as if she
could not believe her ears.

'No, I haven't seen many Hollywood films,' I told her honestly.

'Why?'

'I can't follow the accent,' I told her truthfully. 'I see,' she said slowly
but I could see she wasn't very happy that I worked in Beverly Hills but
never saw Hollywood films. I wanted to tell her that I found our own
actresses far more beautiful: give me Madhubala over a Garbo any day, I
thought. Wisely, I did not tell her that. That evening I told Eileen about
Garbo offering a tip to me.

'And you took it just because you belong to a poor country?' Eileen
asked. 'Do you know how badly the American media portrays your
country?'

'I did not,' I was outraged at her even thinking otherwise. 'That is
why Trotsky was angry with me.'

'Good!' she smiled. 'One should never sell one's self-respect for a
few dollars.'

One day, she showed me her wedding gown, carefully wrapped in
tissue. 'I had so hoped I would give it to my daughter,' she told me.
'But I never had one and the only son I had went to Vietnam and never
came back.' Another time, she pulled out a bottle of perfume her second
husband had presented her.

'Eileen, you are forever talking of husband one two or three, or your lovers from number one to five. Then why are you so critical of Clara Brown?' I couldn't help asking.

'Look, Prabha, in these matters I play from the heart. I love you so whatever you do is acceptable, understand?'

'By that logic, Mrs D should also tolerate her husband's affair with Clara,' I replied.

'Ho, ho, ho,' she laughed. 'I keep telling Mrs D that she is so blindly in love with Dr D that one day that Clara Brown will have to back off!'

I thought of my own predicament: will I have to back off one day?

'Tell me,' she went on, 'when are you planning to go back home?'

'Why? Have I become a burden for you?' 'Don't be silly,' she told me. 'I asked because this place is not for you. Look,' she changed the subject, 'today is the last day of this year. Let's celebrate New Year's eve together, OK?'

'But Mareil had wanted to take me to Disneyland,' I told her.

'Rubbish! I'll take you there, then we'll have pasta at the Farmers' Market and come back.'

Eileen started dressing up for the outing from early evening: she dyed her hair in different colours and painted her toes and fingers in vivid shades, each a different colour. I cannot even describe what the end result was. All the dogs were also dyed and I couldn't help laughing at the sight. The phone rang and it was Mrs D inviting me to a music concert but I refused. 'I'm glad you refused,' Eileen told me as I replaced the receiver. 'What will you do in that gathering of rich people? One should mix with one's own kind.'

Pepe, Tommy, Jimmy, Carla roamed along with us till 2.30 in the morning. Tommy was exhausted by then, so Eileen carried him in her arms. The streets were full of happy people and total strangers would hug and kiss each other, yelling 'Happy New Year!' as they sprayed champagne from bubbling bottles in their hands. We went to an ice-cream parlour, where all of us—including the dogs—gorged on all kinds of flavours before we decided to call it a day. It took us almost an hour to reach home through the crazy traffic.

'Give me a shot of brandy,' Eileen said when we flopped down.

'You've had enough,' I reproached her.

'So what?' she winked. 'I have to toast the new year, Prabha!'

'I'm off to bed,' I said. 'You go ahead and get drunk if you want to.'

'Don't do that, darling,' she coaxed me. 'No one sleeps tonight!'

'When do you ever sleep?' I replied. 'You are up every night as far as I know.'

'I'm afraid to sleep,' she told me. 'Where's Pepe?'

'God knows,' I was getting angry with her now. 'I don't know how you manage to work all day when you never sleep at night.'

'I hardly work, I just keep an eye on Clara Brown and Dr D,' she said. 'The rest of the time, I put my head down on my table and doze off!'

'I'm off! I can't keep awake any longer. Good night, Eileen.'

The next day, there was a New Year party at Dr Dupont's clinic for all the employees and it was also an open-house for all his patients, past and present.

'What did you do to celebrate?' Mareil asked me and I was telling her about the fun Eileen and I had, when Mrs D burst into the room. 'Mareil! Where is Dr D?' she asked.

'Why? What's happened?' Mareil asked.

'Eileen...' Mrs D started to say and then burst into tears. Everyone rushed to the reception desk where Eileen always sat and Dr D announced, 'She is no more!' as he laid her inert body on her table.

'What happened to her? How did she suddenly die?' I asked Mrs D in tears.

'This was bound to happen any day, Eileen had leukaemia, you know,' she told me. 'We all knew she was a walking time bomb.'

'You all knew and no one told me?' I couldn't believe her.

'This is how Eileen wanted it. She managed to drag on for the last few months because of you, I think. She was very fond of you, you know,' Mrs D told me.

'Oh Mrs D!' I wailed. 'I wish you had told me.'

Dr D came over and put a hand on my shoulder. 'We were bound by our promise to her, Prabha,' he said. 'Perhaps you may have refused to stay with her if you knew the truth, and she didn't want to be alone. I think she must have had a drink too many last evening,' he shook his head sadly.

'She did,' I told him. 'And when I told her she was drinking too much, she said she had to toast the new year.'

We laid Eileen to rest on 2 January. We were all standing with our heads bowed when out of nowhere Pepe bounded up to me and rubbed himself against my legs. I bent down and buried my head in his neck. 'She was our mother, Pepe,' I told him and meant every word. I knew Pepe understood and after they had covered her grave with earth, he went and quietly perched himself on it. No one had the heart to remove him from there and for a long time after we had returned from the cemetery, I could not forget his eyes and the pain in them. Who says words alone are eloquent?

Jeff called to say he was out of town and so could not come but he sobbed as he spoke about her. Pepe continued to shed tears and came each day to the clinic to sit quietly by her chair. The minute he saw me, he came and licked my feet. Among the many lessons I learnt from Eileen was to see the human in animals and the animal in humans. Her death opened my eyes to the nobility of the animal world.

SAILABALA DAS

Bilat Prabas

Translated from the Oriya by Jatindra Kumar Nayak

I took out the clothes I would need for the next fifteen days from the suitcase and put them in the almirah in my room. Next, the three of us went on a tour of the ship. It was so big; it seemed like a small city. It filled us with boundless admiration for the brilliance and ingenuity of the British. On board there were a laundry, a shop selling bread, a dispensary, and a post office. Our ship was a mail carrier. The post office contained bags carrying letters sent from different countries. Several Indian and white employees of the post office opened these bags, sorted the letters, and when the ship put in at a port, offloaded letters set apart for it.

Then we went to have a look at the dining hall. Here arrangements had been made to seat and dine four hundred first-class passengers. The hall was beautifully decorated. Much thought had gone into the choice of colour for the pictures of creepers, leaves and flowers with which the wall had been painted. The wall and the ceilings were made of oak panels. Oak is popular in Britain as a building material. The dishes had been laid out neatly and tastefully on the table. The company which owned the ship in which we were travelling made sure its passengers ate well. We sat down to eat. Many types of animals and birds had been killed and cooked with English spices in order to prepare a proper English meal.

We were at a loss to decide whether we would help ourselves to the food before us or admire the gorgeously decked out hall. When the passengers entered the hall for dinner, we looked at them trying to find out if there were any 'blacks' among them. We discovered two 'black' men, but they were utter strangers to us. Even so, we felt happy when we spotted them. After all, they are fellow-Indians. We thought that we would derive some comfort by looking at these faces when we would get fed up of seeing only white faces on the ship day after day. We now started eating. But the dishes were not at all to our taste. We chose a few that we could eat somehow, and got up, feeling discontented.

The ship weighed anchor and slowly sailed out of the harbour into the sea. The sun was about to set. I stood on the deck and fixed my eyes on the shore of India. The sky was overcast, the sea looked yellowish, the shore was but a line of blue, and this line melted into the horizon. Soon the Bombay harbour disappeared from view. The large waves of the Arabian Sea tossed the ship, and it was difficult to remain standing on the dock. So we made our way carefully towards our rooms and took shelter there. We lay on our beds. The other passengers did the same. When the waves toss a ship about, the passengers suffer from bouts of vomiting and head-reeling, which is called seasickness. Sarala and I went down with seasickness. Sarala had never before travelled by ship and did not know that one suffers from seasickness during a sea voyage. So she felt scared and miserable and said, 'Oh god, I would never have come if I had known this would happen to me.' Her words made me smile and I explained to her why she felt as she did. That night we ate nothing at all.

Every room was fitted with a calling bell. If one pressed it, the attendants would come to the passengers. I called a maidservant and said, 'We are in great agony. What should we do?' She smiled and said, 'The sea is very calm today. You need not worry about seasickness any more.' We tried to go to bed, but memories crowded into our minds oppressed us and we could not get any sleep. The long night passed somehow. Next morning, the maidservant came in and said, 'What would you like to have for your breakfast?' When we expressed our unwillingness to eat anything she warned us. 'If you stay on an empty stomach, you will suffer even more.' Saying this, she laid two bowls of cornflakes before us and left.

The attendants brought coffee, tea and some fruit to the passengers every morning. The English passengers helped themselves to all these lying in bed and did not even bother to have a wash. We are never used to eating anything before brushing our teeth. So we got up with great difficulty, had a wash and swallowed two spoonfuls of cornflakes.

Sarala had a bath that day. But, conscious of my delicate health, I desisted from following her example. She rubbed her hair with oil before taking her bath. Then, she put on a sari, and dried her loosened hair, sitting on a chair, putting her legs up. But I lay on a chair covering myself with three blankets and shawls. Sitting erect on a chair was out of the question. In the middle of all this discomfort and unease, the beauty of the big waves of the Arabian Sea never ceased to enchant us. Gigantic waves lashed the ship on all sides and rocked it. It would be difficult to describe this experience to someone who had not actually gone through it. Another wonderful sight took our breath away. Our ship was a mail carrier, it moved at a high speed. The fast moving ship tore through the sea, splitting it. Massive waves rose on either side of the ship and broke into a hundred pieces and crashed back into the sea. The sunlight reflected by the restless water formed hundreds of many-hued rainbows which charmed us. This divine spectacle brought new life into our fatigued bodies, leading us far away from the real world surrounding us. The three of us passed the day somehow, half sitting and half lying on the deck. We felt little appetite. At night we came back to our rooms. In this way we spent five days of our voyage. It was not only we who suffered. Our English women fellow-passengers, too, did not stir out of their rooms during this period. A few male passengers came to the deck once or twice. They would sometimes remark to each other that the weather was fine. This made us laugh.

On 7 September, in the morning, the city of Aden rose like a faint shadow, like a dark cloud, against the horizon far away. Some passengers tried to get a clearer view of the city by looking through a telescope, or their glasses. Slowly, the Arabian Sea grew calm. We approached Aden. What had looked like black clouds from the distance turned out to be hills. We came across a couple of fishing boats. Even the sight of bald low hills gladdened us after five or six days of sea voyage. Our ship put anchor at Aden harbour, where it spent only three hours. Sarala and I stood on the deck and watched Somali children dance.

We also saw letter bags meant for Aden being offloaded from our ship. Now we sailed into the Red Sea, which was very calm. Our ship rocked on more. In my childhood, I thought the waters of the Red Sea were red. But I found out that the colour of its water was no different from that of the water of the Arabian Sea. Here and there arid hills reared themselves from the water. From a distance these hills seemed to stand so close to each other that it seemed they would not allow the ship a passage. But when the ship approached them it was clear that they stood apart and there was plenty of space between them for a ship to sail through. Here we came across small fish with large rings, which shot out of the water and fell back into it after a while. Seagulls chased these. At places we saw large fishes swimming in the sea.

The ship sailed smoothly across the Red Sea, for, unlike the Arabian Sea, it was calm. The passengers felt comfortable now, left their rooms and appeared on the deck. We found that there were forty first-class passengers on the ship. These included a few sahibs, who were highly placed officials in the judicial department. They were accompanied by three white ladies. We made the acquaintance of these sahibs and the memsahibs. Sarala, Fyjee Bibi, these memsahibs and myself often sat together and fell into talk. We got closer to the memsahibs and they now talked freely and intimately with us. One day one of them said to me, 'I am curious to find out if women of your country want to talk to us or socialize with us. I get the feeling that they dislike us.' I replied, 'You are absolutely mistaken. Of course they want to socialize with you, but they hold back for fear that you may look down on them. These days people of your country despise our race so much and treat us so shabbily that we get the impression that they never want to be friends with us. This is why we maintain distance from you.'

Ends

As much as writers reflect on life, societal structures, the self, and the body, they also meditate on the transient nature of life, and its inevitable cessation. Indian women have written powerfully about ill health, ageing and death. This section includes extracts that build a fine web of connections between the breakdown of the body, the mind and how society treats those who are near their end.

Karaikkal Ammaiyar's poems are devotional in intent and spirit, and yet, the verses loom over the reader's mind like a dark portent. She speaks of anger, death, desolation, and the isolation of a woman on the fringes of society. The physical setting of her work is a cremation ground, with burning pyres and corpses, with her 'Heavenly Father' dancing around. Shiva is, after all, the lord of ghouls, the Destroyer.

Salma's story is remarkable in its description of a creeping mania about hygiene, and an incurable illness. The writer uses a subtle approach to examine grief, the anxiety about keeping the body clean and healthy mixed with the fear of judgement.

Manjula Padmanabhan's *Harvest* is a futuristic dystopia where people are trying to cheat death and decay by exploiting each others' bodies—as many people are already doing—through organ harvesting. When there are no longer any limits to what can be extracted from a human being, and when society institutionalizes the practice with the help of an armed force what hope do less privileged people have?

Mahasweta Devi's story 'The Breast Giver' is about a wet nurse who has breastfed dozens of babies for an upper-class household, but finds herself alone and suffering terribly at the end. The world uses one's body in all sorts of ways, but does not necessarily protect it from being overused. This particular extract is about the breast itself, its degeneration into cancer, and the pain of being 'useless' after it can no longer produce milk.

K. R. Meera's story 'Yellow is the Colour of Longing' is an odd sort of romance where two people meet at a hospital and are brought together by ill health, loneliness and the brief opportunity to escape from their families. But bodies are also conduits and transmitters of disease—the source of love and comfort can also be a source of danger.

Enlightenment and renunciation are closely linked to a growing awareness of the transience of the material world, which includes the body. Ambapali, a Buddhist nun, writes of her own beauty with great nostalgia, and compares her present body to a crumbling house. Kisagotami describes the loss of her beloveds, each one snatched by death, and her eventual embrace of the eightfold path which signals the end of all woe. For, as Soyrabai says, 'Who has been spared'?

KARAIKKAL AMMAIYAR

Mutta Tiruppatikam 1

Translated from the Tamil by M. L. Thangappa

2
A female demon
with shrunken breasts
protruding veins
sunken eyes
sticking-out white teeth
hollow belly, reddish hair
lanky legs
and emaciated body
stays in the cremation ground
and wails over her misfortune,
It is there,
His locks of hair swaying
in all directions,
the Lord dances.
Though surrounded by fire
His body is cool.
Such is Thiruvaalangadu
The abode of my Heavenly Father.

3
Stretching her legs
Between a kalli's branches.
she takes a piece of charcoal.
grinds it to a paste
and applies it to her eyelashes.
She laughs in anger,
but she is scared.
She walks, looking from side to side
gets burned in the funeral fire
and jumps away.
In her anger
she scoops up dust
and throws it on the fire,
to put it out.

It is here
the Lord dances.
Such is Thiruvaalangadu,
the abode of my Heavenly Father.

8
Fire-breathing demons
with revolving, red-hot eyes
come together,
dance the Thunangai dance,
rush towards the burning pyres,
remove a corpse from the fire,
eat the flesh
and dance the devil dance.

It is here,
the Lord dances.
With anklets and leg bands tinkling.
Raising his eyes
and going round and round,
He sends out flames
that frighten the foxes.
This is Thiruvaalangadu,
the abode of my Heavenly Father.

9
Those who wander over lands and cities
seeking the path of righteousness
come as corpses to the cremation ground.
They are laid on the pyre,
and covered with firewood.

It is here the Lord stands—
the dancer of puyanga dance
surrounded by his troop of demons.
Holding fire in His hand,
He performs His dance
making forest, oceans, mountains
and all earth and heaven
revolve around Him.

Such is Thiruvaalangadu,
the abode of my Heavenly Father.

The Breast Giver

Translated from the Bengali by Gayatri Chakravorty Spivak

The days would have passed in cooking at the Haldar-house and complaining to the Mother. But that was not enough for Jashoda. Jashoda's body seemed to keel over. Jashoda doesn't understand why nothing pleases her. Everything seems confused inside her head. When she sits down to cook she thinks she's the milk-mother of this house. She's going home in a showy sari with a free meal in her hand. Her breasts feel empty, as if wasted. She had never thought she wouldn't have a child's mouth at her nipple.

Joshi became bemused. She serves nearly all the rice and curry, but forgets to eat. Sometimes she speaks to Shiva the King, 'If Mother can't do it, you take me away. I can't pull any more.'

Finally it was the sons of the eldest daughter-in-law who said, 'Mother! Is the milk-mother sick? She acts strange.'

The eldest daughter-in-law said, 'Let's see.'

The eldest son said, 'Look here! She's a Brahmin's daughter, if anything happens to her, it'll be a sin for us.'

The daughter-in-law went to ask. Jashoda had started the rice and then lain down in the kitchen on the spread edge of her sari. The eldest daughter-in-law, looking at her bare body, said, 'Brahmin sister! Why does the top of your left tit look so red? God! flaming red!'

'Who knows? It's like a stone pushing inside. Very hard, like a rock.'

'What is it?'

'Who knows? I suckled so many, perhaps that's why?'

'Nonsense! One gets breast-stones or pus-in-the-tit if there's milk. Your youngest is ten.'

'That one is gone. The one before survived. That one died at birth. Just as well. This sinful world!'

'Well, the doctor comes tomorrow to look at my grandson. I'll ask. Doesn't look good to me.'

Jashoda said with her eyes closed, 'Like a stone tit, with a stone inside. At first the hard ball moved about, now it doesn't move, doesn't budge.'

'Let's show the doctor.'

'No, sister daughter-in-law, I can't show my body to a male doctor.'

At night when the doctor came the eldest daughter-in-law asked him in her son's presence. She said, 'No pain, no burning, but she is

Ends   311

keeling over.'

The doctor said, 'Go ask if the *nipple* has shrunk, if the armpit is swollen like a seed.'

Hearing 'swollen like a seed', the eldest daughter-in-law thought, 'How crude!' Then she did her field investigations and said, 'She says all that you've said has been happening for some time.'

'How old?'

'If you take the eldest son's age she'll be about fifty-five.'

The doctor said, 'I'll give you medicine.'

Going out, he said to the eldest son, 'I hear your *cook* has a problem with her *breast*. I think you should take her to the *cancer hospital*. I didn't see her. But from what I heard it could be *cancer* of the *mammary gland*.'

Only the other day the eldest son lived in the sixteenth century. He has arrived at the twentieth century very recently. Of his thirteen offspring he has arranged the marriages of the daughters, and the sons have grown up and are growing up at their own speed and in their own way. But even now his grey cells are covered in the darkness of the eighteenth- and the pre-Bengal-Renaissance nineteenth centuries. He still does not take smallpox vaccination and says, 'Only the lower classes get smallpox. I don't need to be vaccinated. An upper-caste family, respectful of gods and Brahmins, does not contract that disease.'

He pooh-poohed the idea of cancer and said, 'Yah! Cancer indeed! That easy! You misheard, all she needs is an ointment. I can't send a Brahmin's daughter to a hospital just on your word.'

Jashoda herself also said, 'I can't go to hospital. Ask me to croak instead. I didn't go to hospital to breed, and I'll go now? That corpse-burning devil returned a cripple because he went to hospital!'

The elder daughter-in-law said, 'I'll get you a herbal ointment. This ointment will surely soothe. The hidden boil will show its tip and burst.'

The herbal ointment was a complete failure. Slowly Jashoda gave up eating and lost her strength. She couldn't keep her sari on the left side. Sometimes she felt burning, sometimes pain. Finally the skin broke in many places and sores appeared. Jashoda took to her bed.

Seeing the hang of it, the eldest son was afraid—if at his house a Brahmin died! He called Jashoda's sons and spoke to them harshly, 'It's your mother, she fed you so long, and now she is about to die! Take her with you! She has everyone and she should die in a Kayastha household?'

Kangali cried a lot when he heard this story. He came to Jashoda's almost-dark room and said, 'Wife! You are a blessed auspicious faithful woman! After I spurned you, within two years the temple dishes were stolen, I suffered from boils in my back, and that snake Golapi tricked

Napla, broke the safe, stole everything and opened a shop in Tarakeswar. Come, I'll keep you in state.'

Jashoda said, 'Light the lamp.'

Kangali lit the lamp.

Jashoda showed him her bare left breast, thick with running sores and said, 'See these sores? Do you know how these sores smell? What will you do with me now? Why did you come to take me?'

'The master called.'

'Then the master doesn't want to keep me.' Jashoda sighed and said, 'There is no solution about me. What can you do with me?'

'Whatever, I'll take you tomorrow. Today I clean the room. Tomorrow for sure.'

'Are the boys well? Noblay and Gaur used to come, they too have stopped.'

'All the bastards are selfish. Sons of my spunk after all. As inhuman as I.'

'You'll come tomorrow?'

'Yes—yes—yes.'

Jashoda smiled suddenly. A heart-splitting nostalgia-provoking smile.

Jashoda said, 'Dear, remember?'

'What, wife?'

'How you played with these tits? You couldn't sleep otherwise? My lap was never empty, if this one left my nipple, there was that one, and then the boys of the master's house. How I could, I wonder now!'

'I remember everything, wife!'

In this instant Kangali's words are true. Seeing Jashoda's broken, thin, suffering form even Kangali's selfish body and instincts and belly-centred consciousness remembered the past and suffered some empathy. He held Jashoda's hand and said, 'You have fever?'

'I get feverish all the time. I think by the strength of the sores.'

'Where does this rotten stink come from?'

'From these sores.'

Jashoda spoke with her eyes closed. Then she said, 'Bring the holy doctor. He cured Gopal's *typhoid* with *homoeopathy.*'

'I'll call him. I'll take you tomorrow.'

Kangali left. That he went out, the tapping of his crutches, Jashoda couldn't hear. With her eyes shut, with the idea that Kangali was in the room, she said spiritlessly, 'If you suckle, you're a mother, all lies! Nepal and Gopal don't look at me, and the master's boys don't spare a peek to ask how I'm doing.' The sores on her breast kept mocking her with a hundred mouths, a hundred eyes. Jashoda opened her eyes and said,

'Do you hear?'

Then she realized that Kangali had left.

In the night she sent Basini for *Lifebuoy* soap and at dawn she went to take a bath with the soap. Stink, what a stink! If the body of a dead cat or dog rots in the garbage you can get a smell like this. Jashoda had forever scrubbed her breasts carefully with soap and oil, for the master's sons had put the nipples in their mouth. Why did those breasts betray her in the end? Her skin burns with the sting of soap. Still Jashoda washed herself with soap. Her head was ringing, everything seemed dark. There was fire in Jashoda's body, in her head. The black floor was very cool. Jashoda spread her sari and lay down. She could not bear the weight of her breast standing up.

As Jashoda lay down, she lost sense and consciousness with fever. Kangali came at the proper time: but seeing Jashoda he lost his grip. Finally Nabin came and rasped, 'Are these people human? She reared all the boys with her milk and they don't call a doctor? I'll call Hari the doctor.'

Haribabu took one look at her and said, 'Hospital.'

Hospitals don't admit people who are so sick. At the efforts and recommendations of the elder son, Jashoda was admitted.

'What's the matter? O Doctor babu, what's the problem?' Kangali asked, weeping like a boy.

'Cancer.'

'You can get cancer in a tit?'

'Otherwise how did she get it?'

'Her own twenty, thirty boys at the master's house—she had a lot of milk—'

'What did you say? How many did she *feed*?'

'About fifty for sure.'

'Fif-ty!'

'Yes, sir.'

'She had twenty children?'

'Yes, sir.'

'*God*!'

KISA-GOTAMI

Therigatha

Translated from the Pali by Caroline Augusta Foley Rhys Davids

Friendship with noble souls throughout the world
The Sage hath praised. A fool, in sooth, grows wise
If he but entertain a noble friend.
Cleave to the men of worth! In them who cleave
Wisdom doth grow; and in that pious love
From all your sorrows shall ye be released.

Mark Sorrow well; mark ye how it doth come,
And how it passes; mark the Eightfold Path
That endeth woe, the Four great Ariyan Truths.
Woeful is woman's lot! hath he declared,
Tamer and Driver of the hearts of men:
Woeful when sharing home with hostile wives,
Woeful when giving birth in bitter pain,
Some seeking death, or e'er they suffer twice,
Piercing the throat; the delicate poison take.
Woe too when mother-murdering embryo
Comes not to birth, and both alike find death.

'Returning home to give birth to my child,
I saw my husband in the jungle die.
Nor could I reach my kin ere travail came.
My baby boys I lost, my husband too.
And when in misery I reached my home,
Lo! where together on a scanty pyre,
My mother, father, and my brother burn!'

O wretched, ruined woman! all this weight
Of sorrows hast thou suffered, shed these tears
Through weary round of many thousand lives.
I too have seen where, in the charnel-field,
Devoured was my baby's tender flesh.

Yet she, her people slain, herself outcast,
Her husband dead, hath thither come
Where death is not!

Lo! I have gone
Up on the Ariyan, on the Eightfold Path
That goeth to the state ambrosial.
Nibbana have I realized, and gazed
Into the Mirror of the holy Norm.
I, even I, am healed of my hurt,
Low is my burden laid, my task is done,
My heart is wholly set at liberty.
I, sister Kisā-gotamī, have uttered this!

AMBAPALI

Therigatha

Translated from the Pali by Caroline Augusta Foley Rhys Davids

Glossy and black as the down of the bee my curls once clustered.
They with the waste of the years are liker to hempen or bark cloth.
Such and not otherwise runneth the rune, the word of the Soothsayer.

Fragrant as casket of perfumes, as full of sweet blossoms the hair of me.
All with the waste of the years now rank as the odour of hare's fur.
Such and not otherwise runneth the rune, the word of the Soothsayer.

Dense as a grove well planted, and comely with comb, pin, and parting.
All with the waste of the years dishevelled the fair plaits and fallen.
Such and not otherwise runneth the rune, the word of the Soothsayer.

Glittered the swarthy plaits in head-dresses jewelled and golden.
All with the waste of the years broken, and shorn are the tresses.
Such and not otherwise runneth the rune, the word of the Soothsayer.

Wrought as by sculptor's craft the brows of me shone, finely pencilled.
They with the waste of the years are seamed with wrinkles, o'erhanging.
Such and not otherwise runneth the rune, the word of the Soothsayer.

Flashing and brilliant as jewels, dark-blue and long-lidded the eyes
of me.
They with the waste of the years spoilt utterly, radiant no longer.
Such and not otherwise runneth the rune, the word of the Soothsayer.

Dainty and smooth the curve of the nostrils e'en as in children.
Now with the waste of the years seared the nose is and shrivelled.
Such and not otherwise runneth the rune, the word of the Soothsayer.

Lovely the lines of my ears as the delicate work of the goldsmith.
They with the waste of the years are seamed with wrinkles and pendent.
Such and not otherwise runneth the rune, the word of the Soothsayer.

Gleamed as I smiled my teeth like the opening buds of the plantain.
They with the waste of the years are broken and yellow as barley.
So and not otherwise runneth the rune, the word of the Soothsayer.

Sweet was my voice as the bell of the cuckoo through woodlands

Ends   317

flitting.
Now with the waste of the years broken the music and halting.
So and not otherwise runneth the rune, the word of the Soothsayer.

Softly glistened of yore as mother-of-pearl the throat of me.
Now with the waste of the years all wilted its beauty and twisted.
So and not otherwise runneth the rune, the word of the Soothsayer.

Beauteous the arms of me once shone like twin pillars cylindrical.
They with the waste of the years hang feeble as withering branches.
So and not otherwise runneth the rune, the word of the Soothsayer.

Beauteous of yore were my soft hands with rings and gewgaws
resplendent.
They with the waste of the years like roots are knotted and scabrous.
So and not otherwise runneth the rune, the word of the Soothsayer.

Full and lovely in contour rose of yore the small breasts of me.
They with the waste of the years droop shrunken as skins without water.
So and not otherwise runneth the rune, the word of the Soothsayer.

Shone of yore this body as shield of gold well-polished.
Now with the waste of the years all covered with network of wrinkles.
So and not otherwise runneth the rune, the word of the Soothsayer.

Like to the coils of a snake the full beauty of yore of the thighs of me.
They with the waste of the years are even as stems of the bamboo.
So and not otherwise runneth the rune, the word of the Soothsayer.

Beauteous to see were my ankles of yore, bedecked with gold bangles.
They with the waste of the years are shrunken as faggots of sesamum.
So and not otherwise runneth the rune, the word of the Soothsayer.

Soft and lovely of yore as though filled out with down were the
feet of me.
They with the waste of the years are cracked open and wizened with
wrinkles.
So and not otherwise runneth the rune, the word of the Soothsayer.

Such hath this body been. Now age-weary and weak and unsightly,
Home of manifold ills; old house whence the mortar is dropping.
So and not otherwise runneth the rune, the word of the Soothsayer.

K. R. MEERA

Yellow is the Colour of Longing

Translated from the Malayalam by J. Devika

'Did you run there from the troops?' He threw her a mischievous look. 'No, ran there to light the torches!' she replied rather gloomily, thinking all the while of her son. It was when he stared at her, startled, that she realized what she had said and to whom. Who is she? Or, what is she? A woman past thirty-five. Her middle was like a freshly swept front yard, all marked with lines like the streaks the broom leaves behind. Her breasts had lost their self-confidence. Her backside wasn't shapely. And her hair was falling strand by strand, like casuarina leaves flying off with every breeze in winter. Which man would fancy such a woman trying to joke? In short, these days, it is terrible for women past a certain age.

They were inside the coffee house by then. He found by himself a place less afflicted by the generator's awful droning.

'I have seen you somewhere.'

'I work at the LIC.'

'Ah! Good!' He smiled.

'What do you do?'

'I'm a teacher. What's your illness?'

'Don't know…' her tone was a disheartened one.

He smiled. 'Lucky lady…'

'What's your sickness?' she inquired.

'Some sort of viral fever. It's almost gone. But I have to get it checked every once in a while.'

The waiter came up with two cups of tea. They drank it in silence. It was he who paid the bill. They were silent until they reached the ward. Her number was called first. She hurried in and described to the doctor some of her symptoms. This doctor too wanted blood and urine reports. She came out, and he went in. Glancing at him as if to say goodbye, she felt a certain perturbation spread to her from him. How many are the different sorts of ailments in this world! Some spread through touch, some through glances. Some through the wind and through messages, letters. Hope Dr Sujith Kumar has remedies for all these.

The lab was crowded. As she stood at the rear of the long queue, he hurried in, looking around as if trying to locate someone in haste. She was amused to see that peculiar demeanour. Who would not be amused to see a man who has greyed a bit, lost some hair, and with a face wrinkled with the burden of worldly cares, look around with adolescence peeping

Ends

out of his eyes? But when she realized that his adolescence was actually seeking her, her face paled and then reddened; then his eyes sought her out, and he rejoiced at finding her. Her heart filled to the brim. For most women, it is like that. When after many years, a woman is sought out by a man's eyes, and when she is sure that they were indeed seeking her and her alone, she will find her heart brimming. That is of course one good thing about women.

Gently, he came to her. In his case too the doctor had asked for several investigations, he told her. There was a blood test to be done. The result would be ready only by two o'clock. He was planning to meet the doctor with it at the evening's OP. Otherwise he would have to come on Wednesday. She told him that she had decided to come another day to meet the doctor. His face fell when he heard that.

'Why bother with another journey?' he asked. 'Wouldn't it be better to meet the doctor today itself?'

His wrinkled face of forty-five years reddened and paled at once. He struggled not to look at her. Maybe he was scared that his eyes may stick to her body parts and then she would take him to be a lecher. That's the problem with men. They can see women only as bodies. They keep worrying how this woman would judge them in bed. In short, it's terrible for men too, after a certain age.

After the test it seemed as though the evening's OP was a long way off. And then, as if trying to crack a joke, mustering up the courage somehow, he suggested: 'We could have gone for a movie if we were younger.'

She smiled. A moment's silence, and then she asked bravely, 'Which theatre has a show this afternoon?'

Before she finished, they saw a poster right in front. *Kaathal Konden.* Noon show. Why not see that film, he asked. She agreed. They found the theatre, bought the tickets, got in and settled in adjacent seats. The show had already begun. But they could soon follow the story. It was a Tamil film. But they could still make out the dialogues. There weren't many people in the theatre. After the intermission, he gently put his arm on her shoulder. She pretended as if she didn't know. After some time, she softly rested her head on his shoulder. He too pretended as if he didn't know.

The movie was over by two-thirty. They had lunch at a nearby hotel. There was a lot more time to kill. Somehow then her head began to spin; she sweated profusely and her eyes rolled back; all around her everything looked yellow. He was alarmed. Was she feverish? He checked her forehead and neck with the back of his palm. It was he who decided that the cure for this was to rest awhile somewhere. She too thought it a good idea.

And that is how, it so seems, they checked into a nearby lodge.

She lay on the white sheets. He sat beside her, caressing her palm. They could see themselves in the mirror just opposite. Two poor souls. People with little time left for love. People too shy to love. Who were too afraid to love. And yet, without the courage to abandon love. She could not take her eyes off his hands. Light-yellow-coloured hands which looked as if they had never even once touched dirt. The nails weren't smudged, like those on the hands she had seen before. They didn't have the yellowish cigarette scar. The palms weren't rough. She looked at her own hands. They were rough, from washing dishes and clothes. The dirt-lined nails had dark borders. What were his wife's nails like? Like hers? He was then thinking of her former husband. Who had given up whom? He, her, or she, him? Wasn't he handsome? Didn't he know how to kiss and cuddle her properly? Who knows women's ways? Some don't like to be kissed. Some can never have enough of it.

He ran his fingers gently down her cheeks. She clasped his hands firmly.

'The yellow, is it gone?'

His tone faltered. 'No...'

She laughed. 'And you?'

'I still have the fever, right? My eyes are red in one corner, black in the other. Still the same old grey.'

He too laughed. Well, one knows too well what all may happen when a man and a woman have a room to themselves and begin to laugh together. They could well laugh until they cried. Laughing is a kind of magic. When she laughed he felt that she was really good-looking; and when he laughed she thought that he was really good-looking. He felt like kissing her; she felt like kissing him. Needless to say more, these two patients with communicable diseases, these two who had met just that morning, they forgot their homes and their haunts, society and its norms, and, to tell the truth, mated, made love. Waking up later, he kissed her wistfully, and she took it the best she could.

When they checked out, the OP at the medical college had closed. The OP of the stars had opened above. Reaching home, she became worse.

Seeing her lying on the bed, terribly weak, her arm pressed on her forehead, her younger child asked, distressed: 'What's wrong, Mother? Are you feeling too sick?'

'Nothing, Son,' she said haltingly. 'Everything looks a bit yellow—that's all.'

That night she became seriously ill. The children were scared. They woke up the neighbours, who got her to the hospital at once.

SALMA

On the Edge

Translated from the Tamil by N. Kalyan Raman

Yesterday, as soon as the plans for the trip were finalized, Nanni had warned her privately:

'Look here. Don't let that woman babble inside the car. Then you must never let her sit next to me. Her whole body stinks because she is not in the habit of bathing. And never put on the air conditioner. That woman will keep farting. If you keep the windows closed, the stink will turn my stomach.'

Such grave concerns! The thought of how much time Nanni must have spent worrying about these things saddened her further. However, since she was well aware of Nanni's special traits, her warnings didn't seem particularly odd to her.

If Raadhi bathed more often than twice a week, it was a miracle. She believed that a person was sure to catch cold from bathing often. All efforts by the people at home to dispel her belief proved futile. Nanni, however, was her exact opposite. She could make anyone who was around her for a day feel extremely unclean.

None of them could bear to watch the outrage of her spending three-quarters of each day in the bathroom. Whenever she found it intolerable, Raadhi would whine to her: 'If I ever wasted water like this, your mother will shoot me dead. Just my bad luck.'

It was true, indeed. Nanni's activities could be a source of great distress for the onlookers. She needed half an hour just to clean her teeth and wash her face in the morning, another two and a half hours if she started bathing at nine, and an hour for her ablutions before each prayer of the day.

Over the past few years, all her time was spent this way, in the company of water. When she hinted once to Nanni about consulting a doctor, Nanni told her: 'Why, do you think I am crazy? I will never do it. If you like, take your Raadhi and show her to a 'loose' doctor.'

Every time she saw Nanni come out of the bathroom, she was seized with wonder. Nanni did glance at the clock before entering the bathroom, but how did she estimate the time for her exit? How was she able to manage the duration so precisely each time?

While in the bathroom, Nanni was in the habit of keeping the door ajar, never fully closing it. When she was bathing, people moving about outside were able to get a good look at her. Nanni was least bothered about it.

To Amma who muttered, 'Why can't you close the door and bolt it from inside,' Nanni replied with disdain, 'Why should I? Won't I feel suffocated? Who is going to turn up here, near the rear entrance?'

It had been her long-time wish to watch Nanni from outside while she was taking a bath.

But since she didn't have enough patience, she thought she would at least watch her perform Olu. So one day she sat down on the stone mortar in front of the bathroom door, a bunch of loose flowers in her lap, well before the scheduled time of Nanni's arrival. The late afternoon sun was sliding down the wall in the backyard.

Nanni arrived exactly at four o' clock to enter the bathroom. When Nanni saw her sitting there, which was quite unusual, she offered a faint smile. 'I am going to perform Olu for Asar,' said Nanni as she shut the door, leaving it ajar. Even the angle at which she left it ajar was always the same. Nanni brushed her teeth once before the Asar prayer.

Stringing the flowers on her lap, she cast a furtive glance around. After the water flowed noisily and filled the bucket, Nanni tilted the bucket suddenly to let all the water flow out. She could guess that Nanni had washed the bucket. Water from the tap began to fill the bucket again. When Nanni squatted on her haunches to pee, she could see Nanni's bare bottom through the half-open door; she lowered her head in embarrassment.

The sound of water was turning into unrelenting noise. As Nanni began to scoop water with a mug again and again to pour it between her thighs and wash herself, she began to count. One, two, three...Nanni was indefatigable...58, 59, 60...at last, Nanni stood up.

Again she heard the sound of the plastic mug dashing against the steel bucket. Nanni begins to perform Olu. She heard the sound of Nanni scooping water and slapping it on her face and hands. The sound of colliding bangles affirmed that she was scrubbing her hands hard. As she began to be amazed that Nanni's body could have so much filth, she was filled with compassion for Nanni instead of anger. Her heart was filled with boundless love for this woman who spent most hours of every day inside the bathroom. The sound of flowing water from the bathroom was unremitting.

Loose jasmine flowers were crumpled unstrung between her fingers. When Nanni came out, her face was slack as an overripe fruit. Smiling placidly at her, Nanni walked towards her room. Planting her pale, water-soaked feet gently on the floor, she walked delicately, like a sauntering bird. At all times, Nanni's room admitted no one but her. She had never seen anyone else being allowed entry into that room. She recalled how anxious Nanni had seemed, uncertain whether to welcome her or turn her away, when she had deliberately entered Nanni's room one day.

'Come, Jassi,' Nanni greeted her half-heartedly, 'sit on this chair.' Nanni pushed a wire-knit chair hastily in front of her. Nanni's voice revealed her anxiety that the visitor must not sit on her mattress.

It was the smallest room in the house. A bed, cupboard and chair—the bit of free space left was sufficient only for spreading her mat for prayer. The washing line was tied between the iron ring above the bed and the window bar above her head. Several pieces of a torn voile sari were rolled up and inserted into the gaps between the window bars. She knew that each rag was meant for a special purpose: one for nose cleaning; another for scrubbing ears; yet another for wiping hands; and still another solely for foot cleaning. Each rag was stuffed into a different gap.

Though it was over five years since the house was built, the walls and the floor sparkled as though they were constructed only yesterday. Nanni, who met her eye uneasily, was growing increasingly restive and anxious. As one edge of the thin Coutraalam towel hanging above her head swayed in the gust of wind from the fan, Nanni moved forward urgently, her face full of worry that it might graze her visitor's head, pushed it to the far end of the line and smiled at her.

In order to appear oblivious to Nanni's predicament, she cast a quick glance around the room, surveying its orderly arrangements.

Unable to grasp the meaning of her glance, Nanni said, 'Why are you looking around as though at something new? This is your house,' and laughed, exposing most of her betel-stained teeth. Even so, Nanni's gaze was directed at her feet which were planted firmly on the floor. After peering at them nervously, worried that they might be filthy, Nanni was steeped in the distress of being unable to reach a firm conclusion.

Reflecting on the way Nanni seemed to be waiting for her to leave the room and how, in the space of a couple of minutes, she had been made to feel like a filthy tramp, she was not clear whether what she now felt for Nanni was pity or anger. Later, emerging out of a long silence, she whimpered, 'Why shouldn't I look around?' in an attempt to ease the situation.

'Why not? Look around all you want. It's your house, after all,' said Nanni and sat on the bed. From the dainty way Nanni sat, it seemed as though she was afraid she might hurt the bed. The whiteness of the bedcover, spread without a single wrinkle, was intended to please the heart. The monthly magazine *Nargis* was lying open and face down on the bed. It was Raadhi who didn't like to read; Nanni read voraciously. Along with several Islamist publications, she also read *Rani, Kalkandu* and children's books; she never left anything out.

Her gaze fell on the sheet of paper spread next to the pillow, and the bit of cloth folded and placed on that sheet of paper. As she gazed intently at the cloth, wondering why it was kept there, Nanni volunteered an explanation: 'That bit is for wiping sweat. I didn't want to keep it on the bed, so I've put it on the paper. The sheet will get dirty, no?'

Lacking the mental strength to sit there any longer, she came out. Her younger brother asked her that evening: 'Why did you do such a thing? After you left the room, did you see how she poured water over the chair you sat on and washed it for an hour? Do any of us enter that room? Why do you go there and humiliate yourself?' She was terribly hurt by his ridicule. So she went up the next day to her mother who was cutting vegetables in the kitchen and asked her anxiously: 'Amma, we have to show her to a doctor. What shall we do?'

Harvest

Act I Scene 2

The same room. OM *and* MA *are sitting upstage centre. A mat is spread on the floor and they are eating the coloured pellets of their new food.* JAYA *is leaning her head and shoulders against the side of the bed.*

The package is open. Its contents are strewn about. There are brightly coloured instruction leaflets, elaborately devised containers for pills and powders and a number of small gadgets similar in size and shape to a slide-viewing device but of obscure purpose.

MA: Tell me again: all you have to do is sit at home and stay healthy?

OM: Well—not *sit* necessarily—

MA: And they'll pay you?

OM: Yes.

MA: Even if you do nothing but pick your nose all day?

OM: They'll pay me.

MA: And what about off-days?

OM: *(shrugs)* Well. *Every* day is off, in one sense—

JAYA: *(suddenly)* Why don't you tell her the truth?

MA   Isn't this the truth?

OM   Jaya—

JAYA   *(swinging herself around, to face them)* Tell her. Tell your mother what you've really done—

MA   Shoo! Don't speak to your husband in that voice—

OM   The walls are thin. Everyone can hear. When you talk like this—

JAYA   Everyone knows already! D'you think you're the only one with this—this *job*? D'you think everyone doesn't know what it means…when the grey guards come? *(tears in her voice)* All that remains to be known is which part of you's been given away!

MA   *(mystified)* What's this, what's this? Who's giving away parts of whom?

JAYA   Which goes first, the brain or the heart, that's what I want to know—

MA   *(to* OM*)* I'm sorry to say, your wife has gone mad. Your sister, I mean—

OM   She's just trying to make trouble—

JAYA   *(bitter laugh)* Huh!

MA	Who cares about her? Wife or sister, Mother comes first! So tell me—these people, your employers, who exactly are they?
OM	It's—it's well, actually it's just one person.
MA	Just one person! With so much money to give away!
JAYA	It's a foreigner. That's why it's so much—
MA	What?
OM	*(sighs)* The money comes from abroad—
MA	Really! *(a sudden doubt)* But...doesn't that mean you'll have to go there? Abroad?
OM	Ma—no one goes abroad these days...
JAYA	Not whole people, anyway!
OM	*(warningly)* I'm warning you now, Jaya—
MA	What's that? What's that? Knot-hole people? What d'you mean— shorties?
JAYA	*(patiently)* Not his whole body. Just parts of it—
MA	*(to OM)* What's your wife saying—not your body, but your what?

JAYA curls herself more tightly into herself.

OM	*(to JAYA's back)* Why're you doing this? Why're you making trouble?
JAYA	*(over her shoulder)* You said it wouldn't affect us—but see what it's done already!
OM	So *tell* me—what? In exchange for your old kitchen you have a new modern one—
JAYA	*(swivelling round)* You call this food? This—*(she indicates the pellets they have been eating)* this—this goat-shit?
MA	It's better than what you make—
JAYA	And calling me your sister—what's that? *(sobs)* If I'm your sister, what does that make you? *(hysterical edge)* Sister, huh! My forehead burns, when, I say that word, 'sister'! *(she smears the red kumkum on her forehead in her torment and succumbs to her tears)*
MA	Shoo! Are you a street woman? To speak in such a voice?
OM	You think I did it lightly. You think it's a heavy price. But at the cost of calling you my sister...we'll be *rich*! Very rich! Insanely rich! What're you saying? *(he gets up to wash his hands and mouth at the kitchen sink, stopping to make his point along the way)* But you'd rather live in this one small room, I suppose! Think it's such a fine thing—*(washes his mouth, spits)* living day in, day out, like monkeys in a hot-case—*(washes mouth again and spits again, wipes face, mouth)* lulled to sleep by our neighbours' rhythmic farting! Dancing to the tune of the melodious traffic!

	And starving. Yes—you'd prefer this to being called my sister on a stupid slip of paper no one we know will ever see!
MA	Why fight over what is finished? Tell me about this rich foreigner, your employer! Who is he? Why does he love you so much? That's what I don't understand—where did he meet you?
JAYA	*(half-sob/laugh)* Ohh—just tell her, tell her!
OM	*(coming back to centrestage)* We've never met, Ma…
MA	What!
OM	He's rich—and old. That's all I know about him. Probably suffering from some illness—
MA	Then why's he paying you so much!
JAYA	Oh *Ma!*—don't you see it? Isn't it obvious?
MA	*(to JAYA)* You're so smart that you can hear the Holy Father himself thinking but I, I need to hear with my ears—*(turns to OM)* Tell me, my son—
OM	*(irritated)* Oh, you won't understand, Ma—
JAYA	I'll tell you! He's sold the rights to his organs! His skin. His eyes. His arse, *(sobs again)*. Sold them! *(holds her head)* Oh god, oh god! What's the meaning of this nightmare! *(sobs. To OM)* How can I hold your hand, touch your face, knowing that at any moment it might be snatched away from me and flung across the globe! *(sobs)* If you were dead I could shave my head and break my bangles—but this? To be a widow by slow degrees? To mourn you piece by piece? *(sobs)* Should I shave half my head? Break my bangles one at a time? *(succumbs to her tears)*
MA	*(only half-comprehending. Turns to OM who stands with his back to the women)* How is it possible?
OM	*(looking up at JAYA)* If you weren't so busy feeling sorry for yourself, you'd have read what they say about respecting the donor—
JAVA	*(bitterly)* Of course! They bathe him in praise while gutting him like a chicken!
MA	But why must they come to us?
OM	See? *(holds up a pamphlet)* Look? In this paper it says that one-third of all donors are left absolutely intact!
MA	Don't they have enough of their own people?
JAYA	And where does that leave you? Two-thirds a man? Half a wit?
OM	*(to MA, distractedly)* They don't have people to spare.
JAYA	And we do, of course. Spare lives! We grow on trees, in the bushes! *What are we, teacher? Oh just some spare lives!*
MA	*(uncertainly)* Well. So long as they don't hurt you …

At this moment, a loud tone sounds. All three react, looking immediately at the globe.

MA   Hai! What's that sound! I must wash my hands! *(she gets up)*

The polygon flickers to life. Each face displays one view of a young woman's face, unmistakeably blonde and white-skinned. She is beautiful in a clear-eyed, unequivocal manner, exuding a youthful innocence and radiant purity.

MA   *(she sees the globe head-on)* Ahhh! Who is this angel?

The room fills abruptly with the pip! of an international phone call about to commence. There is a crackling sound and an audible pause.

GINNI   …hello? Hello?

OM   *(stepping forward self-consciously)* Yes—!

GINNI   I see you!—oh, my Gad! I see you! Is that really you? Auwm? Praycash?

OM   Yes! Yes—it's me, Om! *(he's grinning wide. MA looks bewildered. JAYA looks awe-struck)*

GINNI   Well—hi! That's really great! This is Virginia—Ginni—speaking! Can you see me? How's your reception?

OM   Quite good—quite perfect, I should say! Fantastic!

GINNI   Wow! Yeah … well it's pretty wonderful for me too, you know! I mean, I can't tell you… *(her voice grows breathy with emotion)* I can't *tell you* how much this means to me—

MA   *(to JAYA)* What's it saying? I can't understand when they speak so fast—

OM   No, no, madam! It's our pleasure! Our duty, I mean! Anything we can do to help—

JAYA   *(to MA)* She's saying that she's happy—

GINNI   It's the most beautiful day of my life! I feel I've got hope, at last! And all because of you—

OM   No, no, madam, it is my—our—pleasure.

GINNI   Is it—I mean, can you see me clearly, Auwm?

OM   Perfectly clear.

GINNI   Okay—okay—now you've got to tell me—I'm just switching screens here—okay—there we are—okay! I can see … is that your … your mother? In the pink—*(JAYA flinches; she is wearing a pink sari)* whatdyacallit—sarong?

OM   We call it—*sari*—

GINNI   *(sings an old tune)* 'Who's sari now? Who's sari now?!!'*(laughs to*

Ends   329

	herself) Hehheh—It's magical, it's wonderful! I'm really talking to India—this is really happening! Okay! And your sister—let's see—
JAYA	*(stirring to life)* No! I'm his sister!
OM	*(flustered and confused)* She's my wife—
GINNI	Excuse me?
JAYA	*(hissing to OM)* Sister. I'm your sister.
GINNI	You said just now—
OM	*(still smiling woodenly)* I mean, she is my sister, you see—
GINNI	Auwm—it says here on your form, you're not married.
OM	I'm not. She's my sister.
GINNI	You're sure you're not kidding me or anything?
OM	Sure, sure, of course I'm sure!
GINNI	Because it's important for us to trust one another. I mean, one little slip like that one—and I dunno. I mean, it's hard for me to tell, from so far away—
OM	No, no! I'm telling the truth! I swear on my God!
GIINNI	Okay. I mean, 'coz I've gotta know, you know. If you're married—
JAYA	*(suddenly)* Why?
GINNI	What's that?
JAYA	Why does it matter?
GINNI	Uhh—I'll get back to you on that, okay? Just now...lemme see...there's two more people in your household, am I right, Auwm? There's *(as if checking a list)*...your mother and your brother-in-law. S'right?
JAYA	That is right.
GINNI	Just a moment—uhh—Zhaya? *(the Contact Module swivels towards JAYA, who nods)* Is that your name? Yeah—okay, now honey: I can't handle two people at a time, okay? I mean, it's just this dumb camera, you know, can't look at two people at a time, okay? So—I'm talking to Auwm, well I can't talk to you as well, okay? I mean, no offence—
JAYA	Okay.
OM	My mother is also here—
GINNI	Yes. Okay. I'm turning the scanner around *(the Contact Module turns)* ... I'm panning across the room ... Jeeezus! It's not very much, is it? I mean—oh! Okay! I see her. Hi! Mrs Praycash? Hi! This is Ginni! Can you hear me?
MA	*(shielding her eyes against the light)* What?
GINNI	I said, this is Virginia! I'm—uh, well just look up, if you can—
OM	Ma—just take your hand down—

GINNI	Look towards the Contact Module! You know the thing hanging in the room?
MA	*(to JAYA)* What's happening?
JAYA	Ma—just look at that light—
OM	The light! The light!
MA	*(getting annoyed, straightens up to snap back at OM)* Stop shouting!
GINNI	Ahhright! I see you! Mrs Praycash, glad to meet you!
MA	I can't understand a word of what that thing is saying! Is it a man or a woman?
GINNI	What do I look like to you, Mrs Praycash?
MA	*(cupping her ear)* Ehh?
JAYA	Ma—she wants to know, what she looks like—
OM	Come on, Ma! You've seen foreigners before—
GINNI	Please—Auwm—your mother can answer my questions herself—
OM	She can't understand, you see—
JAYA	*(to MA)* Ma—look up at that light and say what you see—
MA	*(looks up)* I see an angel.
GINNI	*(laughing)* Ha! I look good to you?
MA	Good, bad, I don't know. All I know is I've got to take a leak—*(turns around)*
GINNI	*(embarrassed laugh)* Heh! Mm. But—wait! I'm not through yet!
OM	*(as MA continues moving away, slowly)* Don't go yet, Ma—she's not finished—
MA	Since when did I need anyone's permission to take a leak?
GINNI	I'm sorry, Mrs Praycash, this won't take a minute—
MA	Nothing doing. I'll piss myself if I don't go right away—*(she moves to the door)*
GINNI	Hey! I didn't let you go!
OM	She has some problem, you see—
MA	Wait till you're my age! *(grunts with the effort of opening the door)* Why they can't keep a bathroom on each floor I don't know—

Exit MA.

SOYRABAI

Kiti He Marti, Kiti He Radti

Translated from the Marathi by Jerry Pinto and Neela Bhagwat

How much death. How much weeping.
Who is that laughing on the sly?
We look and we wonder: what is truth?
And why so many pining for a lie?

What is death? What is grieving?
At whom do we aim our thoughtless laughter?
Who has been spared? Who is leaving?
Our fate is common in the hereafter.

Soyra says: I find it odd
Not one among them remembers God.

ACKNOWLEDGEMENTS

I must thank a great many people, starting with hundreds of researchers, linguists, translators, archivists and publishers who did the pioneering work of bringing out new titles or rescuing old ones from obscurity and amnesia. They have not only enabled this anthology but also restored to us our history.

I am grateful to Dr Jayasree for sending me some of the Samyukta journals that had published translations of women writers, and for being so helpful overall.

For letting me have new translations, I thank Arunava Sinha, Rahul Soni, Arjun Choudhuri, Priya Sarukkai Chabria, Neela Bhagwat and Jerry Pinto (who is owed a double debt of gratitude for being so encouraging and for sending hard to find reading material).

I am grateful to Prof. A. R.Venkatachalapathy for his advice and his help in accessing new translations by M. L. Thangappa. Also to Sarah Maguire, Director of the Poetry Translation Centre.

For recommending and giving me books, I thank Desraj Kali, Ahana Lakshmi, Indira Chandrasekhar, Tushar Amin, Sharon Fernandes.

For responding generously to my early tentative emails, and for help with contact numbers, I thank Arundhathi Subramaniam, Mitra Phukan, Aruni Kashyap, Anupama Raju, H. S. Sivaprakash, Mani Rao, Uddipana Goswami, Ashok Vajpayi, Sheela Chungkham, Kannan Sundaram, Ira Pande, Somi Roy, Menka Shivdasani.

For running such a great library, I thank C. S. Lakshmi and the staff at SPARROW.

For building up another great literary resource with so many books by Indian women, and for letting me use it during my week in residence there, I thank Prof. M. Asaduddin of the English Department at Jamia Millia Islamia.

For existing, I thank the vast Sahitya Akademi library in New Delhi. In particular, thanks are due to Mr Padmanabhan who helped me find books when I was overwhelmed by the endless shelves. And to Gitanjali Chatterji of the Sahitya Akademi.

I must thank the team at Aleph, editor Pujitha Krishnan, and especially David Davidar who asked me to take on a project as large as this and thought that I was equal to this mammoth task.

Above all, I must thank the authors, translators and publishers who gave us permission to publish the works represented in this book. Those who did not give me permission but who do publish all genres of vigorous, combative, startling writing by Indian women—I remain grateful to you too.

◆

Grateful acknowledgement is made to the following copyright holders for permission to reprint copyrighted material in this volume.

Extract from 'Mukti' from *Mother Wit* by Urmila Pawar. Reprinted by permission of Zubaan Publishers Pvt. Ltd.

Poems by Nirmala, Soyrabai, Jenabai, Muktabai, Rajai and Bahinabai from *The Ant who Swallowed the Sun* (unpublished) translated by Jerry Pinto and Neela Bhagwat. Reprinted by permission of the translators.

Extract from *Songs for Shiva* by Akka Mahadevi translated by Vinaya Chaitanya. Reprinted by permission of the translator.

Extract from 'Eating God' by Mirabai in *Eating God: a Book of Bhakti Poetry*, translated by Rahul Soni, ed. Arundhathi Subramaniam. Reprinted by permission of Penguin Books India.

Amucha.

Extract from 'Name: Amba Dalmia' by Manju Kapur from *Of Mothers and Others*. Reprinted by permission of Zubaan Publishers Pvt. Ltd.

Extract from *Pebbles in a Tin Drum* by Ajeet Cour translated by Masooma Ali. Reprinted by permission of the author and translator.

'An Infant's Dream' and 'Mother Tongue' by Padma Sachdev translated by Shivnath from *A Handful of Sun and Other Poems*. Reprinted by permission of Sahitya Akademi.

Extract from 'The Yellow Bird' by Lila Majumdar from *Classic Adventures: The Yellow Bird*. Reprinted by permission of Penguin Books India.

Extract from *Mistaken Identity* by Nayantara Sahgal. Reproduced by arrangement with HarperCollins Publishers India Limited. Unauthorized copying is strictly prohibited.

Extract from 'Mushroom Madness' from *The Anger of Aubergines* by Bulbul Sharma. Originally published by Kali for Women, New Delhi, 1997; Reprinted by Women Unlimited, New Delhi, 2004.

'Salad Days', 'Fasting Days' and 'Dessert Days' from 'Salvation' by Prathibha Nandakumar. First appeared in print in the anthology, *Interior Decoration: Poems by 54 women from 10 languages* (2010) Editors: Ammu Joseph, Vasanth Kannabiran, Ritu Menon, Volga, Published by Women Unlimited, New Delhi, an associate of Kali for women, in collaboration with Women's World India. Reprinted by permission of the author.

Extract from *Snakebite and the Distant Window* by Ashapurna Devi translated by Anima Bose. Reprinted by permission of Nupur Gupta on behalf of the author.

Extract from 'In the Flesh' by Nilanjana Roy. Reprinted by permission of *Seminar*.

Extract from *Apradhini* by Shivani translated by Ira Pande. Reproduced by arrangement with HarperCollins Publishers India Limited. Unauthorized copying is strictly prohibited.

Extract from 'Gulabi Talkies' by Vaidehi translated by Tejaswini Niranjana from *Gulabi Talkies*. Reprinted by permission of the author and translator.

Extract from 'Chilli Powder' from *Harum-Scarum Saar & Other Stories* by Bama translated by N. Ravi Shanker. Originally published by Women Unlimited, New Delhi, 2006.

Extract from *The Taming of Women* by P. Sivakami. Reprinted by permission of Penguin Books India.

Extract from *Nectar in a Sieve* by Kamala Markandaya. Reprinted by permission of Penguin Books India.

Extract from *Country of Goodbyes* by Mridula Garg. Published originally by Women Unlimited, New Delhi: 2003.

Extract from *Abhijatri* by Nirupama Borgohain translated by Sajal Dey. Reprinted by permission of Sahitya Akademi.

Extract from 'The Apology' by Rajalakshmi translated by K. R. Jayashree for *Samyukta: A Journal of Women's Studies* (2008). Reprinted with gratis permission from the publisher.

Extract from *Gift in Green* by Sarah Joseph. Reproduced by arrangement with HarperCollins Publishers India Limited. Unauthorized copying is strictly prohibited.

Extract from 'One of My Journeys' from *A Rebel and Her Cause* by Rashid Jahan translated by Rakhshanda Jalil. Published originally by Women Unlimited, New Delhi: 2014.

Extract from *Alma Kabutari* by Maitreyi Pushpa translated by Raji Narasimhan. Reprinted by permission of Katha Books.

Extract from *A Street in Srinagar* by Chandrakanta translated by Manisha Chaudhry. Reprinted by permission of Zubaan Publishers Pvt. Ltd.

Extract from 'Somanatha and Mahmud' by Romila Thapar. Reprinted by permission of the author.

Extract from *Tara Lane* by Shama Futehally. Reprinted by permission of Penguin Books India.

Extract from 'Bibbo' by Mrinal Pande. Reprinted by permission of the author.

'The Black Woman' and 'Wicked Woman' by Nirupama Dutt. Reprinted by permission of the author.

Extract from *Seeing Like a Feminist* by Nivedita Menon. Reprinted by permission of Penguin Books India.

Extract from 'A World Without Men' by K. Saraswathi Amma translated by Dr Lakshmi Devi Menon. Reprinted by permission of DC Books, *Samyukta: A Journal of Women's Studies* (gratis) and the translator.

Extract from 'Indian Women and the Franchise' from *Selected Poetry and Prose* by Sarojini Naidu. Reprinted by permission of Rupa Publications.

Extract from *Fireflies in the Mist* by Qurratulain Hyder. Originally published by Women Unlimited, New Delhi, 2006.

Extract from *Bitter Wormwood* by Easterine Kire. Reprinted by permission of Zubaan Publishers Pvt. Ltd.

Extract from 'The Last Song' from *These Hills Called Home* by Temsula Ao. Reprinted by permission of Zubaan Publishers Pvt. Ltd.

Extract from *Purananuru* by Okkur Macattiyar translated by George L. Hart III. Reprinted by permission of the translator.

Bani Basu, *The Enemy Within*, trans. Jayani Datta (Orient BlackSwan, 2002). Reprinted by permission of the publisher. Originally published in Bangla as *Antarghat*.

Extract from *Killing Days: Prison Memoirs* by Joya Mitra translated by Shampa Banerjee. Originally published by Women Unlimited, New Delhi: 2004.

Irawati Karve, *Yuganta: The End of an Epoch* trans. Irawati Karve (Chennai: Orient BlackSwan, 2007). Reprinted by permission of the publisher. Originally published in Marathi in 1967 as *Yuganta*.

Extract from 'Why Does That Girl Trudge Across?' from *Forest Interludes* by Anita Agnihotri translated by Kalpana Bardhan. Reprinted by permission of Zubaan Publishers Pvt. Ltd.

Extract from *Bapu Kuti* by Rajni Bakshi. Reprinted by permission of Penguin Books India.

Extract from 'To Waris Shah' by Amrita Pritam translated from the Punjabi by Khushwant Singh. Reprinted by permission of Mala Dayal.

Extract from *The River Churning* by Jyotirmoyee Devi translated by Enakshi Chatterjee. Published originally by Kali for Women, New Delhi: 1995; opt. by Women Unlimited New Delhi: 2005.

Extract from *The Other Side of Silence* by Urvashi Butalia. Reprinted by permission of Penguin Books India.

Extract from *Aruna's Story* by Pinki Virani. Reprinted by permission of the author.

Extract from *The God of Small Things* by Arundhati Roy. Reprinted by permission of David Godwin Associates.

Extract from *Adbhuta Ramayana* by Saudamini Devi translated by Arjun Choudhury. Reprinted by permission of the translator.

'Mayamriga, California' and 'Kali' by Rukmini Bhaya Nair. Reprinted by permission of the poet.

'Pandu's Desire for Sons' and 'While Teaching My Son History' by Mallika Sengupta translated by Arunava Sinha. Reprinted by permission of Subodh Sarkar and the translator.

'Viswamitra' from *From the Inner Palace: A Kumudini Anthology* by Kumudini translated by Ahana Lakshmi. Published by Srirangam Srinvasa Thathachariar Trust, 2009. Reprinted by permission of the translator and publisher.

Extract from *Yajnaseni* by Pratibha Ray translated by Pradip Bhattacharya. Reprinted by permission of Rupa Publications.

Extract from *The Fabulous Feminist* by Suniti Namjoshi. Reprinted by permission of Zubaan Publishers Pvt. Ltd.

'Proscribed Blood—1', 'Proscribed Blood—2' by Malathi Maithri translated by N. Kalyan Raman. Reprinted by permission of the author and translator.

'Demon Language' by Malathi Maithri translated by Lakshmi Holmström (from *Wild Girls Wicked Words*, Sangam, 2012). Reprinted by permission of the author and translator.

'Where I Live', '5:46 Andheri Local', 'The City and I' from *Where I Live* by Arundhathi Subramaniam. Reprinted by permission of the author.

'Prayer Flags—2', 'Small Towns and the River' by Mamang Dai. Reprinted by permission of the author.

Extract from 'In the Name of those Married Women' from *Lifting the Veil* by Ismat Chughtai. Reprinted by permission of Penguin Books India.

'A Homeless Sindhi Woman' by Popati Hiranandani translated by Anju Makhija and Menka Shivdasani, with Arjan Shad. Reprinted by permission of Sahitya Akademi.

'Travelling' by Eunice de Souza from *Sweeping the Front Yard* published by SPARROW. Reprinted by permission of the publisher and author.

Extract from 'Chinese Pedlar' from *A Pilgrimage to the Himalayas, and Other Silhouettes from Memory* by Mahadevi Varma. Reprinted by permission of Peter Owen Publishers.

Extract from *A Life Apart* by Prabha Khaitan. Reprinted by permission of Zubaan Publishers Pvt. Ltd.

Extract from *Bilat Prabas* by Sailabala Das. Reprinted by permission of Sahitya Akademi.

Verse from *Mutta Tiruppatikam* by Karaikkal Ammaiyar translated by M. L. Thangappa edited by A. R. Venkatachalapathy. © M. L. Thangappa 2014. Reprinted by permission of the editor.

Extract from 'The Breast Giver' by Mahasweta Devi translated by Gayatri Chakravorty Spivak from *Breast Stories*. Reprinted by permission of Seagull Books.

Extract from 'Yellow is the Colour of Longing' by K. R. Meera translated by J. Devika from *Yellow is the Colour of Longing*. Reprinted by permission of Penguin Books India.

Extract from 'On the Edge' by Salma translated from the Tamil by N. Kalyan Raman. Reprint by permission of the author and translator.

Extract from *Harvest* by Manjula Padmanabhan. Reprinted by permission of the author.

We regret any errors or omissions in the above list of acknowledgements and would like to be notified of any corrections that should be incorporated in future editions of this book.

NOTES

Sangha, Mutta, Citta, Vimla, Ambapali and Kisa-gotami: Verses from the *Therigatha*, the ninth book of the *Khuddaka Nikaya*.

Urmila Pawar: Excerpted from the short story 'Mukti' from the collection *Mother Wit* (2013).

Zeb-un-nisa: Excerpted from *The Diwan of Zeb-un-nisa*, a collection of ghazals by the Mughal princess.

Lal Ded: Excerpted from the poem *Lalla Vakhyani*, a collection of devotional poems.

Bahinabai, Rajai, Jenabai, Muktabai, Nirmala, Soyrabai: Poems by Marathi poet-saints with new translations from the collection *The Ant who Swallowed the Sun* (to be published).

Akka Mahadevi: Verses from *Songs for Siva: Vacanas of Akka Mahadevi* (2010).

Mirabai: Excerpted from the anthology *Eating God: A Book of Bhakti Poetry* (2014).

Andaal: Excerpted from *The Autobiography of a Goddess* (to be published), collection of verses by poet-saint Andaal.

Translator's note:

Ninth-century Tamil mystic Andaal followed the poetic convention of her time by requesting monsoon clouds to act as messengers to her love, the God of the Universe. However, the same conventions demand intense reader engagement. For, besides the literal meaning, each verse embeds parallel and inset meanings that are left to the reader to discover. Thus, simultaneous shifts in meaning dynamize each verse into a literary trompe l'oeil. The second and third renderings of each verse embody the translator's understanding of hidden parallel and inset meanings.

Rosemary: Poem 'What I Have to Tell You' from *Sweeping the Front Yard* (2011), translated from the Malayalam 'Enikku Ninnodu Parayanullathu' first published in *Vakkukal Chekkerunnidam*.

Velli Vitiyar: Verses from the poem *Kuruntokai*, a collection of romantic poems by various poets of the Sangam era.

Avvaiyar: Verses from the poems *Kuruntokai* (a collection of poems dealing with romantic love and separation from the beloved) and *Purananuru* (a collection of poems that deals with war, politics, wealth and daily life). Both include poems by various poets of the Sangam era.

Molla: Verses from the poem *Ramayanam*.

Muddupalani: Verses from *The Appeasement of Radhika: Radhika Santawanam* (2011), an erotic classic.

Krishna Sobti: Excerpted from the novel *Sunflowers of the Dark* (2008), originally published as *Surajmukhi Andhere Ke*.

Yashodhara Mishra: Excerpted from the short story 'A Matter of Choice' from *Body Maps: Stories by South Asian Women*.

Kutti Revathi: Poem 'Breasts' originally published in Tamil in 2002 as 'Mulaigal' in the collection by the same name.

Vibhavari Shirurkar: Excerpted from the novel *Kharemaster* (1993).

Alka Saraogi: Excerpted from the short story 'Death of a Tree' from *The Tale Retold: Selected Stories* (2009).

Attia Hosain: Excerpted from the novel *Sunlight on a Broken Column* (2009).

Rassundari Devi: Excerpted from *Words to Win: The Making of Modern Autobiography* (2013), a translation of major sections of Rassundari Devi's autobiography *Amar Jiban*.

p. 56 **colourfully illuminated** Pages of the manuscripts were not sewn or tied together, but were pressed inside heavy wooden slats. Taking out a page was possible without damaging the book.

p. 56 **master the word** Here she uses the significant word jitakshar, which means 'one who has mastered the word'. There is a word that is somewhat analogous in construction and that is a familiar word in religious discourses: jitendriya or one who has mastered the senses. She probably had that construction in mind and stretched it to substitute 'word' for 'senses'.

p. 56 **how to write** She says this because of her experience of the village school, where students were taught to write out the letters first and then to memorize them one by one. Writing was, then, the first step to reading and one would read what one wrote down. In the absence of blackboards, the teacher did not have to write out anything for the students to read, he would help them with shaping letters. Later, he would recite memorized passages which they would take down to practise writing and spelling.

p. 57 **in silence** Silent reading was unusual. At schools, lessons were recited aloud, and manuscripts—mostly religious or philosophical—were chanted out. With printed books came the habit of silent reading, even though, to this day, lessons are usually loudly recited to help memorize them.

Pundita Ramabai Sarasvati: Excerpted from the memoir *The High-Caste Hindu Woman* (1888).

Ramabai Ranade: Excerpted from the autobiography *Memories of Our Life Together*, originally published in 1910 as *Amchya Ayushatil Kahi Athvani*.

Geetanjali Shree: Excerpted from the short novel *Mai* (2008).

Indira Goswami: Excerpted from the novel *The Blue-necked God* (1976), originally published as *Nilakantha Braja*.

Volga: Excerpted from the short story 'The Experiment' from the collection *The Woman Unbound* (2001).

Kamala Das: Excerpted from the autobiography *My Story.*

Mamta Kalia: Poems 'After Eight Years of Marriage' and 'Brat' from *Nine Indian Women Poets* (1997).

Mannu Bhandari: Excerpted from the novel *Bunty* (1983).

Nabaneeta Dev Sen: Poems 'Antara—1', 'The Twittering Machine', 'Children' and 'Childspeak', some of which were first published in *The Little Magazine*.

Gagan Gill: Poem 'Child, Go Home' translated for The Poetry Translation Centre.

Baby Kamble: Excerpt from the memoir *The Prisons We Broke* (2008).

Cornelia Sorabji: Excerpt from 'The Adoption' from *Sun Babies: Studies in the Child Life of India*, a collection of essays.

Manju Kapur: Excerpted from 'Name: Amba Dalmia' from the anthology *Of Mothers and Others: Stories, Essays and Poems* (2014).

Ajeet Cour: Excerpted from the first volume of Ajeet Cour's autobiography, *Pebbles in a Tin Drum* (1999).

Padma Sachdev: Poems 'An Infant's Dream and 'Mother Tongue' from *A Handful of Sun and Other Poems* (2000).

Lila Majumdar: Excerpted from the story 'The Yellow Bird' from a collection of short stories, *Classic Adventures: The Yellow Bird* (2010).

Nayantara Sahgal: Excerpted from the novel *Mistaken Identity* (2007).

Bulbul Sharma: Excerpted from the story 'Mushroom Madness' from the collection *The Anger of Aubergines: Stories of Women and Food* (2005).

Prathibha Nandakumar: Poem 'Salvation', first published in Poetry International Rotterdam.

Ashapurna Devi: Excerpted from *Ashapurna Devi: Snakebite and the Distant Window: A Critical Study* (2012).

Nilanjana Roy: Excerpted from the essay 'In the Flesh' published in *Seminar* (2006).

Shivani: Excerpted from the collection *Shivani's Apradhini: Women Without Men* (2011).

Vaidehi: Excerpted from the story 'Gulabi Talkies' from the short story collection *Gulabi Talkies and Other Stories* (2006).

Bama: Excerpted from 'Chilli Powder' from the short story collection *Harum-Scarum Saar and Other Stories* (2006).

P. Sivakami: Excerpted from the novel *The Taming of Women* (2012).

Kamala Markandaya: Extracted from the novel *Nectar in a Sieve* (2009).

Mridula Garg: Excerpted from the novel *Country of Goodbyes* (2003).

Nirupama Borgohain: Excerpted from the novel *Abhijatri* (1999).

Rajalakshmi: Excerpted from the short story 'The Apology' from *Samyukta: A Journal of Women's Studies* (July 2008).

Sarah Joseph: Excerpted from the novel *Gift in Green* (2011).

Rashid Jahan: Excerpted from the chapter 'One of My Journeys' from *A Rebel and Her Cause: The Life and Work of Rashid Jahan* (2014).

Maitreyi Pushpa: Excerpted from the novel *Alma Kabutari* (2002).

Chandrakanta: Excerpted from *A Street in Srinagar* (2010).

Romila Thapar: Excerpted from the essay 'Somanatha and Mahmud' in *Frontline* (Volume 16–Issue 8, Apr. 10–23, 1999):

p. 175 **place of pilgrimage** *Vana parvan* 13.14; 80.78; 86. 18-19; 119.1

p. 175 **ninth or tenth century** CE: B. K. Thapar, 1951, 'The Temple at Somanatha: History by Excavations,' in K. M. Munshi, *Somnath: The Shrine Eternal*, Bombay, 105-33; M. A. Dhaky and H. P. Sastri, 1974, *The Riddle of the Temple at Somanatha*, Varanasi.

p. 176 **and the Persian Gulf** V. K. Jain, 1990, *Trade and Traders in Western India*, Delhi.

p. 176 **in the coastal areas** *Epigraphia Indica* XXXII, 47 ff.

p. 176 **extremely prosperous** Muhammad Ulfi, 'Jami-ul-Hikayat,' in Eliot and Dowson, *The History of India as Told by its own Historians*, II, 201. Wasa Abhira from Anahilvada had property worth ten lakhs in Ghazni; impressive, even if exaggerated.

p. 176 **trade in horses** Abdullah Wassaf, *Tazjiyat-ul-Amsar*, in Eliot and Dowson, *The History of India as Told by its own Historians*, III, 31 ff. Marco Polo also comments on the wealth involved in the horse trade especially with southern India. *Prabandhachintamani*, 14; Rajashekhara, *Prabandhakosha*, Shantiniketan, 1935, 121.

p. 176 **according to some sources** Abdullah Wassaf, Eliot and Dowson, op. cit. I, 69; Pehoa Inscription, *Epigraphia Indica*, I. 184 ff.

p. 176 **temple at Multan** A. Wink, 1990, *Al-Hind*, Volume 1, Delhi, 173 ff; 184 ff; 187 ff.

p. 176 **as the Bawarij** Alberuni in E. C. Sachau, 1964 (reprint), *Alberuni's India*, New Delhi, I.208.

p. 177 **as Shaka 947** Ibid., II.9-10, 54.

p. 177 **breaking of the idol** F. Sistani in M. Nazim, 1931, *The Life and Times of Sultan Mahmud of Ghazni*, Cambridge.

p. 177 **pre-Islamic goddesses widely worshipped** *Quran*, 53. 19-20 G. Ryckmans, 1951, *Les Religions Arabes Pre-Islamique*, Louvain.

p. 177 **champion of Islam** Nazim, op.cit.

p.178 **regarded as heretics** A. Wink, 1990, *Al-Hind*, I, Delhi, 184-89; 217-18.

p. 178 **commercial advantage** cf. Mohammad Habib, 1967, *Sultan Mahamud of Ghaznin*, Delhi.

p.178 **a human form** Ibn Attar quoted in Nazim, op. cit.; Ibn Asir in *Gazetteer of the Bombay Presidency*, I, 523; Eliot and Dowson, II, 248 ff; 468 ff. al Kazwini, Eliot and Dowson, I, 97 ff. Abdullah Wassaf, Eliot and Dowson, III, 44 ff; IV. 181.

Shama Fatehally: Excerpted from the novel *Tara Lane* (2006).

Mrinal Pande: Excerpted from the short stort 'Bibbo', first published in *The Little Magazine* (Volume 1, Issue 1).

Nirupama Dutt: Poems 'The Black Woman' and 'Wicked Woman' were featured in The Poetry International Web.

Nivedita Menon: Excerpted from collection of essays *Seeing Like a Feminist* (2012).

Rokeya Sakhawat Hossain: Excerpted from the short story 'Sultana's Dream' (1905).

K. Saraswathi Amma: Excerpted from the essay 'A World Without Men' from *Samyukta: A Journal of Women's Studies* (January 2008).

Sarojini Naidu: Excerpted from the speech 'India Women and the Franchise' from *Sarojini Naidu: Selected Poetry and Prose* (2011).

Qurratulain Hyder: Excerpted from the novel *Fireflies in the Mist* (2008).

Easterine Kire: Excerpted from the novel *Bitter Wormwood* (2013).

Temsula Ao: Excerpted from the story 'The Last Song' from the collection *These Hills Called Home: Stories from a War Zone* (2013)

Okkur Maccatiyar: Excerpted from the *Purananuru*, a collection on secular poems of the Sangam era by various poets.

Bani Basu: Excerpted from the novel *The Enemy Within* (2002).

Joya Mitra: Excerpted from the *Killing Days: Prison Memoirs* (2004), portraits of women who were imprisoned for overstepping boundaries of social norms.

Irawati Karve: Excerpted from *Yuganta* (1967), a study of the main characters of the Mahabharata.

p. 225 **used for serpents** The word is also used for elephants.

Anita Agnihotri: Excerpted from 'Why Does That Girl Trudge Across', a journal entry from *Forest Interludes: A Collection of Journals and Fiction* (2001).

Rajni Bakshi: Excerpted from *Bapu Kuti: Journeys in Rediscovery of Gandhi* (2000).

Amrita Pritam: Poem 'To Waris Shah', an ode addressed to Waris Shah, an eighteenth-century Punjabi poet.

Jyotirmoyee Devi: Excerpted from the novel *The River Churning* (1995).

Urvashi Butalia: Excerpted from *The Other Side of Silence: Voices from the Partition of India* (1998).

Pinki Virani: Excerpt from *Aruna's Story: The True Account of a Rape and its Aftermath* (1998), the book that catalyzed the law on passive euthanasia.

Arundhati Roy: Excerpted from the Booker-prize-winning novel, *The God of Small Things* (1997).

Saudamini Devi: Excerpted from *Adbhuta Ramayana*. This is an alternate version of the epic, and Sita plays a more central and active role.

p. 258 **Kali** also known as Kālikā, is a primarily Tāntrika goddess associated with death, destruction, time and surprisingly, poetry, though the name itself appears as early as the Atharva Veda written 1000 BCE. Kālī is also the name of one of the seven tongues of Agni, the Rig-Veda's fire deity, according to the Muṇḍaka Upaniṣad, and it thus may or may not refer to the goddess directly. In her aspect as a martial goddess, she is popularly pictured as the slayer of many demons like Caṇḍa and Muṇḍa.

p. 258 **Pralaya** The Hindu 'End of Days'. In Hindu cosmology, the word 'pralaya' signifies the dissolution of the manifest universe. During each pralaya, the lower ten realms (loka) are destroyed, while the higher four realms, including Satya-loka, Tapa-loka, Jana-loka, and Mahar-loka are preserved. During each Mahapralaya, all fourteen major realms are destroyed.

p. 258 Asitā Literally, 'dark coloured', an epithet of Kālī. The poet uses this word here in conjunction with the word Sītā to render an obvious poetic effect. Hence the retention of the originals in the translation.

p. 258 Śaṅkara An epithet of Śiva.

p. 258 evil night-walker A translation of niśācara, literally 'one who moves in the night'. A Hindu epithet for all demons and ghouls.

p. 259 ḍākinī A female imp among Kālī's attendants. It feeds on human flesh and has a masculine counterpart called *ḍāka*.

p. 259 yoginī an ambiguous term which may refer to a) a female practitioner of esoteric mysteries, b) a liberated woman, or c) a fierce demi-goddess, or minor goddess in the retinue of the warlike goddesses of the Tantras.

p. 259 Mātṛkā Literally, 'mothers', protective, or malevolent female deities usually associated with childbirth

p. 259 Prabhāvatī... Śobhanā Names of sundry attendants of the goddess, variously called Mātṛkā, Nāyikā, Ḍākinī or Yoginī. Demi-goddesses, or minor goddesses, usually martial in character, as is obvious from the names here.

Rukmini Bhaya Nair: Poems 'Mayamriga, California'and 'Kali' first published in *Yellow Hibiscus: New and Selected Poems* (2004).

Mallika Sengupta: Poems 'Pandu's Desire for Sons' and 'While Teaching my Son History'.

Kumudini: Excerpted from the play 'Viswamitra' from *From the Inner Palace: A Kumudini Anthology* (2009) a collection of short stories, essays, drama and a novelette.

Pratibha Ray: Excerpted from *Yajnaseni: The Story of Draupadi* (1995).

Suniti Namjoshi: Stories excerpted from *Fabulous Feminist* (2012), a collection of feminist fables.

Malathi Maithri: Poems 'Proscribed Bood—1' and 'Proscribed Blood—2' originally published in the collection *Neeli* (2007). 'Demon Blood' originally published in *Wild Girls, Wicked Words* (2012).

Arundhathi Subramaniam: Poems 'Where I Live' from *Where I Live* (2005), '5.46, Andheri Local' from *On Cleaning Bookshelves* (2001) and 'The City and I' from the *Hindustan Times* (2011).

Mamang Dai: Poems 'Prayer Flags—2' from Poetry International Web and 'Small Towns and the River' from *River Poems* (2004).

Ismat Chughtai: Excerpted from the autobiographical piece 'In the Name of those Married Women' from *Lifting the Veil* (2009), a collection of her fiction and non-fiction works.

Popati Hiranandani: Poem 'A Homeless Sindhi Woman' from *Freedom and Fissures: An Anthology of Sindhi Partition* (1998).

Eunice de Souza: Poem 'Travelling' from *Sweeping the Front Yard* (2011).

Mahadevi Varma: Excerpted from the essay 'Chinese Pedlar' from *A Pilgrimage to the Himalayas, and Other Silhouettes from Memory* (1975), a collection of memoirs, sketches and essays.

Prabha Khaitan: Excerpted from *A Life Apart: An Autobiography* (2012).

Sailabala Das: Excerpted from the travelogue *Bilat Prabas* (Journey to England).

Karaikkal Ammaiyar: Verses from *Mutta Tiruppatikam,* a collection of poems addressed to Shiva.

Mahasweta Devi: Excerpted from the story 'The Breast Giver' from *Breast Stories* (1997). English words in the original Bengali story have been italicized in this translation.

K. R. Meera: Excerpted from 'Yellow is the Colour of Longing' from *Yellow is the Colour of Longing* (2011), a collection of short stories.

p. 319 **Did you run** The reference is to a popular saying in Malayalam which goes 'I ran to Pandalam fearing the army; but there was the army lying in wait, their torches all lit.'

Salma: Excerpted from the story 'On the Edge' first published in *Out of Print* (March 2013).

Manjula Padmanabhan: Excerpted from the dystopian play *Harvest* (2003).

Ajeet Cour (b. 1934) is a renowned Punjabi writer who has published several short stories, novellas and a travelogue and has translated several significant works. Her memoir *Khanabadosh* was translated into English as *Pebbles in a Tin Drum*. She has won the Sahitya Akademi Award, and the Padma Shri.

Akka Mahadevi was a twelfth-century mystic-poet who wrote in Kannada. She is believed to have been married to a local ruler, Kausika, but left her home to live in defiance of social convention. She is credited with writing hundreds of vachanas (verses), most of them dedicated to Chennamallikarjuna or Lord Shiva.

Alka Saraogi (b. 1960) did her PhD in Hindi literature on the works of Hindi writer Raghubir Sahay. She has published a collection of short stories, *Kahani ki Talash Mein* ('In Search of a Story'), a novel, *Kalikatha: Via Bypass,* which won the Sahitya Akademi Award.

Ambapali, Citta, Vimala, Mutta, Kisagotami and Sangha were Buddhist nuns who are believed to have lived around 600 BCE whose verses are included in the collection titled *Therigatha.*

Amrita Pritam (1919–2005) is acclaimed as the doyenne of Punjabi literature. Her best-known works are the poem 'Aaj Aakhan Waris Shan Nu' and the novel *Pinjar* (The Skeleton), which was made into an award-winning film in 2003. In 1956, she became the first woman to win the Sahitya Akademi Award for her magnum opus, a long poem, *Sunehe* (Messages); she received the Jnanpith for *Kagaz Te Canvas* (The Paper and the Canvas). In 2004, she was awarded the Padma Vibhushan, as well as the Sahitya Akademi's Lifetime Achievement Award.

Andaal is one of the twelve Alvar or Vaishnav saint-poets. Born around the ninth century, she was adopted by the Alvar saint, Periyalvar. She was devoted to Lord Vishnu and is credited the composition of Thiruppavai, a collection of thirty verses, and Nacciyar Tirumoli, a long poem of 143 verses.

Anita Agnihotri (b. 1956) is an IAS officer with numerous short stories and two novels to her credit, including *Forest Interludes* and *The Awakening.* Her work has been greatly influenced by her travels, particularly through the villages of Orissa and Jharkand. Her book *Seventeen* won the Crossword Award for Translated Fiction. She has been a member of the National Commission of Women.

Arundhathi Subramaniam (b. 1973) is a poet and prose writer of spirituality. She has worked as curator, poetry editor and critic. She is the author of four books of poetry, most recently *When God is a Traveller,* which was shortlisted for the T. S. Eliot Prize and won the Khushwant Singh Memorial Prize. As editor, her most recent anthology is *Eating God: A Book of Bhakti Poetry.*

Arundhati Roy (b. 1961) is a writer and political activist. She won the Man Booker Prize for Fiction for her novel *The God of Small Things.* Her other published works include *The Greater Common Good, An Ordinary Person's Guide To Empire, Listening to Grasshoppers: Field Notes on Democracy,* and *The Algebra of Infinite Justice.* She is also the recipient of the Norman Mailer Prize for Distinguished Writing.

Ashapurna Devi (1909–1995) was one of the most prolific Bengali writers and has published hundreds of books. She is best known for her trilogy: *Pratham Pratishruti, Subarnalata, Bakul Katha.* For her contribution as a novelist and short story writer, the Sahitya Akademi conferred its highest honour, the Fellowship, in 1994. She is the recipient of several prestigious awards, including the Jnanpith and the Padma Shri.

Attia Hosain (1913–1998) was the first woman to graduate from amongst Taluqdari families into which she was born. She was a journalist and a broadcaster and writer of short stories. In 1947 she went to England with her husband and two children. Presenting her own woman's programme on the BBC Eastern service, amongst others, for many years, she also appeared on television and the West End stage. In addition she lectured on the confluence of Indian and Western culture and wrote *Phoenix Fled*, a collection of short stories, and *Sunlight on a Broken Column*, a novel.

Avvaiyar meaning 'respectable women' was the title given to different poets who lived at different periods of time. Avvaiyar I lived during the Sangam era. She is believed to be the author of seven verses including *Kuruntokai* and *Purananuru*.

Baby Kamble (Shantabai Krushnaji Kamble) is a Dalit activist and one of the first Dalit women to write an autobiography. The original Marathi work, *Jina Amucha*, translated as *The Prisons We Broke* describes the lives of the Mahars in an oppressive caste based society.

Bahinabai was a seventeenth-century Marathi poet and a follower of Vithoba. She recorded her life, struggles at home, her spiritual leanings and visions of her guru Tukaram, in the autobiographical *Atmanivedana*.

Bama (b. 1958) is a Tamil writer, teacher and social activist. She is best known for her memoir *Karukku*, which established her as a distinct voice in Indian literature. Her other works in Tamil include two collections of short stories, *Kusumbukkaran* and *Oru Tattvani Erumaiyam*.

Bani Basu (b. 1939) is one of the leading personalities of modern Bengali literature. She was awarded the Tarashankar Award for *Antarghaat*, translated as *The Enemy Within* and the Ananda Purashkar for *Maitreya Jataka*, translated as *The Birth of the Maitreya*.

Bulbul Sharma, writer, painter, birdwatcher, maker of woodcuts, is the author of several books: *Grey Hornbills at Dusk*, *My Sainted Aunts*, *The Perfect Woman*, *The Anger of Aubergines*, *Shaya Tales* and *Tailor of Giripul*. She is a regular columnist for the *Asian Age* and a founder member of Sannidhi, an NGO that works in village schools.

Chandrakanta (b.1938) is a Hindi writer born in Srinagar. She has written seven novels and hundreds of stories. *Katha Satisar* was awarded the Vyas Samman, and she has received the Jammu Kashmir Cultural Academy's Best Book Award multiple times.

Cornelia Sorabji (1866–1954) was the first female advocate from India admitted to Allahabad High Court, the first female graduate from Bombay University and the first woman to study law at Oxford University. She also wrote a number of books, both fiction and essays, including *Love and Life behind the Purdah*, *Sun-Babies: Studies in the Child-life of India*, and *The Purdahnashin*.

Easterine Kire (b.1959) is a poet, novelist, and writer of children's books. Her books include *A Naga Village Remembered*, *A Terrible Matriarchy*, *Mari* and *Bitter Wormwood*. Her work has been translated into German, Croatian, Uzbek, Norwegian and Nepali. She is currently based in Northern Norway where she writes and performs jazz poetry with her band, Jazzpoesi.

Eunice de Souza (b. 1940) is a contemporary poet, literary critic and novelist who writes in English. She has published four collections of poetry, two novels, and four children's books. She has also edited several books including *Nine Indian Women Poets*, *Purdah: An Anthology*, and *Women's Voices: Selections from Nineteenth and Early Twentieth Century Indian Writing in English*.

Gagan Gill (b. 1959) is a Hindi poet who has published four collections of poetry, a volume of essays, and a travelogue. She has also published ten volumes of translations. She is the recipient of the Bharat Bhushan Agrawal Award, the Sanskriti Puruskar, and the Kedar Samman.

Geetanjali Shree (b. 1957) has written four novels: *Mai*, *Tirohit*, *Hamara Sheher Us Baras*, *Khali Jagah*, and two collections of short stories, and *Between Two Worlds: An Intellectual Biography of Premchand*. She is the recipient of the Indu Sharma Katha Sammaan, Hindi Akademi Sahityakar Sammaan and Dwijdev Sammaan.

Indira Goswami (1942–2011) (Mamoni Raisom Goswami) is one of the most celebrated writers in India and has published several creative and scholarly works in Assamese and English. She won several prizes including the Sahitya Akademi Award, and India's highest literary award, the Jnanpith. She was also named a Principal Prince Claus Laureate. Many of her works have been translated into English including *The Blue-necked God*, *The Moth-eaten Howdah of the Tusker*, *Pages Stained with Blood* and *The Man from Chinnamasta*.

Irawati Karve (1905–1970) was a sociologist and writer who wrote in Marathi and English. She was the first Indian woman anthropologist and founded the Department of Anthropology at Poona University. *Yuganta* won the Sahitya Akademi Award for best book in Marathi. Her other Marathi books include *Paripurti*, *Bhovara*, *Amachi Samskruti* and *Gangajal*.

Ismat Chughtai (1915–1991), the grande dame of Urdu literature, was a novelist, short-story writer and essayist who represented the birth of a revolutionary feminist politics and aesthetics in Urdu literature in the twentieth century. Her work has been widely translated and some English titles include *A Life in Words: Memoirs*, *Lifting the Veil*, *Quilt and Other Stories*, and *The Crooked Line*.

Jenabai (Janabai) was a thirteenth-century Marathi poet. Though unlettered, she is credited with the composition of at least 300 verses dedicated to Vithoba, or Vitthala. She worked in the household of the parents of the saint-poet Namdev, and considered him her guru.

Joya Mitra is the author of several novels and collections of poems in Bengali. She was imprisoned for her involvement with the Naxalite movement in the 1970s, an experience she recounts in *Killing Days: Prison Memoirs*. Her poetry collections include *Pratnoprastherer Gaan* (Song of the Ancient Stones), and *Deergha Ektara* (The Long String Instrument). She has translated the works of Amrita Pritam, Bhisham Sahni, Vaidehi and Ajeet Cour into Bengali.

Jyotirmoyee Devi (1894–1988) was a Bengali writer of fiction and essays. She received the prestigious Rabindra Puraskar. Some of her short fiction is available in English

translation as *The Impermanence of Lies* and her novel about the Partition of India has been translated as *The River Churning*.

K. R. Meera (b. 1970) is a Malayalam writer, the author of five novels and six collections of short fiction. She has received the Lalithambika Sahitya Award, the Vayalar Award and the Kerela Sahitya Akademi awards. Her novel *Aarachar* has been translated into English as *Hangwoman*. She also writes screenplays.

K. Saraswathi Amma (1919–1975) was a Malayalam feminist writer. She wrote twelve volumes of short stories, one novel, *Premabhajanam*, a play, *Devaduth*, and a book of essays titled *Purushanmarillatha Lokam* (*A World Without Men*).

Kamala Das (1934–2009) also wrote as Madhavikutty, and later changed her name to Surayya. She wrote novels, poetry and short stories in English and Malayalam. She has received the Kerala Sahitya Akademi, the central Sahitya Akademi Award, the Valayar Award and the Kent Award for English Writing from Asian Countries. She was nominated in 1984 for the Nobel Prize for Literature.

Kamala Markandaya (1924–2004) (Kamala Purnaiya Taylor) was a native of Mysore; she moved to the UK after Independence. Her first novel, *Nectar in a Sieve*, was a bestseller. She wrote several more novels including *Some Inner Fury*, *A Silence of Desire*, *Possession*, and *The Nowhere Man* and *Bombay Tiger*, which was published after her death.

Karaikkal Ammaiyar, believed to have lived around sixth century CE, belonged to a merchant caste. Her original name was Punithavathi. On attaining sainthood she was referred to as 'the venerated woman of Karaikkal'. Her life, full of miracles, is narrated in the twelfth-century Saiva classic *Periya Puranam*. She composed three works, *Arputha Thiru Andhadhi*, *Muutha Thiruppathigam*, and *Thiru Irattai Manimalai*.

Krishna Sobti (b. 1925) was the first Hindi woman writer to receive the Sahitya Akademi Award for her magnum opus, *Zindaginama*. She is also the recipient of the first Katha

Chudamani Award for Lifetime Literary Achievement. Her writings cover a vast range of issues including Partition, upheaval and turmoil in Indian society, man-woman relationship, feudalism and dissolution of human values. Her works have been translated into various Indian and foreign languages.

Kumudini (1905–1986) was one of the earliest women writers of twentieth-century Tamil literature. She translated Rabindranath Tagore's *Yoga-yog* from the Hindi into Tamil. She wrote the novel *Diwan-Magal,* which advocated inter-caste marriage, a revolutionary concept in 1942. She was appreciated for her subtle wit and humour in her stories which were published in *Ananda Vikatan, Kalaimagal* and other magazines. A sincere Gandhian, she spent several months in Sewagram and founded the Seva Sangham in Tiruchi in 1948.

Kutti Revathi (b. 1974) is an influential writer in the feminist space in India. Some of her poems, such as 'Mulaigal' (Breasts), have achieved iconic status all over the world. She is the editor of *Panikkudam,* a literary quarterly for women's writing. Trained in Siddha Medicine, Revathi is also a filmmaker and engages actively in issues of caste and violence against women.

Lal Ded was a fourteenth-century Kashmiri mystic and poet. Also known as Lalla, Lalla Arifa and Lalleshwari, she was born into a Pandit family and married at twelve. At twenty-four, she renounced the material and domestic realm. Her verses, known as vakhs, are some of the earliest literary work in Kashmiri.

Lila (Leela) Majumdar (1908–2007) was a Bengali writer and translator. She wrote several books for children in various genres like detective stories, ghost stories and fantasies. Her book *Holde Pakhir Palok* won the state award for children's literature, *Bak Badh Pala* won the Sangeet Natak Akademi Award, and her memoir *Aar Konokhane* won the Rabindra Puraskar.

Mahadevi Varma (1907–1987) is one of the four 'pillars' of the Chhayavaad (Neo-romanticism) School of Hindi literature. She wrote poetry, fiction and essays. Her poetry collection *Yama* won the Jnanpith award. She received the Padma Bhushan and Padma Vibhushan, India's second-highest civilian award.

Mahasweta Devi (b. 1926) is a noted social activist and Bengali writer. She has published twenty collections of short stories and close to a hundred novels, primarily in Bengali. She has also been a regular contributor to several literary magazines such as *Bortika,* a journal dedicated to the cause of oppressed communities within India. She has won several literary prizes including the Sahitya Akademi Award, the Padma Shri, the Jnanpith Award, the Ramon Magsaysay Award for Journalism, Literature and the Creative Communication Arts, and the Padma Vibhushan.

Maitreyi Pushpa (b. 1944) is a Hindi writer who has published several novels including *Idannammam, Chak, Alma Kabutari,* and *Jhoola Nat* and short story collections. She is the recipient of many awards including the SAARC Literary Award for *Alma Kabutari,* the Premchand Samman and the Sahityakar Samman.

Malathi Maithri (b. 1968) is an acclaimed feminist poet, social activist and public intellectual. She has published four collections of Tamil poetry: *Sankaraaparani, Neerindri Amaiyathu Ulagu, Niili, Enadhu Madu Kuduvai*; and three collections of essays: *Viduthalaiyai Ezhuthuthal, Nam Thanthaiyarai Kolvatheppati, Vettaveli Chirai.* She has edited three anthologies of women's writing and published the feminist political magazine *Anangu.*

Mallika Sengupta (1960–2011) was a Bengali poet and feminist. She published several volumes of poetry, three novels and three collections of essays on gender. She received the Sukanto Puroskar and the Bangla Academy Award among other honours.

Mamang Dai (b. 1957) is a poet and novelist who writes in English. Her books include *The Legends of Pensam, River Poems, Midsummer: Survival Lyrics,* and *The Black Hill.* She received the Verrier Elwin Award for her book *Arunachal Pradesh: The Hidden Land,* and the Padma Shri for her contributions to literature and education.

Mamta Kalia (b. 1940) writes in both Hindi and English and has more than twenty-five books to her credit including four novels and ten collections of short stories. She has written a collection of one-act plays, edited several books and is a regular contributor to leading magazines. She has been honoured with the Sahitya Bhushan Samman, the Mahadevi Verma Memorial Award and the Yashpal Samman.

Manju Kapur (b. 1948) teaches English at Delhi University. Her first novel *Difficult Daughters* won the 1999 Commonwealth Writers' Prize. Her other novels are *A Married Woman*, *Home*, *The Immigrant*, and *Custody*. She also edited *Shaping the World: Women Writers on Themselves*.

Manjula Padmanabhan (b. 1953) is an author/artist living in the US and India. *Harvest*, her fifth play, won the Onassis Award for Theatre. Her books include *Getting There*, *Escape* and *Three Virgins*.

Mannu Bhandari (b. 1931) is known for her two Hindi novels, *Aapka Banti* and *Mahabhoj*, which was later adapted into a play and performed all over the nation. She is a writer of the Nayi Kahani (New Story) style. She also co-wrote the book, *Ek Inch Muskaan* (A Little Smile) with her husband Rajendra Yadav, a pioneer of the Nayi Kahani movement.

Mirabai was mystic poet devoted to Lord Krishna. She is believed to have been born in 1498 into the royal family of Merta in Rajasthan, and was married to Bhoj Raj of Chittor. Against all convention, she mixed with common folk, singing bhajans and dancing in spiritual ecstasy. About 1,300 verses are attributed to her.

Molla was a fifteenth-century Telugu poet, also known as Kummara (potter) Molla, since she came from a potter family. Her translation of the Ramayana from Sanskrit into Telugu is also known as *Molla Bhagavata*.

Mridula Garg (b. 1938) writes in Hindi and English. She has published several novels, short story collections, plays and essays. She is a recipient of the prestigious Sahitya Akademi

Award and the Vyas Sanman. She also won the Hammett- Hellman award for courageous writing given by Human Rights Watch, New York.

Mrinal Pande (b. 1946) taught at the universities of Allahabad, Delhi and Bhopal before switching to journalism. She was India's first woman Chief Editor of a multi-edition Hindi daily, *Hindustan*. She writes in both Hindi and English and her work spans fiction, drama and essays. She has been awarded the Padma Shri, as well as the Red Ink Lifetime Achievement Award by the Mumbai Press Club.

Muddupalani lived in the mid-eighteenth century in Thanjavur. She was a devdasi attached to the court of King Pratapsimha. She wrote *Radhika Santawanam* in Telugu but was a multi-linguist and also wrote in Sanskrit and Tamil. She translated Tamil saint-poet Andaal's *Tiruppavai* into Telugu.

Muktabai was a thirteenth-century Marathi poet, born into a family that established the Varkari tradition. She was the spiritual guide of the Tantric yogi Changdev. She is believed to have attained mahasamadhi when she was just eighteen.

Nabaneeta Dev Sen (b. 1938) has published more than eighty books in Bengali in several genres including poetry, novels, short stories, plays, literary criticism, personal essays, travelogues, and children's literature. She is the recipient of several awards including a Padma Shri, the Celli Award from the Rockefeller Foundation, the Sarat Award from Bhagalpur University, and the Sahitya Akademi Award.

Nayantara Sahgal (b. 1927) is the author of several novels and works of non-fiction. She received the Sinclair Prize for Fiction, the Sahitya Akademi Award, the Commonwealth Writers' Prize, and was awarded an honorary doctorate in literature by the University of Leeds. She was associated with the founding of the People's Union for Civil Liberties and served as its vice-president during the 1980s.

Nilanjana Roy (b. 1971) is author of *The Wildings* (winner of the Shakti Bhatt First Book Prize 2013) and *The Hundred Names of Darkness*, and a columnist who writes on books, gender, culture and food. She is the editor of *A Matter of Taste*, an anthology of food writing. A collection of essays on books and reading, *How to Read in Indian* is forthcoming.

Nirmala was a fourteenth-century Marathi poet. She was a sister of the poet Chokhamela and her husband Banka Mahar also wrote abhangs. Her love for brother Chokha and sister-in-law Soyra is well expressed in her abhangs.

Nirupama Borgohain (b. 1932) is one of the most notable novelists of Assam. Her first novel was *Hei Nodi Niravadhi*. She worked as English lecturer at various colleges in Assam. She also edited *Saptahik Sanchipat* and *Chitrangada*. She was honoured with Sahitya Akademi Award for her novel *Abhijatri*.

Nirupama Dutt (b. 1955) is a poet, journalist, literary and art critic and translator. She writes in both Punjabi and English. She received the Punjabi Akademi Award for her anthology of poems, *Ik Nadi Sanwali Jahi*.

Nivedita Menon is a feminist writer and professor of political thought at Jawaharlal Nehru University. She is the author of *Recovering Subversion: Feminist Politics Beyond the Law* and *Seeing Like a Feminist*. She is also the editor of *Gender and Politics in India* and *Sexualities*.

Okkur Macattiyar was a Tamil poet of the Sangam era, one of the first poets who wrote about secular rather than spiritual love. She has several poems to her credit including *Purananuru, Akananuru* and *Kuruntokai*.

P. Sivakami (b. 1957) has written four novels in Tamil, all centred on Dalit and feminist themes. She translated her own first novel *The Grip of Change* before she left the Indian Administrative Service to start her own political party. Her novel *Anandhayi* has been translated as *The Taming of Women*.

Padma Sachdev (b. 1940) has published several collections of poetry and novels. Her books include *Jammu Jo Kabhi Sahara Tha, A Drop in the Ocean, A Handful of Sun and Other Poems*, and *Where has my Gulla Gone?* She has received a Padma Shri, a Sahitya Akademi Award, and the Kabir Samman for poetry.

Pinki Virani (b. 1959) is a writer, journalist, human-rights activist and author of four bestselling books: *Once was Bombay, Aruna's Story, Bitter Chocolate: Child Sexual Abuse in India*, which won a National Award, and *Deaf Heaven*. *Aruna's Story* brought about a landmark judgment on passive euthanasia in India.

Popati Hiranandani (1924–2005) is Sindhi writer, feminist and social activist. She has published works of poetry, short stories, novels, essays and literary criticism. She has been the recipient of many awards and honours including the Sahitya Akademi Award for her autobiography.

Prabha Khaitan (1942–2008) was a Hindi novelist, poet, an entrepreneur and feminist. She also translated Simone De Beauvoir's *The Second Sex* into Hindi. She was the first female president of the Calcutta Chamber of Commerce. Her autobiography *Anya se Ananya Tak* was translated as *A Life Apart*.

Prathibha Nandakumar (b. 1955) is a poet, filmmaker, journalist and translator. She has published eleven collections of poetry, two collections of short stories, a memoir, *Anudinada Antharagange* and two plays for children. Her poems have been translated into several languages. She has translated Shashi Deshpande's stories, and Padma Sachdev's poems into Kannada.

Pratibha Ray (b. 1943) is an academic and Oriya writer. She is the author of several novels, collections of short stories, and travelogues. She has received several awards including the Orissa Sahitya Akademi Award for her novel *Sheelapadma*, the Moortidevi Award for her novel *Yajnaseni*, the Sahitya Akademi award for her short story collection *Ullaghna*, and India's highest literary award, the Jnanpith.

Pundita Ramabai Sarasvati (1858–1922) was a writer, scholar, and women's rights activist. Besides Sanskrit, she was familiar with Marathi, Kannada, Hindustani and Bengali. She was honoured with the titles 'Pandita' and 'Sarasvati' for her scholarship, and was awarded the Kaiser-e-Hindi medal for community service in 1919. She wrote several articles and essays, but is best known for *The High-Caste Indian Woman*.

Qurratulain Hyder (1927–2007) was an eminent Urdu writer, academic, and journalist. She is best known for her magnum opus, *Aag Ka Darya* (River of Fire). She received the Sahitya Akademi Award for *Patjhar Ki Awaz* (short stories), and the Jnanpith Award for *Akhire Shab Ke Humsafar*. She also received the Padma Bhushan in 2005.

Rajai was a thirteenth-century Marathi poet from the Varkari tradition. She was the wife of the famous mystic Namdev and many of her abhangs express her frustration at living with an unworldly householder.

Rajalakshmi (1930–1965) was a Malayalam writer of poetry and fiction. She taught Physics in various state colleges. She wrote two novels and a few short stories. She won the Kerala Sahitya Akademi Award for her book *Oru Vazhiyum Kure Nizhalukalum* (A Path and a Few Shadows).

Rajni Bakshi is a journalist and author who currently works as the senior Gandhi Peace Fellow at Gateway House: Indian Council on Global Relations. Her book *Bazaars, Conversations and Freedom* won the Crossword Book Award for Non-Fiction. Her other books include *The Long Haul: The Bombay Textile Workers' Strike of 1982-83* and *Bapu Kuti: Journeys in Rediscovery of Gandhi*.

Ramabai Ranade (1862–1924) was a social worker and women's rights activist. At the age of eleven, she was married to Justice Mahadev Govind Ranade, a scholar and social reformer who encouraged her to learn to read and write. Ramabai is best known for her memoir *Amachya Ayushyatil Kahi Athavani*, written in Marathi.

Rashid Jahan (1905–1952) was an Urdu writer and a medical doctor. She trained as a gynaecologist and was an active member of the Communist Party of India as well as the Progressive Writers' Association. She wrote short stories and plays and is best remembered for her contribution to the Urdu anthology *Angaaray*, which was banned.

Rassundari Devi had learned some Bangla and Persian as a child, but was married at twelve and lost much of her learning. She taught herself to read and write at a time when education for women was discouraged. Her autobiography *Amar Jiban* was published in 1876.

Rokeya Sakhawat Hossain (1880–1932) was popularly known as Begum Rokeya. She was a leading feminist and social worker and she wrote in both English and Bangla. She is best known for her satirical work *Sultana's Dream* and *Padmarag*. Her other books include *Pipasha*, *Motichur*, *Oborodhbashini* (The Secluded Women), and *God Gives, Man Robs and Other Writings*.

Romila Thapar (b. 1931) is Professor Emerita in History at the Jawaharlal Nehru University, New Delhi. She is the author of several books including *A History of India*, *Early India: From the Origins to AD 1300*, *Somanatha: The Many Voices of History*, and *The Past As Present: Forging Contemporary Identities Through History*.

Rosemary (b. 1956) is a Malayalam poet, columnist and translator. She has published three collections of poetry and four memoirs. She received the Lalithambika Antharjanam Award for her poetry and the Esenin Award for her Malayalam translation of Russian poets.

Rukmini Bhaya Nair (b. 1952) is an eminent linguist, poet, writer and critic. Her published work include *Yellow Hibiscus: New and Selected Poems*, *The Ayodhya Cantos*, *The Hyoid Bone*, and several academic titles including *Lying on the Postcolonial Couch: the Idea of Indifference*. She is currently a Professor at Humanities and Social Sciences department of IIT, Delhi.

Sailabala Das (1875–1968) was a social worker and politician and believed to be the first woman from Odisha to go to England for higher studies. She was instrumental in the creation of the first women's college in Odisha and also set up Hindu widow's training school to train widows to become high school teachers. She wrote in English and Oriya.

Salma is a writer of Tamil poetry and fiction. Her work speaks about the taboo areas of the traditional Tamil woman's experience. She has written two books of poetry: *Oru*

Maalaiyum Innoru Maalaiyum (An Evening and Another Evening) and *Pachchai Devathai* (Green Angel). More recently, she has also tried her hand at short fiction and the novel.

Sarah Joseph (b. 1946) has published several novels and collections of short stories in Malayalam. Her trilogy *Aalahayude Penmakkal, Mattathi and Othappu* is acclaimed. She has won the Kerala Sahitya Academy Award, the central Sahitya Akademi Award and the Vayalar Award. Her novels *Gift in Green* and *Othappu* are available in English, as is a collection of stories, *The Masculine of Virgin*.

Sarojini Naidu (1879–1949) was a freedom fighter, political activist and poet. She began writing at the age of twelve, starting with a Persian play, *Maher Muneer*. Her poetry collections include *The Golden Threshold, The Bird of Time: Songs of Life, Death and the Spring, The Broken Wing: Songs of Love, Death and the Spring*, and *The Sceptred Flute: Songs of India. The Feather of The Dawn* was edited and published posthumously in 1961.

Saudamini Devi (Soudamini Debi) lived in the latter half of the nineteenth century and wrote verse renditions of religious epics, including *Adbhuta Ramayana*.

Shama Futehally (1952–2005) was a writer and translator. She wrote two collections of short stories. Her novels include *Tara Lane* and *Reaching Bombay Central*. She co-wrote a collection of children's stories with Githa Hariharan, *Sorry, Best Friend*. Her translations include a book of Urdu ghazals, *Slivers of a Mirror* and *In the Dark of the Heart: Songs of Meera*.

Shivani (1923–2003) was one of the pioneers of women-based fiction, and a popular writer in the Hindi magazine industry. She received a Padma Shri for her contribution to Hindi literature in 1982. She garnered a massive following in the sixties and seventies as her literary works were serialized in Hindi magazines like *Dharmayug* and *Saptahik Hindustan*, and in television and films.

Soyrabai was a fourteenth-century Marathi poet from the Varkari tradition. She was married to Chokhamela, who was also a poet devoted to Vithoba. She is credited with writing over sixty abhangs.

Suniti Namjoshi (b. 1941) has several books to her credit. Her poetry, fables, articles and reviews have been featured in anthologies and journals in India, Canada, the USA, Australia and Britain. A deep engagement with issues of gender, sexual orientation, cultural identity and human rights infuses her work. She currently lives in the UK.

Temsula Ao (b. 1945) is a poet and short story writer from Assam who writes in English. She received the Sahitya Akademi Award for her short story collection *Laburnum for my Head*. She is the author of several books of poetry including *Songs from Many Moods* and *Songs from the Other Life*. She has been awarded the Padma Shri and the Nagaland Governor's Award for Distinction in Literature. Her work has been translated into German, French, Assamese, Bengali and Hindi.

Urmila Pawar (b. 1945) is a Marathi writer with several short story collections to her credit. She has also written travelogues, plays, and co-authored a history of Dalit women's movements called We Also Made History. She won the Laxmibai Tilak Award for her autobiography *Aaidan*.

Urvashi Butalia (b. 1952) is an Indian feminist writer and publisher. Her books include *Making a Difference: Feminist Publishing in the South, Women and Right Wing Movements: Indian Experiences*, and *Speaking Peace: Women's Voices from Kashmir*. Her book, *The Other Side of Silence: Voices from the Partition of India*, won the Oral History Book Association Award, as well as the Nikkei Asia Award for Culture.

Vaidehi (b. 1945) is the pen name of Janaki S. Murthy, a Kannada writer and poet. She has written several books including collections of short stories, poems and essays and a novel. She has won numerous awards, including two Karnataka State Academy Awards, the Dana Chintamani Attimabbe Prashasthi, and the central Sahitya Academy Award.

Velli Vitiyar was a Tamil poet of the Sangam era who is believed to be one of the first poets who wrote about romantic love.

Vibhavari Shirurkar (1905–2001) was the

pen name of Marathi writer Balutai Khare. Among her significant works are *Kalyanche Nishwas*, a collection of short stories, and the novels *Hindolyawar*, *Bali* and *Shabari*. *Kharemaster* was a part-autobiographical novel based on her father's life.

Volga (b. 1950) writes fiction, poetry and essays in Telugu. Her novel *Sveccha* was a bestseller and was translated into other Indian languages by the National Book Trust. She has published five other novels, four collections of short stories, and edited the first volume of feminist philosophy in Telugu, *Maku Godalu Levu*.

Yashodhara Mishra is a professor of English and writes in Oriya. She has published five collections of short stories, two novels and several volumes of translations. Her literary awards include the Katha Award for Creative Writing, Jhankar Award for Short Story, Orissa Book Fair Award for Book of the Year, and the Orissa Sahitya Akademi Award.

Zeb-un-nisa (1638–1702) was a Mughal princess, eldest child of Emperor Aurangzeb and Dilras Banu Begum. She wrote poetry in Persian under the pen name Makhfi (the hidden one). She was imprisoned by her father for the last twenty years of her life. In 1724, years after her death, her writings were collected as *Diwan-i-Makhfi*.

Ahana Lakshmi (b. 1963) is an environmental scientist and writer. She has published two works of translation, *From the Inner Palace: A Kumudini Anthology* and *Election Fever and Other Stories*. She has also published a collection of children's stories, *A Balooney Trip and Other Stories*.

Alladi Uma and **M. Sridhar** teach English at the University of Hyderabad and do collaborative work in translation. They published a translation of a collection of short stories by Volga entitled *The Woman Unbound: Selected Short Stories*. They have won the Jyeshtha Literary Award and Katha Commendation Prize for their translations.

Anima Bose is best known for her translation of Ashapurna Devi's work from Bengali to English.

Anju Makhija is an eminent poet, playwright and translator. Her poem, 'A Farmer's Ghost', won the First Prize in the Fifth National Poetry Competition in 1994 organized by The Poetry Society (India) in collaboration with British Council.

Arjan Shad (b.1924) is a prominent Sindhi poet and literary critic. He writes various forms of poetry including nazms, ghazals, azad nazms, rubais, naeem kavita and others. He has also translated Russian poetry into Sindhi, which earned him the Soviet Land Nehru Award.

Arjun Choudhuri (b. 1984) works as an adjunct faculty member at the Department of English in Assam University's Silchar campus. He is the founding editor of *The Four Quarters Magazine*. He was awarded the annual Kavyanandan Award in 2010 by Suranandan Bharati, Kolkata for his book, *Bordering Poetry*.

Arunava Sinha (b. 1962) translates classic, modern and contemporary Bengali fiction and non-fiction into English. Twice the winner of the Crossword translation award, for *Sankar's Chowringhee* and Anita Agnihotri's *Seventeen*, respectively, and the winner of the Muse India

translation award for Buddhadeva Bose's *When The Time Is Right*, he has also been shortlisted for The Independent Foreign Fiction prize for his translation of *Chowringhee*. He was born and grew up in Kolkata, and lives and writes in New Delhi.

B. V. L. Narayanarow is a retired professor of linguistics who taught at the Central Institute for English and Other Foreign Languages, Hyderabad. He has written and translated several Telugu texts.

Caroline Augusta Foley Rhys Davids (1857–1942) was a British Pali language scholar and translator. Her work includes a translation of the *Dhamma Sangini* and the *Therigatha* as *Psalms of the Sisters*.

Enakshi Chatterjee is a bilingual writer, translator and media critic. She has published several books of children's fiction, science fiction, and popular science. She is a Katha-award-winning translator and among other major works, has translated *The River Churning*.

Gayatri Bhattacharya is a former lecturer of English at the University of Guwahati, Assam. She is well-known for translating Birinci Kumar Barua's *Jibonor Batot* into English, another landmark novel in modern Assamese literature. She has also translated Assamese works of stalwarts such as Bhabendranath Saikia and Sarat Chandra Goswami and others

Gayatri Chakravorty Spivak (b. 1942) is a literary theorist, philosopher and professor at Columbia University, where she is a founding member of the school's Institute for Comparative Literature and Society. She is best known for the essay 'Can the Subaltern Speak?' considered a founding text of postcolonialism. She received the Padma Bhushan in 2013.

George Grierson (1851-1941) was a scholar and civil servant who conducted the Linguisitic Survey of India, which he later edited and compiled in eleven volumes. He published several books including *Seven Grammars of the Dialects and Subdialects of*

the Bihari Language, *The Pisaca Languages of North-Western India*, and a monograph, *Lalla-Vakyani*, along with Dr Lionel D. Barnett.

George L. Hart (b. 1945) is a professor of Tamil at UC Berkeley. He has a PhD in Sanskrit and has studied Latin and Greek and several modern European and Indian languages. He is best known for his translations of several Tamil epics into English.

Ira Pande is the daughter of the renowned Hindi writer Shivani. She taught at the Department of English, Panjab University, Chandigarh, for fifteen years and then was an editor at *Seminar, Biblio*, Dorling Kindersley and Roli Books. She is currently chief editor, *IIC Publications*. She is the author of *Diddi: My Mother's Voice* and has recently translated *Shivani's Apradhini: Women Without Men*.

J. Devika is a historian critic, and feminist. She has translated several works of fiction and non-fiction between Malayalam and English, including *Hangwoman* and *Yellow is the Colour of Longing*.

Jai Ratan (1917–2012) was a prolific translator and has translated literary works from languages such as Hindi, Punjabi and Urdu. He has to his credit 600 translated short stories as well as many original stories. He was a winner of the Sahitya Akademi Award for Translation.

Jane Duran (b. 1944) was born in Cuba, brought up in the USA and Chile and moved to England after graduating from Cornell University. Her poems have appeared in anthologies, and selections have been published in *Poetry Introduction 8, Making for Planet Alice* and in *La Generacion del Cordero*.

Jatindra Kumar Nayak is a translator, literary critic, columnist and editor. He has translated several works of Oriya literature into English, including *Yantrarudha*, a novel by Chandrasekhar Rath, as *Astride the Wheel*, which received the Hutch Crossword Book Award 2004 for Indian Language Fiction Translation.

Jayanti Datta teaches English Literature at Kolkata's South City College. Her published works include a novel, *Yearning*, and an English translation of Bani Basu's novel, *The Enemy Within*.

Jerry Pinto (b. 1966) lives and works in Mumbai. He has been a mathematics tutor, school librarian, journalist and columnist. He is now associated with MelJol, an NGO that works in the sphere of child rights. His published works include the award-winning novel, *Em and the Big Hoom*, a book of poems, *Asylum*, and *Helen: The Life and Times of an H-Bomb*, which won the National Award for the Best Book on Cinema in 2007.

Jessie Duncan Westbrook was a translator of Persian, Urdu and Hindi and apart from the ghazals of Princess Zeb-un-nisa has also translated a book of Hindustani lyrics.

Kalpana Bardhan has researched and taught courses on development economics, agricultural economies, and statistics in Calcutta, Delhi, and the University of California, Berkeley. Many of her more recent publications deal with women and development, women's work status and living conditions in South and Southeast Asia.

Kamala Chatterjee, Lila Majumdar's daughter, lives in Kolkata and has undertaken the task of translating her mother's books into English.

Khushwant Singh (1915–2014) was an author, columnist and journalist. He was the founder-editor of *Yojana*, and editor of the *Illustrated Weekly of India, National Herald* and the *Hindustan Times*. He also translated from Hindi, Urdu and Punjabi. He was awarded India's second highest civilian honour, the Padma Vibhushan.

Lakshmi Devi Menon retired as Professor of English after teaching for twenty-eight years at St Teresa's College, Kerala. Her doctoral thesis was on women characters in Post-Independence Indian English Drama and she translated all eighty-four short stories written by K. Saraswati Amma for her Major UGC project. She was awarded the Malayala Manorama Air India Prathibha Puraskaram for Best Teacher in Ernakulam District in 2008.

Lakshmi Holmström (b. 1944) is a writer, literary critic and award-winning translator. She has translated the works of major writers in Tamil such as Mauni, Pudumaippittan,

Ashokamitran, Sundara Ramaswamy, Ambai, Bama and Imayam. In 2000 she received the Crossword Book Award for her translation of *Karukku* by Bama. She is a Founder-Trustee of South Asian Diaspora Literature and Arts Archive.

Lillian Srivastava and **Radhika Srivastava** are Hindi translators who have translated Mahadevi Varma's essays in *A Pilgrimage To The Himalayas And Other Silhouettes From Memory*.

Lucy Rosenstein has an MA in Indology from Sofia University (Bulgaria) and an MA and a PhD in Hindi. She did her PhD on Braj Bhasha verse but since 1997 has been working on contemporary Hindi poetry. This is reflected in the books she has published so far: *Swami Haridas and the Haridasi Sampradaya: A Study of Early Braj Bhasha Verse* and *Nayi Kavita 'New Poetry' in Hindi: An Anthology*.

M. Asaduddin is an author, translator and critic. His work has been recognized with the Sahitya Akademi Prize, the Katha Prize and A. K. Ramanujan Award for Translation. His published titles include *The Penguin Book of Classic Urdu Stories*, *Lifting the Veil: Selected Writings of Ismat Chughtai*, *For Freedom's Sake: Manto*, and *Joseph Conrad: Between Culture and Colonialism*.

M. L. Thangappa (b.1934) is a Tamil poet and taught Tamil in the colleges of the Puducherry government until his retirement in 1994. Two volumes of his translations from classical Tamil poetry have been published in the Penguin Classics: *Love Stands Alone* and *Red Lilies and Frightened Birds. Love Stands Alone* won the Sahitya Akademi award for Translation.

Magan Lal was a translator of Persian and collaborated with Jessie Duncan Westbrook on the translation of the ghazals of Princess Zeb-un-nisa.

Manisha Chaudhry (b. 1947) is a writer, translator, editor and publisher. She has also worked in the development sector as a consultant on issues of gender and primary education. Her English translation of Chandrakanta's *Ailan Gali Zinda Hai*

was published as *A Street in Srinagar,* and of Mridula Garg's *Kathgulab* as *Country of Goodbyes.*

Masooma Ali is a former reader of the Department of English, Miranda House, Delhi University. She has translated several books including *Pebbles in a Tin Drum* by Ajeet Cour, *The Widow of Vrindavan* by Kusum Ansal, *Krishnakali* by Shivani, and *Raavi Paar and Other Stories* by Gulzar (along with Alok Bhalla). Her translation of Govind Mishra's *The House with Five Courtyards* was shortlisted for the Crossword Books awards.

Maya Pandit works at EFL University, Hyderabad. She has taught for over three decades and specializes in feminist studies and translation studies. She has translated several plays, autobiographies, and other Marathi texts into English including Jotiba Phule's *Slavery*. She has also directed a film for the Sahitya Akademi on Marathi Dalit women writers, *Voices from the Margins*.

Menka Shivdasani is a Mumbai-based writer who has published two collections of poetry. She is also Mumbai coordinator for the global 100 Thousand Poets for Change movement and a founding member of Asia Pacific Writers & Translators. In 1986, she had played a key role in founding the Poetry Circle in Mumbai.

N. Kalyan Raman is a translator of contemporary Tamil fiction and poetry. He has published seven volumes of Tamil fiction in English translation. His poetry translations have been published widely in anthologies, literary journals and online publications. He is a regular contributor of essays and review articles to leading magazines and newspapers in India. He lives and works in Chennai.

N. Ravi Shanker is a translator of Tamil and Malayalam. He has translated Bama's *Harum-Scarum Saar and Other Stories* from the Tamil and social activist C.K. Janu's life story from the Malayalam as *Mother Forest: The Unfinished Story of C.K. Janu.*

Neela Bhagwat (b. 1942) is a well-known exponent of the Gwalior style of singing. She studied Marathi and Sanskrit literature as well as sociology. She is known for combining the purity of raga with the folk idiom of poet-saints like Kabir, Shajo and Meera.

Nita Kumar (b. 1951) holds the Brown Family Chair of South Asian History at Claremont McKenna College, California. She has published several titles, including *Friends, Brothers and Informants: Fieldwork Memoirs of Banaras*. Her translation of *Mai* won a Sahitya Akademi award.

Pamela Manasi is a writer and translator. She has published four collections of Hindi short stories and translated Krishna Sobti's *Surajmukhi Andhere Ke* from Hindi to English, and Paulo Coelho's *By The River Piedra I Sat Down and Wept* into Hindi.

Pradip Bhattacharya (b. 1947) is the author of fourteen books of English literature, rural development, homeopathy, children's stories, ancient Indian history and myth. He translated Pratibha Ray's *Yajnaseni* into English. He is a member of the Indian Administrative Service.

Pritham K. Chakravarthy is a researcher, performer and translator between Tamil and English. She has translated P. Sivakami's *The Taming of Women*, both volumes of the Blaft Tamil Pulp Fiction Anthology, and Charu Nivedita's *Zero Degree* with Rakesh Khanna.

Priya Sarukkai Chabria is a poet, writer and translator with five books of fiction, non-fiction and poetry. Her work has been translated into six languages and published in numerous anthologies. Her latest collection is *Another English Anglophone Poems From Around the World*. Her translations of the works of Tamil mystic Andaal (with Ravi Shankar) are forthcoming.

R. K. Jayasree teaches English at Maharajah's College, Ernakulam. A prolific translator, she has a number of published works to her credit. She is actively interested in social support activities and is working on a PhD at the University of Kerala.

Rahul Soni is a writer, editor and translator. He has edited *Home from a Distance*, an anthology of Hindi poetry in English translation, and translated *Magadh*, a collection of poems by Shrikant Verma, and *The Roof Beneath their Feet*, a novel by

Geetanjali Shree.

Raji Narasimhan (b. 1930) writes fiction, literary criticism and translates from Hindi and Tamil into English. Her book *Sensibility under Stress: Aspects of Indo-English Writing* was shortlisted for the Sahitya Akademi Award. The second of her five novels, *Forever Free*, was also shortlisted for the Sahitya Akademi Award. She has two collections of short stories: *The Marriage of Bela and Other Stories* and *The Illusion of Home*. Her other translations include *Unarmed* of Rajee Seth's Hindi novella *Nishkavach* and *Not Without Reason and Other Stories* of Rajee Seth's Hindi stories *Akaran to Naheen*.

Rakhshanda Jalil (b. 1963) is a well-known writer, critic and literary historian. She is best known for her book on Delhi's lesser-known monuments, *Invisible City: The Hidden Monuments of India*, as well as her biographies of Urdu writers Qurratulain Hyder and Rashid Jahan.

Sajal Dey teaches at the English and Foreign Languages University in Shillong. He conducts research and writes on translation studies, languages and linguistics, literary theory and linguistic rights.

Sandhya Mulchandani is a researcher and writer. She is the author of several books including *Kamasutra for Women*, *Erotic Literature from Ancient India* and *The Indian Man: His True Colours*.

Shampa Banerjee is a well-known translator of Bengali literature. She has published several books including Joya Mitra's *Killing Days*, and Shirshendu Mukhopadyay *Woodworm*. She is also the co-author of *One Hundred Indian Feature Films: An Annotated Filmography*.

Shivanath (b. 1925) has an MA in English and is a Dogri scholar and translator. He is the author of *History of Dogri Literature* as well as many other books in original and translation.

Tanika Sarkar (b. 1949) is the professor of Modern History at JNU, Delhi. She has also taught Modern Indian History at the University of Chicago. She has published and edited several books, among them *Words to Win: The Making of a Modern Autobiography*.

She had been awarded the Rabindra Puraskar by the Bangla Academy.

Tejaswini Niranjana (b. 1958) is a translator of fiction and poetry from Kannada to English. Her translation of M. K. Indira's *Phaniyamma* won the central Sahitya Akademi Award. Her academic books include *Siting Translation: History, Post-structuralism and the Colonial Context* and *Mobilizing India: Women, Music and Migration between India and Trinidad*.

Valson Thampu is an educator and translator from Malayalam to English. His translation of *Othappu* (*The Scent of the Other Side*) won the Crossword Award for Fiction in Translation. He also translated Sarah Joseph's *Aathi* as *Gift in Green*.

Vandana R. Singh is an author, editor, literary translator and language educator. She has been an ELT materials developer with NCERT, associate professor with the English Department, Chandigarh Education Service, and language consultant with UN organizations.

Veena Deo is a professor in the Department of English at Hamline University's College of Liberal Arts. She has published articles on African American literature as well as South Asian literatures. Her most recent publication is an English translation of Marathi short stories by Urmila Pawar, *Mother Wit*.

Vinaya Chaitanya writes in English, Malayalam and Kannada, and his translations of Akka Mahadevi have been published by ISLT and Yale University Press.

Yashodhara Maitra has been an educator of the deaf for twenty years in mathematics and the natural sciences in the USA. She has translated works in the genres of biographies, fiction and plays. She has translated into English and performed the play on Kasturba Gandhi, *Jagadamba* by Ramdas Bhatkal in the USA and in India.